D1253297

KARAITE STUDIES

KARAITE STUDIES

Edited and with Introduction

by

PHILIP BIRNBAUM

HERMON PRESS

NEW YORK, 1971

KARAITE STUDIES

HERMON PRESS, New York
L.C. No. 76-136771
ISBN 0-87203-027-X

INTRODUCTION

By Philip Birnbaum

The Karaite movement had a leavening influence on the development of Judaism during the Middle Ages. Well known is the saying of Anan, reputed founder of the sect of Karaites: "Search well in the Torah, and do not rely on my opinion." The controversial issues aroused by the biblical interpretations of the Karaites compelled the spokemen of Rabbinic Judaism to pay more attention to the literal meaning of the Holy Scriptures as against the prevalent aggadic exegesis. Regarding themselves as the intellectuals (*maskilim*) of the time, the Karaite writers repudiated the beliefs in demons and regarded magical formulae and amulets as forms of witchcraft which the Torah prohibits. Karaism was an aggressive force, challenging Rabbinism to self-defense and self-examination. It contributed thereby to the process of clarification of the spiritual values of Judaism. From the heat of the controversy, talmudic Judaism emerged purified and more acceptable by those who were philosophically-minded.

The Karaites never regarded themselves other than an integral part of the Jewish people, sharing its ideas and hopes, its sufferings and struggles. The two camps frequently referred to each other as "our Karaite brethren" and "our Rabbanite brethren." In the ninth century there were numerous cases of intermarriage between the two groups in both Eretz Yisrael and Egypt. Each party to the matrimonial alliance would promise to respect the religious practices of the other. The Karaites became a separate sect when they were expelled from the Jewish fold as heretics, revolting against traditional Judaism.

The Karaites were internally beset by the difficulties of their legalism. They often disputed with one another concerning the visible moon, whether it was the "old" one or the "new" one. This came about because they rejected the constant Jewish calendar, officially introduced by Hillel II in the fourth century C.E. They continued to follow the ancient system, according to which the appearance of the new moon had to be reported by witnesses.

They rejected the Rabbinic mode of calculation and reverted to the actual observance of the new moon. Thus, in one and the same community the festivals were celebrated on different days by opposing factions. The Karaite communities remained small and poor. Intelligent Jews were repelled by the chaotic condition of Karaism. It was impossible to find two Karaites in complete agreement with each other even as late as the middle of the tenth century. The rigorous and ascetic aspect of Karaite practice could have little attraction for the poverty-stricken Jewish masses, whose life was already full of privation and self-denial.

Conflicts and dissensions between the Rabbanites and the Karaites were continuous in those days, when religion and life were so closely connected. The Karaite spokesmen were the aggressors, as their whole movemnt was in the nature of a revolt against the traditional and accepted mode of Jewish life and thinking. An abusive and disparaging tone is to be found in the writings of their scholars, aimed against everything Rabbinic. Daniel al-Kumisi, Salman ben Yeruham, Sahl ben Matzliah, Yefet ben Ali, and others, regularly attacked time-honored Rabbinic practices. Those sectarians carefully studied the talmudic literature in order to pick out strange legends and hold them up to ridicule. Practically all Karaite authors concentrated on attacking the picturesque and highly poetic anthropomorphisms of the *aggadoth* under the general nicknames of idolatry and witchcraft.

This is why Rav Saadia Gaon (882-942) regarded it as his life task to combat Karaism. Already as a young man of twenty-three he wrote a refutation of Anan's *Book of Precepts* (Sefer ha-Mitzvoth). Ten years later, he left his native land, Egypt, for Palestine, where he was able to obtain first-hand information of the sectarian activities. He then developed into the foremost champion of Rabbinism; and for centuries afterward, the Karaites aimed their attacks on him, with a great deal of abuse. Altogether, polemics in those days was highly personal and offensive. Both sides were intensely sincere, since the issues at stake concerned what was dearest to the Jew, namely, the right interpretation of Judaism.

The Karaites were too absorbed in matters of religious law and ritual to keep historical records of their past. At the same time, their Rabbinic opponents saw no reason to preserve early documents dealing with their past. Much of the surviving material, in the form of handwritten fragments, has yet to be deciphered, published, and properly appraised. The largest collection of early Karaite manuscripts is deposited in the State Public Library of Leningrad, and access to it is extremely difficult. It will be the task of future research to discover why a movement so promising in its youth should have been converted into a barren organism, and why Karaism proved unable to produce leaders of sufficient vision and foresight to guide the sect toward a more creative continuity.

The Hermon Press is republishing in this volume several important studies, which originally appeared in various scholarly periodicals and are scarcely accessible. The research material herein included pertains to the origins of Karaism and the teachings of the Jewish sect that rejected talmudic traditions.

* * * *

The late Dr. Bernard Revel (1885-1940), organizer of Yeshiva College in New York, published in 1913 his doctoral dissertation entitled, *The Karaite Halakah and Its Relation to Sadducean, Samaritan and Philonian Halakah.* According to Dr. Revel's thesis, the Karaite sect did not originate from Anan Ben David's desire of revenge for not having been installed as the rightful heir to the Babylonian exilarchy during the second half of the eighth century; nor was the Karaite sect a direct continuation of the Sadducean sect, of the Second Temple period, who differed from the Pharisees in their religious outlook. Instead, he endeavors to prove a similarity between the Karaite laws and those interpreted by Philo, the Alexandrian Jewish philosopher, who died thirty years before the destruction of the Second Temple.

In refuting the Sadducean-Karaitic theory of Abraham Geiger, Revel insists that if the hitherto unnoticed relation of Karaite *halakhah* to the *halakhah* in Philo be well established, we are likely to understand a variety of subjects in the history of Judaism during the early period of Islam. Geiger's theory, however, is well supported by most medieval Jewish authorities, such as Rav Saadia Gaon, Yehudah Halevi and Abraham ibn Daud, who held that Karaism was a revival of the Sadducean sect. Ibn Ezra refers to the Karaites as *tsedokim,* Sadducees. Maimonides writes: "In Egypt they are called Karaites, while in the Talmud they are styled Sadducees" (Commentary to Mishnah Avoth 1:3).

In 1910, Solomon Schechter published the recently discovered *Fragments of a Zadokite Work,* which was considered by Harkavy, Poznanski and Aptowitzer, as sufficient proof of some relation between the Sadducean and the Karaite sects. But according to Schechter, though the term *Zadokites* naturally suggests the Sadducees, "the present state of knowledge of the latters' doctrines and practices does not offer enough points of resemblance to justify the identification of them with our sect." Revel quotes this statement of Schechter, and adds: "In seeking for the origin of Karaism and its *halakhah* we must cut adrift from any theory that would link it with Sadduceeism."

Following are several examples of disagreement between the two sects. The Karaites accept the talmudic tradition that the Sabbath law is suspended in the case of saving a human life. But Schechter's *Fragments* contain a statement of law such as this: "If any person falls into a gathering of water . . . one must not bring him up, during the Sabbath, by a ladder or a cord or any instrument." Schechter's sect prohibited fasting on the Sabbath, whereas most Karaites commend the fasting on the Sabbath. The Karaites maintain that water does not contract ritual impurity, whereas Schechter's sect held that water in a rock, like water in a vessel, is ritually contaminated when touched by an unclean person.

Revel draws comparisons between the laws stated in the writings of Philo and those found in Karaite works, thereby proving the influence of Philo upon the Karaite *halakhah.* Deviating from talmudic law, the Karaites do not require forewarning in any crime; they consider murder punishable even in the absence of intent. According to Philo, intent to murder is punishable by death. Furthermore, those who prepare any poisonous substance with murderous intent must be killed instantly. Both Philo and the Karaites accept the *lex talionis* ("an eye for an eye") literally. The law prescribing the death penalty for the blasphemer is referred by Philo to any disrespectful mention of the divine name at an inappropriate occasion or place. Philo, moreover, contends that, since a false oath involves blasphemy, anyone who swears falsely must die. The Karaites, likewise, set the punishment of death for the sin of taking a false oath. According to talmudic law, however, the penalty incurred by false swearing is thirty-nine lashes (*malkoth*).

An Early Karaite Tract, published by Jacob Mann (JQR, XII, 1922), contains a long discourse about the Tetragrammaton, the four-letter name of God. The author's chief contention being, that the term *nokev* in Leviticus 24:16 does not mean cursing the name of God, but merely pronouncing, uttering. Hence, the mere pronunciation of the divine name involves capital punishment. This interpretation is in agreement with Targum Onkelos as well as the Talmud (Sanhendrin 56a). Anan, too, took the word *nokev* to mean *pronounce,* though he refrained from going to the extreme as to impose capital punishment for the sin of merely uttering the Tetragrammaton. (Dr. Moses Zucker contends that Anan preferred the Rabbanite view to that of Philo as to the interpretation of the verse in question, as well as several other biblical laws cited by Dr. Revel as proof that Karaism was influenced by the teachings of Philo.)

* * * *

Samuel A. Poznanski's (1864-1921) contribution to our knowledge of the history of the Karaite movement and its leaders is unsurpassed. As early as 1898 he published *The Anti-Karaite Writings of Sa'adiah Gaon* (JQR, o.s.X) in which he describes the period between the sixth and the ninth centuries as a vastly important epoch for the intellectual life of Judaism, and at the same time one of the most obscure in Jewish history. Karaism that came into being during that period, along with many other sects that hardly survived their founders, has managed to continue its existence to this very day. Yet, the name Anan is mentioned only once in the entire geonic literature preceding Saadia Gaon.

A great portion of Sadia's checkered life was devoted to his efforts in opposing the Karaite doctrines. His fight against the active and energetic propagandists of the Karaite doctrine required a man with the comprehensive learning, "the sharp, tireless pen, and, above all, the fighting disposition of Saadia, to set himself against the manifold heresies that had invaded the minds of the Jewish people, and especially against the alarming spread of Karaism, which threatened the very existence of traditional

Judaism" (Henry Malter, *Saadia Gaon,* page 261). As to the Geonim who preceded Saadia, it has been stated that they failed to counteract the influence of Karaism because they were preoccupied with the interpretation of the traditional law and the adjustment between the two rival academies which they represented; or, "none of them possessed enough general education and literary skill to take up the fight" (*ibid*).

Saadia's polemical works against Karaism are known to have been four in number, namely: 1) Refutation of Anan; 2) Book of Distinction (*Kitab al-Tamyiz*); 3) Refutation of Ibn Sakawaihi; 4) Refutation of an Overbearing Antagonist. The most important of these works, *Kitab al-Tamyiz,* is frequently quoted by Yefet ben Ali, Saadia's younger contemporary, who cites complete passages verbatim in his Bible commentary. These passages are reproduced herewith in their original Arabic. According to Poznanski, the Karaites eventually lost their vitality and creativity by the absence of a strenuous controversy against them during the centuries following the period of Saadia Gaon.

* * * *

In his other major study, *The Karaite Literary Opponents of Sa'adiah Gaon* (London, 1908), Poznanski asserts that the polemical element existed in the very nature of Karaism. He presents a bibliographical survey of the Karaite polemical literature which, with the advent of Saadia, assumed a tone of bitterness against the Rabbanites in general and against Saadia in particular, continuing through the generations. "Even at a time when all spiritual life in their midst had been stifled, they still roused themselves and brought forth their rusty weapons to attack the execrated Fayyumite" (Saadia).

The Karaites have always accused the Rabbanites of "sins" enumerated by the tenth-century Karaite historian, Jacob Qirqisani, who wrote in his *Account of the Jewish Sects,* translated by Leon Nemoy from the Arabic, as follows: "They permit sexual intercourse on the sabbath, although it has three elements contrary to what we may do on the Sabbath. First, tht excitement and the exhaustion which is contrary to: 'Thou shalt not do any work.' Second, the contraction of impurity, which is contrary to the holiness to be preserved on the Sabbath. Third, the ejaculation of the sperm, which is contrary to the passage: 'Thou shalt rest from ploughing and harvesting' (Exodus 20:10; 34:21) . . . They allow cooking on the Sabbath, provided that the pot is prepared before the Sabbath and placed in the oven, so that the food is cooked and eaten on the Sabbath. They require the circumcision of the dead, which is extremely abhorrent to reason (in case of an infant that died before reaching the age of eight days)."

* * * *

In his *Karaite Miscellanies* (originally in JQR, o.s. VIII), Poznanski presents a number of short fragments from manuscript material which add much to our knowledge of certain obscure aspects of the sect and its exponents.

* * * *

Wilhelm Bacher (1850-1913) in his *Qirqisani, the Qaraite, and His Work on Jewish Sects* (originally in JQR, o.s. VII) was the first to call attention to the work of Jacob Qirqisani, the tenth-century Karaite scholar, which contains important information on Jewish sects and in which quotations from books now lost are preserved. The complete work was later to be translated into English by Leon Nemoy (*Al-Qirqisani's Account of the Jewish Sects,* HUCA, VII).

* * * *

Jacob Mann (1888-1940), another major scholar in the field of Karaitica, contributed to the understanding of Karaite practices with his article, *Anan's Liturgy and His Half-Yearly Cycle of the Reading of the Law* (originally in "Journal of Jewish Lore and Philosophy"). In it is shown that Anan endeavored to imitate the service of the Temple as he conceived it. The Torah readings substituted for the actual sacrificial offerings; hence, they had to be done by a *kohen* (priest) as if offering a *korban* in the Temple. A Levite had to recite the psalm of the day, just as his ancestor had in the sanctuary. The seats of the *kohanim* were arranged so as to remind one of the altar. The *kohanim* had to wear special, distinctive garments.

The final essay in this volume is in a way also its epilogue.

Leon Nemoy's *Anan ben David, A Re-Appraisal of the Historic Data* (originally in "Semitic Studies in memory of Immanuel Low," Budapest, 1947) succinctly sums up the present state of Karaite scholarship when he states that "our abysmal ignorance of the true history of early sectarianism and early Karaism . . . should awaken us to the urgent need for a thorough search in the Karaite manuscript collections . . . for every bit of genuine early material that might shed the least bit of true historical light on Anan and his immediate followers."

The editor and the publishers would be gratified if the present volume will provide the spark needed for rekindling the interest of the scholarly community in the history of the Karaite sect.

BIBLIOGRAPHY

Ankori, Zvi. *The Karaites of Byzantium.* New York: Columbia University, 1959.

Adler, Elkan Nathan. *About Hebrew Manuscripts.* New York: Hermon Press, 1970.

Birnbaum, Philip. *The Arabic Commentary of Yafet Ben Ali the Karaite on the Book of Hosea.* Philadelphia: Dropsie College, 1942.

Ginzberg, Louis. *Geonica.* New York: Hermon Press, 1968.

Ginzberg, Louis. *Geonic and Early Karaitic Halakah. Genizah Studies,* Vol. II. New York: Hermon Press, 1969.

Malter, Henry. *Saadia Gaon.* New York: Hermon Press, 1970.

Mann, Jacob. *Texts and Studies, Vol. II.* Philadelphia, 1935.

Mann, Jacob. "An Early Karaite Tract." *Jewish Quarterly Review,* XII.

Nemoy, Leon. "Al-Qirqisani's Account of the Jewish Sects." *HUCA,* VII.

Schechter, Solomon. *Fragments of a Zadokite Work.* London, 1910.

Steinschneider, M. *Jewish Literature from the Eighth to the Eighteenth Century.* New York: Hermon Press, 1970.

Zucker, Moshe. *Rav Saadyah Gaon's Translation of the Torah.* (Hebrew). New York, 1959.

TABLE OF CONTENTS

Introduction, *Philip Birnbaum* V

The Karaite Halakah and Its Relation to Sadducean, Samaritan and Philonian Halakah, *Bernard Revel* 1

The Anti-Karaite Writings of Sa'adiah Gaon, *Samuel A. Poznanski* 89

The Karaite Literary Opponents of Sa'adiah Gaon, *Samuel A. Poznanski* 129

Karaite Miscellanies, *Samuel A. Poznanski* 235

Qirqisani, the Qaraite, and His Work on Jewish Sects, *Wilhelm Bacher* 259

Anan's Liturgy and His Half-Yearly Cycle of the Reading of the Law, *Jacob Mann* 283

Anan ben David, a Re-Appraisal of the Historic Data, *Leon Nemoy* 309

Acknowledgements

The editor and publishers wish to thank the editors of the Jewish Quarterly Review and the President of Dropsie University for their graceful permission to reprint *The Karaite Halakah* by Bernard Revel from JQR, vols. II and III.

Also, thanks to Dr. Leon Nemoy for his permission to reprint *Anan ben David, a Re-Appraisal of the Historical Data* from "Semitic Studies in Memory of Immanuel Low" (Budapest, 1947).

THE KARAITE HALAKAH

AND ITS RELATION TO SADDUCEAN, SAMARITAN AND PHILONIAN HALAKAH

PART I

BY BERNARD REVEL, M. A., PH. D.

INQUIRY INTO THE SOURCES OF KARAITE HALAKAH

THE causes of the Karaite schism and its early history are veiled in obscurity, as indeed are all the movements that originated in the Jewish world during the time between the conclusion of the Talmud Babli and the appearance of Saadia Gaon.

From the meager contemporary sources it would seem that from the second third of the eighth century until the downfall of the Gaonate (1038) the whole intellectual activity of Babylonian Jewry centered about the two Academies and their heads, the Geonim. Of the early Gaonic period the Jewish literature that has reached us from Babylonia is mainly halakic in character, e. g. *Halakot Gedolot, Sheeltot,* and works on liturgy, which afford us an insight into the religious life of the people. From them, however, we glean very little information about the inner life of the Jews in Babylonia before the rise of Karaism; hence the difficulty of fully understanding the causes which brought about the rise of the only Jewish sect that has had a long existence and has affected the course of Jewish history by the opposition it has aroused.

The study of sects always has a peculiar interest. During the thirties of the last century, the Karaites themselves made accessible to the scholarly world the works of some of their latter-day authorities, and with the publication of Simḥah Pinsker's epoch-making work "Liḳḳuṭe Ḳadmoniyyot" (1860) the attention of Jewish scholarship was turned to Karaism and its literature. Pinsker, blinded by his discovery of an important phase in the development of Judaism, invented a pan-Karaite theory, according to which the Karaites are to be looked upon as the source of all intellectual achievement of mediæval Judaism (*Liḳḳuṭe,* I, 4, 32). The Masorah is a product mainly of theirs, and it is among them that we are to look for the beginnings of Hebrew grammar, lexicography, poetry, and sound biblical exegesis. The Rabbanites, since Saadia Gaon, were merely imitators of the Karaites. Pinsker believed that every Jewish scholar, prior to the eleventh century, who busied himself with the study of Bible alone, was a Karaite, and he transformed, accordingly, more than one Rabbanite into a Karaite.

The question of the origin of Karaism, its causes and early development is still awaiting solution. That Karaism is not the result of Anan's desire to revenge himself on Babylonian official Jewry, need not be said. Karaite literature affords us no data; there is a marked lack of historical sense among them. They have no tradition as to their origin, and their opinions are conflicting (comp. Pinsker, *Liḳḳuṭe,* II, 98). The belief that Karaism is but an echo of a a similar movement during this period in the Islamic world is now generally given up owing to the advance made in the knowledge of the inner development of Islam and, particularly, the nature of the Shiite heterodoxy (see I. Friedlaender, *JQR.,* 1910, 185 ff.).

This question is bound up with the problem of the origin of the Karaite halakah which is of vital importance for the understanding the history of Tradition; as Geiger (*ZDMG.*, XVI (1862), 716) says, it was always the differences in practice, not in dogma, that caused and sustained divisions in Israel. This is particularly true of the Karaites who differ in nothing but religious practices from the rest of Israel.

The solution offered by Geiger that the Karaites are the descendants of the Sadducees and their halakah Sadducean, is accepted with some modification by many scholars (comp. Poznański, *REJ.*, XLIV (1902), 169). On the other hand, the eclectic nature of the Karaite halakah was recognized by several scholars (comp. S. L. Rapoport in *Kerem Chemed,* V (1841), 204 ff., and in Kaempf's *Nichtandalusische* Poesie, II, 240; P. Frankl, *Ersch u. Gruber,* sec. II, vol. 33, 12; Harkavy, in Grätz' *Geschichte,* V.[4], 482 ff.; *id., Jahrbuch f. jüd. Geschichte u. Literatur,* II (1899), 116 ff., and elsewhere). No attempt was, however, made to explain the bulk of the Karaitic halakah, on these lines. I have therefore undertaken the work of tracing the individual Karaite laws to their respective sources, which will, at the same time, be the first exposition of the Karaite laws in general—prefacing it by an examination of the Sadducean-Karaitic theory. The term "Karaite halakah" is used here as a convenient one, though, as Ḳirḳisani has unwillingly shown—and any Karaite code testifies to it—the laws on which all Karaites agree are few. The Karaite laws are discussed here not according to subject matter, but such as have common source are grouped together. I begin with Philo, as the relation of Karaite halakah to that of Philo has remained, to my knowledge, hitherto unnoticed. This relation, if established, may prove helpful in the understanding of other points in the inner history of Judaism during the first centuries of Islam.

For the halakah of Philo, I have used the work of Dr. B. Ritter, *"Philo und die Halacha, eine vergleichende Studie,"* from which most of the citations from Philo in this treatise are taken. Other Philonian laws, not treated by Ritter, are discussed here, but only as they bear on the Karaite halakah.

Not all the early Karaites claimed antiquity for their schism. This is evident from the reply of Salman b. Yeruḥam to Saadia's mention of their late origin (Pinsker, II, 19).[1] Another contemporary of Saadia, Abu Jusuf Yaḳub al-Ḳirḳisani, the most reliable historian among the Karaites, gives a date for what he calls the Rabbanite dissension: Jeroboam, to make permanent the power he had usurped and to prevent the Israelites owing allegiance to the house of David, divided the nation by sowing the seed of dissension, perverted the Law, and changed the calendar (I Kings 12, 32). The followers of Jeroboam in later times are called Rabbanites. Those who remained faithful to the original laws were the ancestors of the Karaites.[2] This fanciful explanation found no credence even among the Karaites.[3]

[1] באמרך בעלי מקרא חדשים ורבותי הישנים הם קדושים . אם בעלי התועבות האלה וכאלה מקודשים סיסרא והמן וזולתם בגן עדן נפושים; comp. also Salman b. Yeruḥam's commentary on Ps. 96, 1 (Winter u. Wünsche, *Jüdische Literatur,* II, 80). See, however, Harkavy in Grätz, *Geschichte,* V[4], 472. That not all the Karaite contemporaries of Saadia claimed antiquity for their sect is evident also from Saadia's fourth answer in his polemical work against Ibn Sāḳaweihi. See *JQR.,* XIII, 664; הקדם, I, 67.

[2] Comp. Poznański, *REJ.,* XLIV (1902), 162 ff.

[3] It was, however, taken up again by the twelfth century Karaite, Elias b. Abraham, in his חלוקי הרבנים והקראים (Pinsker, II, 100 ff.). He

The Karaites felt keenly the need of some account of their origin that would silence the reproach of the Rabbanites and found in the event recorded in the Baraita (Ḳiddushin 66*a;* see Josephus *Ant.,* XIII, 13, 5) a basis for claim of ancient origin for their sect. As stated in that narrative, the disagreement between John Hyrcanus and the teachers of the Law resulted in the extermination of the latter, excepting Simeon b. Shataḥ. As a consequence, ignorance of the Law prevailed until Simeon appeared and reinstated it.

והיה העולם משתומם עד שבא שמעון בן שטח והחזיר את התורה ליושנה
Simeon, say the Karaites, being at that time the sole authority, introduced many innovations upon his return and changed the true interpretation of the Law. To enforce these new laws, he invented the fiction that besides the Written there is also an Oral Law given to Moses on Sinai and handed down from generation to generation, and that the laws proclaimed by him went back to this real tradition.

The people followed him blindly. But some of them, knowing the false basis of these changes, rejected them and adhered to the ancient Tradition in all its purity; those were the Karaites.[4]

adds that those who remained faithful to the original faith migrated מעבר לנהרי כוש and only few of them, because of their attachment to the Temple, remained in Jerusalem. Yet, as Pinsker (II, 98) remarks, Elias himself put little confidence in this myth. For the origin of this legend, see A. Epstein *Eldad ha-dani* (Pressburg 1891), p. L. For later Karaites repeating this story, see Poznański, *l. c.,* p. 163; comp. *ZfhB.,* III, 92 (end) and 93, for the view of a tenth century Karaite (comp. *ib.,* 90 and 172 ff.).

[4] As a striking instance of the purely mythological character of the Karaite beliefs about their origin and past, I shall illustrate the three strata in the development of the last mentioned Karaite theory of their origin. Sahl b. Maṣliaḥ (tenth century) asserts that Karaism goes back to the time of the second Temple, but connects it with no specific event (Pinsker, II, 35). This is still the opinion of Aaron b. Elias (fourteenth century)

On the other hand, most of the Mediæval Jewish scholars seem to agree that Karaism was due to a revival of the Sadducees (Abraham Ibn Daud) or that Sadducean elements are prominent in it (Saadia, Judah Halevi). Saadia Gaon (891-942) was the first to meet the Karaites in open battle[5] and refute their claims for recognition. He states that Karaism is of recent origin (Pinsker, II, 19) and that Anan's breaking with Tradition was due entirely to

in Introduction to his כתר תורה, 4*a*. Elias b. Moses Bashyazi a century later connects the schism with the name of Simeon b. Shataḥ and exclaims: או שהיה שמעון בן שטח נהרג כשאר חחכמים שנהרגו היינו כלנו לעם אחד (intr. to אדרת אליהו, Goslow 1834, 3*a*.). He is followed by his disciple Kaleb Afendopolo in his עשרה מאמרות (quoted in דוד מרדכי, Wien 1830, 9*a*). The sixteenth century Karaite prodigy Moses b. Elias Bashyazi (born 1554 and said to have died 1572) amplified this tale by asserting in his מטה האלהים (quoted in דוד מרדכי, 9*b* ff.) that Judah b. Ṭabbai, who had also survived the king's wrath, opposed the innovations introduced by Simeon b. Shataḥ as also his fiction of an oral law. Judah attracted to his banner all those who remained faithful to ancient traditions. Simeon and Judah each became the head of a school, thus dividing the Jews into two factions. Simeon was succeeded by Abṭalion, Abṭalion by Hillel who systematized the new laws based on the fiction of the Oral Law. Judah b. Ṭabbai was followed by Shemaiah, and Shemaiah by Shammai; those two being the great Karaite teachers from whom the line of succession was never interrupted. Already Jepheth b. Said asserted that Shammai was the teacher of the Karaites (Pinsker, II, 186; comp. *ib.*, I, 6); see also Luzzatto, כרם חמד, III (1838), 223; Geiger, *ib.*, IV, 12; Gottlober, בקרת לתולדות הקראים, Wilna 1865, 5 ff. How foreign this idea was to the early Karaites, is seen from what Salman b. Yeruḥam says of Bet Shammai and Bet Hillel (כרם חמד IV, 13): תועבת ה' גם שניהם.

[5] We know of two Rabbanites who combated Karaism before Saadia: the Gaon Naṭronai b. Hilai (סדר רב עמרם, 38*a*) and the Gaon Hai b. David (Harkavy, *Studien u. Mittheilungen*, V, 108, n. 2; comp. Bornstein, ספר היובל לנחום סאקאלאוו, Warsaw 1904, 158, n. 2, who believes this Gaon to have been Hai b. Naḥshon). For anti-Karaite legislation by Jehudai Gaon see L. Ginzberg, *Geonica*, I, 111, n. 2. For Saadia's anti-Karaite writings, see Poznański, *JQR.*, X, 238 ff., and additions, *ib.*, XX, 232 ff.

personal motives (*ib.*, 103).[6] Yet he adds that the remnants of Zadok and Boethus joined Anan (*l. c.*). About two centuries later, a time which was decisive in the battle between traditional Judaism and the Karaites,[7] the three great lights of Toledo, Judah Halevi, Abraham Ibn Ezra, and Abraham Ibn Daud, each strove to check the Karaite propaganda in Spain[8] carried on at that time with great zeal by Ibn al-Taras, the disciple of Jeshua b. Judah, and they all assert that Karaism is an offshoot of Sadduceeism. Judah Halevi declares that the Karaite schism arose in the time of John Hyrcanus. The Karaites, says he, are superior to the Sadducees in questions of dogma, but agree with them in important religious questions.[9] Abraham Ibn Ezra also identifies them with the Sadducees. In his commentaries on the Bible, which are strongly anti-Karaitic, he usually styles them[10] צדוקים . More emphatic is Abraham Ibn Daud in his *Sefer Hakkabalah,* where he says that "after the destruction of the Temple the Sadducees dwindled to almost nothing until Anan appeared and strengthened them."[11] Likewise, Maimonides, commenting

[6] That Saadia is meant by ולבן דתכם אשר חרף, see Pinsker, p. 98; comp. Poznański, *JQR.*, X, 242.

[7] Comp. Frankl, *MGWJ.*, XXI (1882), 3 ff.

[8] Spain was from early Gaonic times infected with Karaism; comp. Ginzberg, *l. c.*, I, 123, note 1; Frankl. *MGWJ.*, 1888, 6 ff.; and Poznański, *JQR.*, XVI, 768-9. Against the view of Hirschfeld (*JQR.*, XIII, 225 ff.) that some relation existed between the Karaites and the Zahirites in Spain, see Goldziher, *REJ.*, XLIII (1901), 6-7.

[9] Kuzari, III, 65. Judah Halevi's view is shared by Abrabanel, נחלת אבות, and S. Duran, מגן אבות on Abot 1, 3, and II, *21a; 31a.*

[10] Introduction to his Commentaries on the Bible; Lev. 3, 9; 23, 17, 40. As to the relation of Ibn Ezra to the Karaites, see J. S. Reggio, אגרות יש"ר, I (Wien 1834), 42 ff.; see also D. Rosin, *MGWJ.*, XLIII, 76-7.

[11] Neubauer, *Mediaeval Jewish Chronicles,* I, 64. The variant מינים does not affect the meaning of the statement.

(Abot I, 3) on the dissension of Zadok and Boethus, adds: "In Egypt they are called Karaites, while in the Talmud they are named Sadducees and Boethusians."[12]

Elias b. Moses Bashyazi, a fifteenth century Karaite, tells us, in the introduction to his אדרת אליהו, 3*a,* that it is the opinion of all the Rabbanite scholars that the Karaite schism goes back to Zadok and Boethus.

Much confidence, however, was not placed in this testimony of the Mediæval Rabbanites, that the Karaites descended from the Sadducees, as it is evident that the Rabbanites were often actuated by the desire to stamp their opponents in the eyes of the people as descendants of that hated sect which denied divine Providence and resurrection.[13] In the middle of the last century Abraham

[12] See his commentary on Ḥullin I, 3. On the views of Maim. on the Karaites, see ספר היובל למשה בלאך (Budapest 1905), Hungarian part, 164-170; see also the other authors mentioned by Poznański, *REJ., ib.,* 170, to which may be added Estori ha-Pharḥi כפתר ופרח, end of ch. 5 (ed. Luncz, p. 61); David Abi Zimra, *Responsa,* IV, resp. 219; Meiri on Abot I, 3. See also Responsum No. 34 in the Gaonic collection שערי תשובה: ורוב מן החיצונים תלמידי בייתוס.

[13] Comp. David Messer Leon (published by Schechter), *REJ.,* XXIV, 126. See Weiss, דור דור ודורשיו, IV, 53. Joseph al-Baṣir is the only one among the Karaites who identifies the Karaites with the Sadducees (Harkavy, *l. c.,* p. 473). Ḳirḳisani states that the Sadducees revealed part of the truth and that there were no Sadducees in his days (ch. 18, p. 317). Jepheth b. Alī (Poz., *ib.,* 171-2) and Hadassi (Alphabeta 97, 98) speaks of the Sadducees with contempt. The statement by Jacob b. Reuben (Pinsker, II, 84) that the Karaites are the descendants of the Sadducees was, therefore, taken by him from Joseph al Baṣir's כתאב אלאסתבצאר and not from Jepheth b. Ali, as Harkavy (Grätz, *Geschichte,* V[4], 474) suggests. Nor is Harkavy (*l. c.*) right in his assertion that Elias b. Abraham shared this view. See above note 3. Comp. also Pinsker, I, 11-12. The later Karaites claimed that the imputation that they were in some way related to the Sadducees was due to the hatred the Rabbanites bore them. See Kaleb Afendopolo, quoted in דוד מרדכ, 2*b.*

Geiger attempted to prove historically the descent of the Karaites from the Sadducees,[14] and this view constitutes an essential part of his epoch-making theory concerning the internal development of post-exilic Judaism and the history of Jewish sects. His view is accepted by Holdheim,[15] Fürst,[16] Harkavy,[17] Chwolson,[18] and others. A general survey of Geiger's theory[19] will help us better to understand the questions involved.

From the earliest times, says Geiger, two distinct, or, rather, antagonistic currents were at work shaping the history of Judaism. The dualism revealed itself in olden times in the divided nationality of Ephraim (or Joseph) and Judah. Ephraim constituted a worldly kingdom, in constant contact with the neighboring nations and, therefore, in need of a sacrificial and ceremonial religion and a powerful priesthood to protect it from the surrounding heathen influences. Judah, on the other hand, constituted a kingdom politically insignificant, compact and isolated, and less susceptible to foreign influences, with one national sanctuary and a less developed priesthood.[20] Judah escaped the fate of Ephraim and awoke to new life in the sixth

[14] *Des Judenthum u. s. Geschichte,* II, 55 ff.; *Jüd. Zeitchrift,* VIII, 227-233; *Nachgelassene Schriften,* II, 135 ff.; *Urschrift,* index, *s. v.* "Karaiten"; and elsewhere.

[15] מאמר האישות, Wien 1861, 128 ff.

[16] *Geschichte d. Karäerthums* (Leipzig 1862), I, 8 ff.

[17] In Russian periodical "Woschod," 1896, and elsewhere; comp. *id.,* לקורות הכתות בישראל, 4, 19.

[18] *Das letzte Passamahl Christi* (2 ed., Leipzig 1908), pp. 148, 176 ff.; *id., Beiträge zur Entwicklungsgeschichte d. Judenthums* (Leipzig 1910), p. 8 ff.; comp. V. Aptowitzer, *Die Rechtsbücher d. nestorianischen Patriarchen,* 1910, pp. 7-8.

[19] For a more detailed account see Poznański, *Abraham Geiger, Leben u. Lebenswerk,* Berlin 1910, 352-388.

[20] *Jüd. Zeitschr.,* VIII (1870), 279 ff., and elsewhere.

century B. C. With this new life came a struggle, in which priestly aristocracy and sacerdotal rule were antagonized by tendencies towards religious and political democracy that asserted themselves more and more. Since the establishment of the second commonwealth the priests ruled the nation. There stood at the head of the state a high-priest, descendant of the family of Zadok, the chief of the priesthood in the days of David and Solomon (I Kings, 1, 34; 2, 35; I Chron. 29, 22), members of which had exercised priestly functions ever since the building of Solomon's Temple. This family and those related to it constituted the nobility of the nation and since the Return controlled the secular as well as the religious life of the people.

This power, blended with the attribute of holiness, soon led the priestly ruling class to disregard the needs and demands of the people. They stood for the ancient laws and observances, which established and asserted their rights and prerogatives, admitting no modification which the times required. They also allied themselves with the Syrians and cultivated tastes and habits distasteful to the people.[21] With the victory of the Maccabees the government and the high-priesthood passed over to the latter, the Sadducees, the old nobility, joining them. An opposition against them arose among the people, the leaders of which were known as the "Separated" (*Perushim*), descendants of those who in the days of Zerubbabel and again in the

[21] *Ib.*, p. 282 ff.; *Jüd. Zeitschr.*, II, 17 ff.; *ZDMG.*, XIX, 603 ff. An offshoot of the Sadducees, and united with them were the Boethusians, a new aristocratic priestly family called after Simon b. Boethus, high-priest and father-in-law of Herod I (*Urschrift.* 102, 134 ff., 143 ff.). Herzfeld, *Geschichte*, II, 387, accepts the view of Azariah dei Rossi that the Boethusians are the Essenes spoken of by Philo and Josephus. See also *REJ.*, III, 113 ff. and Chwolson, *Das letzte Passamahl Christi*, 28, 129.

time of Ezra separated themselves from heathen surroundings and influences (Ezra 6, 21; 9, 1; Neh. 9, 2). Their aim was to limit the power of priestly aristocracy and turn the government over to the people. The Pharisees recognized the sanctity of priesthood, but contested the centralization of secular power in the hands of the sacerdotal-aristrocratic families.

The difference between these two parties, originally small and of a general nature, widened in time. The spirit of rivalry in this politico-religious struggle brought about laws and regulations on the part of the Pharisees intended to check the authority and diminish the privileges of the priests. Personal purity and sanctity of all the people were to take the place of the sanctity of priesthood. The Pharisees devised new rules of interpretation which enabled them to limit and restrict the biblical laws establishing priestly rights. On the other hand, many laws of purity and observances concerning food, originally intended for the priests and the Temple, they made apply to all the people in and outside of the Temple.[22] So the Pharisees did not adhere to the letter of the Law, but taught and expanded the Law with regard to its inner spirit and the needs of the time, whereby they created a new Halakah differing in content as well as in spirit from the ancient, Sadducean, tradition.[23] The majority of the people followed the new Halakah, but the Sadducean teachings found acceptance outside of Judah proper. The Samaritans, descendants of Northern Israel, were not allowed by the leaders of the national party in the time of Zerubbabel to participate in the further development of Judaism (Ezra

[22] *Jüd. Zeitschr.*, VI, 265 ff.

[23] *Urschrift*, 156 ff., 176, 434 ff.; *Nachgelassene Schriften*, II, 121 ff.; V (Heb.), 112 ff., 142 ff. and elsewhere.

4, 1 ff.). The ancient feud between Ephraim and Judah thus revived. The rejected Samaritans who retained the ancient Israelitish tradition as well as the ancient interpretation of the Law, clung, like the Sadducees, to those traditions and stood for priestly prerogative, characteristic of the religion of Northern Israel and the Sadducees. This accounts for the many practices and interpretations of the law that are common to the Sadducees and the Samaritans.[24]

But, even in Judah, only the political antagonism between the Pharisees and the Sadducees ceased with the destruction of the Temple. The Sadducees, whose existence as the priestly aristocracy and ruling class depended upon the state and the Temple, ceased to control the life of the people. But the religious differences between these two parties did not disappear.

The victorious Pharisees, who ruled the day, rejected all traditions, preserved by the Sadducees, which tended to affirm the exclusive rights of the priests, and the whole body of traditional law was now made to conform to their views. Not all the Pharisaic teachers, however, agreed to these radical changes, and some of them retained their allegiance to the pre-Pharisaic Halakah. Notably among them are Shammai and his school represented by R. Eliezer b. Hyrcanus and Jose the Galilean.[25]

But official Pharisaism did not heed them. It established as a religious norm the interpretations and laws which emanated from the school of Hillel, the great cham-

[24] *Nachg. Schriften*, III, 258 ff., 284 ff.; IV, 65; V (Heb.), 149 ff.; *ZDMG.*, XII, 132 ff. and elsewhere.

[25] *Jüd. Zeitschrift*, VIII, 283 ff. and elsewhere; comp. Hoffmann, *Magazin* 1884, 19.

pion of Pharisaism, who began the systematization of the new Halakah. Hillel's work was firmly established by R. Akiba and brought to completion by Judah Ha-nasi. Two centuries later the center of Judaism was transferred to Babylonia, and soon all consciousness of an earlier and differing Halakah disappeared.[26]

Zealously as the Pharisees of the school of Hillel worked to exclude and annul the laws and traditions tainted with Sadducean views, traces of the latter are still found in some of the apocryphal books; in the Greek version of the Scriptures (LXX); in the Aramaic version, Pseudo-Jonathan;[27] in the halakic midrashim from the school of R. Ishmael, himself a priest and with priestly sympathies,[28] and, to a lesser extent, in the later Palestinian halakic works, Tosefta and Talmud Jerushalmi.[29]

But not only are we able to reconstruct parts of the Sadducean Halakah through the traces in these works, but the Sadducean tradition is still alive, its laws are observed and its practices carried out by their descendants, the Karaites; not only are they the followers and spiritual heirs of the Sadducees, but their physical descendants. Doctrines and practices adhered to and observed by a nation do not disappear at the desire of its leaders. Nor were the Sadducees annulled. The descendants of the once dominant party continued to live according to the traditions of their ancestors. The religious unrest prev-

[26] *Jüd. Zeitschrift,* VIII, 284 ff.

[27] *Urschrift,* 165; 451 ff.; *Nachg. Schriften,* IV, 108 ff.; V (Heb.), 112 ff.; see below.

[28] מכילתא and ספרי; *Urschrift,* 434 ff.; *Jüd. Zeitschr.* IV, 96 ff.; VIII, 284; IX, 8 ff.; XI, 51 ff., and elsewhere.

[29] See *Jüd Zeitschrift,* VIII, 291 ff. For the Jerushalmi comp. *MGWJ.,* 1871, 120 ff.

alent in the Islamic world in the eighth century caused them also to unite and defy their old enemies, the Pharisees. Their leader Anan gave them his name, which was, however, soon changed to the appellation קראים or בני מקרא.

Karaism is, thus, not to be looked upon as a late-day revolt against the authority of Tradition caused by outside influence, but is a survival in a somewhat modified form (as by belief in resurrection) of the pre- and anti-Pharisaic tradition.[30]

[30] D. Chwolson in his *Beiträge zur Entwicklungsgeschichte d. Judenthums* (Leipzig 1910) goes further than Geiger, and asserts that long after the destruction of the Temple, the Sadducees were predominant (pp. 10-22). He bases this view on the assumption that during the time of the Second Commonwealth the Sadducees constituted not only the priestly and secular aristocracy, but also the bulk of the people, their disappearance with the destruction of the State being therefore inconceivable (p. 23 ff.).

Chwolson also believes that it was the people who remained faithful to the Sadducean tradition who are designated in the talmudic literature by the name עם הארץ. This accounts for the mutual hatred that existed between the Am-haareṣ and Pharisaic teachers (p. 9). Chwolson adduces the talmudic account (b. Berakot 47*b* and parallel) of the ceremonies the non-observance of which characterized the Am-haareṣ, as proof of the latter being identical with the Sadducees. It is there said that the Am-haareṣ does not read the *Shema'*; that he does not put on the *phylacteries;* that he does not wear *fringes* on his garments and that he has no *Mezuzah* on his door. Now the Karaites even up to this day observe none of these ceremonies. Some relationship must exist between the Am-haareṣ and the Karaites. As the Karaites are, Chwolson believes, descendants of the Sadducees, a relationship is established between the Am-haareṣ and Sadducees.

The facts are, however, not as Chwolson puts them. The Karaitees have never rejected the biblical precept of ציצית, even if they differ as to the meaning of תכלת and some other details; see, for Anan, Harkavy, ספר המצות לענן, pp. 7-10, and Schechter, *Jewish Sectaries,* II, 25, 1-26, 17; Hadassi, Alph. 241 and 364 (136*b*); Mibḥar, Num., *ad loc.,* גן עדן, 80*b* ff.; לבוש מלכות (Neubauer, *Aus d. Petersburger Bibliothek*), 49*a* ff.; comp. also Ibn Ezra on Num. 15, 38, 39. Nor is it likely that the Karaites have even denied the duty of reading the *Shema'*. Abu Isa Isfahani, from whom Anan borrowed several laws (comp. Poznański, *REJ.,* XLIV (1902), 178), taught, according to Ḳirḳisani (comp. Harkavy, לקורות הכתות בישראל, 9).

The reliability of the traditional account of the origin of the Sadducees and Boethusians (Abot de R. Nathan, ch. 5), rejected by Geiger (*Urschrift,* 105 ff.) as an apocryphal legend, was vindicated by Baneth in *Magazin,* IX (1882), p. 1-37; 61-95, where is also shown how far the view of Geiger—that the Sadducees did not reject Tradition but adhered to a more ancient interpretation of the Law—contradicts the explicit statements of Josephus (*Ant.* XIII, 10, 6; XVII, 1, 4) and all the Talmudic accounts about them.[31]

Before we enter into a discussion of the agreements between the Sadducees and the Karaites which serve Geiger as proofs of the relation of the latter to the former, a few words will not be amiss on the general difficulties connected with the hypothesis, which were ignored by

the duty of reading the *Shema'*, Its reading is enjoined by the later Karaites; see Hadassi, Alph. 15 (15*d*); אדרת אליהו, 59*c*; see Weiss, דור, IV, 88; L. Löw. *Ges. Schr.,* I, 50. Neither can the Am-haareṣ be identified with the Sadducees by his non-observance of the law of Tefillin. The Sadducees accepted the literal interpretation of Deut. 6, 8 (see Weiss, I, 118; Fürst, *Geschichte d. Karäerthums,* I, 10; Graetz, III, 3, 395; comp. also Müller, *Masechet Soferim,* p. 21, note 66). The name צדוקי in Menaḥot 42*b* ספר תורה תפילין ומזוזות שכתבן צדוקי... misled Wreschner (*Samaritanische Traditionen,* Berlin 1888, intr., p. VIII) and J. A. Montgomery (The *Samaritans,*. Philadelphia 1908, 136) to believe that the Sadducees interpreted Deut. 6, 8 symbolically. צדוקי in Menaḥot (*l. c.*) is, as often in the Amoraic literature, equivalent to מין, or was, as usual, substituted therefor by the censor. The parallel passage (Giṭṭin 45*b*) reads מין instead of צדוקי, which is also the reading of Estori ha-Pharḥi, כפתר ופרח, end of ch. 5. Harkavy (ספר המצות לענן, 142, n. 12) believes that Anan interpreted Deut. 6, 9 literally but referred וכתבתם to the עשרת הדברות a view which is held also by the Falashas (Epstein, *Eldad ha-Dani,* 174).

[31] Comp. also Wellhausen, *Die Pharisäer u. die Sadducäer,* Greifswald 1877, 73; G. Hölscher, *Der Sadduzäismus,* Leipzig 1906, pp. 9, 33 ff., 107 ff. The general nature of the Sadducees was recently thoroughly discussed by I. Halevy in his דורות הראשונים, vol. I*c*, pp. 358 ff.

Geiger. Geiger believes that all the differences between the Pharisees and the Sadducees may be brought under one unifying principle, viz., the advocacy of priestly interests by the Sadducees. But if this was the distinctive mark of the Sadducees, what import could this tendency have had many centuries after the destruction of the Temple, when there was no more priestly aristocracy nor prerogative? And how could this issue sustain and keep alive Sadduceeism under the appellative קראים until to-day? Nor can we comprehend how Karaism whose basic principle since the days of its first exponent Anan was חפשו באורייתא שפיר "Search the Scripture,[32] interpret it according to your own reason, and act accordingly," ignoring tradition,—how Karaism could have descended from Sadduceism which, as Geiger himself asserts, was by its very nature conservative, adhering stringently to ancient tradition.

This Sadducean-Karaite theory of Geiger is closely connected with his hypothesis concerning the existence of an ancient Halakah related to the Sadducean and which was therefore suppressed by the later Pharisees, a view that has been accepted by many scholars. A brief discussion of this hypothesis in relation to Karaism is given here.

The Targum Pseudo-Jonathan on the Pentateuch is, as Geiger (*Urschrift,* 162 ff., 451 ff.; *N. S.*, IV, 106 ff.; V (Heb.), 112 ff.) believes, the main depository of remnants and traces of this ancient Sadducean-Samaritan-Karaite Halakah. Ps.-Jon., being a product of Palestine at a time when the more ancient Sadducean traditions had not altogether died out there—though changed to conform to the New Halakah—, still contains much which goes back to

[32] Harkavy ספר המצות לענן, 132, 176; so Sahl b. Maṣliaḥ (Pinsker, II, 33-4); comp. Poznański, *REJ.*, XLIV (1902), 180 ff.

those ante-Pharisaic traditions. As proof of this view, Geiger (*Urschrift,* 176 ff.) attempted to show that several Karaite anti-traditional laws are found among the Samaritans and in Ps.-Jon. The following are the main points of agreement which Geiger finds between the Karaite law and the Targum Pseudo-Jonathan and which he therefore believes to be survivals of the ancient halakah.

According to the traditional interpretation of Lev. 19, 24, the fruit of a tree in its fourth year is, like the "second tithe," to be consumed by the owner within the walls of Jerusalem. This is also the view of Josephus, *Ant.*, IV, 8, 19. Pseudo-Jonathan, however, translates פריו קדש הלולים לה׳ (Lev. 19, 24) by קודשי תושבחן קדם ה׳ מתפרק מן כהנא; so also on Deut. 20, 6.[33] The Samaritans and Karaites also take קדש הלולים to mean that it is to be given to the priest or redeemed by its owner. Geiger (*Urschrift,* 181-184) believes this to have been the view of the ancient Halakah. Since this interpretation agrees with the plain meaning of קדש הלולים (comp. Ibn Ezra *ad loc.*), there is no necessity to assume with Geiger that this interpretation by some [34] Karaites goes back to an ancient tradition.

[33] Comp. Epstein, *MGWJ.*, XL (1896), 142; Gronemann, *Die Jonathan'sche Pentateuch-Uebersetzung in ihrem Verhältnisse zur Halacha,* Leipzig 1879, 48. For the view of the Book of Jubilees 7, 35-7, see B. Beer, *Das Buch d. Jubiläen,* 43-44.

[34] Not all the Karaites, as Geiger (*Urschrift,* 182) thinks; see אדרת אליהו, 70*a*, and כתר תורה, Lev. 54*a*. Geiger refers to Mibḥar, *ad loc.* Aaron b. Joseph, however, contradicts himself; see Mibḥar, Num. 4*b*: ואיש את קדשיו : כגון מעשר שני ונטע רבעי והשלמים שהם לבעלים כמו ממונו ומותר הבעל בהם; comp. however, the super-commentary טירת כסף on Mibḥar, Deut. 16*a*, letter 109. The view that נטע רבעי belongs to the priest is held by Samuel al-Magrabi (M. Lorge, *Die Speisegesetze der Karäer von Samuel el-Maġrebi,* Berlin 1907, 23, end). Geiger finds this view also in p. Soṭah 8, 5; but see Pineles, דרכה של תורה, 176 ff., and Gronemann, *l. c.* For the meaning of that passage see also N. Z. Berlin, in Halevy's דורות

According to Tradition, two tithes were to be taken every year (except the sabbatical year). The "first tithe" (Num. 18, 21 ff.) and the "second tithe" (Deut. 14, 22 ff.) are to be taken in the first, second, fourth, and fifth years; the "first tithe" and the tithe for the poor (Deut. 26, 12 ff.) in the third and sixth years of every cycle of seven years. Geiger (*Urschrift,* 176 ff.) contends that the ancient Halakah required the taking of all these three tithes in the third and sixth years, as the Karaites hold.[35] He

ענינים שונים הנוגעים לתקופת הראשונים, III, 313-4; comp. also Poznański, הגאונים, 16 ff. Hadassi (Alph. 205 (18*c*) and 303 (112*d*)) also holds that the fruits of the fourth year belong to the priests. As was pointed out already by Maimonides (מאכלות אסורות 10, 18) the mistaken view of some Geonim that the fruits of the fourth year are not to be eaten—even when redeemed—during the fourth year was caused by Lev. 19, 25: ובשנה החמשית תאכלו את פריו which seems to prohibit the enjoyment of the fruits of the fourth year during that year (Tosafot Rosh ha-shanah 10*a, s. v.* ופירות; ר"ש to Maaser Sheni 5, 1 and Asheri, ה' ערלה, end, quote this view from Halakot Gedolot. See also She'eltot No. 10, but see Kaminka, הקדם, II, 21). This accounts also for the interpretation of verse 24 by Ps.-Jon., many Karaites, and even Ibn Ezra (*ad loc.*) to mean that the fruits of the fourth year are to be given to the priests and that the owner is to enjoy the fruits of the *fifth* year (v. 25). For the view of Geiger see also *Jüd. Zeitschrift,* II, 183; *Nachgel Schr.,* IV, 38, 107.

[35] Not all; see כתר תורה, Deut. 18*a*: ויש מבעלי מקרא אומרים שבשנה ראשונה ושנית נותן שתי מעשרות ובשלישית מוציא שלש מעשרות תוספת מעשר עני; comp. H. Olitzki, *Flavius Josephus und die Halacha,* Berlin 1885, 16-19. See also Mibḥar, Deut., 12*a*; 23*b*; and טירת כסף to the last mentioned place, letters 27-28. According to Anan (Schechter, *Jewish Sectaries* II, p. 5 ll. 10-19) *two* tithes are to be taken every year. This seems to be the meaning of his words: ובארץ יש' מפרשינן [מנהו] ב' ב' מעשר חד מעשר ללוים וחד מעשר אכלין ליה מ[רואתיהו] דכ' עשר תעשר וג' ואכלת לפני יי' אלהיך ב' א' י' לשכן שמו ש[ם והאי] מעשר ישראל אכלין ליה דקא אמא ואכלת לפני יי' אלהיך והלא מע[שר ללוים] דכ' ולבני לוי אלא על תנין מעשר קאים מישום האכי אקד[ם עשר תעשר] בתרין לישאני לאפרושי תרין מעשר חד מעשר ללוים וחד מעשר [אכלין] בעלים בבית המקדש כי היכי דאמרן. A similar view is mentioned in כתר תורה on Deut., 18*a*: ויש אומרים שבשנה שלישית מה שיותר מן המעשרות ראשון

bases this opinion on Tobit 10, 7, 8 (against which see F. Rosenthal, *Vier Apokryphische Bücher*, Leipzig 1885, 117, note), Josephus *Ant.* IV, 8, 22, Sifre to Deut. 12, 17; 14, 28 (against which see Weiss, דור דור וד׳, I, 126, note); but mainly on Ps.-Jon. to Deut. 26, 12-13: ארום תשיצון לעשרא ית כל מעשר עללתך בשתא תליתיתא דשמיטיתא ותתנון מעשרא קמאה לליואי מעשרא תניינא הוא מעשר מסכיניא לגיוריא ליתמיא ולארמלתא וייכלון בקרווך ויסבעון : ומעשר תליתאי תיסק ותיכול קדם ה׳ אלהך ותימר הא אפרשנן קודשיא מן ביתא ולחוד יהבנן מעשרא קמאה לליואי מעשרא תנינא לגיורי ליתמא ולארמלא הי ככל תפקידתך דפקידתני לא עברית חדא מן פקודייך ולא אנשיית. As was already pointed out by M. Olitzki (*Flavius Josephus und die Halacha*, 18, note) and Bassfreund (*MGWJ.*, XL 1896), 5 ff.), there is nothing in Ps.-Jon. to these two verses to justify the view of Geiger. What Ps.-Jon. adds to the translation of the text is entirely in agreement with tradition (Sifre, II, 109 and 302) that in the שנת הבעור all the tithes from the last three years must be removed, the first tithe given to the Levite and the "second tithe" carried to Jerusalem. (See also on the whole Pineles, דרכה של תורה, 173-6, and Gronemann, p. 161 ff.).[36]

ושני מוציאם בשער הלוי לוקח שלו והעני מן השני. Harkavy's suggestion (ס׳ המצות לענן, 142, note 18) that Ibn Ezra on Deut. 14, 28 meant Anan and the Karaites is thus proved erroneous; comp. also Book of Jubilees 32, 11. For a full refutation of the view of Geiger, see Bassfreund, *MGWJ.*, XL (1896), 5-8.

[36] Geiger, on the basis of his theory that R. Eliezer b. Hyrcanus and R. Ishmael represent the ancient Halakah related to Sadducean Tradition (see above), sees also in every agreement of Ps.-Jon. with the interpretation of R. Eliezer or R. Ishmael ancient laws, which were changed by the school of R. Akiba (*Urschrift*, 447, 472 ff.; *Nachg. Schriften*, IV, 106-7). It was however shown by Gronemann (119, note 2; see also 103, note; 139-140, notes; comp. also Epstein, *MGWJ.*, XL (1896), 142) that Ps.-Jon. does not always follow the interpretation of the school of R. Ishmael against that

An agreement between Pseudo-Jonathan and many Karaites, not noticed by Geiger, is their interpretation of Lev. 18, 21 ומזרעך לא תתן להעביר למלך as referring to marriage with a Gentile woman;[37] see Ḳirḳisani 11, 23; Hadassi (Alph. 324): עוד אמר ומזרעך לא תתן להעביר למלך וגו׳... פתרון שני נאמר כי אסור על אנשי הדת שלא יקחו מבנות העכ"ומז; see *ib.*. Alph. 278, 313 and 364; see also כתר תורה, *ad loc.* (49*a*). This interpretation, though censured in the Mishnah (Megillah 3, 9; comp. תוספות יום טוב *ad loc.*), is given in the name of[38] תנא דבי רבי ישמעאל (Megillah 25*a*; p. Sanhedrin 9, 7, see also Sifre II, 171) and as Friedmann, *Bet Talmud,* I, 336-7 (comp. Ginzburger, *MGWJ.,* 1900. 6 ff.), points out, the Mishnah simply meant that this verse is not to be interpreted in this way in public as it adds to the text.

of R. Akiba, his acceptance of the former being mostly conditioned by their being nearer to the plain meaning of the verse; comp. also the view of D. Hoffmann, *Zur Einleitung in die halachischen Midraschim,* pp. 74-76.

[37] This verse, as Frankel (*Einfluss,* 156) remarks, gave rise to many divergent interpretations. Anan also interpreted this verse allegorically; see Harkavy, ספר המצות לענן, 207, and Schechter, *Jewish Sectaries,* II, 32. The interpretation in the Book of Jubilees 30, 7-10 of this verse as referring to one who effects a union between a Jewish woman and a Gentile and that such action is punished by death is found also among the Karaites; so Samuel al-Magrabi (Book of Precepts called אלמרשד, a unique MS. of the Hebrew translation of the אלמרשד written in 1722 by Samuel b. Solomon ha-Kohen (see Pinsker, II, 144-5; Gottlober, בקרת לתולדות הקראים, 202, note) now in the library of the Jewish Theological Seminary of America), 222*a*: ויש אומרים כי הרצון בזה המאמר כי האדם מישראל לא יבעל אחת מן הגוים בין בזנות ובין בנשואים ויתן בה בגופה... וכן מי הוציא זרעו לאומות העולם בבעילתו או בזנותו באשה מהם או בחזוק איש מהם כי יבעל באשה מבני ישראל העושה המעשה הזה הוא מחלל שם ה׳ וגזר על העושה זאת ברגימה באבנים על ידי עם הארץ.

[38] Comp. Rashi, *ad loc.*; Aruk, *s. v.* ארם; S. L. Rapoport, נחלת יהודה, Krakau 1868, p. 231 ff.; Geiger, *Urschrift,* 304; *Nachg. Schriften,* IV, 106; Berliner, *Onkelos,* II, 88 ff. and literature quoted there.

The Karaites agree with Ps.-Jon. to Lev. 1, 4 and 3, 2, (against Sifra to 16, 21; Menaḥot 93*a*; Tosefta *ib.*, 10, 3; so also Philo, II, 241) that סמיכת קרבן is with the right hand only. See Mibḥar, Lev., 3*a*: וסמך ידו: הימנית... בידו האחת יסמוך ואין סמיכה בשתי ידים רק על שעיר המשתלח ואשר אמרו בעלי הקבלה הכתוב מתגבר על קבלתם [בשתי ידים]. So also Mibḥar, Lev., 27*a*, and כתר תורה on Lev. 1, 4 (3*b*, end). But see D. Hoffmann, *Zur Einleitung in die halachischen Midraschim,* Berlin 1887, p. 75, who contends that this interpretation of Ps.-Jon. (which is also favored by the פשט; see Ibn Ezra on Lev. 1, 4) goes back to the school of R. Ishmael.

Ps.-Jon. translates אשה חדשה in Deut. 24, 5, against Sifre *ad. loc.* and Soṭah 44*a,* by בתולתא חדתא. This is also the interpretation of חדשה by many Karaites. See גן עדן, 154*b*: ובאמרו אשה חדשה רומז בזה שלא נשאת עדיין... אבל אלמנה או גרושה מן הנשואין לא תקרא אשה חדשה. So also כתר תורה, *ad loc.* (27*b*). See, however, Mibḥar *ad loc.* (20*b*). Samuel al-Magrabi (MS. 95*a*) states that the Karaites are divided on the interpretation of אשה חדשה. This deviation of Ps.-Jon. and *some* of the Karaites from the talmudic interpretation of חדשה rests on the plain meaning of that word. See Ibn Ezra *ad loc.;* comp. Gronemann, *l. c.,* p. 67.

While, as we have seen, the proofs adduced by Geiger do not establish relationship between the ancient Halakah, believed by him to be contained in Pseudo-Jonathan, and the Karaite Halakah, the following consideration, not hitherto noted, arises against any attempt at connecting the Karaite law with the ancient Sadducean Halakah which is believed to be represented in Ps.Jon.:

If the deviation of Ps.-Jon. from our Halakah go back to ancient tradition related to Sadduceism, then we should expect the Karaites—a later name for Sadduceism, according to this view—to be in agreement with such deviations of Ps.-Jon. The following examination of the main halakic divergences of Ps.-Jon. from our Halakah and of the view of the Karaites on these points will show how untenable this view is.[39]

According to Tradition (Mekilta, Mishpaṭim, 1, ed. Fried., 74*b;* Arakin 18*b;* p. Ḳiddushin 59*a*; Maim. עבדים, 4, 4) the seventh year in which the Jewish male or female

[39] Ginsburger's edition of Ps.-Jon. (Berlin 1903) is followed here. Most of the differences between Ps.-Jon., and our Halakah are collected by Gronemann, *ib.* He includes, however, renderings of some passages not being aware that Ps.-Jon. followed in their interpretation the Jerushalmi. Comp. *ib.*, p. 48, in reference to Deut. 17, 5, אל שעריך, which is the interpretation of the רבנן in p. Sanhedrin 6, 1. See also Onkelos, *ad loc.*, and Ps.-Jon. on Deut. 22, 24; comp. *MGWJ.*, LII (1908), 217, note 1. This also explains Ps.-Jonathan's rendering of Lev. 11, 11 ואת נבלתם תשקצו by וית ניבלתהון תשקצון ומן הנייתהון תתרחקון which Hoffmann (*ZfhB.*, VII, 1903, 47; comp. Reifmann, *Bet Talmud,* I, 314) considers to be anti-traditional. But see p. Shebiit 7, 1: כתיב טמאים הם [לכם] מה ת״ל וטמאים יהיו לכם אלא אחד איסור אכילה ואחד איסור הנאה the meaning of which, as is evident from what follows there, is that איסורי אכילה are not to be made objects for trade and gain (see b. Pesaḥim 23*a*). Ps.-Jon. in his ומן הנייתהון תתרחקון thus follows the Jerushalmi; comp. also the fragment of a commentary to p. Shabbat published by Poznański in הקדם, II, 49 and n. 4, and Saadia Gaon on Lev. 11, 11 published by Hirschfeld in *JQR.*, XIX, 140, beginning, ויכתבון ליה סביא in Ps.-Jon. to Deut. 17, 18 (comp. Reifmann, *l. c.*, p. 348) may be a reference to p. Sanhedrin 2, 6 (20*c*; comp. Tosefta *ib.*, 4, 7; *Maim.*, מלכים 3, 1): ומגיהין אותו מספרי עזרה על פי בית דין של ע״א.

Ps.-Jon. translates also Deut. 21, 7 in accordance with the *Palestinian* interpretation as referring to the murderer. See p. Soṭah 9, 6; comp. b. *ib.*, 38*b* and Rashi, *ad loc.* See also on the Halakah of Ps.-Jon. J. Reifman, *Bet Talmud,* I, 215 ff., 347 ff.; A. Büchler, *Die Priester und der Cultus,* Wien 1895, 151 ff.; D. Hoffmann, *Zur Einleitung in d. haláchischen Midraschim,* 74-76; *id., in ZfhB.*, VII (1903), 46-48.

slave is to be released (Ex. 21, 2; Deut. 15, 12) refers not to the Sabbath year (שנת השמטה), but to the seventh year from the commencement of their servitude.[40] Ps.-Jon., however, seems to interpret וּבַשְּׁבִעִת "the sabbatical year" (Ps.-Jon. to Ex. 21, 7; 22, 2; but see Ps.-Jon. to Ex. 21, 2 and to Deut. 15, 12). The Karaites differing among themselves on the laws of slavery agree with Tradition that ובשבעת refers to the seventh year of servitude. See משאת בנימין, 1*d*: ישראל שנמכר לא יעבוד יותר משש שנים שלמים [שנ'] שש שנים יעבד ובשבעת יצא לחפשי חנם; Samuel al-Magrabi (S. Gitelsohn, *Die Civil-Gesetze der Karäer von Samuel al-Magrabi,* Berlin 1904, 2, line 1); Afendopolo's appendix to אדרת אליהו 9*c*: עבד שנמכר בשש שנים אם ביניהם שמטה אינו יוצא כי השנים האלו מעת ביאתו על סדר לא בשנות השמטה.

Geiger holds (*Urschrift,* 190 ff.) that the ancient Halakah did not distinguish between paid and gratuitous guardians, as does Tradition (B. M. 93*a*) but made the difference in responsibility depend on the nature of the goods entrusted. It referred Ex. 22, 6-8 to things light in which case the guardian is liable only for lack of ordinary care, and verses 8-13 to things heavy for which the

[40] So also Josephus (H. Weyl, *Die jüdischen Strafgesetze bei Flavius Josephus,* Berlin 1900, 122; Olitzki, *Magazin,* XVI (1889), 78). On the view of Philo, see Ritter, 59, and Weyl, *l. c.*, note 19. The Samaritans also interpret וּבַשְּׁבִעִת as the seventh year of the *servitude* (Klumel, *Mischpatim, Ein samaritanisch-arabischer Commentar zu Ex.* XXI-XXII, 15 *von Ibrahim ibn Jakub,* Berlin 1902, p. II). They disagree, however, with Tradition in referring Ex. 21, 2-7, to a proselyte (*l. c.*) a view which is also represented among the Karaites (Jepheth b. Ali quoted in Mibḥar, Ex. 40*a*; גן עדן, 148*d;* כתר תורה, Ex. 68*b;* אדרת אליהו (Odessa 1870), 189*d;* Samuel al-Magrabi (Gitelsohn, p. 1, 5). The Samaritans take ועבדו לעולם (v. 6) literally (Klumel, p. VII) as do also some Karaites (see אדרת אליהו, 90*a;* Samuel al-Magrabi (Gitelsohn, 5)).

guardian is responsible even if they were stolen. Ps.-Jon. taking vs. 9-11, against the talmudic interpretation (Mekilta, *ad loc.;* Baba Meṣi'a 94*b*) as referring to a gratutious guardian בלא אגר נטיר and v. 11, with the Talmud, to a paid guardian דהוה ליה עמיה אגר נטיר, represents according to Geiger (*ib.*) an intermediate state in the development of the law of guardians.[41]

All the later Karaites accept fully the traditional interpretation of Ex. 22, 6-15 as referring to four kinds of guardians, so Mibḥar, *ad loc.,* 44*b*-45*a;* כתר תורה, *ad loc.,* 75*a-b;* גן עדן, דין ארבעה שומרים, 182*b*-184*c;* Samuel al-Magrabi, MS., 136*a* ff.

Ps.-Jon. interprets Lev. 5, 1 against Tradition (Sifra *ad loc.*) interpret this verse like Tradition, as referring another person swearing falsely or breaking an oath and conceals it (comp. Reifmann, *l. c.,* 313, and Hoffman, *Leviticus,* I, 199, note).[42] The Karaites (מבחר and כתר תורה, *ad loc.*) interpret this verse like Tradition, as referring to שבועת העדות.

Geiger (*Urschrift,* 477) finds support for his view that according to the Sadducees all the work connected

[41] See RaSHbaM on v. 6; comp. Reifmann, *Bet Talmud,* I, 219. The view of Gronemann, 77 ff., is improbable, comp. *ib.,* note. For Philo's and Josephus' interpretation of these verses see Ritter, p. 61 ff., and Weyl, p. 130 ff. Hadassi (Alph. 370) refers verses 6-10 to מטלטלין and verses 10-13 to בעלי חיים. Benjamin Nehawendi seems also to make this distinction (משאת בנימין, 2*b*) but contradicts himself. He says (*ib.,* 3*b*): המלוה חייב לשלם דמי העבוטות ומשתלם חובו ממנו בעבור כי הוא דומה לשומר וחייב בגנבה שנאמר ואם גנוב יגנב מעמו וגו', thus referring verse 11 to מטלטלין.

[42] Philo makes such reticence a *capital crime* (II, 275; Ritter, p. 47; comp. *Werke Philos,* II, 114, note 4). This interpretation of Ps.-Jon. seems to have escaped Ritter (*l. c.*).

with the Red Heifer was to be done by priests only[43] in Ps.-Jon. to Num. 19, 9. 18 ויכנוש גבר כהין דכי (comp. also Brüll, *Bet Talmud,* I, 270).

The Karaites, however, agree with Tradition in the interpretation of איש טהור (so also Philo II, 253); and Mibḥar (*ad loc.,* 18*b*) records the opinion of some Karaites that even שרפת פרה (v. 5), which according to Tradition is פסול בזר (see note 43), does not require a priest:

ויש אומרים השורף יתכן להיותו כהן או זולת כהן

Ps.-Jon. adds to יוציא מחוץ למחנה (Lev. 16, 27) the words יתפקון באסלין על ידיהון דטליא דכהניא... which is against the Halakah, as Büchler (*Die Priester und der Cultus,* 153) remarks. The Karaites agree with Tradition. See Mibḥar. *ad loc.* (28*a*):

יוציא אל מחוץ למחנה : יוציא דמוציא ולא כהן.[44]

Ps.-Jon. differs from Tradition, Yoma 6, 6, in the interpretation of ושלח את השעיר (Lev. 16, 22) in ascribing the death of the goat to non-human agency. Geiger (*N. S.,* V, Heb., 115) believes this to have been the ancient interpretation (failing, however, to indicate the reason that

[43] Comp. Brüll, *Bet Talmud,* I, 273. Geiger (*l. c.*) quotes also Ps.-Jon. on verses 3, 5, 7, but in the interpretation of v. 5, Ps.-Jon. is in full agreement with Tradition, which also requires שרפת פרה to be by a priest (Brüll, *l. c.,* 271, n. 5, notwithstanding). See Parah 4, 4; Tosefta, *ib.* 4, 6; Maim., פרה אדומה, 3, 2; 4, 17. The view that שחיטה בכהן (Ps.-Jon. on verses 3, 7) is represented also in Yoma 42*a*. As to the slaughtering of sacrifices in general if it need be by a priest, see Ritter, pp. 110-11; see also Büchler, *Die Priester und der Cultus,* 138 ff., and p. 101, n. 2, and p. 155, n. 2. See Yoma 27*a* and Zebaḥim 32*a;* see also Lev. Rabba 22, 4: תני דבי ישמעאל לפי שהיו ישראל אסורים בבשר תאוה במדבר ... והכהן שוחט ומקבל.

[44] See also Geiger, *Urschrift,* 173 (and Büchler, *l. c.,* 154) as to Ps.-Jon. Ex. 29, 37; 30, 29; against which see the just remarks of Gronemann, 48, note.

might have caused the change in the interpretation of this verse). The Karaite interpretation agrees with that of the Talmud. See Mibḥar, *ad loc.* (27*b*) ...ומשליכו משם, comp. also כתר תורה, *ad loc.*

According to Tradition שלמי נדר ונדבה (Lev. 7, 16-18) are eaten only two days and the night between (Sifra *ad loc.;* Zebaḥim 5, 7; Pesaḥim 3*a;* Maimon., מעשה הקרבנות, 10, 6). It construes וממחרת והנותר (v. 16) so that יאכל refers to ממחרת. Ps.-Jon. refers יאכל to the night after the second day so that שלמים are eaten two days and two nights (comp. Ps.-Jon. to Lev. 19, 6). The Karaites are divided on this question. See Mibḥar, *ad loc.* (11*b*): ממחרת. שנאכלים לשני ימים ולילה אחד והנותר מבשר הזבח ביום השלישי באש ישרף: ביום השלישי דבק עם באש ישרף לא עם והנותר... But see כתר תורה, *ad. loc.* (18*b*): והנה שלמי נדר ונדבה נאכלים לשני ימים ושתי לילות לא שני ימים ולילה אחת... הוא הדין גם בשלמי נדר שיום המחרת תופש גם הלילה של אחריו. In a fragment of a commentary on Lev. which Schechter published in his *Saadyana,* 144 ff., the author of which Schechter believes to be the famous ninth century Karaite Daniel al Ḳumṣi, the same view is held (*ib.,* p. 146):[45] ...כן נדר ונדבה יאכל ממחרת וליל שלישי...

[45] Aaron b. Elias, however, contradicts himself. See גן עדן, fol. 39*c*. l. 7 from bottom: והשלמים נאכלין לשני ימים ולילה אחת. Philo, as is evident from the third reason given by him for the law of Lev. 19, 6 (II, 245), agrees with Ps.-Jon. See also Geiger, *Nachg. Schr.,* IV, 38; Reifmann, *Bet Talmud,* I, 314. Chwolson, *Das letzte Passamahl Christi,* 35, believes this to have been the *Sadducean view;* comp. *ib.,* 32, 34. The interpretation of Ps.-Jon. seems to have escaped Chwolson. Another Karaite view is found in the fragment mentioned in the text. Daniel says that the words אדם כי יקריב מכם קרבן (Lev. 1, 2) excluded Gentiles from bringing any sacrifices to be offered for them in the Temple. Other Karaites hold the same view (Mibḥar, Lev. 39*a*, and טירת כסף, *ad loc.,* כתר תורה 62*a;* but see תטיב דעת by the Karaite

Ps.-Jon. interprets ולא ירבה לו סוסים (Deut. 17, 16) to mean that he should not have more than two horses (לחוד לא יסגון ליה על תרין סוסוון) which is against the talmudic interpretation that the King is not to keep more horses than he actually needs (Sifre, *ad loc.*, 105*b;* Sanhedrin 21*a*, comp. Brüll, *Bet Talmud,* II, 25-26). The Karaites agree with the talmudic interpetation. See Mibḥar, *ad loc.* (14*b*) : ולא ירבה לו סוסים : אלא כדי מרכבתו.

Tradition interprets ומת הנביא ההוא (Deut. 18, 19) as death by strangulation (Sanhedrin 10, 1; Sifre, *ad loc.*, 108*a*). Ps.-Jon. translates death by sword.[46] The Karaites agree with Tradition. See כתר תורה, *ad loc.* (22*a*): אך הנביא אשר יזיד : זהו נביא שקר וגם יכלול מי שהוא מן מגנבי דברי השם והמתנבא בשם עבודה זרה והנה שלשתם בחנק.[47]

As was already remarked by Jonathan Eibeschütz (אורים ותומים, 9, 2) Ps.-Jon. in his translation of Deut, 24, 1 יכתוב לה ספר תירוכין קדם בי דינא requires the presence of a court for the execution of a bill of divorce. The Karaites agree with Tradition (see Baba Batra 174*b;* Arakin 23*a*: אטו כל דמגרש בבי דינא קא מגרש; but comp. פירוש ר׳ גרשום, *ad loc.;* see the literature in L. Löw, *Ges. Schr.*, III, 235-244) against Ps.-Jon. Anan requires the presence of ten, which constitutes a court according to the early Karaites (see *REJ.*, XLV, 67; 69 note) in case of marriage (סה"מ לענ ed. Harkavy, p. 113) but not for a divorce (*l. c.*, p. 119). See also Benjamin Nahawendi,

M. Sultanski, Goslow 1858, 118). The later Samaritans shared this view (Wreschner, 61-2). This Karaite law is based on no tradition; see Schürer, Division II, Vol. I (Engl. transl.), 299 ff.

[46] Ps.-Jon. interprets יומת in Deut. 13, 6 also by יתקטל בסייפא, which is against the Mishnah, Sanhedrin 10, 1.

[47] Aaron b. Joseph (Mibḥar, Deut. 15*a*) believes that death here is בידי שמים, basing his view on Jerem. 28, 16.

משאת בנימין, *6c*, ll. 9-12, and גן עדן, 155*b*. Elias Bashjatzi (אדרת אליהו, ע̅ נשים, פ׳ י״ב) states: ולכן התקינו בתי דינים שינתן [הגט] בב״ד כדי שיהיה הדבר מפורסם

It is, however, most probable that in many instances a writ of divorce would be given in the presence of a בית דין to insure legality and publicity, to which custom Ps.-Jonathan's קדם בי דינא may be due. In a recently discovered Assuan papyrus a divorce is said to be announced בעדה. See *Jahrbuch d. jüdisch-literarischen Gesellschaft*, VII, Frankfurt a-M. 1910, p. 378.

Ps.-Jon. (so also Fragment Targum) interprets ובאת אל הכהן אשר יהיה בימים ההם (Deut. 26, 3) against Tradition (Bikkurim 3, 12; Sifre, *ad loc.;* so also Josephus, IV, 8, 22) as referring to the high priest (תעלון לות כהנא די יהוי ממני לכהין רב). The Karaites agree with Tradition. See Mibḥar, *ad loc.*, 23*a*. So also כתר תורה,[48] *ad loc.* 29*b*).

[48] The Karaites, relying on Nehem. 10, 36, contend that the firstlings (בכורים) are to be offered from all kinds of earth and tree fruits (Mibḥar and כתר תורה, *l. c.*). According to Tradition (Bikkurim, 1, 3) they are offered only from the "seven kinds" enumerated in Deut. 8, 8. Philo, II, 298 states that they are brought from the fruits of trees (see *Werkes Philos,* II, 168, n. 2; but see Philo, II, 391); comp. also Book of Jubilees 21, 10 and Josephus *Ant.* IV, 8, 22.

I will now turn to the differences known or supposed to have existed between the Sadducees and the Pharisees and examine Karaite halakah on these disputed points.

The interpretation of Lev. 16, 12-14 constituted one of the earliest differences between the Pharisees and the Sadducees. The Sadducean view and practice was (Tosefta Yoma 1, 7) that the kindling of incense in the vessel (v. 13) was to take place before the high-priest entered the Holy of Holies, maintaining that otherwise the high-priest when entering it would see the Ark,—which contravenes כי בענן אראה על חכפרת (v. 2).[49] The Pharisaic ruling and practice was that the incense is to be put on the coals in the Holy of Holies itself (T. K. Aḥare Mot, 3; Tosefta Yoma 1, 7; Yoma 19*b*; 53*a*; p. *ib.*, 1, 5 (39*a*)). The Karaites agree with the Pharisaic interpretation of these verses. See Mibḥar, *ad loc.* (27*a*): ונתן את וגו׳ : אחר הכנסו מיד שלא יראה הכפרת; so also כתר תורה, *ad loc.* (42*b*): כנראה שקטורת מכניסה על ידי כלי אחר ובהכנסו נותנה על המחתה.

The authenticity of Megillat Taanit (ed. Neubauer, ch. 4), according to which the interpretation of וירקה

*Continued from New Series, vol. II, 517 ff.

[49] See כתר תורה, Lev. 41*b*, for the anti-Sudducean interpretation of this verse: ואין הטעם שלא אראה רק בענן הקטורת. Comp. Geiger, *Jüd. Zeitschrift*, II, 29 ff., and Oppenheim, *Bet Talmud* IV, 269 ff.

בפניו (Deut. 25, 9) constituted a difference between the Pharisees and the Sadducees, is admitted by Geiger (*Jüdische Zeitschrift,* II, 28; comp. *ib.,* 95). The latter in their adherence to the letter of the Law required the יבמה to spit in his face (ממש) while the Pharisees in case of *ḥaliṣah* caused her to spit before him (Yebamot 106*b*). The Karaites agree with the Pharisees in the interpretation of וירקה בפניו.[50] See Mibḥar, *ad loc.* (22*a*) וירקה בפניו בארץ כנגד היבם וי"ל בפני הנעל. Comp. טירת כסף, *ad loc.*

The responsibility of a master for damage caused to others by his servants constituted, as already recorded in Mishnah (Yadaim 4, 7), an issue between the Pharisees and Sadducees. The latter applied the law of Ex. 21, 35 also to damage done by one's servants. The Karaites agree with the Pharisees and reason like them. See גן עדן (180*c*): נזקי עבד ואשת איש אשר הזיקום אחרים משלמין אבל הם פטורים.... אבל במה שיש תשלומין אינו דין שיפרע הבעל או האדון... ואין להקיש נזקי העבד בנזקי השור כי העבד יש לו דעת ואפשר שירע לבבו מאדוניו ויפסיד ממון אחרים וימצא משלם; comp. G. Hölscher, *Der Sadduzäismus* (Leipzig 1906), 30 ff.; Geiger, *Urschrift,* 143 ff.

The Pharisees and the Sadducees differed on the law of inheritance. According to Num. 27, 8 when there are sons and daughters, the sons are the heirs. But if the son died before his father, the son leaving a daughter, the Sadducees held that the daughter shares with her brother's daughter the inheritance. The Pharisees held that the son and all his descendants, male or female, should precede the daughter in the right of inheritance (Meg. Taanit 5,

[50] See Rapoport, דברי שלום ואמת (Prag. 1861), 11 ff.; Weiss, I, 117, note 2. Josephus (*Ant.* IV, 8, 23) translates with the Sadducees בפניו literally. See, however, Anan (Harkavy, 116): ויירקא באפיה. Comp. also *Testament of Twelve Patriarchs,* Zebulun, 3, 4, ff.

(Neubauer, II, 10); Tosefta Yadaim 2, 20; Baba Batra 115*b*-116*a; p. ib.,* 8, 1).[51]

The Karaite law of inheritance, as they themselves confess (גן עדן, 165*b*), is confused, and difference of opinion exists among them on essential points. The prominent ninth century Karaite, Daniel al Ḳumṣi, held that the daughter when sons are left receives a third of the inheritance (Pinsker, II, 85; comp. אדרת אליהו, 101*a*).[52] Joseph b. Abraham ha-Kohen was of the opinion that the daughter's right to inheritance is equal to the son's (*ib.*, 101*c;* גן עדן 165*d*); this, he reports in the name of David b. Boaz, was also the view of many others.[53] These views disagree with

[51] See V. Aptowitzer, *Die syrischen Rechtsbücher und das Mosaisch-Talmudische Recht*, Wien 1909, 82. His assertion that the law of Timotheos quoted there is Sadducean is mistaken. The equal rights of a daughter's son and another daughter's daughter never constituted an issue between the Pharisees and the Sadducees.

[52] Wreschner, 41, suggests that it was taken by some of the Karaites from the Samaritans, who follow the Mohammedan law and give the daughter, when there is a son, a third of the inheritance. The Karaite law: ממון כל שאין לו קרוב וגואל הוא לכהן הגדול המשרת המקדש (Benjamin Nahawendi, משאת בנימין, 2*d*: so also Hadassi, Alph. 369) might have also been borrowed from the Samaritans (see Wreschner, 42). For a similar view, see Schechter, *Jewish Sectaries,* I, p. 9, lines 14-15. Tradition makes no provision for the case of a man dying without heirs and considers it impossible (Sifre to Num. 5, 8; Baba ḳamma 109*a*). According to Philo (II, 291) the tribe inherits his property.

[53] An opinion identical with that of Joseph b. Abraham is quoted in p. Baba batra 8, 1 in the name of חכמי גוים. Aaron b. Elias (גן עדן, 166*a*) states that by "many others" David b. Boaz meant the *Sadducees* and reads in Baba batra 115*b* כל האומר תירש בת עם הבן אפילו נשיא בישראל אין שומעין לו instead of כל האומר תירש בת עם בת הבן; see also the reading in Neubauer's edition of Megillat Taanit (*l. c.*); comp. Hoffmann, *ZfhB.*, IX (1905), 135. For the view of Anan on ירושת הבת, see Hadassi, Alph. 256 (98*b*); comp. Grätz, *Geschichte,* V[4], 187; D. H. Müller, *Syrisch-römische Rechtbsücher u. Hamurabi,* 31.

The opinion of Wreschner, 39, that חכמי גוים refers to the Samaritans

the Sadducean as well as with the Pharisaic practice. Those Karaites who do accept the traditional view that daughters do not share with sons in inheritance,—and this is the view of nearly all later Karaites (Hadassi, Alph. 252, 256; גן עדן, 166*a*, and מבחר and כתר תורה to Num. 27, 8)—agree also with the *Pharisees* against the Sadducees, that the son's children, female as well as male, are the sole heirs even when the deceased has left daughters. See Hadassi, Alph. 252 and 256: ואמר ובן אין לו והעברתם את נחלתו לבתו בתורתך: "פתרונו בן קודם לבת וכל יוצאי ירכו של בן קודמים לבת; so also אדרת אליהו 102*d*: ...ולפי זה בת הבן קודמת מן הבת...; so also כתר תורה, Num. 41*b*: ...ופרחי הבן, בין זכר ובין נקבה קודמין מן הבת.

Hadassi (Alph. 97) informs us that the Sadducees "absolutely forbade divorce." Geiger (*Zeitschrift*, 1836, p. 99) doubted the authenticity of this report. Ḳirḳisani reports it in the name of David b. Merwan Almukameṣ (ed. Harkavy, 304, l. 3; 305, l. 12). S. Holdheim in his מאמר האישות (Berlin 1861, p. 43 ff.) finds support for this assertion in the fact that the Karaites, who, as he believes with Geiger, descend from Sadducees, also prohibit divorce except in case of suspicion of adultery in the wife, and quotes (p. 53, note) אדרת אליהו. Holdheim, however, misstated the facts. The author of אדרת אליהו (96*c*) as well as all the other later Karaites (Hadassi, Alph. 366 (141*c*); מבחר and כתר תורה on Deut. 24, 1; Gan Eden 154*d* and לבוש מלכות (A. Neubauer, *Aus d. Petersburger Bibliothek*, 54)), does not like the School of Shammai (Gittin 90*a*) take ערות דבר (Deut. 24, 1) to mean sexual immorality, but an

is forced. He and Aptowitzer (*JQR.*, XIX, 609) overlooked Shabbat 116*b*. For the expression אפילו נשיא בישראל, see החלוץ, VIII, 78; נשיא בישראל may also refer to R. Gamaliel II who was the supposed litigant (Shabbat 116*b*).

"intolerable thing" as, for instance, the wife's becoming (after the marriage) deaf or blind or contracting an incurable disease; anything of such a nature is legitimate cause for divorce. But even this view was rather an innovation of later Karaites. As we now know, according to Anan, marriage may be dissolved at the wish of either of the parties, by a writ of divorce. See his ספר המצות (Harkavy, 119): וקא אמא והיה אם לא תמצא חן בעיניו כי מצא בה ערות דבר דאי לא שפרא בעיניה דאשכח בה מילי סניתא ולא ניחא ליה בגוה מגריש לה בין דלא צבי בה הוא ובין דלא צביא ביה היא.[54]

Benjamin Nahawendi (משאת בנימין, 5*b*), considered the right of divorce to be vested in the husband alone. Samuel al Magrebi tells us of the following three opinions among the Karaites as to the husband's right of divorce. He says (MS. 97*b*): כי מצא בה ערות דבר: דע כי התחלפו חחכמים בזה הדבר מהם מי אמר כי ישוב להדת ועניו לא תמצא ח בעיניו לאשר מצא בה כי היא מקלה במצות.... ומהם אמר כי זה המאמר יכלול כל אשר ימצא האיש באשתו מאשר ימנע האיש כי תמצא האשה חן בעיניו ואין הבדל אם יהיה המום מפני דרכי הדת אם מפני דרכי העולם מפני היצירה או הצורה ומהם מי לא ישים זה המאמר תנאי בגרוש כי בדעתם מאז יאמר אני שנאתי [את אשתי] יאָמֵר לו תן לה המוהר המאוחר שלה ותגרשנה וגם ראיתי את אנשי זמני דורכים בזה הנתיב.

[54] See Harkavy in Grätz, *Geschichte,* V[4], 487. This view of Anan seems to have escaped Poznański, *ZfhB.,* XI (1907), 72. It is possible that Anan in this law raised to the dignity of a biblical law the תקנת מורדת enacted about a century before Anan. See Sherira Gaon, *Epistle,* ed. Neubauer, 35, l. 11; *id.,* חמדה גנוזה, Resp. 140; comp. Grätz, V[4], 129-130; Weiss, *Dor,* IV, 5, 9, 37; A. Schwarz, *Moses b. Maimon,* Leipzig 1908, 342-345. Hadassi (Alph. 335) stands alone in his opinion that מום לאחר קדושין is not sufficient cause for divorce. For the Samaritan interpretation of ערות דבר comp. *MGWJ.,* LIV (1910), 433; Philo and Josephus agree with the view of Beth Hillel (Ritter, 70, n. 1).

The practice of the Karaites of his day thus coincided with the opinion of R. Akiba[55] (Gittin 90*a*): אפילו מצא אחרת נאה הימנה.

The preparation of the Red Heifer was, according to Num. 19, 9, to be done by one ceremonially clean: ואסף איש טהור. The interpretation of איש טהור constituted one of the essential differences between the Pharisees and Sadducees. The Pharisees considered the unclean man who has bathed in the day time, and awaits sunset, in accordance with Lev. 22, 7, to be טהור and eligible to prepare the ashes of the Red Heifer. The Sadducees considered him unclean

[55] Still more erroneous is the assertion of Holdheim (*l. c.*, 57 ff.), that the Karaites considering the marital bond similar to that of God and Israel allow the husband to forgive and take back an adulterous wife, while Tradition demands the dissolution of the marriage by a writ of divorce. *The reverse is true.* According to the Karaite law, even the אנוסה is considered defiled and forbidden to her husband whereas the talmudic law requires divorce only in case the husband be a priest (Ketubbot 51*b;* the reason of the opinion of אבוה דשמואל (*l. c.*) is שמא סופה ברצון; for Ps.-Jon. on Deut. 22, 26: אלא גברא יפטירינה מיניה בגיטא, see Chayes, אמרי בינה, 9; comp. also שערי צדק, IV, 4, 4). See Benjamin Nahawendi (משאת בנימין 5*a*): ואם אשת איש היא ואנוסה דינה כמו של מאורשה אבל על בעלה אסורה; שנ׳ משבילי נ״ע אמרו בין אנוסה אחרי אשר הוטמאה; so also Hadassi, Alph. 329: בין מפותה אסורה על בעלה; comp. also Alph. 364 (135*b*); גן עדן 152*b;* 155*a;* אדרת אליהו, 93*b;* לבוש מלכות, 47. Jepheth b. Ali held that in case of defilement no writ of divorce is necessary; for the marriage is *ipso facto* dissolved (גן עדן, 155*a*); but see Hadassi, Alph. 5. lett. ק. Holdheim (*l. c.*, 112) contends that the *Sadducees* did not consider a captive (שבויה) even when אשת כהן defiled. Yet the *Karaites* hold that even an אשת ישראל שבויה is forbidden to her husband. See Hadassi, Alph. 365 (141*d*). Josephus (*Contra Apionem* I, 7) agrees with Tradition (Ketubbot 27*a*). Holdheim (*l. c.*, 53, note) states that while the Karaites consider man and woman equal in their spiritual duties, the Mishnah (Berakot 3, 2) confines the duty of prayer to man. The *very* Mishnah which he quotes states that women *are* included in the obligation of prayer.

and barred him from assisting in the preparation of it.[56] This issue could have arisen only if we interpret והיה לפנות ערב ירחץ במים in Deut. 23, 12 to mean "from the time that the sun begins to decline" allowing the unclean to take the ablution after midday,[57] a period thus intervening between the purification bath and sunset, during which he was considered by the Pharisees clean and suitable to prepare the אפר פרה.

Most of the Karaites, however, take לפנות ערב to mean the last part of the day and assign the ablution to the hour which immediately precedes sunset, see Harkavy, ספר המצות לענן, 143, n. 9; see also כתר תורה, *ad loc.* (27*a*): והיה לפנות ערב: סמוך לערב וכן לפנות בקר לא כדעת בעלי הקבלה שהטעם מעט שיפנה הערב יהיה ראוי לרחוץ כל היום וזה טבול יום. See *ib.*, Lev. 39*b*; Hadassi, Alph. 295 (110*c*). So also אדרת אליהו, 71*d*: ובטהרת המים אמרו החכמים כי צריך להיות סמוך לערב כאשר כתוב בבעל קרי והיה לפנות ערב ירחץ במים ... וביארו החכמים שפנות ערב סמוך לערב ... לכן פסקו שטהרת הטמאים כולם במים צריך להיות סמוך לערב. ... . So also Samuel al Magrabi (MS., 191*b* ff.): ועת פנות ערב התחלפו החכמים בו ... ואמר זולתם כי הוא בקרוב הערב והוא כשיעור שיתרחץ הטמא ויצא וישאר מעט מהשמש על ראשי ההרים כמאמר הכתוב וטמא עד הערב אחר מאמרו ורחץ במים. Comp. also the anti-Karaite ordinance of Maimonides (ed. Friedlaender, *MGWJ.*, 1909, 476): ומנהם מן תתואכי בהדא אלסבב אן יכון בין השמשות בחסב אעתקאד אלמינים; see also גן עדן 110*b, c, d;* 115 *c, d;* comp. also Sahl b. Maṣliaḥ, Pinsker, II, 28. According to them, such state of uncleanness as

[56] Parah 3, 7; Tosefta, *ib.*, 3, 8; Yoma 2*a* and parallels; comp. Grätz, III[4], 447 ff. G. Hölscher, *Der Sadduzäismus*, Leipzig 1906, 20-21 wholly misunderstood this controversy.

[57] Comp. Geiger, *ZDMG.*, XX, 567; Maim., ה' מקואות, 1, 6, and ראב"ד and כ"מ *ad loc.*

טבול יום—one who has bathed (for purification) in the *day time*—does not exist at all; the Karaites thus differ in the question of טבול יום as much from the Sadducees as they do from the Pharisees.

The law of false witnesses constituted one of the earliest differences between the Pharisees and the Sadducees. The latter restricted the application of Deut. 19, 19 to the case when the accused has already been executed in consequence of their false testimony. The Pharisaic view and practice were that false witnesses are liable to equal punishment after the judgment had been passed but not carried out (Sifre, *ad loc.*, ed. Friedmann, 109*b;* Makkot, 1, 6; Tosefta Sanhedrin 6. 6; p. *ib.*, 6, 3 and parallels).

Geiger (*Urschrift,* 140) and Weiss (I, 138) consider apocryphal the report of the Baraita Makkot 5*b* that the Pharisees did not apply the law of false witnesses in case the wrongly accused was already executed. The issue between the Pharisees and Sadducees was, according to them, the case where the testimony was found to be false *before* the execution of the alleged offender.[58]

Most of the Karaite exegetes and codifiers agree with the Pharisees in this disputed point; see Mibḥar, *ad loc.* (15*b*): ואימתי יעשה לו כאשר זמם; אחר שינמר הדין; comp. טירת כסף,

[58] Comp. also Pineles, דרכה של תורה, 172; Friedmann, *Beth Talmud,* V, 233 ff.; Herzfeld, *Geschichte,* III, 387; Graetz, III[3], 99. The Book of Susannah was according to Brüll, *Jahrbücher,* III (1877), 63 ff. (comp. also Hoffmann, *Magazin,* IV (1877), 157 ff.) written as a protest against this Sadducean practice. For the view of Philo see Ritter, 26, n. 1. Josephus accepts the Pharisaic view (Weyl, 85). For the Samaritans see Wreschner, Intro., p. VIII, note 5. For attempts to explain the talmudic view הרגו אין נהרגים (see Geiger, *Urschrift,* 140, note), which is also the view of the Karaite Aaron b. Joseph (Mibḥar, Deut. 16*a*) see *Magazin,* XX (1893), 88 ff.; Rapoport, דברי שלום ואמת, p. 7. L. Löw, *Ges. Sch.,* I, 284, is to be corrected accordingly.

ad loc. (let. 95): ... ואף על פי שבעדות הזוממים לא נהרג המועד יקבלו העונש מיד ב"ד כאשר זממו לעשות; comp. גן עדן, 194*d*: וכן אמרו בעלי הגמרא אין העדים הזוממין נהרגין אלא אחר שנגמר הדין: לא הרג נהרגין הרגו אין נהרגין וחכמי הקראין אומרים לא כל שכן והם אומרים אין דנין לבא מן הדין ....; comp. also Hadassi, Alph. 357, and כתר תורה, Deut. 26*a*, l. 1: ..... וצריך שאם היה אמת יהרג הוא; see, however, גן עדן 177*c*: ... ואם לא נהרג אינם חייבים ואפילו שנפסק דינו ועדיין לא נהרג.

The two daily burnt offerings (עולת תמיד) being pubic offerings, had to be provided at the expense of the public, from the תרומת הלשכה of the half-shekel tax (Sheḳalim 4, 1; Sifre I, 142).[59] The Sadducees claimed (basing it on the singular form את הכבש אחד תעשה in Num. 28, 4) that the daily burnt offerings may be offered by individuals. Menaḥot 65*a* and Megillat Taanit, 11 (Neubauer, *Mediaeval Jewish Chronicles,* II, 3): שהיו צדוקים אומרים מביאים תמידים משל יחיד זה מביא שבת אחד וזה מביא שתי שבתות וזה מביא שלשים יום; comp. Geiger, *Urschrift,* 136.

The Karaites, in agreement with the Pharisees, consider the perpetual offering a public sacrifice to be offered at the expense of the people, though they hold that, in all duties incumbent on the people at large, if an individual anticipates it, the duty is discharged. See Mibḥar to Ex.

[59] So also Josephus, *Ant.* III, 10, 1 and *Contra Ap.*, II, 6. Philo also considers the קרבן תמיד a public sacrifice (II, 239). Comp. M. Zipser, *Flavius Josephus' "Ueber das hohe Alter des Jüdischen Volkes gegen Apion,"* Wien 1871, 113. The fact that King Hezekiah defrayed the expense of the תמיד (II Chron. 31, 3; comp. Schürer, II, I, 284, Engl. transl.) is not against this view, as even according to Tradition an individual is allowed to bring the תמיד, if he first turns it over to the people (Rosh hashanah 7*a*); see Maim., כלי המקדש, 8, 7: אף כל קרבנות הציבור שהתנדב אותן יחיד משלו כשרים ובלבד שימסרם לציבור, comp. משנה למלך, *ad loc.* and ר"ש to Parah 2, 3. This escaped Ratner, ספר היובל in honor of N. Sokolow, Warsaw 1904, 502.

27, 20 (57*a*): וזו המצוה אם קדם אחד לעשותה נפטרו כל ישראל וכן התמידים והמלח ועצי העולה והנסכים ומצות רבות כך. Similarly to Num. 19, 2; comp. טירת כסף, *ad loc.*: ... אף על פי שהיא מתחייבת להעשות מממון של צבור יספיק בהבאתה על ידי איש אחד ויהיו פטורים כל ישראל כי יצאו ידי חובתם; see also כתר תורה, Ex. 95*b*, and אדרת אליהו, 101*b*.

The view of Geiger (*Jüdische Zeitschrift*, I, 24; *Nachgelassene Schr.*, V, Heb., 161; *ZDMG.*, XX, 560 and elsewhere; comp. Poznański, *REJ.*, XLV, 63) that the Samaritan interpretation of Deut. 25, 5 ff., which was also held by some early Karaites, goes back to the Sadducees, cannot be accepted. The Samaritans took החוצה (v. 5) to be an adjective, referring to אשת המת translating it "the outer wife," i. e. the betrothed who had not as yet entered her husband's house, and restricted the law of levirate marriage to the betrothed woman whose husband died without living issue (Ḳiddushin 75*b*-76*a*; p. Yebamot 1, 6 and Giṭṭin 1, 4; comp. Frankel, *Vorstudien*, 197, note *b*). If the Sadducees, like the Samaritans, would have applied the law of *yibbum* only to the betrothed, but not to the widowed wife, marriage would have been prohibited with them, as the cause of the exclusion of the Samaritans from the Jewish community and of marriage being prohibited with them, was that they referred the law of levirate marriage to the betrothed only. See Ḳiddushin 75*b*.[60]

An agreement of great importance, as Geiger thinks, between the Sadducees and the Karaites is their rejection of the device known as *'erub*, by which restraint on walk-

[60] Against this view of Geiger see also L. Löw, *Gesammelte Schriften*, III, 162; Geiger's opinion (*Urschrift*, 148) that many of the Pharisees were against intermarriage with Sadducees is not proved; see, to the contrary, N. Krochmal, מורה נבוכי הזמן, Warsaw 1894, 65; L. Löw, *l. c.*, 160. קבוצת מאמרי גייגער ed. Poznanski I, 87, n. 3, end and 84, n. 1.

ing and carrying on the sabbath is lightened.[61] Geiger sees in the institution of *'erub* a result of the Pharisaic desire to imitate the priestly sacerdotal meals eaten in חבורות. The sacrificial meals constituted a religious act. To afford the priests an opportunity to assemble for such repasts, which were usually held on holidays and sabbath, the regulations concerning walking distances and carrying food from one precinct to another (מרשות לרשות) were disregarded. The Pharisees also instituted common repasts (originally of companies of ten peoople, as in the eating of the Paschal Lamb). These meals, though of profane food, חולין, were eaten על טהרת הקדש and in connection with them were practised rites and observances usually associated with sacerdotal meals. To facilitate such gatherings, i. e. participation by those who lived outside the city limits in such consecrated meals (usually held on holy days), they devised the fiction of *'erub,* through which members could come from distances and food be carried from one precinct to another on sabbath. The Sadducees opposed this device (Erubin 6, 2; *ib.,* 68*b*). The rejection of this "evasion law" by the Samaritans (Erubin 31*b*) and the Karaites (Hadassi, Alphabeta 182, 183, 242, see also authors quoted below) thus goes back to their common source—the Sadducees. This hypothesis of Geiger is due to misunderstanding the above quoted Mishnah. As has been shown by I. Halevy in his *Dorot Ha Rishonim* (1*c,* pp. 436 ff.; so also Weiss, *Dor,* I, 119),[62] the Sadducees are mentioned there as מי שאינו מודה

[61] *Jüd. Zeitschr.,* II, 24, *Nachg. Schriften,* III, 290; V, Heb., 145 ff. and elsewhere. Against the view of Geiger concerning חבורות of ten people to which he ascribes much importance (see references above and *Urschrift,* 121 ff.; *Nachg. Schr.,* IV, 107), see A. Büchler, *Der Galiläische Amhaareṣ,* 208, n. 2; comp. also, for Ps.-Jon. on Exod. 12, 4, Frankel, *MGWJ.,* 1846, 114.

[62] לא היו מודים [הצדוקים] בעירוב והכחישו איסור הוצאה בשבת (עירובין פ"ו מ"א). Weiss overlooked, however, Horayot 4*a;* comp. also Geiger himself,

בעירוב, which means "one who does not believe in the device of *'erub,"* i. e. one who ignores as invalid the rabbinic injunctions against יציאה חוץ לתחום and הוצאה בחצר on sabbath. Thus, while the Sadducees did not consider יציאה and הוצאה forbidden, the Karaites prohibit them and reject the "evasion law" of *'erub* (Hadassi, *l. c.*, and authors quoted below). The early Karaites Anan,[63] Benjamin Nahawendi (גן עדן, 31*a* ff.) and Sahl b. Maṣliaḥ (*l. c. and* אדרת אליהו, 29*c*) interpreting Ex. 16, 29*b* שבו איש תחתיו literally, forbade[64] leaving the house on sabbath save for physical needs

Urschrift, 147-8; *Nachg. Schr.,* V, Heb., 147, ll. 5 ff. This is also the meaning of מי שאינו מודה בעירוב in Erubin 31*b* (concerning the Samaritans). See Niddah 57*a* and Rashi, *ad loc., s. v.* לאתויי; see also Wreschner, 15; comp. S. Hanover, *Das Festgesetz d. Samaritaner nach Ibrahim ibn Jakūb,* Berlin 1904, 21. For the Sadducees, comp. also Schürer, Div. II, vol. II (Engl. transl.), 37, n. 102.

[63] See גן עדן, 31*b;* אדרת אליהו, 29*c;* comp. also Harkavy, ס"המ לענן, 129, n. 1; 139, n. 3. This is also the view of Hadassi; see Alph. 144 (54*c*) and 247 (94*d*). Some Karaites forbade, like the later Samaritans (Wreschner, 15), leaving the house on sabbath even for physical need or a religious object; see Hadassi, Alph. 144. See also Reifmann, *Beth Talmud,* I, 385; Harkavy, *Magazin,* VI (1879), 121.

[64] The later Karaites, including Levi b. Jepheth ha-Levi, Joshua b. Judah, Samuel al-Magrabi, and Aaron b. Elias, accepted the rabbinic (see Mekilta to Exod. 16, 29; Alfasi and Asheri to Erubin 1, end; Tosafot *ib.,* 17*b, s. v.* לאו; Maim., שבת, 27, 1) restriction of the sabbath way to two thousand yards outside the city limits, תחום שבת, making thereof a biblical ordinance. See also Joseph al Baṣer, Pinsker, II, 87.

It may also be pointed out here that *only* R. Akiba, the champion of the New Halakah according to Geiger (*Urschrift,* 153 ff. and elsewhere), is of the opinion that the restriction of אלפים אמה is biblical (Soṭah 5, 3)! See also Schechter, *Jewish Sectaries,* I, p. 10, l. 21; p. 11, l. 6.

It was also R. Akiba, the antagonist of the Sadducean-*Samaritan* halakah according to Geiger, who held the Samaritans to be genuine converts, גרי אמת (Kiddushin 75*b;* comp. Frankel, *Einfluss,* 245), while R. Eliezer and R. Ishmael who, according to this view, partly adhered to the Sadducean-Samaritan halakah, held the Samaritans to be only lion-converts, גרי אריות; see Kiddushin, *l. c.;* Shebiit 8, 10; p. *ib.,* and פני משה *ad loc.*

or some religious object.[65]

Geiger (*Jüd. Zeitschr.*, II (1863), 43 ff.) holds that the Sadducees prohibited the sacrifice of the Paschal Lamb (קרבן פסח) on sabbath. Derenbourg (*Orientalia,* I, 184 ff.), Holdheim (מאמר האישות, 160 ff.), Chwolson (*Das letzte Passamahl Christi,* Leipzig 1908, 28 ff., 140, 161; comp. Bacher, *JQR.*, VI, 680 ff. and *REJ.*, XLV, 176 ff.) claim that the similar view held by Anan and *some* other early Karaites goes back to the Sadducees. See against this view A. Schwarz, *Die Controversen der Schammaiten und Hilleliten,* I, Wien 1893, p. 17, note. It may also be pointed out that it is hardly probable that the Sadducees distinguished, as Geiger (*l. c.*) and Chwolson (*l. c.*, 21; 29, n. 2; 43, 140) claim, between the "perpetual offering" (קרבן תמיד) as a *public* offering (קרבן צבור), and the קרבן פסח as a *private* offering (קרבן יחיד), since, according to the Sadducees themselves, the קרבן תמיד was also to be offered by an individual. See Menaḥot 65*a;* comp. Geiger, *Urschrift* 136, and above. Moreover, many early Karaite authorities agree with Tradition that the קרבן פסח takes precedence over the sabbath. So Benjamin Nahawendi (סה"מ לענן, 153; comp. also the views of Daniel al Ḳumṣi and Jepheth b. Ali, Harkavy, *l. c.*). So also Aaron b. Joseph (Mibḥar, Exod. 16*b*); Samuel al Magrabi (ed.

[65] The Karaites differ among themselves also on the source of אסור הוצאה on sabbath. Jepheth b. Ali (Pinsker, II, 21) and Joseph al Baṣīr (אדרת אליהו, 29*d* ff.) follow Tradition and consider it to be a מלאכה and therefore forbidden. Ḳirḳisani thinks that carrying is not מלאכה and its prohibition is *traditional* and attested by Jerem. 17, 22 (גן עדן, 26*b;* comp. also the views of Joshua b. Judah and of Aaron b. Elias, גן עדן, *l. c.*). Levi b. Jepheth stands alone in his opinion that the carrying of light things is not forbidden (אדרת אליהו, 29*c*).

Junowicz, *Fast-und Festgesetze d. Käräer,* Berlin 1904, 6); Elias Bashyazi (אדרת אליהו, ע' פסח, ch. 8).

Geiger (*Nachgel. Schriften,* III, 315; V, Heb., 149 ff.; *ZDMG.,* XVI, 717 ff.; comp. Cohn, *ZDMG.,* XLVII, 678) holds that the Karaite view that עור נבלה, like בשר נבלה, communicates uncleanness goes back to Sadducean Tradition. It escaped Geiger that the *earliest* Karaites, the Ananites, were of the opinion that no separate part of the carcass is capable of communicating uncleanness. See אדרת אליהו, ע' טומאה, beg.: אמנם החכמים נחלקו על שיעור הנבלה מהם אמרו והם הענניים שנבלה בכלל תאמר על כלל הגוף המת אמנם חלקי המת לא יקרא נבלה .... והנה לפי דעתם אם יכרת אבר אחד מהבהמה לא תקרא נבלה. So also גן עדן, 99*b,* end; comp. also *JQR.,* XIX, 151, l. 11; for Anan's opinion see also Jacob b. Reuben (Pinsker, II, 84); Harkavy, סה"מ לענן 59; 153, n. 12; Schechter, *Jewish Sectaries,* II, 23; comp. also *REJ.,* XLV, 56, n. 4. See also Geiger, *Urschrift,* 135, that the Boethusians allowed ספרים תפילין ומזוזות to be written on עור בהמה טמאה which proves their agreement with Tradition that עור נבלה is not מטמא. Geiger's interpretation of Shabbat 108*a* (*N. S.,* V, Heb., 151) is forced; comp. also Schorr, החלוץ, IV, 33.

The view of Geiger (*Jüd. Zeitschr,* I, 51; II, 27; *N. S.,* III, 316; V, Heb., 138 ff.; 163 ff.) that the Samaritan and Karaite interpretation of Lev. 12, 4, 5 (ימי טהרה) goes back to the Sadducees is not proved. See Wreschner, *l. c.,* 38, in favor of whose view it may be pointed out that the *Book of Jubilees* (3, 13) seems to agree with Tradition that a woman during ימי טהרה is excluded only from ביאת מקדש and אכילת קדשים; see also Schwarz, *l. c.,* 94 ff.

The only view common to the Boethusians (a latter-day Sadduceeism) and the Karaites is the interpretation of

ממחרת השבת and the time of the Feast of Weeks. The Feast of Weeks is, according to Lev. 23, 15-16, to be observed on the fiftieth day after the waving of the sheaf. The "wave-sheaf," עומר, is to be offered "on the morrow after the sabbath" ממחרת השבת יניפנו הכהן. Tradition interprets ממחרת השבת "from the day after the holy convocation," i. e. from Nisan the sixteenth. The Boethusians interpreted ממחרת השבת to mean the day after the weekly sabbath that occurs during the feast of the unleavened bread, so that Pentecost is celebrated always on the first day of the week (Menaḥot 65*a;* Megillat Taanit 1, 2; Sifra on Lev. 23, 15 and parallels). This is also the Samaritan[66] and Karaite[67] interpretation of ממחרת השבת.

But to adduce this Karaite view as evidence of the Karaite descent from the Sadducees is hardly justifiable. As Geiger himself (*Urschrift,* 138-139); Wellhausen (*Die Pharisäer und die Sadducäer,* 59 ff.); Schürer (II, 334); Poznański (*Abraham Geiger, Leben u Lebenswerk,* 365) pointed out, this Boethusian interpretation of ממחרת השבת does not go back to Sadducean tradition but originated in the animosity of the Boethusian priests-aristocrats against the Pharisees after having been deprived by them of their

[66] See Wreschner, Intr., XXIII; S. Hanover, *Das Festgesetz der Samaritaner nach Ibrahim ibn Ja'kūb,* Berlin 1904, text, p. VII; comp. *ib.,* 62-63; Geiger, *Nachg. Schr.,* III, 294-296. The Samaritans and the Karaites differ, however, in the following essential question, namely, when to count if the fifteenth of Nisan occurs on Sunday. The Karaites begin on it to count the seven weeks. The Samaritans would begin counting on the first of the next week and thus offer the עומר *post festum.* See Geiger, *l. c.,* 296; Hoffmann, *Leviticus,* II, 164. For the Falashas, see A. Epstein, *Eldad ha-Dani,* 154 ff.; *id., REJ.,* XXII (1891), 13 ff.

[67] See on it lastly Poznański, *Gedenkb. zur Erin. an D. Kaufmann,* 173 ff. Some Karaites trace their interpretation of ממחרת השבת to R. Phinehas b. Jair. See Pinsker, II, 16-7; comp. Frankl, *MGWJ.,* 1876, 115 ff.: Epstein, *Eldad ha-Dani,* 158, note.

prerogative to regulate the calendar and was never carried out in practice.

The only agreement between the Sadducees and the Karaites known to us is their rejection of "water libation," נסוך המים, on the Feast of the Tabernacles.[68] See Jefeth b. Ali (Pinsker, II, 23): נסוך המים לא צוה יושב הכרובים לא בפנים לא בחוצה: האומרים במצות נסוך המים הוסיפו על מאמרו הוא הדבר אשר ה׳ לא דברו...; see also Mibḥar, Num. 28*b*, and טירת כסף, *ad loc*.

Thus, as we have seen, in all the differences between the Sadducees and Pharisees recorded in Talmud and Megillat Taanit the Karaite halakah (as far as Karaite opinion is known to us), with the exception of ממחרת השבת and נסוך המים, either agrees with the Pharisees against the Sadducees, or is in itself undetermined by reason of divergent views among the Karaites themselves.[69]

The mention by the Karaites Ḳirkisani and Ḥassan b. Mashiaḥ of a work (or works) composed by Zadok the founder of the Sadducean party, is considered by many scholars[70] proof of some relation existing between Sadduceeism and Karaism.

Schechter has established close relation of "*Fragments of a Zadokite work*" discovered and published by him (*Jewish Sectaries*, Cambridge 1910, vol. I.) with the כתאב

[68] Sukkah 48*b*; Yoma 26*b*; comp. Maim. Commentary on Sukkah 4, 9. See on it lastly Feuchtwang, *MGWJ.*, 1911, 49 ff.

[69] See also Grätz, V[4], 495. This examination of the relation of the Karaite halakah to the Sadducean views known to us discloses how unfounded are the assertions of Weiss (*Dor*, IV, 85); Neubauer (*Aus der Petersburger Bibliothek*, 2); Fürst (*Geschichte d. Karäerthums*, I, 13 ff.); Harkavy (Grätz, *Geschichte* V[4], 477 and elsewhere); Poznański (*REJ.*, XLIV (1902), 173) and others who follow Geiger, that the Karaites agree with the Sadducees in the differences between the latter and the Pharisees.

[70] See Harkavy, *l. c.*, 776; Poznański, *REJ.*, *l. c.*, 176-7; V. Aptowitzer, *Die Rechtsbücher der nestorianischen Patriarchen u. ihre Quellen*, 8.

אלצדוקיה mentioned by the above-named tenth century Karaites. As Schechter himself says: "The term Zakokites naturally suggests the Sadducees; but the present state of knowledge of the latter's doctrines and practices does not offer enough points of resemblance to justify the identification of them with our sect" (*Intr.*, XXI). However, if these fragments *do* contain Sadducean traditions and practices,[71] they afford no support of the Sadducean-Karaite theory, but rather disclose further proof that in seeking for the origin of Karaism and its halakah we must cut adrift from any theory that would link it with Sadduceeism.

One of the two main and specfic accusations of this Sect against their antagonists is polygamy (p. 4, ll. 20 ff.) which nearly all Karaites allow if it does not interfere with the husband's duties to his first wife and is not לצרור.[72] See

[71] See Israel Lévi, *REJ.*, 1911, 162 ff.; K. Kohler, *American Journal of Theology*. 1911, 432; comp., however, G. F. Moore, *Harvard Theological Review*, 1911, 358, 270, and Poznański, *Jewish Review*, September 1911.

The suggestion of Bacher (*ZfhB.*, 1911, 19) that these Zadokites represent a group of Sadducean priests who, not long before the destruction of the Temple, in consequence of the victory of the Pharisees, left Palestine, is based on the theory of Büchler-Chwolson that not until a decade before the national catastrophe did the Pharisees control the national life of the people—a theory which is still to be proved; comp. A. Epstein, *MGWJ.*, XL (1896), 139-140. Kohler (*l. c.*, 431) states that "The Fragments of a Zadokite Work" discovered by Schechter "strongly confirms the theory of Abraham Geiger as to the relationship of Samaritanism and Karaism to Sadduceeism" and that "Professor Schechter has made it highly probable, if not certain, that the Document brought to light by him formed the very source of Anan's system, which, as Ḳirḳisani relates, was founded upon the books of Zadok" and: "We thus possess in this Document the connecting link between the ancient Sadducean and Samaritan lore and the doctrines of the Karaites in a far more direct form than Geiger and Harkavy could expect" (*l. c.*, 432-3). The following examination of the halakah contained in this Document will show how erroneous these assertions are.

[72] Comp. Leḳaḥ Ṭob to Deut. 21, 15 referred to by Schechter, XVII, n. 16. Gittelsohn, *Civil-Gesetze der Karäer*, Berlin 1904, 11, n. q, is to be corrected accordingly.

Harkavy, סה"מ לענן, 105, 115, 109, 127; Hadassi (Alph. 324 (119*d*); comp. also Alph. 321-2, 365 (135*b*)); Aaron b. Joseph (Mibḥar, Lev. 33*b*); Samuel al Magrabi (MS., 214*b*); Aaron b. Elias (גן עדן, 146*d*, 154*b*; כתר תורה, Lev. 49*a*); Elias Bashyazi (אדרת אליהו, נשים, ch. 5); Mordecai b. Nisan (לבוש מלכות, 46). A present day Karaite, Samuel b. Shemariah Pigit, Ḥazzan in Ekaterinoslav, writes: כאלו ... חכמינו ע"ה אסרו לקחת שתי נשים, הם לא אמרו זאת מעולם כי אין אצלנו חרם רבנו גרשון רק הם חייבו על פי הכתובים למלאות איש חובתו כנגד נשיו והיא שאר כסות ועונה (אגרת נדחי שמואל, St. Petersburg 1894, I, 176); comp. also Schechter, *l. c.*, p. XIX, n. 22.

According to this Sect "Fish may be eaten only if while still alive they have been split open and drained of their blood" (p. 12, ll. 13-14; comp. p. LI, n. 23), not requiring that the fish be *caught* by an Israelite. Anan (*JQR.*, XIX, 143; comp. *ib.*, 138) and many other early Karaites[73] (Hadassi, Alph. 235 (89*d*); Jacob b. Reuben quoted in טירת כסף to Mibḥar; Num. 10*b*, lett. 55) held, in agreement with the Samaritans (Wreschner, 51), that only fish caught

Schechter (pp. XVII, XIX, XXXVI, n. 3) believes that this Sect prohibited divorce and regarded a second marriage during the life-time of the first husband or wife, even after divorce, as fornication (comp. *JQR.*, 1911, 138). This view is as foreign to the Karaite halakah as to Tradition; see above. This Sect decries also the Pharisaic regulation of the calendar. If the calendar of this Sect was a solar one (comp. Schechter, XVI, XX and Kohler, *l. c.*, 429), the Karaites differ in this important point from this Sect as much as the Rabbanites.

[73] It may be pointed out that a similar view is quoted in Midrash (Gen. r., 7, 2 and parallels) in the name of Jacob of כפר נבוריא who seems to have been suspected of some מינות (comp. Eccl. r. 7, 47; המגיד, vol XIV, 245). The later Karaites rejected this view. See כתר תורה, Num. 15*b*: אם את כל דגי הים יאסף : נאמרה אסיפה בדגים כפי רוב המנהג לא שהאסיפה [ב]מקום השחיטה שאם כן צריך להיות אסיפת ישראל מכשרת ולא אסיפת גוי; so also גן עדן, 101*b*: comp. also Samuel al-Magrabi, *l. c.* The requirement that the blood be drained from the fish before it is eaten suggests, as Schechter p. LI, n. 23, points out, that this Sect prohibited the eating of

by an Israelite may be eaten. Moreover, "splitting open the fish while still alive," which is required by this Sect, is *expressly forbidden* by most of the Karaites. See Samuel al Magrabi, ed. M. Lorge, *Die Speisegesetze der Karäer von Samuel el Margrebi,* Berlin 1907, 21; Hadassi, Alph. 234 (89*d*); comp. also *JQR.*, XIX, 143, beg. אדרת אליהו, ע' שחיטה, ch. 23; אפריון, 25.

Schechter (pp. XVIII, XLIX, notes 16, 24, LX) pointed out several agreements between the Karaite halakah and that of this Sect in the details of sabbath-observance. Extreme sabbatarianism is, however, a general sectarian propensity. Moreover, the Karaites differ from this Sect in the following laws of the sabbath.

According to this Sect (p. 11, ll. 16-17) "if any person falls into a gathering of water or unto a place of .... he shall not bring him up by a ladder or a cord or any instru-

the blood of fish. This is also the view of Daniel al-Ḳumṣi (Ḳirḳisani, ed. Harkavy, 316). So also Hadassi, Alph. 234, end and Aaron b. Elias (גן עדן, 93*c;* כתר תורה, Lev. 19*a*). Comp. Bacher, *MGWJ.*, 1874, 272. Many Karaites, however, oppose this view. See Mibḥar, Lev. 12*a*, and טירת כסף, *ad loc., lett.* 65; Samuel al Magrabi, *l. c.*, 16. Kohler's contention (*l. c.*, 427) that the Book of Jubilees agrees on this point with Tradition against this Sect is not proved; see Book of Jubilees, 6, 10; 7, 28.

Many Karaite authorities agree with the law of this Sect (p. 12, ll. 14-15) that locusts are to be killed in water. See Hadassi, Alph. 235 (89*d*); Jacob b. Reuben (*ZfthB.*, IV, 73); Samuel al-Magrabi, *l. c.*, 9, 21; גן עדן, 101*c;* אדרת אליהו, ע' שחיטה, ch. 24. Schechter (XXIV, LI, n. 20) believes that this Sect considered honey to be אבר מן החי and therefore prohibited it. It is, however, more probable that מעגלי הדבורים (p. 12, l. 12) refers, as Schechter himself (*l. c.*) suggests, to the particles of the bees which are mixed up with the honey and is, perhaps, to read מרגלי הדבורים. See Asheri, on Aboda Zarah, 68*b*: תימה היאך אנו אוכלין הדבש והלא רגלי הזבוב מעורבין בו. Anan (Harkavy, 3) and the later Karaites allowed the use of honey (גן עדן, 92*d*, 93*a*). It is, however, doubtful whether this was also the view of the earlier Karaites many of whom prohibited even eggs as אבר מן החי; see Hadassi, Alph. 232 (89*c*) and Alph. 308 (114*c*). The view of Lesynsky (*Die Sadduzäer,* Berlin 1912, 40) that the Sadducees prohibited honey is untenable; he overlooked Judg, 14, 8-9.

ment." (See Schechter, XLIX, n. 39; I. Levi, *REJ., l. c.* 198, n. 14; Moore, *l. c.*, 365; Kohler, *l. c.*, 425). This law is against the Karaite halakah as well as against Tradition. The Karaites agree[74] with Tradition (Shabbat 18, 3; Yoma 84*b* ff.; Mekilta on Exod. 31, 14 and parallels) that for the saving of a human life the sabbath is to be desecrated. See Hadassi, Alph. 148; 179; Mibḥar, Exod. 38*a;* גן עדן, 34*a;* אדרת אליהו, ע׳ שבת, ch. 21; אפריון, p. 9.

This Sect, like the *Book of Jubilees* (50, 12, comp. v. 9), prohibited[75] fasting on sabbath. Most of the Karaites, however, allow and even commend fasting on the sabbath. See Hadassi, Alph. 150 (56*d*); comp. Alph. 244 and 264. So also Samuel al Magrabi, ed. Weisz, *Traktat über den Sabbat bei den Karäern,* Pressburg 1907, 14; comp. also גן עדן, 36*a;* Elias Bashyazi in his אגרת הצום and in אדרת אליהו, ע׳ שבת, ch. 11, but see אפריון, p. 8. It may also be pointed out that the two most important Karaite devia-

[74] Grätz (*Geschichte,* V[4], 186) states that Anan prohibited medical treatment on the sabbath. I do not know his authority for this statement. See Hadassi, Alph. 301, letters צ, ק (112*b*) and Levi b. Jepheth quoted by Harkavy, ספר המצות לענן, 132. Anan relying on Exod. 15, 26 prohibited *altogether* the use of medicine and of physicians (Ḳirḳisani, quoted by Harkavy in Grätz, V[4], 487; comp. Hadassi, Alph. 207 (82*a*)). It is only in case of ספק פקוח נפש that some Karaites hold that it is not דוחה שבת. See Hadassi, Alph. 179 and Alph. 364 (135*a*) and Joseph b. Abraham quoted in גן עדן, 34, and in אדרת אליהו, ע׳ שבת, ch. 2; see, however, Maim., ה׳ שבת, 2, 3.

Aaron b. Joseph (Mibḥar, Exod. 38*a*) quotes I Sam. 21, 7 as proof that פקוח נפש דוחה שבת. This verse is adduced also in Matthew 12, 4 and in Yelamdenu (Yalḳuṭ, II, 30) in this connection.

[75] This seems to be the meaning of אל יתערב איש מרצונו בשבת (p. 11, ll. 4-5; comp. p. XLIX, n. 19; I. Levi, *REJ., l. c.*, 197; Bacher, *ZfhB.*, XV, 21, n. 5; Kohler, *l. c.*, 424.) reading יתרעב for יתערב; comp., however, Moore, *Harvard Theological Review*, 1911, 246. The Falashas postpone even the Day of Atonement when it occurs on sabbath.

tions from Tradition in the laws of the sabbath, namely, the prohibition to have fire in the house on the sabbath and the prohibition of cohabitation on the sabbath-day, which Geiger (*Nachgel. Schriften,* III, 288 ff.) and Harkavy (Grätz, *Geschichte,* V[4], 478) believe,[76] go back to Sadducean Tradition, are *not* shared by this Sect.

The law of this Sect that water in a rock not sufficient for immersion is contaminated, like water in a vessel, when touched by an unclean person (p. 10, ll. 13-14) is against the Karaite principle that water does not contract uncleanness. See Ḳirḳisani (quoted by Harkavy, Grätz, *Geschichte,* V[4], 488) who states that this was the view of Anan. So also Hadassi, Alph. 235, 286, 295; Mibḥar, Lev. 28*d;* גן עדן, 98*d* and 105*c;* כתר תורה, Lev. 28*a;* אדרת אליהו 72.[77]

[76] See also Fürst, *Geschichte d. Karäerthums,* I, 11. While the opinion that the *Sadducees* also prohibited cohabitation on sabbath may be justified on the hypothesis of Geiger that any divergence from traditional halakah which is common to the *early* Samaritans and the Karaites goes back to a pre-Pharisaic (Sadducean) tradition, since we find the early Samaritans holding this view (Frankel, *Einfluss,* 253, stands alone in his opinion that this prohibition was adopted by the Samaritans from the Karaites; comp. Wreschner, 18-19), there is *no* reason to assume that already the early Samaritans prohibited having light in the house on sabbath. The arguments adduced by the Samaritans Manugga (Wreschner, 16, 17) and Ibrahim b. Ja'ḳūb (who knew the Karaite view; comp. Geiger, *N. S.,* III 289) for this prohibition which are *borrowed from the Karaites* (Wreschner, 18) tend to show that this prohibition was accepted by the later Samaritans from the Karaites. Nor is it probable that this prohibition resulted from the ancient interpretation of the concept מלאכה (Geiger, *l. c.;* comp. Poznański, *REJ.,* XLIV 174 ff. in connection with which see the claim of the tenth century Karaite Ibn Saquie, who, like Geiger, believed in the existence of a more ancient Halakah (*JQR.,* XIII, 664; הקדם, I, 1908, 125), as to the reading in Tosefta Shabbat 1, 23; אין פותקין מים לגינה; comp. *JQR., l. c.,* 662; הקדם, *l. c.,* 120).

[77] See, however, the view of Joseph b. Abraham (quoted in Mibḥar, *l. c.*) that מים תלושין contract uncleanness. The view of this Sect agrees

According to this Sect (p. 10, ll. 11-12) no man ritually unclean shall cleanse himself in the water of a vessel. As Schechter (XLVIII, n. 3) remarks, this law is directed against מים שאובים. The Karaites, however, not only allow מים שאובים (comp. *MGWJ.*, 1909, 469) but, as Ḳirḳisani informs us (quoted by Harkavy, *l. c.*), it was the view of Anan that one who does *not* bathe in a vessel remains unclean.[78]

The two laws contained in p. 12, ll. 15-19 are, as Schechter (p. LI, n. 27) remarks, against the Traditional view that only כלי and תלוש are capable of contracting and communicating Levitical uncleanness.[79] The Karaites agree with Tradition *against* this Sect. See Anan: ודק קרא וכתב אשר יעשה מלאכה בהם לאודעך דכל מאנא דלא גמר מאניה למעבד ביה עיבידתא לא מיטמיא (סה"מ לענן ed. Harkavy, p. 51;

partially with Miḳwaot 1, 1 ff. (according to the interpretation of Maim. in his commentary *ad loc.* and טומאת אוכלין, 15, 1) that water less than ארבעים סאה (אשר אין בו די מרעיל, p. 10, ll. 12-13 may also mean less than מ' סאה) contract uncleanness if בכונה even when מחובר.

Ps.-Jon's rendering of Lev. 11, 36: וגובין בית כנישות מיין נבעין is against our halakah. It may also be pointed out that the Dositheans held, like this Sect, that water is מקבל טומאה; comp. Kirchheim, כרמי שומרון, 25.

[78] The Samaritans, according to p. Abodah Zarah 5, 4. agree with Tradition on מים שאובים; comp., however, ר"ש to Miḳwaot, 8, 1.

[79] It must, however, be pointed out that the law of this Sect (p. 12, ll. 17-18): וכל כלי מסמר או יתד בכותל אשר יהיו עם המת בבית מטמא בטומאת אחד כלי מעשה (r. כטומאת) agrees with the view of Hadassi, Alph. 290, 292, that in the case of Num. 19, 18 (טומאת מת) טומאה is contracted and communicated even when מחובר. This view is not shared by the other Karaites. See Mibḥar, Num. 10*b;* כתר תורה, Num. 29*b;* גן עדן, 122*c;* אדרת אליהו, ע' טומאה וטהרה, ch. 20. Even in case of תנור וכירים (Lev. 11, 35; see Rashi and Naḥm. *ad loc.*, Shabbat 125*a;* Maim., כלים, 15, 6 and commentary to כלים 5, 1) it is the opinion of most of the Karaites that it is not מקבל טומאה when מחובר. See כתר תורה, *ad loc.* (28*a*); גן עדן, 106*a;* but see Hadassi, Alph. 292 and Mibḥar, Lev. 18*a*. Ps.-Jon and Yalḳut on Num. 19, 18.

comp. *ib.*, p. 58 and 133; Hadassi, Alph. 286; Mibḥar, Lev. 17*a*, 20*a*; כתר תורה, Lev. 26*b*, 28*b*; גן עדן, 103*b*, ff.; אדרת אליהו, 71*b*; אפריון, p. 21).

The Influence of the Works of Philo upon the Karaite Halakah

PENAL LAWS

1. In the laws of homicide the Karaites widely deviate from Tradition. According to Tradition, murder is punishable only when felonious intent to kill has been proved (Sanhedrin 78*b* ff.).[80] Beside intent, antecedent warning immediately before the commission of the crime and its acknowledgment by the offender (התראה) are required (Mekilta on Ex. 21, 12; Sifre on Num. 15, 33 and Deut. 22, 24; Sanhedrin 80*b*; Makkot 6*b* and parallels). The Karaites do not require forewarning in any crime[81] and consider murder punishable even in the absence of intent. See משאת בנימין, 2*a*: המכה אדם ומת מן אותה המכה יומת ואפילו אין מתכוין להרגו שנא׳ מכה איש ומת. So also Samuel al-Magrabi (Gitelsohn, 22). Intent to kill is required by the Karaites only when the missile by which the killing has been effected was not likely to cause death. See גן עדן, 176d: והרוצחים חלקם הכתוב לשלש מעלות יש רוצח שרצח את הנפש .... אך הכתוב הפליג בענין זה הרוצח שאם כון להכותו לבד והכהו בדבר אשר לא יתכן למות בו והוא מת זה יקרא רוצח בשגגה · אך אם הכהו בדבר שימות בו ומת זה נמנה בחזקת רוצח מזיד שטעם מזיד שלא בדק אם

[80] According to R. Simeon (Sanhedrin 79*a*) and Rabbi (Mekilta, Mishpaṭim, 8) murder is not punishable even in case of miscarried felonious intent, i. e. when a man intending to *kill* a person killed another instead.

[81] Mibḥar, Exod. 42*a*: וכן אמרו אינו חייב עד שיתרה בו וכן כל חייבי לאוין והייש התראה יתירה מן לאו שבתורה; so also גן עדן, 177*c*. This seems also the opinion of Philo; see *Werke Philos,* II (Breslau 1910), 263, n. 2.

ימות בו או לא ימות. (Comp. also Mibḥar, Exod. 32*b* and כתר תורה, Numb. 49*b* and Samuel al Magrabi (Gitelsohn, 14) in which case the offender would, according to Tradition, not be punishable at all (Mekilta to Ex. 21, 18; Sifre to Num. 35, 17 (ed. Friedmann 61*b*); Sanhedrin 79*a;* Maimonides, רוצח, 3, 1-3.).[82] Tradition punishes murder only when the murderer has laid his hand on the victim and the death has resulted from such *direct* assault; handing another poison, unless actually forcing it in his mouth, or leading him to a place where in a short while a force of nature or a beast will kill him, is thus not punished by death (Sifre to Num. 35, 17; Sanhedrin 76*b* ff.; Maim., רוצח, 2, 2 ff.). The Karaites do not require the death to be the direct result of the action of the murderer. The Karaites accept the view of R. Judah b. Bathyra (Sanhedrin 78*a*) in case of murder committed by several people simultaneously. See משאת בנימין, 2*a*: והנהרג ע"י אלף אנשים ויותר כלם חייבים מיתה. See also Hadassi, Alph. 152 and Alph. 166; גן עדן, 177*c;* and Samuel al Magrabi, MS., 84*a*: ואין הפרש אם ההורג לנפש אם הוא אחד או רבים בחיוב זה ... הכל מחויבים בהרינה ...; and the opinion of Beth Shammai (Ḳiddushin 43*a*) concerning murder committed through an agent. See גן עדן, 177*b*: ואחד אם יעשהו האדם בעצמו או על ידי צווי; comp. Hadassi,

[82] Nor do the Karaites, in case of the defendant's confession of any crime, require witnesses to establish guilt. See Benjamin Nahawendi, משאת בנימין 1*c*: ולפני בית דין הודאת פיו כשני עדים נאמנים; so also Hadassi (Alph. 357ת): תודת חוטא אשר יודה הוא על עוונו הוא כשני עדים; see also Alph. 370; so also Samuel al-Magrabi (MS., 105*b*): דע כי אם ידבר בעל הריב על נפשו ויאמר אני עשיתי כן וכן לא יצטרך לעדים וזה בהפך מדעת המחליפים; comp. also Mibḥar, Num. 5*a;* גן עדן, 194*d;* אדרת אליהו, 98*a*. The talmudic principle is אין אדם משים עצמו רשע, no man can incriminate himself, confessing of guilt not being admitted as evidence (Sanhedrin 9*b* and parallels; Maimonides, סנהדרין, 18, 6; but comp. Weiss, I, 22-3).

Alph. 269 ff.; comp. also Weiss, I, 150. They also consider accessories, accomplices, and counselors to murder punishable equally with the principal. See Hadassi, Alph. 274: וכן המלשין לחברו בין בסתר בין בגלוי להרגו ונהרג הוא הוא הרוצח וכלם רשעים הם ויהרגו בדרישה בבית דינך . . . See כתר תורה, Exod. 64*b*-65*a*: וכבר בארנו בספר מצות אופני הדרכים שמצדם יקרא האדם רוצח ויתחיב בין שיהרגנו בעצמו בין על ידי זולתו בין ע"י סם המות בין בעדות שקר בין שיסבב מיתתו או שירצה בהריגתו ...; so also גן עדן, 177*b*. See also Samuel al Magrabi (MS. 84*b*): ההריגה תפול על אופנים ממנו הכאה ביד .... ומהם כי ידחה האדם את רעהו ויפול ממקום גבה או לשלג או למים או לאש ... ומהם כי ישקה האחד את חברו סם או יהיה בו חולי וירפאהו בזולת העקרים הראוים לאותו החולי בצדיה ... ומהם כי ירגל האדם ברעהו ויהיה סבה להריגתו... ואין הפרש בכל אשר דברנוהו אם האדם יעשה אותו בנפשו או אומר לזולתו לעשות כי האומר והעושה לא ביניהם הפרש במשפטי התורה ... So also Mibḥar, Exod. 38*a*.

These Karaite laws approach the view of Philo according to whom intent to kill even when not carried out is punished by death (I, 314, Mangey, comp. B. Ritter, *Philo und die Halacha,* Leipzig 1879, 23 ff. and *Werke Philos,* II, 209, note 3).[83]

[83] Josephus (*Ant.* XII, 9, 1) agrees with Tradition that only *action* is punishable. Philo states in this connection (II, 315) that those who with murderous intent prepare poison or any other deadening substance are to be killed *instantly* (Josephus, *Ant.* IV, 8, 34, considers even the keeping of poison punishable by death in which, as Weyl, p. 66 ff., has shown, he followed the Roman law (*Lex Cornelia de sicariis*)). As suggested by Ritter (p. 28), Philo based this law on Exod. 22, 17. The Septuagint translates מכשפה by *φαρμακους* which has also the meaning of "poisoners." Ritter fails, however, to indicate the source of Philo's assertion that the Law commands that the poisoner is to be executed *immediately*. The peculiar expression לא תחיה instead of the usual מות תמות (comp. רשב"ם and Naḥm., *ad loc.*) must have been taken by Philo to mean "do not suffer him to live even a moment." This interpretation of לא תחיה is also found among the Karaites. Samuel al-Magrabi (MS., 141*b*) says that

2. Ransom for death caused by the unguarded property of a man or through his instrumentality is required, according to Tradition, only in the case of the goring ox (Exod. 21, 29-31), the provision not applying to death caused by any other property or by any cause of danger created by him (Baba ḳamma 5, 6; b. *ib.*, 53*b;* Maimonides, נזקי ממון, 12, 16). The Karaites interpret the law of ransom (v. 30) to apply to all cases where a person meets death through the negligence of the owner of the property or the creator of the cause of death. Thus, whether it be a pit (Ex. 21, 33-35), or a fire kindled on one's premises that spread beyond (*ib.*, 22, 5), or failure of the owner of a house to build a battlement for his roof (Deut. 22, 8)—and a person was killed as a result of such negligence—in all these cases the Karaites hold that the owner of the property or the maker of the fire or pit is to pay ransom, according to Exod. 21, 30. As Hadassi says: תורת השונג ששגג ולא שמר שורו : אשר הועד ולא כסה לבורו ואשר לא עשה מעקה לגגו[84] ותולד מהם מיתה יחד יכשר לתת כֹּפֶר כתורתך (Alph., 274). See *ib.*, Alph. 270 and 370. See also משאת בנימין, 2*c*: המטמין פח ומצודה וחבל הנחנק בהם א׳ מן בני אדם ויענש בדמין וכה״א כי נמצאו בעמי רשעים וגו׳ · ואם מבקשים כופר נותן ככר וינצל. See also גן עדן, 180*d*: ואולם הנזק הבא מצד הגרמותיו בין בנפש

though the Law reprieves the condemned pregnant woman, in case of מבשפה the execution is not to be postponed since the Law says ואמר לא : לא תחיה תחיה ולא אמר מות תמות הודיענו בזה המאמר כי לא יכשר לנו לאחר מיתתה מעת לעת ואם היא הרה מעוברת כי היא כמו החרם.

[84] Comp., however, Mibḥar., Exod. 43*b*. The Karaites agree also with Philo (II, 324), against Mekilta *ad loc.*, in the interpretation of והמת יהיה לו (v. 34) as referring to the מזיק; Philo (323) and Hadassi, Alph. 273, interpret also והמת יהיה לו in v. 36 as למזיק. So also Benjamin Nahawendi, משאת בנימין, 2*c*, l. 1, but see Mibḥar, *ad loc.;* כתר תורה Lev. 74*a;* comp. also גן עדן, 181*b*.

בין במומים כן יעשה לו ואם לאו יתן כופר ע״על רציחתו הזכיר הכתוב ולא תקחו כופר לנפש רוצח ולא על רציחת הגרמותיו · והנה על רציחת שורו אמר השור יסקל וגם בעליו יומת · ואמר אם כופר יושת עליו ונתן פדיון נפשו ככל אשר יושת עליו · והתורה הזכירה ארבע אבות נזיקין והוא הדין לכלם שאם נהרג נפש באחד מהם יתן כופר. Comp. *ib.*, 178*d*, 181*c*, 182*b* and Samuel al Magrabi, Gitelsohn, 39-40. Further fol. 133*a* (not published) he says: ואם היו שם אנשים או נפשות והשיגה אותם האש ונשרפו ומתו יתחיב בכופר נפשם.

A view similar to this Karaite anti-traditional law—that also other cases of criminal negligence are punishable—is held by Philo.

Expounding the law of Ex. 21, 33 (II, 324), Philo says that if a man fall into the pit and die the court shall decide what punishment the digger is to suffer or what fine he is to pay (οτι χρη παθειν η αποτισαι). He also says about the law of Deut. 22, 8, that those who fail to make a battlement to their roof commit a crime equal to that of one who digs a pit, and declares: κολαζεσθωσαν γουν εν ισῳ τοις αχανη τα στομια των ορυγματων καταλειπουσιν; comp. Ritter, 52 and notes.

Philo and the Karaites agree also in the interpretation of v. 29*b* וגם בעליו יומת. Tradition interprets it to mean that the owner, if he does not redeem himself, shall suffer death at the hand of God[85] מיתה בידי שמים (Mekilta, Mishpaṭim, X;

[85] Frankel (*Einfluss,*, 93) believes that the translation of the Septuagint indicates the traditional interpretation, against which see Ritter, 48, n. 2 and 124 ff. and H. Weyl, *Die Jüdischen Strafgesetze bei Flavius Josephus*, Berlin 1900, 153 ff. The view of Geiger (*Urschrift*, 448 ff.) that the ancient halakah interpreted וגם בעליו יומת as מיתה בידי אדם was already shown by Pineles (דרכה של תורה, 193-6) and Weyl (*l. c.*, 144-153) to be unfounded; comp. also Poznański, *Abraham Geiger, Leben u. Lebenswerk*, 378, n. 1.

Sanhedrin 15*b;* comp. Ps.-Jon. to v. 29). The Karaites uphold the literal interpretation of וגם בעליו יומת (i. e. בידי אדם) and take ואם כפר יושת עליו (v. 30*a*) to mean that the nearest kinsmen (גואלֵי הדם) of the killed are to decide whether to execute him or to take ransom. See Benjamin Nahawendi, משאת בנימין, 2*c*: ואם הוא נודע [השור] ובעליו מועד וממית אדם הוא יסקל ויומת גם בעליו וכה"א השור יסקל וגם בעליו יומת · ואם גואלי הדם רוצים ליקח ממנו כפר יתן וינצל בעבור כי הרינה זו על ידי הבהמה לפיכך הרשות בידם אם רוצים הורגים ואם רוצים לוקחים כפר : שכה"א אם כפר יושת עליו . See also Hadassi (Alph. 270, 370); גן עדן, 177*d,* and כתר תורה, *ad loc.* (73*b*); Samuel al Magrabi (Gitelsohn, 35-36).

Philo holds the same view, and in his exposition of this law (II, 323) says that the owner of the goring ox is guilty of the man's death. He shall be put to death or pay ransom. The court shall decide his punishment. The Karaites thus agree with Philo and differ only as to the question with whom rests the option of death or ransom; while according to Philo (so also Mekilta, *ad loc.*) the court is to decide, the Karaites hold that it rests with the גואלי הדם.

3. Tradition interprets the law of Ex. 21, 24-26 and Lev. 24, 19-21 to mean money indemnity (Mekilta *ad loc.,* (Mishpaṭim 8); Sifra on Emor, 24, 19; Baba ḳamma 8, 1; Ketubbot 35*a* and parallels; comp. Maimonides, חובל ומזיק I, 1 ff.).

Philo takes these verses literally and in several places vigorously advocates the practice of *lex talionis.* See Ritter, *Philo und die Halacha,* p. 18 ff. The *lex talionis* is accepted in all its severity also by nearly all the Karaites. Benjamin Nahawendi interprets עין תחת עין literally. See Benjamin Nahawendi, משאת בנימין, 2*d;* העשה כל מכה ומום בחבירו

נפרע שנאמר כאשר עשה כן יעשה לו. So also Ben Zuta, a Karaite contemporary of Saadia Gaon (Ibn Ezra on Exod. 21, 24); Jepheth b. Ali (*MGWJ.*, XLI, 1897, 205); Hadassi (Alph. 275 (104*c*); 370 (146*b*); 373 (149*c*); comp. also Alph. 170); Aaron b. Joseph (Mibḥar, Exod. 42*a*); Aaron b. Elias (גן עדן, 179*a* ff.; כתר תורה, Exod. 71*b* ff.); Samuel al Magrabi (Gitelsohn, *l. c.*, 28-9); Abraham b. Josiah (אמונה אמן, 24*b*); Solomon Troki (אפריון, 39).[86]

[86] See also Rapoport, בכורי העתים, 1831, p. 34. L. Löw, *Gesammelte Schriften*, I, 287 is to be corrected accordingly. Harkavy, ס"הם לענן, 198, believes that Anan also upheld *lex talionis;* comp. also Schechter, *Jewish Sectaries*, II, 7, ll. 5-7. The Samaritans also interpret עין תחת עין literally (Klumel, *Mischpatim, ein samaritanisch-arabischer Commentar*, XX; *JQR.*, 1911, 210 is to be corrected accordingly). Some Karaites restrict the application of *lex talionis* to intentional permanent injury; still others leave it to the discretion of the court to pronounce sentence of equal punishment or indemnity; comp. Mibḥar, Exod. 53*a;* כתר תורה, Exod. 71*b* ff. According to the Scholion of Megillat Ta'anit ch. 4 (Neubauer, *Mediaeval Jewish Chronicles*, II, 8; comp. Grätz, III[4], 693) the *Boethusians* extended their literalism to *lex talionis*. Geiger at one time (*Urschrift*, 148, but see *id.*, *Sadducäer u. Pharisäer*, 22; *Nachg. Schriften*, V, Heb., 162), Rapoport (דברי שלום ואמת, 15), and Ritter (133-4) deny this report any historical basis (comp. Jost, *Geschichte d. Judenthums*, I, Leipzig 1885, 221; L. Löw, *l. c.*, 286; Büchler, *MGWJ.*, L (1906), 679, n. and the literature adduced by Ritter, *l. c.*). Such an important difference would not have been left unnoticed in the talmudic literature. It is also improbable that Josephus, who was an avowed Pharisee (*Vita*, II, end) and who in all the differences between the Sadducees and the Pharisees, as far as his opinion is known to us, sides with the Pharisees (except in the interpretation of באש תשרף in Lev. 21, 9; see Olitzki, *Flavius Josephus und die Halacha*, Berlin 1885, 42, 44, 54 and Ritter, 26), would have accepted the literal interpretation of עין תחת עין (*Ant.* IV, 8, 35) if it were anti-Pharisaic.

Geiger (*Nachg. Schriften*, V, Heb. 162) claims that the ancient halakah also interpreted עין תחת עין literally, as R. Eliezer held this view (Baba ḳamma 84*a;* see the version of R. Eliezer's opinion in Mibḥar, Exod. 42*a*, which he seems to have taken from Mekilta, Mishpaṭim, 8, reading R. Eliezer for ר' יצחק; comp. Geiger, *l. c.*, and L. Löw, *l. c.*, 287, n. 2). See I. Halevy, דורות הראשונים, vol. I*c*, 425 ff. for elucidation of the traditional view and that of R. Eliezer; comp. S. Munk, *Guide des Égarés*, 371, n. 1. Philo (II,

Philo (II, 323, end) states that the owner of an animal that killed a slave is to pay the *full value* of the slave. Ritter (49) considers this view of Philo to be against Exod. 21, 32: שלשים שקלים יתן לאדניו. Many Karaite authorities agree with Philo and hold that v. 32 establishes the minimum fine and that if the value of the slave be more than שלשים שקל, the owner is to be paid the full value of the slave. Other Karaites hold that by שלשים שקל the law indicates the value of the average slave and that in all cases the owner of the animal is to pay the full value of the slave. See גן עדן, 181*a*: ואם המית עבד דן הכתוב לתת שלשים שקלים לבעל העבד. ובעלי הקבלה אמרו שעליו יש להקל ולהחמיר אחד עבד שבפחותים ואחד עבד שבחשובים ערך אחד גדולים וקטנים עבד ושפחה אע"פ שיש מחכמי הקראים חולקים בזה: יש מהם אומרים שזה ערך הפחות אבל יש להוסיף עליו. ומהם אומרים ע"ה ערך בינוני ויש להוכיף ולגרוע. So also כתר תורה, Exod. 73*b*.

The Karaites agree with Philo also in the interpretation of Exod. 21, 19 אם יקום והתהלך בחוץ על משענתו. Tradition (Mekila *ad loc.* (Mishpaṭim, 6); Onkelos and p. Ketubbot 4, 4 (28*c*; but see Ps.-Jon. and Naḥm. *ad loc.*), taking על משענתו figuratively, interprets it to mean that the offender is not liable for death consequent on a blow, if in the interval the injured party has so far recovered that he is able to walk about "on his own strength," i. e. without others' assistance. Philo (II, 317; Ritter, 32, note 3) takes על משענתו literally, namely, that even when the injured party required the support of a staff or of a man the offender is

313; Ritter, 22) holds (against Mishnah Sanhedrin 9, 1; Mekilta on Exod. 21, 12) that the murderer is to be killed in the same manner in which he committed the crime (so also Book of Jubilees 4, 32). This is also the view of many Karaites. See S. Gitelsohn, *Civil-Gesetze der Karäer von Samuel al-Magrebi*, 14, ll. 13-15; see, however, גן עדן, 177*c*. The opinion of Büchler (*MGWJ.*, L (1906), 679 n., 692, 706) that this was also the view of the Sadducees is not supported by any proof.

to be acquitted. The Karaites interpret על משענתו, like Philo, literally; see כתר תורה, Exod., 71*a*: על משענתו ... ובעלי הקבלה אמרו במשענֶת עצמו ואינו נכון. So also Mibḥar, *ad loc.;* גן עדן, 180*b;* Samuel al Magrabi (Gitelsohn, 23).

The Karaites interpret also Deut. 25, 12 וקצות את כפה against Tradition (Sifre *ad loc.;* comp. Midrash Tannaim. ed. Hoffmann, 168 ff.) literally; see Mibḥar *ad loc.* (22*b*); כתר תורה *ad loc.;* Samuel Al Magrabi, (Gitelsohn, 29). So also Philo (II, 328): Εστω δε η δικη χειρος αποκοπη της αψαμενης ὢν οὐ θεμις.

4. Philo deviates in his exposition of Exod. 21, 22 ff. from Tradition which refers אסון in verses 22-23 to the woman and holds the man guilty of murder if he killed the mother, but not punishable for the deadly effect of the blow on the unborn child, regarding the foetus only as part or limb of the mother (*pars viscerum matris*) and without an independent existence (Mekilta *ad loc.;* Baba ḳamma 48*b* ff.; see also Ohalot 7, 6 and Ps.-Jon. to v. 22). Philo (II, 317 comp. 319, beg.) takes this law to refer to the embryo and interprets these verses: If the foetus miscarried by the blow was not formed at the time of the blow the offender is not liable for murder (verse 22), but if the embryo has assumed a distinct shape and is completed the offender shall die for the death of the child (verse 23).[87] Philo, though considering the unborn child to be a part of the mother (II, 319), holds that the law of Lev. 22, 28

[87] Philo follows the Septuagint in the interpretation of these verses; see Ritter, 35. Josephus (*Ant.*, IV, 8, 33) agrees with Tradition and refers אסון to the mother only; comp. Geiger, *Urschrift*, 436-7. Yet he holds, like the Karaites (Hadassi, Alph. 270 (103*b*)), causing abortion to be murder. See *C. Ap.*, II, 24; comp. M. Zipser, *Des Flavius Josephus Werk... gegen Apion*, 164. Some Karaites follow Tradition in the interpretation of אסון. See Benjamin Nahawendi, משאת בנימין, 2*d;* כתר תורה, Exod. 71*b*, below.

includes the prohibition of sacrificing a pregnant animal, a law unknown to Tradition (II, 398; comp. Frankel, *Ueber palästinische u. alexandrinische Schriftforschung,* 32, n. 6; Ritter, 109 and notes). Philo (*l. c.;* comp. Ritter, *l. c.,* n. 3) seems also to believe, against Tradition (Arakin *7a;* comp. Ps.-Jan. to Deut. 22, 22), that the law reprieves a pregnant woman condemned to death. These anti-traditional views of Philo are found also among the Karaites. The Karaites, like Philo, consider the killing of an embryo murder punishable by death (Hadassi, Alph. 238פ, 270מ, 275י; see also references given below) and interpret אסון in verses 22, 23 to refer to the embryo or to the mother and the embryo. See Ḳirḳisani (ed. Poznański) in *Gedenkbuch zur Erinnerung an David Kaufmann,* Breslau 1900, 186; Hadassi, Alph. 238; 270; Mibḥar, Exod. *42b;* כתר תורה, Exod. *71b* ff.; גן עדן, *177d; 179c-d;* Samuel al Magrabi, ed. Gitelsohn, 27 ff. They also consider the killing of a pregnant animal violation of Lev. 22, 28 and go even further than Philo in prohibiting the שליל a foetus found in a killed animal, for food. See Ḳirḳisani, ed. Harkavy, 291; and ed. Poznański, *l. c.,* 184 ff.; Sahl b. Maṣliaḥ (Pinsker, II, 28; comp. *ib.,* 30, 83); Salmon b. Jeruḥam (Poz., *l. c.* 186-7); Hadassi, Alph. 238-240; 308 ; 360 ; 364 (134*d*); Mibḥar, Lev. *15b; 39a;* כתר תורה, Lev. *24a; 62b;* גן עדן, 83*d.* ff.; Samuel al Magrabi, ed. Lorge, 10-11; אדרת אליהו, 64*b* ff.; אפריון, 23; לבוש מלכות, 47; comp. also Ibn Ezra, Mibḥar, and כתר תורה on Gen. 25, 22 and Leḳaḥ Ṭob on Lev. 11, 13 and 12, 8.[88] Many Karaites

[88] See also Frankel, *MGWJ.,* VIII, 400. The Samaritans also apply the law of Lev. 22, 28 to שליל; see Geiger, *Nachg. Schriften,* III, 263-4; 302, V, Heb., 114; Wreschner, Intr., XXVII. Geiger's view (*Nachg. Schr.,* V, Heb., 112 ff.; comp. also Büchler, *MGWJ.,* L (1906), 674, note) that this Samaritan-Karaite opinion is based upon the principle of : עובר לאו ירך אמו. a view which, as Geiger (*l. c.*) believes, was held also by the ancient

prohibit also the execution of a pregnant woman. See Mibhar on Deut. 22, 22 and טירת כסף *ad loc.*[89] Samuel al Magrabi (MS. 86*a*) states: ואם יאמר אומר אם היא מעוברת היכשר כי תהרג והיא מעוברת, יאמר לו לא יכשר כי תהרג והיא מעוברת אבל יאחרוה לאחר שתלד ואחר לידתה תהרג ואם לא כן נהיה הורגים שתי נפשות והמשפט אל נפש אחת בהריגה.

5. Tradition interprets: ונקב שם ה׳ מות יומת (Lev. 24, 16) to mean the cursing of the Divine Name (Sanhedrin 7, 5; Sifra *ad loc.*; comp. Ps-Jon. *ad loc.*: ברם מאן דמפרש ומחרף);[90] so also the Septuagint (comp. Frankel, *Einfluss*, 132) and Josephus (*Ant.* IV, 8, 6). Philo (*Vita Mosis*, II, § 206 ff.) refers this law to any disrespectful mention of the name of God at an inappropriate occasion or place. To this untraditional interpretation of ונקב by Philo, goes back the view of Philo (Tischendorf, *Philonea*, 79; comp. Frankel, *Eidesleistung d. Juden*, Dresden 1840, 21; Ritter, 45-7) that the law punishes a false oath with death. As Philo (*l. c.*, 80) argues, a false oath involves the dishonor of the Divine Name therein employed (comp. Lev. 19, 12)

halakah, is erroneous. The question of עובר ירך אמו is applied in the Talmud to animals and slaves but not to free persons. See also against this contention of Geiger Pineles, דרכה של תורה, 190 ff.; L. Löw, *Ges. Schr.* III, 401; Gronemann, 122, note. It must also be pointed out that most of the Karaites mentioned above do not distinguish in the interpretation of אסון between a finished and an unfinished embryo.

[89] Ḳirḳisani agrees with Tradition that the execution is not to be postponed (ed. Poznański, *Gedenkbuch zur Erinnerung an D. Kaufmann*, 185). Samuel al-Magrabi (ed. Gitelsohn, 38) states that the Law reprieves even a pregnant animal condemned to death! See above, note 83.

[90] For Onkelos *ad loc.*: ודי מפרש שמא see Geiger, *Urschrift*, 274. Chwolson, *Das letzte Passamahl Christi*, 119, overlooked the view of R. Meir (Sanhedrin 56*a*) that מקלל בכנוי is also punished with death. (M. Duschack, *Josephus Flavius u. d. Tradition*, 23 is to be corrected accordingly.) See, however, the opinion of R. Levi פסיקתא דרב כהנא ed. Friedmann, 184*a*: כל מי שהוא מפרש שמו של הקב״ה חייב מיתה שנא׳ ונוקב שם ...

and he applies to it the law of Lev. 24, 16, according to his interpretation of this verse. Most of early Karaites agree with Philo in the interpretation of ונקב שם ה׳ (v. 16). See Anan (ed. Harkavy, 13); ... ואקדים ליה כי יקלל לאדעך דעל מאן דאדכר שמיה דרחמנא בקלילותא קאים דמחייב קטלא.[91] The Karaites, like Philo, also set the punishment of death for false oath.[92] See Hadassi, Alph. 346, 347; Mibḥar, Exod. 37*a*; כתר תורה, Exod. 62*b*; comp. *ib.*, Deut. 24*b*; Samuel al Magrabi (MS., 67*a*); שבועות, אדרת אליהו, ch. 6. They follow also the reason given by Philo. As a false oath involves the dishonor of the name of God the penalty therefor is death in accordance with Lev. 24, 16.[93]

[91] Harkavy's note to it (*ib.*, 198, *s. v.* דברי) is unintelligible. The later Karaites abandoned this interpretation of ונקב; comp. Mibḥar, Lev. 44*b*. For the Samaritan interpretation of ונקב see Grünbaum, *ZDMG.*, XVI (1862), 401 ff.

[92] According to Tradition (Tosefta Makkot 4, 5; b. Shabuot 20*a*) the penalty of a false oath is מלקות; comp., however, תנחומא, וישב, 2 and Naḥm. on Lev. 27, 29. See Schechter, *Jewish Sectaries*, I, p. 16, l. 8 and notes, that according to the sect which Schechter designates as Zadokite (see above) "one is to keep a vow pledging him to a particular commandment *even at the risk of death.*" The view of Kohler (*American Journal of Theology*, 1911, 417), that according to that sect the penalty of *any* false oath is death is not proved. The Zadokite sect (*l. c.*, p. 15, ll. 1-3) agrees also with Philo (*l. c.*; comp. Frankel, *Eidesleistung*, 19-20) that oaths are not to be taken by God's name. See Schechter, *l. c.*, LIV, as to the Samaritan manner of oath, against which see Kohler, *l. c.*; but see L. Löw, *Ges. Schr.*, I, 193 ff.; comp. also Grünbaum, *l. c.*, 404.

[93] See Afendopolo's appendix to אדרת אליהו, Odessa 1870, 209*cd*: ורוב החכמים וגדוליהם פסקו ודנו מיתה למי שעבר על שבועתו או שקר בה וחללה .... ואמר הרב רבנו לוי ע״ה כי המפר השבועה חייב מות ... ואמר ועם זה כי הראיה יוציא המשפט כי מי יחלל קדש משפטו הוא המות שנאמר ואוכליו עונו ישא כי את קדש ה׳ חלל ונכרתה ומקל וחומר מי חלל שם ה׳ וכן דעת הרב רבנו יהודה האבל ע״ה וחכמים אחרים גדולים עמהם כרבנו ישועה ויפת הלוי ע״ה והחכם האלהי הרב רבנו אהרן הראשון עמהם ... In Lev. 19, 8 quoted by Levi b. Jepheth and Samuel al-Magrabi (*l. c.*) as proof that the penalty of the dishonor of the name of God is death only כרת punishment is mentioned. The

Based on this Philonian-Karaite interpretation of Lev. 24, 16 is the view of the early Karaites that every antinomian utterance or action is punished by death. See Anan (ס"הם, *l. c.*): ומאן דאמא מימר מצות לאו מידי אינון או אוריתא לאו מידי היא או דאמא מי יי׳ מיחייב קטלא ורגמין ליה כל ישראל; so also Hadassi, Alph. 267: טיב המגדף הוא המפר מצות עשה מעשותו: ביד רמה בזדון הפיר מצותו ודנו בו רגימה בנקמתו; comp. also Alph. 372ה, 373ח, so also Samuel al Magrabi (MS., 108*b*): ודע כי נחלפו החכמים במצות אשר לא נזכר להם משפט בנקימה: מהם מי אמר כי כולם להם משפט מות וכי האדם אם ימרה אשר האמירו ית׳ בהם בצדיה יחויב מיתה והביא ראיה על זה ממאמרו כי דבר ה׳ בזה ואת מצותו הפר ואמר אחר כי זה המאמר בראיה המביאים אותה כי היא נאמרה על מי אשר כחש במצות התורה או מי יאמר כי המצוה הזאת איננה חוב או יאמר מנין יחויב זה המאמר על דרך הבזיון כי אמר עליו את ה׳ הוא מגדף:[94] That this Karaite

early Karaites, however, took כרת to mean death by court, מיתה בידי אדם, against the traditional interpretation of the concept כרת as heavenly visitation (comp. Sifra on Lev. 23, 29; Sifre on Num. 19, 13; Moed ḳaṭan 28*a;* p. Bikkurim 2, 1; Maim., תשובה, 8, 1; Ibn Ezra on Gen. 17, 14; Naḥm. on Lev. 18, 29 and Abrabanel on Num. 15, 30). See Hadassi, Alph. 266: ... כי כל בעלי כרת ביד שופטיהם חייבים במשפט ה׳ אשר צוה בתורתך: מסורים ביד כהניהם מלכיהם שופטיהם ושוטריהם: ידי עדיהם תהיה בם בראשונה ... Death in כרת punishment is by stoning (*ib.,* Alph. 267). See also Ibn Ezra on Lev. 20, 20 and Harkavy, ספר המצות לענן, 141, n. 14, and טירת כסף to Mibḥar, Lev. 37*a*, letters 63, 69. S. Munk, *Palestine* (German ed. by M. Levy, II,438) is to be corrected accordingly. The latter Karaites agree with Tradition; see Mibḥar, Lev. 34*b;* כתר תורה, Gen. 47*b;* Lev. 56*b;* גן עדן, 125*d;* אפריון, 7.

[94] Every antinomian action or utterance involves the dishonor of God's name which is, according to the Karaites, punished by death. See Hadassi, Alph. 373 (149*c*): ... ואם חלול שם ה׳ ותורתו על האיש ההוא מיתה ככתוב כי את דבר ה׳ בזה ואת מצותו הפר וגו׳. See also Book of Jubilees 30, 8-7. According to some Karaites failure to pray is also punished by death (in accordance with II Chron. 15, 13). So Samuel al-Magrabi (MS., 57*a*): והעוזב את התפילה ולא יעשנה מהבוגדים ויעשה בצדיה וזדון ועל דרך הבזיון הוא חייב מיתה, ויש מהחכמים ז"ל שאמר כי העוזב אותה על כל פנים חייב מיתה.

view is not due to their fondness for exaggeration but is based on the above-mentioned Philonian interpretation of Lev. 24, 16 and Num. 15, 30 (for Num. 15, 30, see Philo, II, 252 and 404) is evident from the fact that a similar view is held by Maimonides who, in disagreement with the talmudic interpretation (Sifre, *ad loc.;* Horayot *8a;* Keritot *7b;* comp. Rashi, Rashbam, and Naḥm., *ad loc.;* comp. also Mibḥar, Num. 15*a;* כתר תורה Num. *22b*), refers Num. 15, 30 to all *antinomian actions.* See מורה נבוכים, III, 41 (Eng. translation by M. Friedlander, London, 1904, 348-9): "If a person sins presumptuously so that in sinning he shows impudence and seeks publicity; if he does what is prohibited by the Law, not only because of his evil inclination but in order to oppose and resist the Law, he 'reproacheth the Lord' (Num. 15, 30) and must undoubtedly be put to death. ... Even if an Israelite eats meat (boiled) in milk or wears garments of wool and linen, or rounds off the corners of his head, in spite against the Law, in order to show clearly that he does not believe in its truth, *I apply to him the words 'he reproacheth the Lord'* and (I am of the opinion) that he must suffer death as an unbeliever. .. According to my opinion, all the members of an Israelitish community which has insolently and presumptously transgressed *any of the Divine precepts* must be put to death."[95]

6. According to Tradition, cursing parents is punished by death (Ex. 21, 17; Lev. 20, 9) only when the Divine

The Karaites, relying on Lev. 4, 2: מכל מצות..., hold (against Tradition; see Sifra *ad loc.*) that a sin-offering is to be brought for the involuntary transgression of *any* law. See Pinsker II, 73 (the meaning of this passage escaped Poznański, *Karaite Literary Opponents of Saadia Gaon*, 66); Mibḥar, Lev., *6b;* כתר תורה, Lev. *9a;* גן עדן, 176*a*, end. See also Philo, II, 246.

[95] See also Maim., רוצח, 4, 10; Z. Chajes, תורת נביאים, Zolkiew 1836, 18*b* ff.

name is used (Sanhedrin 7, 12; Mekilta *ad loc.*). Striking parents is punished by death (Ex. 21, 15) only when the blow is a מכה שיש בה חבורה (Sanhedrin 10, 1; Mekilta, *ad loc.*). Death for the latter offense is by strangulation (*l. c.*). Philo (Tischendorf, *Philonea,* 77) makes death the penalty for *every* manner of insult to parents, and death by stoning the penalty for striking parents (*l. c.* and Frag., II, 629). The Karaites[96] agree with Philo and refer Ex. 21, 15 to *any* physical violence against parents; see Mibḥar, Exod., 41*b*: ומכה אביו ואמו : בכל מיני מכה בין שיש בה חבורה ובין שאין בה חבורה; so also כתר תורה, Exod., 70*b* and Samuel al Magrabi, ed. Gitelsohn, 17. Nor do the Karaites in Exod. 21, 17 condition the use of the Divine Name. See Hadassi, Alph. 272ט (103*d*); Mibḥar, Exod. 42*a;* כתר תורה, Exod. 70*b,* and Samuel al Magrabi, *l. c.,* 19. They agree also with Philo in making death by stoning the penalty for violence to parents. See Hadassi, Alph. 267ד (102*c*) and כתר תורה, Exod. 70*b*; comp. Samuel al Magrabi, ed. Gitelsohn, 19, Büchler, *MGWJ.,* L (1906), 683.

Philo (II, 330; but see *Quaest. in Ex.* II, § 6) states that distinction is to be made in punishment between insult to a public officer and a private person. Tradition makes

[96] For the Samaritan view comp. *ZDMG.,* XLVII (1893), 681. Mark 7, 10 ff. and Matthew 15, 5 ff. (comp. commentaries) perhaps refer to this older interpretation of Exod. 21, 17: that *every* manner of insult to parents is punished by death. Comp. Wünsche, *Neue Beitiäge,* 181-6.

The Karaites decry what they falsely ascribe to the Rabbanites: the opinion that punishment is inflicted only when the curse or blow affected *both* parents; Hadassi, Alph., 249, says: הורו כך במכה אביו ואמו מות יומת אינו חייב אלא עד שיכה את שניהם בבת אחת ובן בקללה עד שיקללם בבת אחת; so also Alph. 250ס; see also Salmon b. Jeroḥam quoted by Neubauer, *Aus d. Petersburger Bibliothek,* 111. See Sanhedrin, 85*b;* Mekilta on Exod. 21, 17: Sifra on Lev. 20, 9.

no such distinction.[97] This view, however, is found among the Karaites. Jepheth b. Ali (quoted in Mibhar, Exod. 42*b*) punishes cursing מלך or נשיא with death. Hadassi (Alph. 343ס) states that cursing a righteous Judge is a *capital* crime; so also Samuel al Magrabi (ed. Gitelsohn, 21) who also states (MS., 147*b*) that even the cursing of the patriarch of a tribe or family is punished by death.

MARRIAGE LAWS

7. The issue of a prohibited alliance[98] is a bastard (ממזר) and the law enjoins concerning him: לא יבא ממזר בקהל ה׳ (Deut. 23, 3). Tradition (Yebamot 8, 3) refers it to marriage. Philo, as was pointed out by Ritter (91, n. 5),

[97] Weiss, *Dor*, I, 126, note, relying on Ḳiddushin 66*a*: הדיוט שבישראל כך הוא דינו ואתה מלך וכהן גדול, believes this to have been the *Sadducean view* (the מלקות there was not, as Weiss *l. c.*, states, in accordance with Deut. 22, 18, but because Judah (or Eleazar; see Josephus, *Ant.* XIII, 10, 5) was a single witness; see Pesaḥim 113b: נגדיה לזיגוד ...). See also Josephus, *C. Ap.*, II, 23 that disobedience to the high-priest is punished like impiety toward God (comp. *Ant.* IV, 8, 14). It is, however, possible that Josephus had in mind the law of Deut. 17, 12; see Grätz, III[3], 110, note 1; comp. Maim., Maim., פ"המש, Sanhedrin, 10, 5: ולכן חייבתו תורה [לזקן ממרא] מיתה לכבוד בית דין ומעלתה כמו שחייב המקלל אביו ואמו מיתה לכבוד אביו ואמו.

[98] Against Geiger's anti-traditional interpretation of ממזר (*Urschrift*, 54 ff.; 350) see Rapoport, נחלת יהודה, 78 ff. For the Septuagint see Frankel, *Einfluss*, 204, and for Philo see Ritter, 91, n. 5. Most of the later Karaites agree with the accepted talmudic interpretation of ממזר (Sifre, II, 248; Yebamot 4, 13; Ḳiddushin 3, 12; see p. Ḳiddushin 3, 2; Tosafot Yebamot 49*a*, *s. v.* שמעון; Maim., איסורי ביאה, 15, 1; Frankel, *Grundlinien d. mosaisch-talmudischen Eherechts*, 5, n. 21 is to be corrected accordingly); see Mibḥar, Deut. 19*b*; so also גן עדן, 149*c*: ואיזה הוא ממזר הנולד מאיסורי ערוה מחייבי כריתות; but see Hadassi, Alph. 278צ (105*d*) and Samuel al-Magrabi, ed. Gitelsohn, 11, l. 14. For a peculiar interpretation of the concept ממזר by some early Karaites as referring to the Chazars see Harkavy, *Semitic Studies in memory of Dr. Kohut*, Berlin 1897, 246-7.

interprets this verse, verses 2, 4 (II, 261), and v. 9 (II 393) to mean that the ממזר is not to mingle with the community of Israel and does not refer to marriage. In his exposition of v. 9, (II, 393) he says: "... *καλειν εις εκκλησιαν και μεταδιδοναι θειων λογων, ους θεμις τους αυτοχθονας και ευπατριδας ιεροφαντεισθαι* ."[99] This view, as Samuel al Magrabi informs us, was held by many Karaites (MS., 91*b*) ודע כי אשר דברנוהו הוא על דעת רוב החכמים ז"ל וגם התיר קצתם זאת הבעילה על תנאי כי יהיה זרעם פחות והוא כי ששן נתן בתו לירחע עבדו והיה מצרי ... ובדעתם כל הנאמר בו לא יבוא לא ירצה בו הבעילה אבל רצונו בזה בעתות הקרבנות והשמחות בחופות חתנים ומילות ובקהלות האומה והביא ראיה ממאמרו אשר ציויתי לא יבואו בקהל לך אחר אמרו כי ראתה גוים באו מקדשה.

This is the view of many early Karaites. See Hadassi, Alph. 365 (140*b*): "דוק המשפט של ילד הנולד מן ערוות ומן אשת איש ומן גויה ומכל דרך אסור בזמן זו גלות נדודי: להוציא הילודים ואמותם מיחס זרע הקדש ... ואם יש חפץ לאחד מישראל להתחתן עמהם יכתב בכתובתם כעורם וקלקול ייחוסם לדורות להחרידי כאשר כתוב ולשישן עבד מצרי .....; so also Alph. 373ר (148*d*). Aaron b. Joseph (Mibḥar, Deut. 19*b*) states that Sahl b. Maṣliaḥ (second half of the tenth century) held that marriage with a ממזר is not forbidden: ולא ידעתי טעם לדברי רבנו סהל שאם יחפוץ ישראל יקחנו [את הממזר]. Sahl b. Maṣliaḥ, evidently, also interpreted לא יבא ממזר בקהל, as did Philo, Hadassi, and the Karaites mentioned by Samuel al Magrabi, to mean that the ממזר is not allowed to mingle in the community.[100] See also Mibḥar, *l. c.*: לא יבא בקהל ה׳: בכל דבר והנכון בנשואין לבד; comp. טירת כסף, *ad loc.*

[99] See Michaelis, *Mos. Recht*, II, § 139; Ewald, *Alterth. des Volkes Israel*, 247; comp. also Rapoport, נחלת יהודה, 46.

[100] The interpretation given by Geiger (אוצר נחמד, IV, 21-2) to this view of Sahl is forced and unnecessary. Geiger's reference (*l. c.*, 22) to Sahl's opinion quoted in Mibḥar, Deut. 6*b*, has no bearing on his view

8. In the exposition of the law of Deut. 21, 10-15 concerning marriage with a female captive of war, Tradition makes no distinction between a married woman and the unmarried (Sifre, *ad loc.;* Ḳiddushin 21*b*: אשת — ואפילו אשת איש). So also Josephus, *Ant.* IV, 8, 23. The Karaites hold that this law refers only to the case when the captive

here. Sahl's interpretation there of החרם תחרים אתם (Deut. 7, 2; comp. טירת כסף to Mibḥar, Deut. 6*b*, letter 115) is held by many Rabbanites; see e. g. Naḥm. on Deut. 20, 10. The Karaite anti-traditional view (see Ḳiddushin 3, 13; Yebamot II, 5 and parallels) that children born to a Jew from a Gentile woman are considered to be Jews which caused the early Karaites to interpret להוציא in Ezra 10, 3 as referring to the mothers onlv (Pinsker, II, 23, n. 12; Geiger. *l. c.;* see also Benjamin Nahawendi, משאת בנימין, 6*b*: אבל מבנות עכו"מז ואמהות בני בלי שם לא נקראים אלא על שם אביהם שנ' רגשות להוציא כל נשים והנולד מהם; similarly Hadassi, Alph. 366' (141*d*): הילודים שנולדו מן הערוות ואשת איש ואשה נכרית ושפחה הוא זר ונקרא על שם אביו הזונה; yet he adds: ועל בני נכריות ושפחות כתוב להוציא כל נשים והנולד מהם, so also Alph. 365ד (140*b*)) goes back to talmudic times and was held by Jacob of כפר נבוראי (p. Yebamot 2, 6; p. Ḳiddushin 3, end; G. rab., 7, 3 and parallels) who seems to have been suspected of some מינות (see above, note 73). See also the early Bible critic (ed. by Schechter), *JQR.*, XIII, 362, lines 22-25, and note on p. 371.

The assertion of M. Friedmann (*Beth Talmud,* I, 106) that the Karaites. like Tradition (Yebamot 8, 4, b. *ib.*, 76*b* ff. and parallels), interpret Deut. 23, 4: עמוני ולא עמונית is erroneous. All Karaites attack this traditional view. See Elias b. Abraham (Pinsker, II, 105); Mibḥar and כתר תורה *ad loc.;* גן עדן, 146*b;* 149*d ff.;* אדרת אליהו, 93*c;* אורח צדיקים, 17*b;* A. Firkowitsch, חותם תכנית (appendix to the מבחר ישרים. Goslow 1835), 51*a;* comp., however, Hadassi, Alph. 323' (119*b*). The legitimacy of David (descendant of Ruth the Moabitess) they save by asserting that Deut. 23, 4 refers only to those who do not embrace Judaism.

Schorr (החלוץ, IV, 43) claims that Maimonides is inconsistent in considering (איסורי ביאה, 12, 18; not 12, 9) the law of עמוני ולא עמונית as הלכה למשה מסיני as this law is disputed, and quotes Yebamot 8, 4; ואם לדון יש תשובה and Tosafot, *ib.*, 77*b*, *s. v.* הלכה. Schorr apparently overlooked the fact that ואם לדון and Tosafot by him quoted refer to the question of מצרית ואדומית and have nothing to do with the law of עמוני ולא עמונית.

was unmarried or a widow. See Hadassi, Alph. 281 ; Mibḥar, Lev. 34*a*, and Deut. 17*a* and טירת כסף, *ad loc.;* כתר תורה, Deut. 24*a* (but see גן עדן, 147*d*). So also אדרת אליהו, 92*b*: ולכן אמרו חכמינו בשבויה שהיא אלמנה .... לא לפי דעת בעלי הקבלה שאמרו שאין אישות לגוי; so also Abraham b. Josiah Jerushalmi in his אמונה אמן (Goslow 1846), 24*a*. Samuel al Magrabi (MS. 222*a-b*) states: דע כי זה מאמרו בעשרת הדברים לא תנאף יגוש אסור כל אשה בעלת איש אם הוא מאנשי הדת או מזולתם מהאומות.... ומי יתלה את עיניו ונפשו באשת יפת תאר ובספור הכתוב עליה ואמר אולי יהי אישה עודנו בחיים יאמר לו זאת התליה אין בה טענה חזקה כי אנשי זו העיר אולי נהרגו .... וגם כי בודאי יהי חקירה על זה הענין קודם התחברו עם האשה הנזכרה למען יעשה כפי חפץ הכתוב. That this is also the view of Philo was shown by Ritter, 75.

9. The penalty of adultery with a married woman is according to Tradition (Sanhedrin 10, 1; Sifra קדושים, 9 (ed. Weiss, 92*a*) strangulation. Many Karaites, however, hold that the law of Deut. 22, 24 applies not only to the betrothed, but also to a married woman; the punishment being stoning in both cases. So Samuel al-Magrabi speaking of adultery and its punishment says (MS., 6*a*): ואם יאמר אומר איך הריגתם יאמר לו הריגתם באבנים כי ידענו זה ממאמרו על המאורשה והוצאתם את שניהם אל שער העיר ההוא וסקלתם אותם באבנים ומתו כי לא הפריש בין הבעולה והמאורשה במשפט כי המאורשה נקראת אשת איש; see also L. Cohn, *Des Samuel al-Magrebi Abhandlung über die Pflichten d. Priester u. Richter,* Berlin 1907, 10, and Mibhar on Lev. 18, 20 (34*a*), and טירת כסף, *ad loc.,* letter רלב: ... וגם בבת ישראל אשת איש הנואפת בין בעולה בין מאורשה ענשן אחד שהרי גם המאורשה נקראת אשת איש; comp. also כתר תורה, Lev. 58*b* and גן עדן, 194*d*. That this is also the view of Philo is evident from the fact that he

sets death by stoning even for the *unmarried harlot;*[101] see II, 308, where he says: *παλιν πορνην κατα τον ιερον λογον οὐ παραδεχεται η πολιτεια ... Ὡς λυμη ουν και ζημια και κοινον μιασμα καταλυεσθω.*[102]

[101] See Ritter's comment on this law of Philo (p. 92); but see Book of Jubilees 20, 4 which also seems to punish unchastity of an *unmarried* woman with death (by burning, in accordance with Gen. 38, 24). The early Karaites also considered unchastity of a פנויה to be ניאוף; see Salmon b. Jeroḥam quoted by *Pinsker,* II, 62: ומלל לא תנאף : באשת עמיתך וזה כדרך הריבונין; comp. also the opinion of Saul b. Anan quoted there (the authenticity of the מקדמא is, however, disputed; comp. also Poznański, אוצר ישראל, VI, 88*a*). See also the Samaritan reading of Deut. 23, 18: לא תחיה קדשה (comp. Klumel, *Mischpatim,* p. VI). See also Brüll, *Jahrbücher,* III (1877), 39, n. 104. It is, however, possible that the Karaites, in fixing stoning as the penalty for adultery, were influenced, as in many other instances (Steinschneider, *Beschneidung d. Araber u. Mohammedaner,* 26-7; *id., Polemische Literatur d. Juden,* 398, n. 1; Wreschner, 41, 44), by the Mohammedan law which also punishes adultery with stoning; comp. *ZDMG.,* LIII (1899), 161.

[102] Noteworthy in this connection is the agreement between the view held by the earliest Karaite authorities (Anan and Benjamin Nahawendi) and the practice in vogue among the Alexandrian Jews in the first century B. C. I refer to Tosefta Ketubbot 4, 9; Baba meṣi'a 104*a;* p. Ketubbot 4, 8: כשהיו בני אלכסנדריא מקדשין נשים אחד (or אחר) בא וחוטפה מן השוק which seems to indicate that the בני אלכסנדריא considered betrothal not so binding as נשואין (A. Brüll, *Fremdsprachliche Redensarten in den Talmuden u. Midraschim,* Leipzig 1869, 32, note, wrongly translates this passage: "Wenn die Alexandriner sich Frauen angelobten, nahmen sie sie *gerade von der Strasse weg.*"). Büchler (*Festschrift zu Israel Lewy's siebzigstem Geburtstag,* Breslau 1911, 123, n. 3) justly remarks: "Vielleicht war hierin hellenistischer Einfluss wirksam" (Büchler, *l. c.,* thinks that the words לכשתכנסי לחופה (or לביתי) were inserted in the שטר כתובה to make the ארוסין unbinding. But, then, what was the purpose of the ארוסין and of the כתובה?). Philo also states (II, 311) that there are many who do not consider unchastity with a betrothed woman to be adultery, though he himself agrees with Tradition (comp. Frankel, *Grundlinien d. mos.-tal. Eherechts,* XXIV ff.) that bethrothal is as binding as marriage (*ib.,* and II, 229). See also p. Hagigah 2, 2: היו בני ירושלים כותבין : מירושלים הגדולה לאלכסנדריא הקטנה : עד מתי ארוסי יושב אצלכם where ארוסי (p. Sanhedrin 6, 6 reads: בעלי, but see Halevy, דורות הראשונים, I*c,* 478, note) is perhaps an allusion to the view of the בני אלכסנדריא

10. Philo (II, 310) states that violation of a widow or divorced woman is a crime approaching adultery and the court shall decide upon the punishment whether it be physical chastisement or pecuniary fine.[103] Tradition, as Ritter (90-91) observes, makes no distinction between a divorced woman or widow and a woman who has never been married. A view similar to that of Philo is held by the Karaites, some of them even making carnal intercourse with a widow or divorced woman a *capital* crime while most

concerning ארוסין as not being binding. This view of the Alexandrian Jews was held also by the earliest Karaites who maintained that the betrothed can sever their connections without a writ of divorce and that, in general, betrothal does not have the force of marriage. See Anan (ס״המ, ed. Harkavy, 118) קא אמא: כי יקח איש אשה ובעלה אלמא אי לא בעלה לא צריך ספר כריתות ובעדים סגיא ליה למפטרה; so also Benjamin Nahawendi, משאת בנימין, 5*b*: שלוח מאורשות דין בעדים שלא פרש בהן בגט המקרא שנ׳ כי יקח איש אשה ובעלה והיא לא בעולה; so also Hadassi, Alph. 365 (141*a*); comp. also גן עדן, 154*c*.

Geiger, relying on the view of Beth Shammai: אין ממאנין אלא ארוסות (Yebamot 13, 1), claims that the older halakah distinguished in a similar manner between ארוסין and נשואין (*Jüd. Zeitschr.*, II, 97; *Nachg. Schr.*, V, Heb., 162). As the marriage of a minor by her mother or brothers is only a *Rabbinic* institution, the view of Beth Shammai concerning מיאון does not prove much. Ḣadassi, Alph. 250 כ (96*b*) and 334-5 (123*ab*) falsely states that according to the Rabbanites a minor given to marriage by her *father* (Deut. 22, 16) is free to annul her marriage through מיאון and reads in Yebamot 108*a*: אי זהו מיאון ... אי אפשי בקידושין שקדשוני אבי ואמי ... ! (Holdheim, מאמר האישות, 53, note, erroneously ascribes this view to Elias Bashyazi; see to the contrary, his אדרת אליהו, נשים ע׳, ch. 2). For another misrepresentation of a traditional law by Hadassi see above, note 96; see also Bacher, *MGWJ.*, XL (1896), 21, n. 5.

[103] Büchler's suggestion (*MGWJ.*, L (1906), 674, note) that this law of Philo goes back to the more ancient view (represented by Beth Shammai) allowing divorce only in case of the wife's adultery and considering the divorced woman to be still to some extent an אשת איש, is not plausible as it does not account for Philo's view concerning אלמנה. Moreover, Philo and the Karaites do not share the view of Beth Shammai and allow divorce for any cause. See, for Philo, Ritter, 70, note 1 and, for the Karaites, above.

of them are, like Philo, satisfied that a special penalty be imposed on the offender, such as the court may deem best. See Hadassi, Alph. 278: ...וזנות חלק הג׳ הוא הזונה עם האלמנה או עם הגרושה גדול עוונו ומעלו ... ויותר מחמירים עליו משפט מות כי הן נשי איש תקראנה שנ׳ אשת נבל הכרמלי תאמר תורתך: יען כי הלא נבל מימים רבים מת ועוד היתה אשת נבל: וכן שאמר אשר ינאף את אשת איש וגו׳ בין שהוא חי בין שהוא מת כי בא עליה בלי צווי ותנאי אלהיך כן זאת אלמנה גרושה הן נשי פלוני נשי איש וגרש או מת אסורות והבתולה; so also גן עדן, 158*c*: וחמורות הן בלי תנאי ואירושי איש שהיא גרושה או אלמנה אף על פי שאינה שכובה מרבית החכמים דנו אותן הבא עליהן כדין הבא באשת איש שהוא מחויב מות...; so also Samuel al Magrabi (MS. 86*b*): וגם אמר קצת מהחכמים ז״ל כי האלמנה והגרושה נכנסים גם הם בזאת האזהרה [לא תנאף] אם יתעלל בהם בלא קידושין ובדעתו כי השוכב מנאף ויחויב מיתה.

11. Tradition (Soṭah 1, 1; Sifre on Num. 5, 13) makes warning by husband and subsequent סתירה of wife with the man against whom she has been warned condition precedent to subjection of the woman to ordeal of Num., 5, 15 ff.[104] Philo, speaking of this law (II, 308), says that in case the husband suspects his wife of adultery they are to bring the matter before the court in the Holy City (comp. Soṭah 1, 4) and if the court is undecided the woman is to submit to the ordeal; Philo, evidently, not considering necessary suspicion of a particular man, warning (קנוי) and סתירה.[105] This is also the view of the Karaites. See Hadassi, Alph. 328, end and 239; Mibḥar, Num. 5*a*: כתר תורה, Num. 7*a;* so also גן עדן, 157*b*: ואין הטעם כדעת בעלי

[104] One of these must be before witnesses (Soṭah 1, 1). The accepted norm (Maim., סוטה, 1, 1-2) requires witnesses for both.

[105] Ritter (pp. 81-85) discusses this law as given by Philo; he fails, however, to notice this essential deviation of Philo from Tradition.

הקבלה שאמרו שנסתרה כשיעור ביאה ואומרים שצריכה עדי קנוי ועדי סתירה ואז ראוי להשקות.[106] ...

12. Tradition takes Deut. 22, 20: אם אמת היה הדבר to mean that in case adultery *during betrothal* has been established by the testimony of *witnesses,* penalty is death (v. 21) in accordance with Deut. 22, 24 (Sifre, *ad loc.;* Ketubbot 46*a;* comp. Frankel, *Der gerichtliche Beweis,* 49). Philo, in his exposition of this law (II, 313), says that if the husband's charge be found true, the parents of the woman are guilty of having deceived the husband at the time of the *betrothal.* Philo, evidently, held that the accusation of the husband, whose substantiation involves death, was *unchastity before betrothal.*[107] This is also the view of most of the Karaites. See Hadassi, Alph. 366 (141*b-c*) that the mere absence of the בתולים is sufficient to convict her: "חייבים אב ואם שלה להכין על היצוע שמלה .... טענתו עוד אם לא יכינו האם והאב או הנמצאים בעת ההיא את השמלה על המטה והוא צועק ומגיד בבעילה ראשונה כי לא מצאתי בתולים לנערה ..... כיון שמבקשים את השמלה ולא היא נמצאת בסקילה חייבת היא הנערה: טעמו שאמר: לא נמצאו בתולים לנערה: והוציאו את הנערה; see also Alph. 365 (140*c*): "דרוש ידרשו הדיינים ואם יש שמלה ופרשו השמלה וגו' והאמת יגידו ... ואם אמת היה הדבר לא נמצאו לה בתולים אם מוכת עץ היא או מכל מכה או מחולי ועדים על זה יעידו ... ואם אין

[106] In case the suspected woman refuses to submit to this ordeal she is, according to Tradition (Soṭah 1, 3), to be divorced and forfeits her dowry. Some Karaites consider such refusal *prima facie* evidence of her guilt and say she is to be put to death as an adulteress; see אדרת אליהו, 98*a*: אמנם אם באה לנקות עצמה ומאנה בשתיה נהרגת; comp. *ib.,* 98*b.* All Karaites agree that in case the woman confesses her guilt, it is sufficient to convict her; see Mibḥar, Num. 5*a*: ואם הודית [שזינתה] שוברת כתובתה ויוצאת ולדעת חכמי הקראים נהרגת והוא הנכון כי פיה כמאה עדים; comp. also כתר תורה, Num. 7*b;* גן עדן, 156*d;* אדרת אליהו, 98*b* and above, note 82.

[107] See *Werke Philos,* II, 207, n. 3. Ritter (p. 77) overlooked this deviation of Philo from Tradition. For the view of Josephus, see Weyl, 87, 105.

זה ולא זה מחויבת היא סקילה כדין תורה. See also Mibhar, Lev. 38*b;* comp. טירת כסף, *ad loc.*: ... שהרי מצינו גם בבת ישראל דין כזה המוציא שם רע על בתולת ישראל ואם באמת לא נמצאו בתולים לנערה חייב לה הכתוב סקילה בפתח בית אביה בלי הסגיל תנאי אם זינתה קודם הארושין או אחר הארושין;[108] so also *ib.* to Mibhar, Deut. 19*a,* letter 77. So also Samuel al Magrabi (Ms., 97a): ואמר קצתם כי לא תהרג אלא בשני עדים עליה בזנות וזה רחוק ממאמר הכתוב כי הכתוב יגוש זולת זה. The later Karaites agree with Tradition that *negatio virginitatis* is not *prima facie* evidence of her guilt. See אדרת אליהו, 96*ab*: ואם תביא עדות שזינתה או נאנסה קודם הארושין אין לה מות. אמנם אם לא תביא נחלקו החכמים. מהם אמרו והם הרוב שאין לה משפט מות אם לא יעידו שזינתה אחר הארושין ... וקצתם אמרו שכל זמן שלא תביא ראיה שזינתה קודם הארושין היא בחזקת שזינתה אחר הארושין וחייבת

[108] Related to this Philonian-Karaite interpretation of Deut. 22, 20 is the Karaite interpretation of Lev. 21, 9. Tradition refers this law to a betrothed or married daughter of a priest (Sifra, *ad loc.;* Sanhedrin 50*b* ff.; Ps.-Jon., *ad loc.*). The Karaites maintain that this law—שרפה for unchastity in a priest's daughter—refers also to the unmarried. See Hadassi, Alph. 330 (121*d*); Mibḥar, Lev. 38*b*: ... ובדעת הקראים בפנויה הכתוב מדבר; so also כתר תורה, Lev. 58*b*. Samuel al-Magrabi (L. Cohn, *Des Samuel al-Magrebi Abhandlung über die Pflichten d. Priester u. Richter,* 9) even asserts that this law applies also to בן כהן guilty of unchaste conduct with a woman married or unmarried; comp. also Mibḥar, Gen. 60*a* and טירת כסף *ad loc.* and to Mibḥar, Lev. 34*a,* letter 232. This is also the view of Philo (? Hoffmann, *Leviticus,* II, 90) and Josephus (*Ant.,* IV, 8, 23; comp. Ritter, 81; P. Grünbaum, *Die Priestergesetze bei Flavius Josephus,* Halle 1887, 18, n. 2; Weyl, 106). Comp. also B. Beer, *Das Buch d. Jubiläen u. sein Verhältniss zu den Midraschim,* Leipzig 1856, 58. The view of Büchler (*MGWJ.,* L (1896), 681, n. 2) that this was also the view of R. Eliezer (Sanhedrin 51*a*) is very improbable; comp. also Weiss, *Dor,* I, 151.

For the mode employed in the execution of בת כהן (באש תשרף; Lev. 21, 9) which, according to Rab Joseph (Sanhedrin 52*b*), was taken by the Sadducees (so also Josephus, *Ant.,* IV, 8, 23) literally (comp. Brüll, בית תלמוד, IV, 7 ff.; Weiss, *Dor,* I, 151; Büchler, *l. c.,* 549 ff., 557 ff.) the Karaites disagree among themselves; see Samuel al-Magrabi, *l. c.;* comp. also Hadassi, Alph. 324ק.

משפט מות; the later Karaites thus disagreeing among themselves only as to the mode of proof of the woman's guilt or innocence *after* betrothal.[109]

13. Num. 36, 6-10 provides that when a man dies without male issue and his daughter inherits his property, the heiress is to marry only within her tribe so that the allotment of one tribe might not pass over to another. According to talmudic interpretation (Baba batra 120*a* ff.; comp. Pseudo-Jonathan on verse 6: דא פתגמא דפקיד ה' לא לדריא דעתידין למיקום בתר פילוג ארעא אלהן לבנת צלפחד and Geiger, *Urschrift*, 447) this rule applied only to the "generation of the conquest," while according to Samuel (B. b. 120*a*) even in the case of the daughters of Zelophehad it was not a command, but merely counsel: עצה טובה השיאם הכתוב (but comp. Ritter, 97, n. 1, and Ibn Ezra, *ad loc.*, v. 8).

Philo[110] states that in case a daughter inherits she is to marry one of her *relatives* (based perhaps on Num. 36. 11), in the absence of which she must at least not marry out of her tribe, thus applying the law of Num. 36, 6-10 to all generations.

[109] According to the scholion of Megillat Taanit (ch. 4) the Boethusians interpreted ופרשו השמלה literally (ממש). Rapoport (דברי שלום ואמת, 14); Geiger (*Urschrift*, 148) and Ritter (133 ff.; comp. Büchler, *l. c.*, 680, note; comp. Weiss, *Dor.*, I, 117) consider this report unauthentic as this view is held also by R. Eliezer b. Jacob (Sifre, II, 237; Ketubbot 46*a*); see, however, Halevy, דורות הראשונים, Ic, 415-18.

[110] See Treitel, *MGWJ.*, XLVII (1903), 409. Philo explains also the law of *yibbum* (Deut. 25, 5-11) as a means that the allotment of one might not pass over to another (II, 443; Ritter, 69, n. 3 errs in asserting that Philo mentions nowhere the law of יבום) which is also the prevailing view among the later Karaites (comp. Poznański, *REJ.*, XLV (1902), 62). Josephus also considers the law of Num. 36, 7 as applying to all times (*Ant.*, IV, 7, 5; comp. Ritter, 96-7). This view is shared also by the author of Tobit 6, 12-13; comp. M. Rosemann, *Studien zum Buche Tobit*, Berlin 1894, 3 ff. and F. Rosenthal, *Vier apokryphische Bücher*, Leipzig 1885, 116, note.

The Karaites, like Philo, apply the law of Numb. 36, 6-10 to all times; see Hadassi, Alph. 260 (99*a*); Mibḥar, *ad loc.* (33*a*), and כתר תורה, Num., 50*b*: וכל בת יורשת נחלה בא להתמיד הדבר לדורות על כן לא יתכן מאמר בעלי הקבלה ... עד שאמרו שהמצוה לשעתה אלא אח"כ תסוב הנחלה; comp also גן עדן, 171*b;* so also Samuel al Magrabi (MS., 263*a*): ודע כי הבת וזולתה מהנקבות אם יתהוה להן ירושה מנחלת ארץ לא יכשר להן כי יהיו לנשים מזולת השבט שלהן למען לא יתהוה להן זרע מזולת השבט ויירש אותן אחר מותן ותצא הנחלה הנזכרה לזולת השבט ...

14. The law of Lev. 21, 2-3 enjoining the priests not to defile themselves by approaching a dead body says, "But for his kin that is near to him. . . ." (v. 2*a*), כי אם לשארו הקרוב אליו.

The talmudic interpretation finds in the words כי אם לשארו support for the tradition that a priest is to defile himself by approaching the body of his wife[111] (Sifra, *ad loc.*: אין שארו אלא אשתו שנ' שאר אביך הוא; Yebamot 22*b*). The Karaites, rejecting this interpretation of שארו,[112] forbid the

[111] See Maim., אבל, 2, 7: ואינו מטמא לה אלא מדברי סופרים; comp. commentaries and לחם משנה, *ib.*, 2, 1. Weiss (*Dor*, I, 46, note) quotes: ... וטימאוהו בעל כרחו (Zebaḥim 100*a;* Sifra, Emor, 1; Semaḥot, ch. 4) as proof that the law of טומאת כהן לאשתו was not universally accepted. Weiss apparently overlooked the fact that the wife of יוסף הכהן died בערב הפסח (*l. c.*) and defilement would have barred him from participation in the קרבן פסח, whereas טומאת כהן לאשתו is, according to many, only רשות; see Zebaḥim, *l. c.;* and Tosafot Soṭah 3*a*, *s. v.* לה; comp. Büchler, *Der Galiläische Am-ha-Areṣ*, 205 and n. 2.

[112] Most of the Karaites reject also the talmudic interpretation of לשארו in Num. 27, 11 (Baba batra 8, 1; Sifre, *ad loc.;* Maim., נחלות, 1, 8 accepts the view (Ketubbot 84*a*) that ירושת הבעל is only מדברי סופרים) and hold that the husband does not inherit his wife; see Mibḥar, Num., 37*a;* גן עדן, 170*d* ff.; כתר תורה, Num. 42*a;* אפריון, 28; לבוש מלכות, 50. Mordecai b. Nisan (לבוש מלכות, *l. c.*) states: ואמרו כי מאמר ויירש אותה היא מצוה בפני עצמה והרצון שהבעל יורש את אשתו ...... והם החליפו הכתוב מעיקרו ...

defilement of a priest in case of wife's death; see Mibḥar *ad loc.* (38*a*) (comp. טירת כסף, *ad loc.*: כי אם לשארו הקרוב אליו : לא יתכן להיות אשתו ומנגד לבעלי הקבלה שאמרו אין שארו אלא אשתו והתירו לכהן ליטמא באשתו); so also כתר תורה, *ad loc.* (58*a*): ובעלי מקרא אמרו שאסור ליטמאות באשתו; comp. also Hadassi, Alph. 206ר and אדרת אליהו, 171*a*; Philo (II, 230) speaking of the law of Lev. 21, 2-3 mentions the six blood-relations, enumerated in these verses, as those for whom the priest is to defile himself, evidently excluding like the Karaites the wife.

15. Philo and the Karaites also agree in the interpretation of Lev. 21, 14. Philo (II, 229) interprets this law to mean that the high-priest must choose his wife from priestly lineage.[113] That this is also the interpretation

(?) ואפילו חכמיהם האחרונים אינם מסכימים לפירוש זה; Benjamin Nahawendi agrees with Tradition (ס"המ לענן, ed. Harkavy, 179). Hadassi (Alph. 365ה (140*a*); 367ח (142*c*) holds that the husband inherits his wife if they have children; Samuel al-Magrabi (MS., 269) states: ותדע כי החכמים נחלפו בענין : מי שם ירושתה לאישה אם היא תחת ממשלתו ורשותו והם בני משנה וקצת מחכמינו ז"ל ומהם והם הרבים מחכמינו ז"ל לא ראו בכן; comp. Weiss, *Dor*, I, 46, note.

[113] See Ritter, 73, n. 2 and Hoffmann, *Magazin*, VIII (1881), 56. It is, however, possible that Philo recorded here a custom which he believed to be a law. Büchler (*Die Priester u. d. Cultus*, 88-9; comp. also Berakot 44*a;* Pesaḥim 49*a;* Rashi, Yebamot 84*b*, *s. v.* מאי) has collected instances which tend to show that also ordinary priests married only daughters of priests (comp. also Grätz, *MGWJ.*, 1879, 499 and Krauss, *JQR.*, VIII, 671). The custom to marry within the family was considered praiseworthy even for non-priests and is commended by the Rabbis; see Tosefta Ḳiddushin 1, 2; Yebamot 62*b;* p. Ḳiddushin 4, 4; Gen. rabba 18, 5; see also Book of Jubilees 4, 15-33; 8, 5-6, 9, 7; but see Kohler, *JQR.*, V (1893), 406, note); comp. also Tobit, 6, 12-3 and *MGWJ.*, 1879, 507, 510 ff. For the view of Josephus see M. Zipser, *Des Flavius Josephus Werk: Gegen Apion,* Wien 1871, 30; Ritter, 73 and P. Grünbaum, *Die Priestergesetze bei Flavius Josephus,* 29-30.

To the Karaite authorities mentioned by Geiger (*l. c.*) that the high-priest is to marry the daughter of a priest may be added Jacob B. Reuben, ספר העשר, on Ez. 44, 22 and Samuel al-Magrabi (ed. Cohn, 12, l. 24 ff.; Cohn, *ib.*, note 111 remarks: "Diese Ansicht ist nur karäisch vielleicht nur des Authors"!).

of most Karaites was already observed by Azariah de Rossi (מאור עינים, ed. Wien, 68*a*) (comp. Geiger, *ZDMG.*, XX (1866), 561 ff.; *Nachgelassene Schriften* III, 311-14 V, Heb., 133 ff.; *Jüd Zeitschr.*, VI, 265).

CEREMONIAL LAWS

16. Philo, speaking of the First of the seventh month (II, 295), says that it is called Day of Trumpets, as trumpets are blown that day at the offering of the sacrifices. Their sounding is a commemoration of the giving of the Law. The trumpet being an instrument of war, symbolizes the war between the different forces of nature and humanity, for the pacification of which man must be greatful to God. Philo makes no mention of the traditional interpretation of יום תרועה (Num. 29, 1), i. e. that the "Shofar" (Sifra on Lev. 25, 9; see Hoffmann, *Leviticus,* II, 247) is to be sounded everywhere (except on sabbath; R. ha-shanah 29*b*) in Israel on that day and seems to have identified יום תרועה in Num. 29, 1 with ותקעתם בחצצרת, the blowing of trumpets every holiday at the offering of sacrifices (Num. 10, 10).[114] The Karaites also reject the traditional interpretation of תרועה and explain it as loud praises to God (Hadassi, Alph. 225; 364 (136*a*); גן עדן, 58*a* ff.; כתר תורה Lev. 67*a*; אדרת אליהו, 48*a*; אפריון, 13; לבוש מלכות, 48-9) or

[114] Nor does Josephus (*Ant.* III, 10, 2) mention the law of תקיעת שופר; comp. also Book of Jubilees, ch. 6. The Samaritans, like the Karaites, reject the traditional interpretation of יום תרועה, differing among themselves as to its meaning; see Geiger, *ZDMG.*, XX, 570; Hanover, *Das Festgesetz der Samaritaner nach Ibrahim ibn Jakub,* text, pp. X-XI and *ib.*, 28, 68. Some Karaites take יום תרועה to mean the blowing of any instrument on that day (Mibḥar, Lev., 42*b*; גן עדן, *l. c.*). Samuel al-Magrabi (MS. 41*a*) states that תרועה is the sounding of *ḥaṣoṣrot* by priests and, in absence of authenticated priests and *ḥaṣoṣrot*, not to be observed now.

as the sounding of חצצרת on every holiday (comp. גן עדן, 58*d;* Hadassi, 136*a*).

The Karaites also reject the traditional interpretation of ולקחתם לכם ביום הראשון (Lev. 23, 40) (see Josephus, *Ant.* III, 10, 4) and claim that the "four species" are for the construction of the "booths" mentioned in verse 42, deriving support for this view from Nehem. 8, 14 ff. See גן עדן, 56*ab* (where the views of Anan, Benjamin Nahawendi, and Daniel, al Kumṣi are quoted); Hadassi, Alph. 168 (64*b*); 225-6; 364 (136*a*); Mibhar, Lev. 43*a;* כתר תורה, Lev. 67*b;* אדרת אליהו, 47*b* (where the opinion of Jepheth b. Ali is quoted); Pinsker II, 96; אפריון, 14; לבוש מלכות, 34, 49.[115] Philo, speaking of the Feast of Tabernacles (II, 297), makes no mention of the law of "four species." Philo, as Treitel (*MGWJ.*, 1903, 512) suggests, must have understood verse 40 not as a separate commandment but,[116] like the Karaites, as prescribing material for the booths.

17. Tradition (Zebaḥim 5, 8; Maim., ה' בכורות, 6, 4) interprets Lev. 27, 32 to mean that the animal-tithe, מעשר בהמה

[115] Some Karaites agree with Tradition in the interpretation of ולקחתם לכם; see גן עדן, 55*b* and the opinion of Joseph ha-Kohen (*l. c.,* 55*d;* כתר תורה, Lev. 67*b;* אדרת אליהו, *l. c.*).

The Samaritans agree with the Karaites; see Geiger, *ZDMG.,* XX, 544; Hanover, *l. c.,* 16 and 62 (Hanover, 31, n. 2, relying on the words of Ibn Ezra on Lev. 23, 40: והצדוקים אמרו כי מאלה תעשו סוכות והביאו ראיה מנחמיה, believes that the Sadducees shared this view, unaware that by והצדוקים Ibn Ezra refers, as usual, to the Karaites (see above, note 10); see, how- M. Duschack, *Josephus Flavius u. d. Tradition,* 27 and Grätz, III, note 10). Josephus agrees with Tradition (*Ant.,* III, 10, 5); so also the Falashas (Epstein, *Eldad ha-Dani,* 162). See also Book of Jubilees 16, 4 and B. Beer, *Buch d. Jubiläen,* 47.

[116] It must, however, be pointed out that Philo (*l. c.*), in contradistinction to Josephus (comp. M. Olitzki, *Flavius Josephus und die Halacha,* p. 25, n. 31 and p. 50), does not seem to require the construction of *special* booths for the Feast of Tabernacles.

like the "second tithe," is to be eaten by the owner within the walls of Jerusalem. Philo (II, 234, 391; comp. Ritter, 123; Driver, *Deuteronomy,* 170, note is to be corrected accordingly) states that the animal-tithe is to be given to the priests.[117] The Karaites agree with Philo. See Mibḥar, Lev. 51*a;* כתר תורה, Lev. 76*b*.

18. Tradition applies the law of Lev. 22, 19 (תמים) to animal sacrifices only (Sifra to Lev. 1, 14; Menaḥot 6*a* and parallels). Philo, as is evident from the reason given by him for the law of תמים (II, 238) holds that תמים refers also to תורים ובני יונה. The Karaites agree with Philo. See Mibḥar, Lev. 3*b,* ואמרו בעלי הקבלה אין המומין פוסלין בעוף .... והנכון שאלו הפרשיות למדות זו מזו; see also כתר תורה, Lev., 5*a*.

19. Philo (II, 256; comp. *Werke Philos,* II, 93, n. 1) states that all the lights of the sacred candle-stick (מנורה) were extinguished in the morning. According to Tradition (Tamid 6, 1; Sifre on Num. 8, 2; Tosefta, Soṭah 13, 7; Yoma, 39*a*[118] and parallels; comp. also Naḥm. on Ex. 27, 20 and Tosafot Menahot 86*b s. v.* ומנה; comp. M. Duschak. *Josephus Flavius u. d. Tradition,* Wien 1864, p. 4, which is to be corrected accordingly) one light was left burning the whole day (נר המערבי). Josephus (*C. Ap.,* I, 22) also states that the lights were never extinguished (see *Ant.*. III. 8, 3 that *three* lights burned in the Temple during

[117] So also Book of Jubilees 32, 15 and Tobit 1, 6. Ritter, 123 overlooked that Philo (II, 234) disagrees with Tradition (Bekorot 9, 1) also in requiring מעשר בהמה to be given from all domestic animals. See also Schechter, *Jewish Sectaries,* II, 4, ll. 13-15; comp., however, Hadassi, Alph. 205.

[118] See Tosefta Soṭah 13, 7; Yoma 39*a;* p. *ib.,* 6, 3: ארבעים שנה ששמש שמעון הצדיק .... והיה נר מערבי דולק [כל הלילה] מכאן ואילך פעמים דולק פעמים כבה; but see Weiss, *Dor,* I, 82, note 1, that this refers to שמעון הצדיק who lived about forty C. E.: see Maim., תמידין ומוספים, 3, 12 and כ"מ *ad loc.:* comp. ת' הרשב"א, ed. Wien, No. 309.

daytime!) The Karaites hold, like Philo, that no lights burned in the Temple during the day. See Mibḥar, Exod. 57*a* and כתר תורה, Lev. 85*b*.

20. The Karaites reject the ancient traditional law[119] that vows made and oaths taken without due consideration of the circumstances involved may be annulled by a court as those of a daughter by her father (Num. 30, 5-6) and that of a wife by her husband (*l. c.*, v. 7 ff.). See Hadassi, Alph. 139-141, 364 (135*a*); Mibḥar, Num. 29*a;* לבוש מלכות, 51; comp. also Maim. commentary on Nedarim, ch. 10, end; ... שזה אצלינו בערי המערב ר״ל היתר השבועות מעשים בכל יום לפי שבמקומינו אין נובעין בהן מים הרעים ר״ל המינות; and *id.*, משנה תורה, הל' שבועות, 12, 12. This seems to be also the view of Philo who seems to express his objection to the law of annulment of vows by the statement (II, 273; comp. *Werke Philos,* II, 112, n. 2) that *"no man is competent to heal vows."*[120]

[119] Weiss (*Dor,* I, 81) believes that the law of התרת נדרים was inaugurated in the time of Simon the Just. This opinion of Weiss is based on his view (*l. c.*, 80; so also Geiger, *Urschrift,* 31-2) that שמעון הצדיק did not favor the making of vows; see, however, Rapoport, נחלת יהודה, 23 ff. We do not know whether the law of התרת נדרים was even contested by the Sadducees; comp. p. Berakot 7, 2; Gen. rabba 91, 3. Schechter (*Jewish Sectaries,* I, XVIII; comp. *ib.*, p. 16, ll. 7-8 and notes) believes that the sect which he designates "Zadokite" (see above) held that vows cannot be annulled; comp. also K. Kohler, *American Journal of Theology,* 1911, 425-6.

[120] The later Karaites accepted, with slight modifications, the law of התרת נדרים; see Kaleb Afendopolo's appendix to אדרת אליהו, Odessa 1870, 227*a* ff. It is, however, possible that in rejecting התרת נדרים the early Karaites, as in several other instances, turned into a law the general sentiment among the Babylonian Jews during the Gaonic period against the annulment of vows. Jehudai Gaon (quoted by Naḥshon Gaon) states: דאנן לא' גרסינן נדרים ולא ידעינן לאסר ולהתיר בה לא נדר ולא שבועה; see הלכות פסוקות, ed. Müller, No. 122; comp. *ib.*, Nos. 117, 120; חמדה גנוזה, Nos. 6, 44, 75; שערי תשובה, Nos. 38, 137, 143, 145-6; תורתן של ראשונים,

21. The Karaites agree with Philo also in the interpretation of לא תבשל גדי בחלב אמו (Exod. 23, 19; 34, 26; Deut. 14, 21) as prohibiting the seething of a kid or—by analogy—of any other animal in the milk of *its* mother. See Philo II, 399; comp. Ritter, 128.[121] See Hadassi, Alph. 240 (91*cd*); 360ח (132*d*); Mibḥar, Exod. 47*b;* כתר תורה, Exod. 79*ab*.[122] לבוש מלכות, 41.

22. The law of Ex. 13, 13; Num. 18, 15 enjoins the redemption of the firstling of an ass with a lamb, and that, if the owner fails to redeem, the firstling is to be killed by having its neck broken. According to Tradition this law refers only to an ass but not to the firstling of any other unclean animal (Mekilta, *ad loc.;* Sifre on Num. 18, 15; Bekorot 5*b*). Philo makes this law apply to all *domestic*

ed. Horowitz, I, Nos. 12, 14; so also Sar Shalom Gaon: כך ראינו שאין בדורות הללו מי שיכול להתיר נדרים וכ"שכ שבועות, (שערי תשובה No. 141: תשובות הגאונים, ed. Lyck, No. 37; see however, *ib.,* No. 11 end; שערי תשובה, No. 48 and איי הים, *ad loc.*).

[121] See Ḥullin 8, 1 ff.; Mekilta on Exod. 23, 19; Sifre on Deut. 14, 21. The Samaritans agree with Tradition; see Geiger, *Nachg. Schr.,* III, 303-4; Wreschner, *Intr.;* XXVI. For the view of the ancient Samaritans see Geiger, *l. c.,* 305-6 and *Nachg. Schr.,* IV, 66, 126. For the LXX see Frankel, *Vorstudien,* 183. The practice of the Falashas agrees with the view of Philo and the Karaites (Epstein, *Eldad ha-Dani,* 130, 173; Epstein, *l. c.,* 129-131 believes that this was also the view of Eldad ha-Dani; but see No. 35 of Eldad's Halakah, ed. Epstein, 121). Against the view of Rapoport ערך מלין, 101*a* (comp. Ritter, 128) that the law of בשר בחלב was not universally known in Babylonia even long after the destruction of the Second Temple see Halevy, דורות הראשונים, I*c,* 128.

[122] For Anan's interpretation of לא תבשל גדי בחלב אמו see Harkavy, ס"הם לענן, 152, n. 1. For other interpretations of this verse by some early Karaites see Hadassi, Alph. 240 (91*cd*); Jacob b. Reuben (Harkavy, *l. c.,* 155) and Ibn Ezra on Exod. 23, 19. Most of the later Karaites accept the traditional interpretation of לא תבשל; see Geiger, *Nachg. Schr.,* III, 303; comp. also כתר תורה, Exod. 79*a;* Samuel al-Magrabi, ed. Lorge, 20-22; אפריון, 24.

animals (II, 233; Ritter, 119 ff.).[123] This is also the view of the Karaites. See Anan (ed. Schechter, p. 7, ll. 8-15): הטמאה (Num. 15. 18b) טפי בה הי מ[שום דכתיב ופטר] חמור תפדה בשה טפי האכא הי לאדעך דעל כל ב[המה קאי] והאיי דפרט התם בחמור מישום דכל בהמה טמאה [בכלל חמור] דכת' שורך וחמרך וכל בהמתך אמא מבהמה טהור[ה שור ומבהמה] טמאה חמר ואמא בתריה וכל בהמתך באלה [כללה ?] לבהמ[ה טהורה בהדי] שור ולבהמה טמיאה בהדי חמור ומישום הכי כת' וכל ב[המתך] לאדעך דעל כל פטר רחם דבהמה טמאה קאים; comp. *ib.*, p. 8, l. 15 ff. So also Hadassi, Alph. 204; כתר תורה, Exod. 35*a*: ופטר חמר : כי נראה שלא הקדיש מבהמות הטמאות כי אם פטרי חמור לבד וכן דעת בעלי הקבלה ובני מקרא אומרים זה הקש לכל בהמה טמאה.

[123] So also Josephus, *Ant.*, IV, 4, 4. As Olitzki suggests (*Flavius Josephus und die Halacha,* 29) this anti-traditional view of Josephus may be due to his desire to remove any suspicion that the ass occupied a favorable position in Jewish law. This may also account for the view of Philo. Philo omits the law of וערפתו (Exod. 13, 13; comp. Ritter, 120; Olitzki, *Magazin,* XVI, 178.). Nor do all the Karaites accept the literal interpretation of וערפתו; see the opinion of Sahl b. Maṣliaḥ quoted in Mibḥar, Exod. 19*b* (comp. Ibn Ezra, *ad loc.*). Aaron b. Joseph (Mibḥar, *l. c.* and Num. 17*b*) agrees with Tradition that only the ass is to be redeemed. Comp. also Weiss, Dor, I, 51.

The contradiction between Exod. 13, 2 (פטר כל רחם בבני ישראל באדם ובבהמה לי הוא) and Deut. 15, 19-20 (לפני ה' אלהיך תאכלנו) and between Lev. 27, 26 (לא יקדיש איש אותו...; the firstling is קדוש *ipso facto*) and Deut., *l. c.* (הזכר תקדיש...; the בכור is to be *declared* קדוש by the owner) led many Karaites to refer Deut. 15, 19-20 to בכור עדר of clean animals which, as they believe, in contradistinction to בכור פטר רחם is to be declared קדוש by the owner and, like the "second tithe," to be consumed by him within the walls of Jerusalem or redeemed; see Hadassi, Alph. 204-5; Mibḥar, Deut.. 12*b;* כתר תורה, Deut. 19*a* (Ibn Ezra on Deut. 12, 17 refers to *this* Karaite view; Harkavy, ס"המ לענן, 142, n. 16, is to be corrected accordingly). Anan tried to reconcile the above mentioned contradictions by claiming that the firstling whose conception and birth were while its mother belonged to an Israelite is קדוש *ipso facto* and to be given to the priests (Exod. 13, 2; Lev. 27, 26, Num. 18, 15), whereas the בכור who was owned by an Israelite only at the time of its birth is to be made קדוש by the

The Philonian halakah, in general, is a problem still to be solved. Philo lived in Egypt where as we now know from the papyri recently discovered in Assuan and Elephantine (Sayce-Cowley, *Aramaic Papyri discovered in Assuan*. London 1906; Sachau, *Drei aramäische Papyrusurkunden aus Elephantine*, 1908), the Jews were permanently settled in the sixth century B. C. (comp. Schürer. *Geschichte des Jüdischen Volkes*, III [4], 24 ff.).[124]

Alexander the Great transplanted many Jews into Egypt in 332 B. C. (Josephus, *Bell. Jud.* II, 18, 7; *Contra*

owner and belongs to him (Deut. 15, 19-20). See Anan's *Book of Commandments* (ed. Schechter, p. 6, ll. 7-18): וקא [א]מא לי הוא ואף על גב דלא מקדש [יתי]ה וכתב כל הבכור [אשר יולד בבקרך ובצאנך] הז׳ ת׳ ליי׳ אלהיך קא אמא אשר יולד לאדעך דעל בכור [דא]ת[י]לודי ביני יש׳ קאים ולאו דמזדרע אזדרועי וקא אמא [תקדיש לה׳] אלהיך דצריכת לאקדושיה וקא אמא בתריה לפני ה׳ אלהיך [לאודע] לך (?) דהאיי בכור דאתילודי הוא דאתיליד ביני יש׳ ולאו [דמזד]רע ביני יש׳ מרואתיה נאכלוה בבית המקדש ... וכת׳ אך בכור אשר [יבכר קא א]מא אשר יבכר ל׳ בבהמ׳ לאדעך דעל בכור דמן כד אזדרע [בקדוש]תא קאים והינו בכור דמזדרע אזדרועי ביני יש׳ וקא אמא[לא יקדיש אי]ש אתו דלא צריך אקדושיה וכ׳ כל פטר רחם לכל בשר [וק]א אמא באדם ובבהמה יהיה לך קא אמא לך דבכד מזדרע [אזדרועי ביני] יש׳ לכהן יהבינן ליה; comp. also *ib.*, p. 8, ll. 15-26 and p. 9, ll. 9-10, 21 ff. Ḳirḳisani alludes to this view of Anan (ed. Harkavy, 248) and states that the authority for this law of Anan was found in one of Jannai's liturgical compositions. Harkavy, *Studien u. Mittheilungen*, V, 107, note, is to be corrected accordingly.

124 See also Rapoport, נחלת יהודה, 128-9; *id.*, ערך מלין, 100*b* ff.; Ritter, 6, 8-9. Herzfeld, *Geschichte*, III, 463; Frankel, *Vorstudien*, 10, and notes; *id.*, *MGWJ.*, 1852, 40.

On the Egyptian Jews and their relation to Palestine see the literature quoted by Schürer, *l. c.*, 147 ff., and in Sweet's *Introduction to the Old Testament in Greek*, Cambridge 1902, 3 ff. In the third and fourth centuries C. E. there were still some Amoraim in Alexandria; see p. Erubin 3, 9; p. Ḳiddushin 3, 14; comp. Frankel, מבוא הירושלמי, 77*a*. It may also be pointed out that Judah b. Ṭabbai, to whom the later Karaites (see above, note 4) ascribe the beginning of Karaism, lived in Alexandria; see p. Ḥagigah 2, 2; p. Sanhedrin 6, 6; comp. Frankel, דרכי המשנה, 34-5; Weiss, *Dor*, 128, n. 1; Halevy, דורות הראשונים, I*c*, 474 ff.

Ap., II. 4; comp. Schürer, *l. c.*, 35 ff.; 40). The city of Alexandria early became a great center of Jewish activity, second only to Jerusalem. The existence of the Temple of Onias did not affect the loyalty of the Jews in Egypt to the Sanctuary in Jerusalem (Frankel, *Einfluss,* 157; Schürer, *l. c.,* 147-8). Palestinian scholars often visited Alexandria (Rapoport, ערך מלין, 101*b*). The Palestinian interpretation of the Law and the practices in vogue there were not unknown to them (Frankel, *Vorstudien zu der Septuaginta,* 185-186; comp. Halevy, דורות הראשונים, I*c*, 127, note; 129, note) and the influence of Palestinian exegesis is patent in that great monument of the Jews of Egypt, the Septuagint (Frankel, *Vorstudien zu der Septuaginta; Ueber den Einfluss d. paläst. Exegese auf d. alex. Hermeneutik; Ueber paläst. und alex. Schriftforschung;* but see Herzfeld, *Geschichte,* III, 548 ff.). Philo, the great representative of Egyptian Jewry, knew of the existence of an oral tradition and considered it as binding as the Written Law (see the references by Ritter, 14-5; comp. Neumark, *Geschichte d. Jüdischen Philosophie des Mittelalters,* II, Berlin 1910, 418, note; see, however, *Werke Philos,* II, 289, note).[125] He also visited Palestine and there saw the people living according to that Tradition (Grätz, *MGWJ.*, 1877, 436 ff.). How are we then to account for the interpretations and decisions in which Philo deviates from traditional halakah? Are such deviations subjective opinions of Philo?[126] Do they reflect the actual practices

[125] See also Ritter, 16-7. For Philo's *eruditio hebraica* see the references by Ritter, 10, n. 2 and by Schürer, *l. c.*, 699; comp. also L. Löw, *Ges. Schr.*, I, 7, 303.

[126] See Treitel, *MGWJ.*, 1903, 415; but see Ritter, 15-16.

in vogue among Egyptian Jewry[127] or do they go back to a peculiar tradition?[128]

But be this as it may, the fact, which I have attempted to demonstrate, that *in most of Philo's deviations from Tradition the Karaites hold the same view,* points to some kind of dependence of the latter on Philo, or to common descent from a particular tradition. The former view gains in probability from the following:

The Hellenic or Alexandrian method of interpretation of the Scriptures did not remain unknown to the Palestinian teachers of the law and the works and views of Philo found their way to the Palestinian schools.[129] Moreover, the general belief that Philo and his works were lost to the Jews of the Middle Ages until Azariah dei Rossi, about

[127] So Ritter 16-17; comp. *ib.,* 28, 63 ff., 90, 93; but see *Werke Philos,* II, 48, n. 2; 202, n. 3; 258, n. 1. Frankel (*Über palästinische u. alexandrinische Schriftforschung,* 32, nu. 6; *Einvuss,* 157 see *ib.,* 33, n. 9 and pp. 190-201) believes that Philo's exposition of the sacrificial ritual goes back to the practice of the Temple of Onias; comp. also Grätz, *MGWJ.,* 1877, 436; but see Ritter, 109, n. 2; 112.

[128] See L. Cohn, *Werke Philos* I, 14. The view of Büchler (*MGWJ.,* L (1906), 706; see also Lauterbach, *Jewish Encyclopedia,* X, *s. v.* Philo, 16*b*) that Philo's deviations from traditional halakah represent an earlier halakah (that of Beth Shammai) is still to be proved. Geiger who scanned Jewish literature and that of its sects for traces of ancient halakah took no account, as already remarked by Poznański (*Abraham Geiger, Leben u. Lebenswerk,* 372, n. 1), of Philo. Philo's deviations from Tradition cannot be brought into relation with Sadduceeism and the supposed ancient halakah related to it; comp. Rapoport, ערך מלין, 101*a*. Philo interprets ממחרת השבת like the Pharisees (Frankel, *Einfluss,* 137). He considers (II, 230) like the Pharisess (Menaḥot 65*a*) the קרבן תמיד a *public* offering; allows divorce without ערות דבר (Ritter, 70, n. 1) and seems to agree with the Pharisees also in the law of עדים זוממים (Ritter, 26, n. 1).

[129] See Freudenthal, *Hellenistische Studien,* I, 68 ff.; C. Siegfried, *Philo von Alexandria als Ausleger des Alten Testament,* Jena 1875, 278 ff.; Weinstein, *Zur Genesis der Agada,* II, 29 ff.; D. Neumark, *Geschichte der Jüdischen Philosophie des Mittelalters,* II, 70 ff., 84 ff.

the end of the sixteenth century, reintroduced him in Jewish literature, is now proved to be unfounded. The tenth century Karaite, Abu Yusuf al-Ḳirḳisani, in his work *Kitāb al-anwār wal-marākib* (written 937), speaks of a Jewish Sect named "the Magarites" (אלמגאריה). This sect, says Ḳirḳisani, sprang up before the rise of Christianity. The adherents of the sect make the biblical passages that speak of attributes of God refer to an angel who, according to them, created the world (ed. Harkavy, 304). Among them are the works of the "Alexandrine" (אלאסכנדראני) which are the best of the "Books of the Cave" (*ib.*, 283). The same author, speaking of Benjamin Nahawendi whom he considers the second founder of Karaism, says that Benjamin's belief that an angel created the world is similar to the view held by the Alexandrine (*ib.*, 314). Harkavy ingeniously suggested that these "Magarites" are the Egyptian Essenes, known as the Therapeutae. The "Alexandrine" whose works they so highly estimated is *no other than Philo* (*ib.*, 256 ff.) and Nahawendi's "Angel" goes back to Philo's "Logos" (comp. Poznański, *REJ.*, L, 1905, "Philon dans l'ancienne littérature judéo-arabe," where all the material is collected and discussed). The view that some of the works of Philo were known to the Jews in the eighth, ninth, and tenth centuries—the period of religious unrest among the Jews and the birth of Jewish religious philosophy—is shared by many scholars. See Bacher, *JQR.*, VII, 701; Hirschfeld, *ib.*, XVII (1905), 65 ff.; Poznański, *l. c.* (see *id.*, אוצר ישראל, III, 128*a*); Eppenstein, *MGWJ.*, LIV (1910), 200; D. Neumark, *Geschichte der jüdischen Philosophie des Mittelalters*, I, Berlin 1907, 128, 133, 560, 568; II, 372 and 466 ff. Among Philo's (the "Alexandrine's) works—which, as Ḳirḳisani informs us, were eagerly studied,—might have been those that contain Philo's expositions of biblical laws; Philo thus influencing, not only the theological views of the first Karaite philosophers (Benjamin Nahawendi and his followers), but also their interpretation of biblical laws and their practices.[130]

[130] The allegorical method of interpretation, characteristic of Philo, was popular also among the Karaites; see Weiss, *Dor,* IV, 86 and Poznański, *MGWJ.*, 1897, 208, n. 1; comp. also H. Hirschfeld, *Jefeth b. Ali's Arabic Commentary to Naḥum,* London 1911, 8 and 10 ff. The Karaites share also the view of Philo that the Decalogue is the text on which the whole Law is but a commentary (this view is found also in the later Midrashim; see the references by L. Löw, *Ges. Schr.*, I, 42. A similar view is found in p. Sheḳalim 6, 1. Reifmann, בית תלמוד, I, 350 and Weiss, *Dor,* IV, 141 are to be corrected accordingly). Saadia Gaon proved to them by it the possibility of an oral law (comp. Weiss, *Dor,* IV, 141) and the Karaites Nissi b. Noaḥ (eleventh century; see lastly Harkavy, ס"המ לענן, intr., VII) and Judah Hadassi (twelfth century) arranged their works, like Philo, according to this view. Comp. also Müller in *Oeuvres complètes,* XI, intr., XIX; Bacher, *Jewish Encyclopedia,* X, 583*b*.

The Karaite Zeraḥ b. Nathan (end of sixteenth century) was much interested in the works of Philo (Neubauer, *Aus der Petersburger Bibliothek,* 75, 125). The famous nineteenth century Karaite Abraham Firkowitsch indeed asserts that Philo was a *Karaite* (preface to מבחר ישרים, *2a*), but, according to him, Jesus was a Karaite likewise (חותם תכנית, appendix to מבחר ישרים, 54*a*, 56*a;* Ḳirḳisani, ed. Harkavy, 305, 9 and Hadassi, *JQR.*, VIII (1896), 436 state that Jesus was a Sadducee); comp. I. B. Levinsohn, תער הסופר, Odessa 1863, 18-9.

KARAITE STUDIES

THE ANTI-KARAITE WRITINGS OF SAADIAH GAON.

THE period between the conclusion of the Babylonian Talmud and the activity of the last Geonim, extending from the sixth till the ninth century, although not totally destitute of literary documents, is yet one of the most obscure epochs in Jewish history. That space of time was, nevertheless, of vast importance for the intellectual life of Judaism. The period comprises the activity of the Massoretes, the introduction of our system of punctuation, the production of a number of Midrashim, and a series of mystical writings. The liturgy assumes fixed forms [1], and—which is of special importance—in the second half of that period new doctrines arise, diverging from official, traditional Judaism, and new sects spring up. It is true, many of these sects hardly survived their authors, yet many of them succeeded in living, at least for some time; whilst one of them, that of the Karaites, continues to exist even to the present day.

The period also was productive of many riddles, that have not been solved even yet, one of which is the attitude of the Geonim towards the Karaite doctrines. These official representatives of the Judaism of the day, did nothing to avert the danger that threatened from the part of the Karaites. They neither tried to warn the people against the opinions of the Karaites, nor did they endeavour to regain the apostate sectarians for traditional Judaism, or to rebut the Karaite teachers. Nor is it certain that the

[1] The fixing of our constant calendar dates also probably from that time. Cf. my essay on Ben Meir in the JEWISH QUARTERLY REVIEW, Oct., 1897.

Geonim appealed to the secular authorities against the Karaites[1], and, perhaps, they only made some arrangements which had an anti-Karaite tendency[2]. It is a fact, that the name of ʿAnân appears only once in the whole literature before Saadiah, in a *responsum* of Natronai b. Hillai, and the passage proves that the latter knew ʿAnân's code of laws only from hearsay[3]. The only Gaon, perhaps, who, before Saadiah, entered occasionally upon the attacks of the Karaites, was Hai b. David[4].

We are, as I mentioned before, too little acquainted with the internal history of the Judaism of that period, to be able to discover and form a judgment on the motives by which the Geonim were guided. If the Geonim were of opinion that the movement would be nipped in the bud by being ignored, or that the heresy was only a transient phenomenon, incapable of striking root among the people, and that, in consequence, it was superfluous to combat it—if they thought this, they were thoroughly mistaken. Karaism is still in existence, after more than a thousand years, although its condition is only a poor one. During the first century of its existence, however, the movement seems to have made proselytes among the Rabbanites, so that even Sahl b. Mazliach and Tobia b. Moses mention Rabbanites, who subsequently joined the Karaites[5].

But the work that had been neglected by the Geonim of Babylon, was taken up with great ardour by a young scholar of Egypt, namely Saadiah al-Fajjumi. When a young man of twenty-three, he stood up as an opponent

[1] Cf. Schorr, *Hechaluz*, VI, 70 sqq.

[2] Vid. Weiss, *Dor dor wedorschaw*, IV, 107 sqq.

[3] Vid. סדור רב עמרם גאון, f. 38 a: ··· ותלמידי ענן ירקב שמו אבי אביו של דניאל חוט המשלש ברשע ובמינות שאמר לכל התועים והזונים אחריו עזבו דברי משנה ותלמוד ואני אעשה לכם תלמוד משלי ··· וראה מרנא ורבנא אלעזר אלוף ז"ל ספר תועבות שלו שקורין אותו ספר מצות כמה תחבולות יש בו וכו'.

[4] Vid. Harkavy, *Studien u. Mittheilungen*, V, 108, note 2.

[5] Sahl's words in Pinsker, *Likkute Kadmonioth*, p. 33; those of Tobia in *Hashachar*, VII, 217, and *Monatsschrift*, XXX, 471.

of ʿAnân, the founder of the sect of the Karaites[1], and a great portion of his chequered life was devoted to combating the Karaite doctrines. His appointment as Gaon at Sora he owed, probably, in part to his activity in that direction, in spite of the usage that had been hitherto in force, to give that dignity only to a scholar from the school of the Geonim[2]. Later authorities were also grateful to him for his having made a stand against heresy in general, and against the Karaites in particular[3], and Moses di Rieti opens the Paradise for Saadiah for his polemics against the Sectarians[4].

Besides the polemical dissertation against ʿAnân, Saadiah also wrote some other anti-Karaite works, none of which has been preserved. I shall now try to fix the number and contents of such works from quotations that are still extant[5].

1. The first anti-Karaite work of Saadiah, was, as already said, his polemical essay against ʿAnân, entitled

[1] Vid. infra.

[2] I say "in part," for there is no doubt that the fame of his other writings, which he composed in Egypt, had come as far as Babylonia. It is even said that in the year 921 a question was directed to him from Babylonia, for the purpose of refuting the dicta of a certain Ben Meir in reference to the Festivals. Vid. Harkavy, l. c., 212 sqq. Abraham ibn Daud's notice in his Chronicle (ed. Neubauer, p. 65), (ובמחבואו חבר (רב סעדיה כל ספריו, has long been recognized to be incorrect; vid. Grätz, *Geschichte*, V, note 20.

[3] Vid. e.g. Abraham ibn Daud's words (l. c., p. 66): ועשה טובות גדולות לישראל והשיב תשובות על המינים ועל הכופרים בתורה וכו׳.

[4] *Mikdasch Meat*, ed. Goldenthal, f. 95 a: רב סעדיה גאון עם ספריו. ותשובות למינים מאיר אישון.

[5] I have already mentioned Saadiah's anti-Karaite writings in my "Karaite Miscellanies" (Jewish Quarterly Review, VIII, 689–691). Before that time, Dukes (*Beiträge*, &c, II, 32, 33) and Steinschneider (*Cat. Bodl.*, cols. 2165–2168) gave a list of those writings. The latter compiled methodically and exhaustively everything that was known on the subject before 1860, and my exposition was partly based on his. But I was obliged to differ from him on many points, and most particularly in the arrangement of the writings, in consequence of fresh material, and many additions.

כתאב אלרד̃ עלי ענן, written in his twenty-third year, i.e. 915. For, as Luzzatto[1], and Geiger[2] have shown, it is to this writing that the verse: כתבו בן שלש עשרים להפר עצת ענן אשר קשר ומרד, quoted by Abraham Ibn Ezra (יסוד מספר, ed. Pinsker, p. 170), refers. The essay is, as far as I know, cited by name only by Saadiah himself in his Commentary to Gen. viii. 3, and to Lev. xxiii. 15. The former passage, quoted by Jefeth b. 'Ali in his Commentary ad loc., reads as follows[3]: קאל ראס אלמתיבה קד דכרנא פי כתאב אלתמייז ופי כתאב אלרד̃ עלי ענן אקואל ואסעה̈ מן אלרד̃ עלי מן אסתשהד בקצה̈ ותנח התיבה עלי אן אלהלאל אדא לם יר פיגב אן יחסב אלשהר ל̇ אלך. 'Anân inferred from the circumstance that the Flood lasted five months—150 days—that, whenever the moon was invisible from any cause whatever, the month had always thirty days, without any regard to the preceding months; for Noah counted the five months as 150 days, because he could not see the new moon in the Ark. Saadiah refuted that view at great length[4]. The other passage, also quoted by Jefeth ad loc., reads thus: וקולה למועד חדש האביב לים יגב אן גלתמס אלאביב ענד כל שהר ניסן ואנמא הו עלאמה̈ לוקת כרוגהם אנהם כרגו מן מצר וכאן אביב במצר לקולה הנאך כי השעורה אביב או לגיר דלך . . . . ופי הדא חגג כתירה̈ נכתצר תדוינהא האהנא וקד אתבתנאהא פי כתאב אלרד̃ עלי ענן אלך. This refers, therefore, to the question of considering the ripeness of the new ears of corn when an

[1] In Pinsker's *Einleitung in d. babyl. Punktationssystem*, p. 206.

[2] *Kerem Chemed*, IX, 64. Harkavy, l. c., p. 199, conjectures that this was a verse of Saadiah himself, and that it was contained in the fourth chapter of his ספר הגלוי.

[3] Communicated by Munk, *Additions à la notice sur Saadja* (at the end of his edition of Tanchum to Habakkuk), p. 106.

[4] Here is not the place to dwell on this subject, and I will only say briefly that, as far as I know, this opinion is not mentioned in the older Karaite literature, nor, as it seems, was it ever put into practice. Something similar is found in Bashiatschi's *Adereth Elijahu*, ענין קדוש החדש, chapter 11: כשיקרו עבים חדש אחר חדש ולא יראה הישן והחדש הנה נעשה ד' מלאים זה אחר זה לא יתר והראיה מן הכתוב מה שנאמר בענין נח. Cf. also Ibn Ezra's full commentary to Genesis vii. 13 (ed. Friedländer, p. 53).

intercalary month was to be fixed. This essay is also, without doubt, alluded to by Salmon b. Jerucham in his controversy against Saadiah, c. 14, letter ר׳[1]: ויראּ · · · · (ר״ל סעדיה) כי לא יכול למו, על ספר החכם המאור תפארת סגולת י״י רבינו ענן יעׂ נבׂ הריק חרמו. ״שיניו יחרוק על רבינו ענן, כי חציו ברבותיו שנן וכו׳ Besides, Qirqisâni is thought by Harkavy[2] to quote it in his *Kitâb al-'Anwâr* anonymously. Whether the report in חלוק הקראים והרבנים (Pinsker, p. 103), in the name of a Rabbanite, as to the low motives that induced 'Anân to come forward, and the objectionable means he employed, is directly copied from this writing of Saadiah, as Pinsker[3] and Harkavy[4] assume, must remain an open question, for we have no exact information about the authorship, the time, and the trustworthiness of that Karaite chronicle[5]. It must however be observed, that it is expressly stated in an old Karaite commentary to Exodus, which Harkavy thinks was written by Sahl b. Mazliach, that Saadiah accused 'Anân that the only reason the latter had for fixing the new moon from observation was a desire to flatter the Caliphs[6]. Saadiah was also called the author of the same accusation in a Karaite fragment[7], whose author, as Frankl proved[8], was not Tobia b. Moses, but Jehudah Hadassi. We learn from that fragment, that Ben-Mashiach had already written on this subject against Saadiah. At all events, the fact that no other author, except Saadiah himself, quotes this controversial writing by name, sufficiently proves that must have been lost already at a very early date. If we find, therefore, in later Karaitic writings some allegations from Saadiah's books, which he wrote against

[1] Vid. Pinsker, *Likkute Kadmonioth*, p. 18.

[2] l. c., p. 107.

[3] l. c., p. 98.

[4] "Zur Entstehung des Karaismus" (in Grätz's *Geschichte*, V, 3rd edition).

[5] Vid. Steinschneider, *Hebr. Bibliogr.*, V, 49; XX, 91; *Cat. Lugd.*, 104; Schorr, l. c., 77.

[6] Vid. Harkavy, *Stud. u. Mittheil.*, V, 225. Cf. also his edition of Qirqisâni, 254, note 4.

[7] In Pinsker, p. 95.

[8] *Monatsschrift*, XXXI, 77–81.

'Anân, this particular book was not their source. The following points are, as far as I know, those about which Saadiah wrote against 'Anân.

Qirqisâni, in the 29th chapter of the eleventh section of his *Kitâb al-'Anwâr*, gives information about Saadiah's controversy against 'Anân on the subject of the prohibited degrees of relationship[1]. Such controversy could have been contained in the pamphlet under discussion, Qirqisâni having been a younger contemporary of Saadiah, and having undoubtedly known it. On the other hand, it is possible that it was contained in Saadiah's Commentary to the Pentateuch or in his ספר עריות. Saadiah's repudiation of 'Anân's opinion, that an animal, which dies before it is eight days old, did not defile, was quoted and confuted at length in the MS. of a Karaite Commentary of Leviticus in Arabic, of the year 1050[2]. But in this case also, Saadiah's Commentary of the Pentateuch may have been the source. This is, probably, also the case with another controversy of Saadiah against 'Anân on the subject of the laws of menstruation, as cited in another MS. of an Arabic Commentary of Leviticus (MS. Brit. Mus. Or. 2595, f. 182 b)[3]. No more can it be said with certainty, in which of his books Saadiah wrote against 'Anân on the subject of forbidden fat, a controversy particularly dealt with by Tobia b. Moses in his אוצר נחמד[4], on the conception and application of מליקה[5], and on 'Anân's prohibition of eating meat in the Diaspora[6]. Moses Ibn Ezra relates also in his

[1] Cf. *Steinschneider-Festschrift*, p. 201.

[2] Cf. ibid., pp. 209, 215.

[3] Only fragments of this Commentary have been preserved (Lev. xi. 1–xv. 25). No one is cited there except 'Anân and Saadiah.

[4] Vid. Steinschneider, *Cat. Bodl.*, 2168; *Steinschneider-Festschrift*, p. 203, note 3.

[5] Cf. Weiss, l. c., 139.

[6] 'Anân, and many Karaite authorities after him, prohibit the use of meat in the Diaspora. Vid. Hadassi, *Eshkol Hakkofer*, Alphab. 236, letter ז sqq. Saadiah combats that view in his Commentary to Daniel (communicated by Mathews in his edition of the *Comm. on Ezra and Nehemiah by R. Saadiah*,

Art of Poetry, that ʿAnân was mistaken in his views about the application to the laws of the Torah, of the method of Analogy (קיאס, היקש), and that Saadiah confuted them in *several of his works*. He then cites a passage from Saadiah's commentary to the section קדושים, in which, however, ʿAnân is not mentioned[1]. It is hardly possible that Moses Ibn Ezra was still in possession of Saadiah's pamphlet, and that it is this he alludes to. Saadiah quotes also and confutes in his philosophical work[2], a view of ʿAnân's about the seat of the soul, but does so without any animosity. It is not likely that Saadiah treated this point also in his polemical work, otherwise he would undoubtedly have quoted the latter, as he does in his polemic against Hiwi-al-Balchi. Besides, in his controversy against ʿAnân, he probably confined himself to questions of the Law. Should, however, the passage from the Commentary, attributed to Sahl, and from the חלוק הקראים והרבנים, also have occurred there, the inference would be that Saadiah's attack against ʿAnân not only had reference to the controversial topics, but was also directed against ʿAnân in person. It follows from all that has been said here, that it is impossible to gain an accurate notion of the contents of this pamphlet of Saadiah.

2. But the most important and voluminous work against the Karaites seems to have been the כתאב אלתמייז (Hebrew: ספר ההכרה or ספר המבחן), "the Book of Distinction." This work was written in the year 926, there-

Preface, p. xvi, and by D. S. Margoliouth in his edition of Jefeth to Daniel, Preface, p. vii), without mentioning ʿAnân. It is possible that Saadiah treated this point also in his polemical writing against ʿAnân. Cf. also my remarks in the *Monatsschrift*, XXXIX, 443, and in *Steinschneider-Festschrift*, p. 204.

[1] *Kitâb al-Muḥâḍara* (MS. of the Bodleian, Cat. Neub. 1974), f. 108: ואעלם אן קד גלט אלנאס קדימא פי אלקיאס · · · והנא סקט ענן ושיעתה · · · וקד רד עליהם רב סעדיה פי כתיר מן תואליפה · · · קאל פי שרח פרשת קדושים אלך. The passage is reproduced from the Oxford MS. in the original by Steinschneider (*Cat. Bodl.*, 2166), and in Hebrew from a St. Petersburg fragment, translated by Harkavy (חדשים גם ישנים, VII, 31).

[2] Cap. VI, at the commencement (ed. Slucki, 96; ed. Landauer, 190).

fore in Egypt, as is shown by the following passage of Abraham b. Chija (ספר העבור, p. 96): ומצאנו הגאון ר׳ סעדיה ז״ל זכר המחלוקת הזה בחבורו הנקרא ספר ההכרה ואמר בלשון ערבי דברים אשר יהיה פירושן על הענין הזה השנה הזאת אשר אנו עומדים בה היום היא שנת אלף רלה למלכות אלכסנדרוס והיא שנת דתרפו לבריאת עולם לחשבוננו ויש אחרים שחושבים היום לבריאת עולם תרפז[1]. The work is quoted by Saadiah himself in his Commentary to Gen. viii. 3 (vid. supra), and by the Rabbanites, besides Abraham b. Chija, by Mebasser Hallevi, a contemporary and opponent of Saadiah[2], by Moses Ibn Ezra in his כתאב אלחדיקה פי אלמגאז ואלחקיקה (Heb. ערוגת הבושם)[3], and by Abraham Ibn Ezra in his Commentary to Exod. xxxv. 3[4]. But most frequently it is quoted by Jefeth b. ʿAli in his Commentary on the Bible, and he cites whole passages *verbatim* (חרף בחרף). In order to obtain a clear notion of the contents and form of the work, I reproduce here all passages which I know, and of which two only (Exod. xii. 2 and Lev. xxiii. 15)[5] have been hitherto printed[6]:—

[1] Cf. about this passage Rapoport, *Erech Millin*, s. v. אלכסנדר מוקדון, p. 87 b sqq.

[2] Vid. Harkavy in the *Israelitische Monatsschrift* (Supplement to the *Jüd. Presse*), 1891, p. 6.

[3] Communicated in ציון, II, 37: אך התימה הגדול על חברינו המודים בנו שחולקים עלינו (l. על) קהל המינים כי גם הם הסכימו עמם על זאת המחשבה הרעה ברוב זדונם ועזות פניהם לדבר גדולות על דבור הקרושים ז״ל בראותם כי הלכו ברוב דבריהם ע״ד העברה הנמצאות בכתוב . . . ורבינו סעדיה הגאון ז״ל כתב בספר המבחן [ו]בתשובותיו על בן סקויה האפיקורוס ועל זולתו החולקים ומאריכים לשון על התורה ועל הקבלה מה שיספיק לכל שומעיו מן המאמינים וכו׳. Cf. on this book of Moses Ibn Ezra, Harkavy (חדשים גם ישנים, VII, 32-34), who has found a large fragment of the Arabic original.

[4] We read here, it is true, והגאון רב סעדיה חבר ספר נכבד תשובות על החולקים על קדמונינו על נר שבת, but that "book" is only a chapter of the כתאב אלתמייז, vid. Pinsker, p. 18 (cf. also, infra, the quotation from Jefeth to Deut. xxv. 4). In Ibn Ezra's short Commentary (ed. Reggio, p. 111) we read: והשם יכפיל שכר הגאון שהשיב תשובות גמורות על הצדוקים האוסרים נר בשבת.

[5] Cf. infra.

[6] I only quote those passages which are distinctly designated as taken from the כתאב אלתמייז, or which are sure to have been taken from that work. All extracts are reproduced, partly from the MSS. in the British Museum, and partly from Pinsker's copies (at present in the Vienna *Beth*

Gen. i. 14.

· · · ומן אדל̈ דלילא אנה (אי ראס אלמתיבה) מכ̇אלף ללאג̇מאע קולה פי אלרד̈ עלי אלקראיין בוהיו לאותות ולמועדים פקאל הד̇ה אלאלפאט̇ חרף בחרף פקאל אן קולה והיו לאותות ימכן אלעטף בה עלי אליום ואללילה דון אלמאורות לאנה קאל יהי מאורות ברקיע השמים פעלהא להבדיל בין היום ובין הלילה פלמא ד̇כר אליום ואללילה קאל עליהמא והיו לאותות ולמועדים וכאן הד̇ה אלקול אול מא לאח לי ממכנא פקט פלמא ג̇יידת תאמ̈לה ראיתה ואג̇בא[1] פהד̇ה מא את̇בתה אלרג̇ל פי כתאבה אלמלקב̈ בכתאב אלתמייז · · ·

· · · וקד קר̈ ראס אלמתיבה אן אלרבאנין יכ̇תלפו פי עצרנא הד̇א פבעצ̇הם יקול אן אלעבור ליסה ען אלנבי [והד̇א קולה] חרף בחרף פי כתאב אלתמייז וד̇לך אני שאהדת נאס מן אלרבונין פצ̇לא ען אלעאמה̈ ועלי מכ̇אלפיהם יתוה̈מון אן קד כאן שהר ניסן יקע פי אלסלף מן אלזמאן פי איאם ליס יקע אלאן פיהם והם עלי צ̇רבין מנהם מן יקול כאן אלפסח יקע יום אלג̇מעה̈ לא לאת̇נין ולא לארבעה̈ ומנהם מן יקול כאן יקע איצ̇א פי אליום אלאת̇נין ויום אלארבעה̈ ת̇ם ד̇כר אחתג̇אג̇הם והו קול אלחכמים פי אלפסח העצמות והגידים והנותר ישרפו בששה עשר חל ששה עשר להיות בשבת ישרפו בשבעה עשר וקולהם העומר בא בין בשבת בין בחול משלש סאין וקולהם עצרת שחלה להיות בשבת[2] · · · פקד נאקץ̇ נפסה פי מא קאל קבל הד̇א אלפצל והו קולה ואקול אן אלג̇מאעה̈ ינקלון מד̇הבא למערפה̈ אלשהור נקלא ומכ̇אלפיהם אכ̇רג̇ו בעד ד̇לך ט̇ מד̇אהב · · ·

ווג̇דת לה פי הד̇א אלכתאב איצ̇א פצל אכ̇ר עג̇יב ג̇דא ממא יצ̇עף דעואה

Hamidrash). In the following explanatory notes I confine myself to what is absolutely necessary. I reserve a full treatment of these materials for another occasion.

[1] MS. ואגבה. The Karaites wish to derive from Gen. i. 14 the commandments of observing the first appearance of the moon, and of fixing the beginning of the month accordingly. They explain the verse thus: The luminaries in the firmament of the heavens must serve as signs, to distinguish by them the various times (מועדים is taken to mean "new moons"). Saadiah objects, *inter alia*, that, in that case, ולחדשים would be required, and that יהיו refers to the immediately preceding "day and night." Cf. my remarks in Jewish Quarterly Review, VIII, 702, and *Monatsschr.*, XLI, 208–210.

[2] Cf. infra.

אן אלעבור כאן קדימא והו אסתדלאלה עלי אלעבור באנה כאן ביד בני
אסראיל והו קולה חרף בחרף וד̇לך אני ראית פציח אלנאס מן בני אסראיל
קד כאנו יתכ̇דון ראס שהר יומין ולם אג̇ד הד̇א אלא פי מד̇הב אלרבאנין
פעלמת אן עמל בני אסראיל לם יזל עליה ואצבת איצ̇א פי כ̇בר אלמתקד̈מין
אנהם כאן יעלמון[1] מן קבל חלול ראס אלשהר הל הו יום ואחד או יומין מן
קול דוד ליהונתן הנה חדש מחר ואנכי ישב [אשב] עם המלך לאכול ושלחתני
ונסתרתי בשדה עד הערב השלישית פכלאמה הד̇א ידל̈ עלי אן ראס אלשהר
כאן אלי ערב השלישית וד̇לך יומין ת̇ם לם אקנע[2] בהד̇א אלקול חתי
וג̇דת ויהי ממחרת החדש השני ויפקד מקום דוד ויאמר שאול אל יהונתן
ותמאם אלקול או יצרף קולה החדש השני אלי שהר ת̇אני בעד כ̇ט̇ יום
או ל̇ יום לאנה קאל גם תמול גם היום לכני פצחת וקלת לעל הד̇א אליום
אלב̇ מן אלשהר והו חול או[3] יכון אלשהר נפסה הו שהר ב̇ מן אלסנה̈ פוג̇דתה
פי אכ̇ר אלקצה̈ ויקם יהונתן מעם השלחן בחרי אף ולא אכל ביום החדש
השני לחם פסמא אליום אלת̇אני חדש כמא סמא אלאול פצח̈ צחה̈ בלא
שך̈ מעהא אן אליומין ג̇מיעא יקאל להמא חדש פלו כאן פימא בין אלאמה̈
מד̇הבאן או ג̇ פיהא אן ראס אלשהר יכון יומין כאן אלחק̈ פי אחדהמא
ולם יכן נעלם פי א̈יהם הו מן הד̇א אלוג̇ה פלמא לם נג̇ד פי מא בין
אלאמה̈ מד̇הבא פיה אן ראס אלשהר יומין סוי מד̇הב אלרבונין צח̈ ענדנא
אנה מד̇הב אלאבא והו אלחק̈ . . .[4] ת̇ם קאל בעד הד̇א קול הו אעג̇ב מן
הד̇א והו קולה ואי̈ד הד̇א אלמד̇הב ענדי איצ̇א למא לם נג̇ד פי נץ̈ אלמכתוב
במא ד̇א תוכ̇ד רוס אלשהור וכאן מן אלואג̇ב אן לא יכ̇לי אלחכים
אמ̈תה מערפתהא פלמא לם יוג̇ד דלך פי אלמכתוב כאן באלצ̇רורה̈ פי
אלמנקול . . . ת̇ם קאל בעד הד̇א פאן תשבה לבעץ̇ אלנאס אן ד̇לך מנצוץ
פי אלכתאב פאני סאד̇כר פי הד̇א אלבאב ג̇מיע תלך אלשבהה̈ ואביין
אנכסארהא . . . ת̇ם קאל בעד הד̇א בל ראית אלנץ̈ ישיר אלי אנה
ההנא עלמא בהא תערף אלאעיאד ולצנאעתהא קום כ̇ואץ מן אלא̇מה̈
בקולה ומבני יששכר יודעי בינה לעתים לדעת מה יעשה ישראל [ראשיהם]
מאתים וכל אחיהם על פיהם ואלעתים אלד̇י יג̇ב עלי ישראל פיהא אלעשייה
פהי ג̇ אולהא חג המצות בקולה ועשית פסח ליוי אלהיך ת̇ם חג שבועות
קאל פיה ועשית חג שבועות ליוי אלהיך ת̇ם חג הסוכות [קאל פיה חג
הסכות] תעשה לך שבעת ימים פמן קולה יודעי בינה לעתים עלמנא אן

[1] MS. יעמלון. [2] MS. אקע. [3] MS. אן̇.
[4] Cf. Hadassi, Alphab. 197, letter ר sqq.

S 2

הדׄא [אלעתים] בחסאב תעמל ולדׄלך פרד להא עלמא וחכמא ולו כאן ברויא אלהלאל תעמל לם יעו̈ל פיהא עלי אלעלמא[1].

Gen. xlix. 14.

· · · וארי אן אדׄכר בדׄיא מא דׄכרה אלכׄצם ואסתד̈ל עלי אן אלעבור כאן מסתעמל ביד ישראל קדימא קאל הדׄא אלמצ̈ל נפסה בדיא פי כתאבה אלמלק̈ב כתאב אלתמייז בל ראית אלנג̈ ישיר אלי אנה האהנא עלמא · · · [2]

Exod. xii. 2.

· · · פקאל ראס אלמתיבה פי כתאבה אלמלק̈ב בכתאב אלתמייז פצל פי הדׄא אלבאב והו קולה חרף בחרף ויתאי̈ד קול אלגמאעה̈ אנה לא ילזמהם טלב אלסנבל ועלי אן פי אלתורה דׄכר אביב לאנה לו כאן כמא יקול כׄצומהם לכאן אלחכים אחכמה פי תוראתה אלמקד̈סה̈ מן אי מכאן יטלב פי אי יום וכם מקדאר כמיתה ומא הו צורתה פלמא לם תוגד חדוד הדׄה אלמעאני פי כתאבה תבי̈ן אנה ליס בשריעה̈ · · · [3]

[1] This proof of Saadiah (i. e. from 1 Chron. xii. 33) is also quoted in his name by Sahl b. Mazliach in his polemic (Pinsker, pp. 37, 41), and it was undoubtedly also taken by him from the כתאב אלתמייז, and not from a Commentary of Saadiah to the Chronicles, as Kaufmann (*Notes to Jehuda b. Barzilai's Jezira-Comm.*, p. 336) conjectures. Saadiah's proof is also cited by Levi b. Jefeth in his ספר המצות (vid. *Kerem Chemed*, VIII, 56), and, anonymously, by Aaron b. Elia (*Gan Eden*, f. 4 c). Cf. Munk, *Additions*, &c., p. 108.

[2] Here follows the same passage as to Gen. i. 14. Pinsker (pp. 38, 39) reproduced here Saadiah's words, together with Jefeth's refutation, in Hebrew. Cf. also Munk, l. c.

[3] This passage has already been communicated by Munk, l. c. (cf. also *Isr. Annalen*, 1841, 77). The Karaites maintained that the ripening of the ears (אביב) only had to be regarded at the intercalation of a month, according to Deut. xvi. 1, and try to harmonize this verse with Gen. i. 14, according to which the course of the sun (therefore also the תקופה) would have to be regarded. Vid. Hadassi, Alphab. 187 sqq., and *Gan Eden*, f. 16 d sqq. Saadiah, by his theory of the Sinaitic origin of the Jewish Calendar, was compelled to insist that the cycle of nineteen years, with constant calculation, was of remote antiquity, and to explain away the requirement of the אביב. Let it also be noticed that Jefeth, in his commentary to our verse, mentions Saadiah's polemical writing a second time, without, however, quoting anything from it: · · · ואיצׄא אן ראס אלמתיבה תכלם פיה האהנא (אי פי תפסיר החדש הזה) נׄטיר מא תכלם בה פי סדר בראשית ופי כתאב אלתמייז אלדׄי אלפה ופי כתאב אלרד עלי בן סאקויה אלךׄ.

Lev. xxiii. 5.

· · · אלקול אלאול פי והיו לאותות אנה אלקצד בה אלי אלמאורות
לא אלי אלליל ואלנהאר כמא אדעא אלפיומי פי כתבה אלדי ענד מא
קצד מעאנדה̈ אלקראיין פי אחתגאגהם ללרויה̈ בקו׳ והיו לאותות ולמועדים
פמנע אן יכון והיו לאותות ישיר אלי אלמאורות וגעלה̈ אשארה̈ אלי אליום
ואללילה̈ וד̇אך קו׳ פי כתאבה אלדי לקבה בכתאב אלתמייז הד̇ה אלאלפאט
חרף בחרף קאל אן קולה והיו לאותות · · ·[1]

· · · וקד כנא רדדנא עלי אלפיומי פי מא ד̇כרה פי כתאבה אלדי
לקבה בכתאב אלתמייז מן אלרד עלי אצחאבנא פי מא יעתקדונה מן
אנה געל אללה עלאמה̈ אלראשון אלאביב ואורינא אנה ד̇כר מד̇אהבהם
וצנפהא ותחאמל פי בעצ̇הא עליהם פי מא ד̇כרה ענהם מא לם יקולוה
ואנה מע ד̇לך לם ירד עליהם אכת̇ר ממא ד̇כר מד̇אהבהם פקט וסמאה
רד וליס אכ̇תלאפהם ממא ידפע אן יכון אלאביב עלאמה̈ אלראשון ורדדנא
עליה פימא געל חדש אביב אסם ללשהר ואן ליס אלאביב אסם זרע
ואורינא אנה כ̇אלף אגמאע אליהוד פי ד̇לך ואחצ̇רנא מן כתב אצחאבה
אנהם יקולון באלאביב מת̇ל מא נקול וד̇כרנא מא קאלוה פי מכאלה̈ (=מכילתא)
החדש הזה לכם ראש חדשים אנהם יעמלון אלפסח עלי אלאביב ואנהם קד
יכבסו כביסה̈ עלי כביסה̈ פי תאכ̇ר אלאביב ען אלשהר אליג׳ פי אלסנה̈ אלתי
כאנו קד כבסוהא פי אלעאם אלאול ממא יטול אעאדתה[2].

Ibid. (Second Recension)[3].

· · · וקד אקר ראס אלמתיבה פי אלכתאב אלדי לקבה בכתאב אלתמייז
אן בעץ׳ אלרבונין יקול אן הד̇א אלחסאב מחדת̇ ואן אלקדמא כאן עמלו
עלי אלרויה̈ ואן ללשיוך אן ידברו אמר אלאעיאד כיף שאו ואורא אנה
יתענב מן קולהם הד̇א · · ·

· · · ואמא זעם ראס אלמתיבה פי כתאבה אן אללה תע׳ אפתרץ׳ פי

[1] The same passage follows as to Gen. i. 14. Cf. also Neubauer, *Aus d. Petersburger Bibliothek*, p. 16.

[2] Saadiah objected, *inter alia*, that חדש האביב need not necessarily mean "month of the ripening of the ears"; אביב may also be a proper noun, as e.g. in Ez. iii. 15. Vid. *Gan Eden*, f. 16 d (Saadiah's name is not mentioned by Hadassi, Alphab. 190, letter ס sqq.).

[3] Jefeth himself testifies that he had composed two recensions of his commentaries, e.g. to Exod. xxxiv. 18: וקד רדינא עליה (אי עלי ראס אלמתיבה) פי החדש הזה לכם פי אלנסכ̇ה̈ אלאכ̇רה̈ במא פיה כפאיה̈.

אלגלות מסך יומין מן אגל אן אלאבא עצו פי אעיאד אללה פאוגב אללה אן נמסך יומין . . .[1]

Lev. xxiii. 15.

. . . פאמא אלפיומי פקד תכלם פי הדא אלבאב במא לא יתחצל מנה שי ודלך אנה געל קאנון כלאמה עלי אית שבת הי אלתי יגב אן יכון אלעדד גדהא ולם יעלם אן ליס בנא חאגה אלי מערפה אית שבת הי ואנמא יגב אן נערף אית מחרת הי פמא תקדם בה אלקול פאכד יתכלם עלי אלשבת ויקסמהא כק׳ פי כתאבה אלמלקב בכתאב אלתמייז פי אנה ליס תכלו הדה אלשבת מן אחד כמסה . . .[2]

Deut. xvi. 1.

. . . ואמא מא דכרה [אי בעץ אלמצלין] מן מדאהב אצחאב אלאביב פי אלכמיה ואלכיפיה ופי אי יום הו מן אלשהר וגמיע מא דכרה פי כתאבה אלמלקב בכתאב אלתמייז פאנה לו צדק פי גמיע מא דכרה מן אלמדאהב למא כן בצרר אד אלכל אעני אלאמה באסרהא מגמעה עלי אן אלאביב אסם לזרע ואנה דליל אדא וגד פי ארץ ישראל . . .

וראית לה פי הדא אלמעני אמרא עגיבא והו אנה אנכר בדיא אן יכון אלאביב דלילא לראשון ואן אלכבאים גאריה עליה וקאל בעד הדא אלגמאעה לם יעידון אלא ואלאביב מוגוד פי ארץ ישראל וליס יכבסו ויוגד אביב פי אלשהר אלג׳ והו קולה חרף בחרף ווגדת לה אן יקולון למא כאנת כבאיסנא מאכודה ען אלאנביא ען אללה תע יגב אן יקול אן עאלם אלגיב לם יגוז בהדא אלכבאים לעלמה באן אלאביב לא בד מן [אן] יקע מנהם ויכון הדא דלאלה עלי אן מכאלפיהם אית סנה הי לנא בסיטה וקאלו הם

[1] כתאבה here does not perhaps indicate Saadiah's כתאב אלתמייז, but his polemic against Ibn Saqûje, which is also quoted by Jefeth (vid. infra). Be it observed, by the way, that the conception, according to which the observance of two festival days is to be considered as a punishment, is mentioned already in the Talmud. Cf. Jeruschalmi, *Erubin*, III, 9, and parallel passages: מי גרם לי להיות משמרת שני ימים בסוריא על שלא שמרתי יום אחד בארץ.

[2] This passage was already printed in Hirschfeld's *Arabic Chrestomathy*, pp. 109-116. Cf. also Neubauer, l. c. In this verse, the כתאב אלתמייז is also quoted by Jacob b. Reuben in ספר העשר (vid. Steinschneider, *Cat. Lugd.*, 2[illegible]; Pinsker, p. 85; Munk, l. c., p. 109), but it is known that this Karaite commentary is only an extract from Jefeth (vid. Pinsker, p. 80).

לם נגד אביב אנהם קד אכ̇טו אלט̇לם ולם יג̇דו אלחקיקה לאן אלנבי מא קאלה לא בד״ מן אן יכון . . .[1]

Deut. xxv. 4.

וקו׳ בדישו ליס יריד בה לא תכ̇טמה פי חאל דיאסה פיג̇וז אן יכ̇טם קבל אלדיאס וידכ̇ל אלי אלדיאס מכ̇טומא ואנמא יריד בה לא יכון מכ̇טום פי חאל מא הו פי אלדיאס וכד̇אך קו׳ אללה לא תבערו אש בכל מושבותיכם ביום השבת ליס יריד אן לא ישעל אלנאר פי אלסבת ויג̇וז אן תשעל קבל אלסבת ותבקא פי אלסבת ואנמא יריד בה אן לא תכון אלנאר משתעלה פי יום אלסבת וקד זעם בעץ׳ אלמצ̇לין אן בינהמא פרק וד̇כר ד̇לך פי כתאבה אלמלקב בכתאב אלתמייז פקאל אן אלפרק בינהמא הו אן טפי אלנאר פי אלסבת חראם כאשעאלהא וליס חאל אלכ̇טאם פי אלדיאס חראם בשדה . . .[2]

Deut. xxxiii. 18.

. . . וארי אן אד̇כר בדיא מא ד̇כרה אלכ̇צם ואסתדל עלי אן אלעבור מסתעמל ביד ישראל קדימא קאל הד̇א אלמצ̇ל לנפסה בדיא פי כתאבה אלמלקב בכתאב אלתמייז בל ראית אלנג̇ ישיר אלי אנה האהנא עלמא . . .[3]

I Sam. xx. 27.

. . . פאמא מא ד̇כרה אלפיומי פי כתאבה אלמלקב בכתאב אלתמייז אן קולה ולא אכל ביום החדש השני לחם ידל עלי תצדיק אלרבאנין דון גירהם מן פרק אליהוד אלד̇ין לא יתבתון יומין ראס אלשהר פאן פי מא ד̇כרנאה מן אלביאן יסקט קולה וקד אוסענא אלרד עליה פי כתבנא מנהא פי בראשית ומנהא פי זאת הברכה ופי ספר המצות פלד̇לך אכ̇תצרנא ען אעאדתה פי הד̇א אלמוצ̇ע.[4]

The first point to be observed is the calm tone which

[1] The text seems to be incorrect here. The words ווגרת לה make it appear as if Saadiah addresses himself to a particular person. The whole passage is perhaps taken from the polemic against Ibn Saqûje, which Jefeth here also cites (vid. infra).

[2] This argument of the Karaites was also refuted by Saadiah in his Commentary to Ex. xxxv. 3 (cited by Jefeth, ad loc.). Cf. also Ibn Ezra, *Mibchar* and *Keter Torah*, ad loc.

[3] Follows the same passage again as to Gen. i. 14 and xlix. 14.

[4] Cf. Pinsker, 183. Jefeth alludes here undoubtedly to the Commentary to Gen. i. 14 and Deut. xxxiii. 18.

prevails all through, and this work bears, altogether, the character of defence rather than of attack. The few passages that are preserved show also that almost all points of divergence between Rabbanites and Karaites were discussed in it; thus, questions referring to the calendar (Jefeth to Gen. i. 14, xlix. 14; Exod. xii. 1; Lev. xxiii. 5; Deut. xvi. 1, xxxiii. 18; 1 Sam. xx. 27) which must have formed the greatest portion of the controversial matter; further, questions about the lighting of light on Sabbath (Jefeth to Deut. xxv. 4, and Ibn Ezra to Exod. xxxv. 3); about the date of the Feast of Weeks (Jefeth to Lev. xxiii. 15), and about the validity of the Tradition (Moses Ibn Ezra). According to Steinschneider, it was particularly Salmon b. Jerucham and Jeshua b. Jehuda, that wrote against this work. In reference to the latter, we possess only a small part of his comments against Saadiah, and of Salmon b. Jerucham, I have already shown that he probably did no such thing. Grätz's opinion that this work of Saadiah's was a reply to Salmon's attacks, I have already shown, both from historical and chronological data, to be impossible [1].

3. Another anti-Karaite work of Saadiah, of which it is not known, when it was written, is the כתאב אלרד̈ עלי אבן סקויה, "Writing in confutation of Ibn Saqûje (or Sâqeveihi)." I know of only authors that quote this work by name. Firstly, the above-mentioned Mebasser Hallevi in his controversy against Saadiah: ופי כתאב רד̈ה עלי אבן סאקויה קאל אן נט̈ם אלוידי עויתי פשעתי חטאתי הו קול ר׳ מאיר ואמא סאיר אלחכמים פאנהם יקולון חטאתי עויתי פשעתי [2]; secondly, by Moses

[1] Cf. Jewish Quarterly Review, VIII, 689, 690.

[2] Communicated by Harkavy in the *Zapiski* (Memoirs of the Oriental section of the Russian Archaeological Society), 1891, p. 208. It is, of course, difficult to say in which connexion Saadiah treated this theme. In Isaac ibn Gajjath's *Halachoth* (שערי שמחה, ed. Bamberger, 62) we read: כיצד היה מתודה אנא השם עויתי פשעתי וחטאתי לפניך דברי ר׳ מאיר וחכ"א חטאתי עויתי פשעתי . . . בהלכות פסק כרבנן . . . ורב (אך רב .l) חפץ ומר רב סעדיה פסק (פסקו .l) כר׳ מאיר וכו׳. May perhaps Ibn Gajjath have had our writing of Saadiah's

Ibn Ezra in his כתאב אלחדיקה[1]; and, thirdly, by Jefeth b. ʿAli in three places in his commentary on the Pentateuch, namely:—(1) To Exod. xii. 2: וקד קר ראס אלמתיבה פי אלכתאב אלדי רד פיה עלי בן סאקויה אן אלאואיל כאנו יעברו סנתהם עלי אלאביב וגירה והו אלפירות ואלתקופות אלך. (2) To Lev. xxiii. 5 (second recension), after the passage cited above on p. 249, in which it is said that Saadiah had himself admitted that, according to some Rabbanites, the origin of the Calendar was of a later date: ולקד אקר אלפיומי בהדא אלקול אלדי תעגב מנה ואתבתה פי כתאבה אלדי רד בה עלי אבן סאקויה. (3) To Deut. xvi. 1: ולקד אקר צאחב הדא אלקול פי כתאב אלרד עלי אבן סאקויה וזעם אן אלאביב הו אצל תעמל עליה אלכבאים מתל אלתקופות אלך[2]. It is evident that this work did not exclusively deal with the importance of the ripening of the ears (מציאת האביב) when a month had to be superadded, as Pinsker (p. מג) assumed[3]. Yet, it appears that this theme was here dealt with at length, and Munk's conjecture[4], that a passage, cited by Abraham b. Chija from an anti-Karaite work of Saadiah, was taken from this particular book, gains in probability. This is the passage (ספר העבור, p. 94): אבל הגאון הגדול רבינו סעדיה ז״ל דבר בזה הענין על דרך אחרת בספר אשר חבר להשיב על המינים אמר כך אחד מן המינים טען עלינו בהלכה זו והיא ת״ר אין מעברין את השנה אא״כ היתה התקופה חסרה רובו של חדש וכמה רובו של חדש י״ו יום · · · ואמר המין הזה אתה מוצא אם כן מן ההלכה הזאת ארבעה שיעורים · · · השיבו ר׳ סעדיה ז״ל ואמר אין זה מחלוקת ביניהם וכו׳.

before him? In a *responsum* of Sherira's on this theme (תשובות גאוני מזרח ומערב, No. 144) Saadiah is not mentioned. Cp. also Saadiah's *Œuvres complètes*, IX, 154, note 1.

[1] Vid. supra. In another place of this writing of his, Moses Ibn Ezra names Ibn Saqûje together with Chivi al-Balchi; vid. Harkavy, חדשים גם ישנים, VII, 33.

[2] Cf. also supra.

[3] Cp. also the words of the Karaite Chronicler Ibn al-Hiti (Jewish Quarterly Review, IX, 435): ובן סקויה רה את רד עלי אלרבאנין ועלי אלפיומי פי אלהלאל ואלאביב ואלענצרה ואלאליה ואלשחם ואלתקליר ואבטל נקלהם (cf. *Zeitschr. f. hebr. Bibliogr.* II, 79).

[4] *Additions*, p. 112.

We see that the question is here also about the intercalary month. Suppose this passage had been taken from the כתאב אלתמייז, Abraham b. Chija would not have omitted quoting that book by name (ספר ההכרה), as he does on another occasion (vid. supra, p. 245).

We do not know who this Ibn Saqûje was[1], but so much is certain that he was a Karaite, and this is sufficient to refute Lebrecht's assumption, that he was identical with the Exilarch David ben Zakkai[2]. Pinsker is of opinion that the first name of this Karaite was Samuel, but this assumption is, as was shown already, based upon a misunderstood and badly translated passage of Joseph al-Baṣir's כתאב אלא סתבצאר[3]. In the same way, I consider Geiger's hypothesis to be highly improbable, according to which בן סאקויה was the Arabic name of Salmon ben Jerucham, and this work identical with another anti-Karaite work by Saadiah, quoted by Nissim b. Jacob (נטעי נעמנים, Hebrew part, fol. 16 b), namely:—

4. כתאב אלרד̈ עלי מתחמ̈ל היום (?) (Heb. ספר התשובה על הטוען), "Book of refutation of the attacking writer" (?). Apart from historical and chronological data, the contents of these books make it impossible to declare them to be one and the same. We have seen that the other book dealt chiefly with the subject of the Calendar, whilst the subject of this book was, probably, only the anthropomorphic Agada. This follows from Nissim's words: ומה ששאלת לענין מה שנמצא בדברי חכמינו ז״ל מן התיבות (?) הנה על צורה מה שנחשב עליהם בדבר זה כבר רבי׳ סעדיה ז״ל דבר על זה בפיו (l. בפי׳) ובחיבורו דברים משנים (?) ושלמים ובספר התשובה על הטוען הנקרא בלשון ישמעאל בתאב (l. כתאב) אורד (l. אלרד̈) עלי מתחמל היום פי׳ זה וביאורו

[1] The ending ויה need not, by any means, point to Persia as his home. In Nöldeke (*Persische Studien*, in the *Sitzungsberichte d. Wiener Akademie*, 1888, p. 399 sqq.), and Justi (*Iranisches Namenbuch*, Marburg, 1895), I have not found the name סאקויה. Cf. also my essay on Meswi al-Okbari in the *Revue des Études Juives*, XXXIV, 161, note 2.

[2] *Ltbl. d. Orients*, I, 131. Cf. Steinschneider, *Cat. Bodl.*, 2168.

[3] Vid. Jewish Quarterly Review, VIII, 690.

בטענות מפורשות מפורסמות וראיות מקויימות שמסירות הספקות ודוחות הדמיונות וכו׳. This book is, without doubt, the same as the one cited by Jehuda b. Barzilai in two places of his Commentary on Jeẓira (ed. Halberstam, pp. 20, 34). In the former passage it is said expressly, that a heretic asserted of the Talmudists, that they attributed to the Creator form and shape, and that Saadiah, in a book written for the purpose, refuted these attacks. By these heretics he means, of course, Karaites, for none of them, from Qirqisâni and Salmon b. Jerucham till Mordechai b. Nissan and Abraham Firkowitsch, fail to attack the Talmudists, on the ground of anthropomorphic passages of the Agada, which they take in their literal meaning, induced thereto either by ignorance or malice. And these very two passages of the Agada, the interpretation of which are cited by Jehuda b. Barzilai, were attacked by the two older Karaites, named before. The one (p. 20), about the vision of Ishmael, mentioned in Berachot, 7 a, is quoted by Salmon b. Jerucham [1], the other (p. 34), about the passage מניין שהקב״ה מתפלל, is quoted by this author [2], and by Qirqisâni [3]. But it must be observed that, whilst Qirqisâni directs his attacks against the Rabbanites in general, Salmon, in his flippant way, attacks Saadiah personally, and makes him responsible for whatever he finds fault with. I have already said that Saadiah wrote this pamphlet after the *Emunoth*, and therefore after 933 [4].

5. Ibn Ezra makes, in two passages of his commentary, mention of a dispute of Saadiah with the otherwise unknown Ben Zuta. The first passage (Exod. xxi. 24) deals with the *lex talionis*, and the second (Lev. xxiii. 15,

[1] Cap. 15, letter פ. [2] Ibid., letter צ.

[3] *Kitâb al-'Anwâr*, I, 4 (ed. Harkavy, p. 298). Cf. also Hadassi's *Eshkol Hakkofer*, Alphab. 78, letter ה; Alphab. 81, letter ו.

[4] Vid. Jewish Quarterly Review, VIII, 691. Cf. also Kaufmann, *Gesch. d. Attributenlehre*, p. 61. On the theme of the created light, as treated by Saadiah, vid. Epstein, החוקר, II, 37 sqq., to which the passages in Jehuda b. Barzilai, pp. 119, 175, are to be added. Cp. also חרשים גם ישנים, X, pp. 17, 52.

in the fragment of a second recension in Friedländer's *Essays on the writings of Abraham Ibn Ezra*, Hebrew Appendix, p. 70) with the frequently discussed phrase ממחרת השבת. It cannot be inferred from either passage that Saadiah had written a book against that Karaite, the former rather leads to the conclusion that there was no more than a verbal discussion. עין תחת עין אמר רב סעדיה לא נוכל לפרש זה הפסוק כמשמעו ··· אמר לו בן זיטא והלא כתוב במקום אחר כאשר יתן מום באדם כן ינתן בו והגאון השיב לו יש לנו בי"ת תחת על ··· ובן זיטא השיב לו ··· והגאון השיב ··· ובן זיטא השיב ··· והגאון השיב ···. Ben Zuta not being quoted by any of the Karaite writers, it is probable that the source of Ibn Ezra was Saadiah, and most likely the latter's commentary on the Pentateuch. I shall endeavour to show in another place that Ibn Ezra's other quotations of Ben Zuta's opinions (Commentary to Exod. ii. 2, xx. 23, xxi. 35, xxii. 28; ספר העבור f. 7 a) were all taken from Saadiah, and that all of them were subjects of controversy between the latter and the former[1].

6. Besides the above-mentioned special writings, Saadiah combated the Karaites also in his large commentary on the Pentateuch. He says, in the preface to his second translation of the Pentateuch, with so many words, that he was asked to reproduce the simple meaning of the words of Scripture, without linguistic digressions or polemics against the heretics[2]. As a matter of fact, some remnants of Saadiah's polemic, taken from that commentary, have been preserved. Salmon, in his controversy, informs us that Saadiah had produced, in his commentary on Genesis, seven proofs of the necessity and divine character of the Tradition[3]. Jefeth ben 'Ali also cites

[1] Vid. my "Miscellanies on Saadiah," II (*Monatsschrift*, XLI, 203–212), where the proofs can be found for all that is brought forward here.

[2] Ed. Derenbourg, p. 4: לאן בעץ̇ אלראגבין סאלני אן אפרד בסיט נץ אלתורה פי כתאב מפרד לא ישובה שי מן אלכלאם פי אללגה̈ ··· ולא ידכ̇ל פיה קול מן מסאיל אלמלחדין ולא מן אלרד עליהם אלך̇. Cf. *Monatsschrift*, XLI, 205.

[3] Vid. Geiger's *Wissensch. Zeitschr. für jüd. Theol.*, V, 133.

anti-Karaite passages from Saadiah's commentary, e.g. Gen. i. 14, viii. 9; Exod. iii. 2, xii. 2, 16, xxi. 33, xxiii. 15, xxxv. 3; Deut. xvi. 9, &c.[1] We learn from a *Responsum* of Hai Gaon, that Saadiah maintained in his commentary that the constant calendar was of remote antiquity, in doing which he failed not to contradict the Karaites[2]. Tobia b. Moses, in his אוצר נחמד, cites a passage from Saadiah's commentary to Exod. xxiv. 12, in which the divine character of the Mishna and Talmud is vindicated[3], and another passage from the commentary to Leviticus, in which the Karaite notions about prohibited fat are confuted[4]. Moses ibn Ezra communicates, in his *Art of Poetry*, a passage from Saadiah's commentary to the section קדושים, in which 'Anân's method in reference to the application of the inference by analogy (קיאס, היקש) is combated[5]. Finally, we have already pointed out the probability that many controversial passages against 'Anân, and also against Ben Zuta, were contained in the commentary on the Pentateuch.

7. Saadiah, in his philosophical work, cites, it is true, an opinion of 'Anân and Benjamin-al-Nahawendi, which he confutes[6], but without any polemical heat, and, on the whole, he abstains in that work from all controversy with the Karaites. Of only two passages, in which he speaks of the opinions of "people who call themselves Jews," or "who are called Jews" (אנשים שנקראים יהודים · קום ממן יתסמון באליהודיה), I believe that I have shown that a section of the

[1] Cf. Munk, l. c., 104 sqq.

[2] Vid. *Responses of the Geonim*, ed. Lyck, No. 1: כי ר"ס ז"ל כתב בפירושו כי אין ספק מעיקרא אלא הקב"ה ציוה את משה עבדו והוא אמר להם לישראל כי בארץ יהיה להם יום אחד ובחו"ל שני ימים וכן היו מעולם כל ישראל עושין · · · כן ראינו כי זה שאמרתם שכתב ר"ס ז"ל קנה הוא שדחה את אפיקורוס וכו'.

[3] MS. Bodl., Opp. fol. 26, f. 96 a: והירושה אשר תזכור אותה היא אצלך המשנה והתלמוד וזולתם מן ספרי הרבנים והדומה להם כאשר זכרו (l. וזכרת) בפתר' פסוק עלה אלי ההרה והיה שם וכו'.

[4] Vid. Steinschneider, *Cat. Bodl.*, 2168.

[5] Vid. supra, p. 244.

[6] Ed. Slucki, pp. 96, 100; ed. Landauer, pp. 190, 201.

Karaites were alluded to [1]. The assumption that the second version of the seventh chapter, on the resurrection of the dead, on which Ibn Tibbon's translation was based, was directed specially against the same portion of the Karaites is, as recently shown by Bacher [2], plausible enough. Yet, as already said, a direct controversy against the Karaites is not to be found in the work. Several scholars have tried to explain this circumstance. Thus Kaufmann [3] believes the absence of all controversy to be attributable to Saadiah's consideration of Mahommedan readers, to whom he wished to represent Judaism as an undivided unit, without schism. But this suggestion is unacceptable, because controversy, both against Islam and against erroneous exegetical doctrines within Judaism, is by no means a rare thing in *Emunoth* [4]. More plausible is Guttmann's view [5], adopted also by Bacher, that there was no room in *Emunoth* for any polemic against the Karaites, in as far as the latter were in accord with the Rabbanites on the fundamental ideas that form the subject of the book. But this explanation is not quite satisfactory either, for the belief in the divine origin of the Tradition was to Saadiah a fundamental principle also. We shall have to rest for the present without an explanation. But the work mentioned above, under No. 4, and which was written after *Emunoth*, shows that Saadiah, even when advanced in years, had not lost his readiness for controversy.

8. As far as I have found, no controversy against the Karaites occurs in the other, still extant, writings of Saadiah's. It is true that Schechter [6] suggested that Saadiah's

[1] Vid. my "Miscellanies on Saadiah," I (*Monatsschrift*, XXXIX, 441–446).

[2] *Steinschneider-Festschrift*, p. 224.

[3] *Gesch. d. Attributenlehre*, p. 80 sqq. Cf. also *Revue des Études Juives*, XXVII, 271.

[4] Vid. Bacher, *Die Bibelexegese d. jüd. Religionsphilos. vor Maimuni*, pp. 35–44.

[5] *Die Religionsphilosophie d. Saadia*, p. 29, note 1; cf. also ibid., p. 17, note 1; p. 155, note 1.

[6] *Beth Talmud*, IV, 237. Cf. also the preface of the late Joel Müller to his edition of this commentary of Saadiah in the *Œuvres complètes*, Vol. IX.

commentary on the Thirteen Rules of R. Ishmael may have had an anti-Karaite tendency, but this conjecture is not supported by a single passage of the book. The assumption is all the more improbable, since both 'Anân and his followers also applied those rules [1]. As for Saadiah's lost works, the following may have contained anti-Karaite passages :—

(*a*) ספר עריות. Nothing is known of this book, except a rather lengthy quotation in the book with the same title by Jeshua ben Jehuda, first completely edited by Steinschneider in the magazine מגד ירחים, III, 76, and, again, partly in *Cat. Bodl.*, 2163 [2]. In this passage, Saadiah also rejects the application of the Analogy (היקש, קיאס) to the prohibited marriages, a method of which the Karaites made constant use. I also conjectured before, under No. 1, that Saadiah s polemic against incest was perhaps contained in that book.

(*b*) On the margin of a MS. in Oxford (Cod. Pococke, 256, Cat. Neubauer, 1533), a work of Saadiah is quoted under the title of כתאב אלקיאס עלי אלשראיע אלסמעה̈ [3], which Lebrecht designates, without any foundation, as an apologetical and polemical work [4]. But Steinschneider correctly identifies it as Saadiah's work כתאב תחציל אלשראיע אלסמעיה̈, quoted by Moses ibn Ezra [5], and it is, without doubt, identical with the כתאב אלשראיע mentioned in the Fihrist. Several conjectures were made in respect to that work, and Bacher proposed to identify it with the *Kitâb al-'amanât* [6]. Munk's opinion appears to be the only correct one, namely, that it was a compendium of laws (ספר המצות),

[1] Vid. *Steinschneider-Festschrift*, p. 208.

[2] The whole passage was also reprinted with explanatory notes by Joel Müller in Saadiah's *Œuvres complètes*, l. c., pp. 171–173.

[3] Vid. Munk, *Notice sur Saadja*, p. 14.

[4] Vid. Steinschneider, l. c., 2166.

[5] Ed. Kokowzow (Specimen in *Wostotchnija Zamjetki*), p. 219, where, however, one line in the quotation from Saadiah is missing. Vid. my remark in the *Zeitschr. f. hebr. Bibliogr.*, I, 30, note 6.

[6] *Abr. ibn Esra's Einleit. zu s. Pentateuchcomm.*, p. 20.

and this view has become more probable through a recently discovered citation from the same book, communicated by Neubauer[1]. Although no anti-Karaite matter occurs in either of these quotations, yet it is more than likely that Saadiah had in this book frequent opportunities of defending the Tradition and attacking the Karaites.

(*c*) כתאב אלעבור והו אלתאריך. This work is also mentioned in Fihrist, and its subject was, as the title shows, probably, the Knowledge of the Calendar and the Jewish Chronology. The little we know about it was collected by Rapoport[2], Luzzatto[3], and Steinschneider[4]. The work being quoted mostly by authors who wrote in Hebrew, none of whom mentioned its title, Luzzatto is of opinion, that Saadiah had written it in Hebrew, under the title of ספר העבור, a name which Ibn Nedim translated into Arabic by כתאב אלעבור, to which he added והו אלתאריך, for the better understanding of his Arabic readers[5]. Luzzatto further assumes that the book was unknown to Abraham b. Chija, since he never quotes it. In the absence of fuller information, nothing positive can be asserted; yet it must be observed that Ibn Bal'âm, in his Arabic commentary to I Kings vi. I, reproduces a passage from Saadiah's כתאב אלתאריך, which certainly deals with chronology[6]. It is also more than probable that the passage quoted by Abraham b. Chija in name of Isaak b. Baruch was, as the contents show, taken from this book. The כתאב אלתמייז could also be thought of in this connexion, but Abraham b. Chija would not, in that case, have omitted quoting it by name, as he knew this book

[1] Jewish Quarterly Review, VI, 707. It is certainly possible, also, that the words קאל ענה פי כתאבה פי אלשראיע cited there, do not allude to Saadiah, but to בר פרקאן, who is also mentioned there.

[2] *Biography of Saadiah*, note 23.

[3] *Orient*, XII, 101–103; 132–134.

[4] *Cat. Bodl.*, 2170. Cf. also היונה, 19; *Bibliotheca Mathematica*, 1894, 103.

[5] It is also possible that Saadiah himself gave his book a Hebrew and an Arabic title, as with the ספר האגרון. Vid. also, for other instances, Harkavy, חדשים גם ישנים, VII, 15.

[6] Cited by Neubauer, *Mediaeval Jewish Chronicles*, II, p. xi.

of Saadiah, a passage from which he cites, under the title of ספר ההכרה. It follows, at all events, that the כתאב אלעבור was no longer known to Abraham b. Chija. If we do not assume that Ibn Bal'âm had translated the Hebrew title into Arabic, his citation leads to the conclusion that Saadiah wrote this, like all his other works, in Arabic. Rashi's quotation, Rosh Hashana, 20 b[1], proves nothing, for he either may have quoted from a Hebrew extract, or he may have meant another book[2]. Nor are there any sufficient grounds for explaining why Saadiah should have written this particular book in Hebrew[3]. The Genizot in Egypt, which constantly supply fresh surprises, will perhaps still throw some light on this matter, and we have, perhaps, even now already a fragment of this work before us. It is, at any rate, more than probable, that Saadiah combated the Karaites in this very book, since questions in connexion with the knowledge of the Calendar are, so to say, the *perpetuum mobile* in the polemics between Saadiah and the Karaites.

9. We have seen that all Saadiah's anti-Karaite writings, with the exception of a few scanty fragments, are lost without leaving any trace. But a little fragment from one of them may, perhaps, have been rescued, namely, two loose sheets, contained in a Codex of Fragments in the Bodleian Library (MS. Hebr. 45, fol. 1–2), and which have come from Egypt, like all recent acquisitions made by the Library. I shall first communicate both text and translation of these two sheets,

[1] כך ראיתי ביסודו של רבינו סעדיה ז"ל.

[2] The same is the case with the נקוד דרב סעדיה, cited by Rashi to Ps. xlv. 10.

[3] In regard to those books of Saadiah that were written in Hebrew, we also know a reason for their having been composed in that language; thus, the ספר הגלוי and the ספר המועדים, because Saadiah wished to present them in Biblical garb, with vowel-points and accents (vid. Harkavy, *Stud. u. Mittheil.*, V, 133 sqq., 212 sqq.). He could not have written his polemic against Chivi al-Balchi in Arabic, vid. the quotation from Bachja's *Ma'ani al-nafs*, in *Revue des Études Juives*, XXV, 249 (cf., on this point, Kaufmann, ibid., XXVII, 271; in Broydé's translation of תורות הנפש, p. 20, ערבית must be altered into עברית, and עברית into ערבית. Cf. also *Monatsschrift*, XLI, 247, note 1).

and then proceed to give the arguments that induced me to set up this hypothesis.

· · · [1 a] לחד מן היה דבר ייי ביד[1] חגי הנביא לאמר פתוה̈ם עלי
מא סבק אלי ט̇נ̇ה אן קולה ביום עשרים וארבעה לחדש בששי הו[2] בשביעי
בעשרים ואחד לחדש והו יום ואחד מנסוב אלי שהרין פג̇על[3] אלשהר אלאול
מנסובא אלי שהור[4] אלשמס ואלשהר אלת̇אני מנסובא אלי שהור אלקמר
ולם יעלם אן יום עשרים וארבעה ליס הו יום עשרים ואחד ואנמא המא
יומאן מכ̇תלפאן מן שהרין מתואליין ופי כל ואחד מנהמא פעל ג̇יר אלאכ̇ר
והו אן קולה ביום עשרים וארבעה מוצולא במא קאל קבלה ויבאו ויעשו
מלאכה בבית ייי צבאות אלהיהם וכאן אול מא אבתדו באלבנא פי ארבעה̈
ועשרין מן אלול פאקאמו עלי תלך אלחאל אלי ואחד ועשרין מן תשרי פלמא
כאן יום ואחד ועשרין מן תשרי והו יום ערבה קאל אללה לחגי קל להם מי
בכם הנשאר אשר ראה את הבית הזה בכבודו הראשון ומה אתם ראים
אתו עתה הלוא כמוהו כאין בעיניכם פקד אוצ̇חנא אן ביום עשרים וארבעה
יקתצ̇י מא קבלה ויום ואחד ועשרין יקתצ̇י מא בעדה ואנכסר קול מן ג̇עלהמא
יומא ואחדא[5] ובנא לה מד̇הבא עלי שבהה̈ צעיפה̈[6] ואמא אלתפליסי וג̇ירה
מן אהל זמאננא הד̇א ממן אקר̈ באלחסאב לכנה אדעי אן וקת נהאיה̈ דקאיק
כל שהר הו יום תרתיבה פאן אלנקץ̇ עליה סהל וד̇לך אנה רג̇ל מסתדל̈ ליס
נאקל פאד̇א קיל לה מן אין קלת הד̇א אלקול לא ג̇ואב לה ולאצחאבה[7]
אכ̇תר מן אן יקול אשבהה באלצבי אלד̇י אד̇א ולד וקד בקי מן אלנהאר
דקיקה̈ נחסב לה ד̇לך אליום יומא תאמא ויכתן [1 b] פי מת̇לה וכד̇לך אלנדה
תרי פי אכ̇ר יום ויחסב להא יום תאם[8] וכד̇לך ג̇מיע אלטמאות ולכ̇צומה
אן יקולו לה קבל אלמקאיסה̈ אכ̇ברנא מא דלילך עלי וקת אלנהאיה̈ ומא
עלמך ען[9] כמיה̈ אלשהר [אלתי] הי הד̇ה אלתסעה̈ ועשרין יומא ונצוף והד̇ה
אלכסור פאנה לא חילה̈ לה ילג̇א אליהא אלא אחד ת̇לת̇ה̈ אמור אמא אן
ידעי פי ד̇לך מן אלמקרא ולא יג̇ד פיה שיא מנה או[10] ידעי אעתבאר אלרצד
ואלמחן אלתי אכ̇רג̇הא אלמנג̇מון והד̇א חסאב לא ימצ̇י עלי שי מן אקואל
אלמנג̇מין לאנה לם ישארכה וסט מסר אלקמר ולא מסירה אלמעד̈ל פקד
כ̇רג̇ מן צנעה̈ אלנג̇ום[11] וליס לה אלא אלוג̇ה אלת̇אלת̇ והו אן יקול כד̇א
נקלוה בנו אסראיל ען אלרסול פאד̇א הו צאר אלי הד̇א אלקול קיל לה

[1] MS. אל.
[2] MS. המהו.
[3] MS. פגהל.
[4] MS. אלשהור.
[5] MS. ואחדה.
[6] MS. צעיפא.
[7] MS. ולא צחאבה.
[8] MS. תאני.
[9] MS. אן.
[10] MS. אי.
[11] MS. אלנטם.

פאן נאקליה יזעמון אן אלרסול אמרנא באלענאיה בנהאיה גמלה אלסנה אלי ראס תשרי לנמתתל פיהא חלך אלשרוט ובין לנא אנא לא נבאלי במא סוי דלך מן אלשהור תקדם או תאכר פאן כאנת יהודיא[1] תסנד אלי הדה אלנקלה[2] פהדא קולהא וזעמהא ואן כאן לך נאקלון אכר פדלנא עליהם חתי נעתברהם ודלך מא לא יגדה פאדא לם ימכנה אקאמה אלברהאן עלי דעואה סקטת ואסתגנינא ען קיאסה וען נקצה   ופי אלאמה צנף אכר פי עצרנא הדא יעדון עלי אלאהלה ויזעמון אנהם עלי מדאהב אלרבונין ואן אלאואיל מן אלרבונין כאנת הדא חאלהם ואנהם כאנו ינאדון פי אלאמה פיסתחצרון אלשהוד[3] אלדין ראו אלהלאל ויסאלונהם ען דלך תם אדא צחת להם אלשהאדה קדסו וקאלו מקודש וכאנו איצא אדא צחת להם רויתה אשעלו . . .

. . . [2 a] ואן לם יכן מן האולי ולא האולי אלא אנה יקר באלמקרא פאלכלאם עליה מתוגה[4] אכתר מן אלגמיע ודלך אן פי אלמקרא מן הדא כתיר דלך קול[5] אלנבי אם אסק שמים שם אתה וג׳ ומחאל אלצעוד אלי אלסמא וקול אללה אם יחתרו בשאול וג׳ וממתנע אלאכתפא פי אלתרי וקולה לעשו אם תגביה כנשר ואם בין כוכבים שים קנך וגו׳ וקולה ליכניהו [כי] אם יהיה כניהו בן יהויקים מלך יהודה חותם על יד ימיני וקולה אם יעמד משה ושמואל לפני ומחאל קיאמהמא אלא באדנה וכמא וצף נגעים פי אלמנאזל ונגעים פי אלתיאב והי גיר מוגודה ואנמא הדה אלאקואל כלהא מבאלגה ותנאהי פי אלמעני כדאך קו אלחכ זכ לב הדה אלאקואל פי אלמשנה תגאיי ותבאלג פי אלקול ליערפו חכם מא ימו פי דלך ואנמא אתבת האהנא קול אלמנטקיין ואלגדליין לאפהם אן גמיע אלנאס קד אתפק פי אלכוץ פי אלמבאלגה ואלתנאהי פי אלאשיא ועלי אן דלך גיר מוגוד פרד עלי מן יטען עלי אלחכמים ואדחץ דעואה. והדא אלפריק כתירא מא יסאל מא באלניסן[6] לא יקע פי בדו פנקול פי דלך אולא קולא מן גהה אלנקל ואדא אכטרתה עלי באלך וגדתה צחיחא והו אן אלדליל אלדי נצבה אללה לידלנא עלי רצאה מא הו פי אמר מרחשון וכסלו וכל סנה למא כאן יקטע איאם אלגמעה קטעא גיר מתסאויה ויחכם לכל ואחדה מנהא בחכם מא וצפנא

[1] MS. יאהדא. [2] MS. אלנאקלה. [3] MS. אלשהור.

[4] MS. מתנה. Cf. Dozy, s. v.: فذلك من لا يتوجه هذا الخطاب عليه "ce discours ne s'adresse pas à lui."

[5] MS. בקול.

[6] Perhaps למא ו׳א אלניסן. The whole passage seems to be somewhat corrupt.

צארת אלשהור תמרד בעצ̇הא בעצ̇א פילחק כל ואחד אין מא לחק ד̇לך לאן
אלמרתב בעד מא ית̇בת הד̇ין אלשהרין עלי חאל [2 b] מא פלא חילה̈ לה פי
באקי אלשהור בעד ד̇לך בזיאדה̈ ולא נקצאן לאן אלעשרה̈ אלבאקיה̈ מחכמה̈
פלמא כאן אלאמר כד̇אך בטל קול מן זעם אן ניסן או תשרי ירחיאן[1]
לכנה הו חסאב לא ינאהי ניסן אלי איאם אזואג̇ בל אלי איאם פראד והו
א̇גה̈ז ומת̇אל ד̇לך כאלכ̇מסין אלתי לא תטיק אן תקסמהא עלי סבעה̈ אפראדא
אבדא או כאלכ̇מסה̈ ועשרין אלתי לא ימכנך אן תקסמהא עלי ארבעה̈ אזואג̇א
אבדא לאן אלחסאב ימתנע מן אכ̇ראג̇ ד̇לך באלטבע כד̇אך הד̇א אלחסאב[2]
ימתנע מן מנאהאה̈ ניסן אלי אלאיאם אלאזואג̇ באלטבע אלד̇י לה. ואקול פיה
בעד ד̇לך קולא אכ̇ר מן ג̇הה אלכתאב וד̇לך באן אקד̇ם קבלה מקדמה̈ עלי
מד̇הבנא ואקול אן כל פרץ̇ נזלה אללה קבל פרץ̇ פלם יג̇ז אן יאתי אלת̇אני
פינקץ̇ אלאול בל לא יקע אלת̇אני אלא עלי מא לם ידכ̇ל תחת אלאול
ד̇לך כאלמילה אלתי הי קבל אלסבת פאמרנא אללה אן נכ̇תן כל יום פלמא
אמר בעד ד̇לך באלסבת כאן לא יקע עלי אלמילה אלמאמור בהא כל
יום פינסכ̇הא וכאלקרבן עולה איצ̇א אלמפתרץ̇ קבל אלסבת כאן נקרב בכל
יום פלא יג̇וז אן ימנעה אלסבת פאלפסח איצ̇א אפרץ̇ קבל אלסבת יג̇ב פלד̇לך
יג̇ב פעלה פי אלסבת ואמא מא נזל מן אלשראיע בעד אלסבת פלא יג̇וז פעלה
פיהא אלבתה̈ ת̇ם נקול אנא ראינא אללה עז וג̇ל קד רסם לנא פי אלמועדות
שראיעא לא בד̇ מן פעלהא פלם ירסמהא פי תלך אלאוקאת אלא לעלמה
אנהא לא תקע פי סבת פנמנע[3] מן פעלהא אד̇ הי מן בעדה שרעת פמן
האהנא נעלם אן אלחסאב אלד̇י עלמנאה רסולה הו . . .

". . . [1 a] His error lay in the verse: 'The word of God came by the prophet Haggai, saying' (Hag. ii. 1), and he erroneously thought, as we said already, that both dates 'the 24th of the sixth month' (ibid. i. 15) and 'the 21st of the seventh month' (ibid. ii. 1) were identical, and referred to two different sorts of months. He thought the former to refer to the solar, and the latter to the lunar month. But he did not know, that these two dates, the 24th and the 21st, are two different days, falling in two consecutive months, and that a different event occurred on each of them. For the words 'on the 24th' [&c.] are the continuation of the preceding verse: 'and they came and did

[1] Perhaps ירחיאן. [2] MS. אחסאב. [3] MS. פימנע.

work in the house of the Lord Zebaoth their God' (i. 14). Thus, they commenced building on the 24th of Elul, and continued till the 21st of Tishri. On that very day, the day of the *'Arâba*, God said to Haggai: 'Speak to them: Who is left among you that saw this house in its former glory, and how do you see it now, is it not in your eyes as nothing?' (ii. 3). We have thus made it clear that the 24th of Elul must refer to the preceding verse, but the 21st of Tishri refers to that which follows. The words of him, therefore, who considers these two dates to mean the same day, and who bases his opinion upon doubtful and weak arguments, are of no value [1].

"Now Tiflîsi—and many of his contemporaries follow him—keeps to the reckoning of the Calendar; only, he thinks that the end of the minutes of every month was, at the same time, the day of the order [of the new month?] [2].

[1] This passage seems to be directed against the assertion that the Bible reckons also according to the solar months. Jehuda ha-Parsi is here perhaps alluded to, who taught that we had to reckon by solar months, as mentioned by Ibn Ezra (Introduction to the Commentary on the Pentateuch; Comm. to Gen. viii. 3; Exod. xii. 1; Lev. xxv. 9; Sefer ha-Ibbur, 8 a; Iggeret ha-Shabbath, in *Kerem Chemed*, IV, 163). Ibn Ezra does not, however, quote the proof from Hag. i. 15 and ii. 1. It is remarkable that the older Karaites inform us, that among the Sadducees every month had thirty days, and that they, consequently, had solar months, thus, e. g. al-Qirqisâni, *Kitâb al-'anwâr*, I, 7 (ed. Harkavy, p. 304; and, probably, thence Hadassi, Alphab. 97, letter ת), Jefeth to Lev. xxiii. 5: וחכי ענהם אנהם כאנו יתבתון שהורהם שמסיה לא קמרייה אלך (אי ען אלצרוקיה). I hope shortly to return to this subject.

[2] The name of this sectarian was Mûsa al-Zafrâni, or 'Abû 'Imrân at-Tiflîsi. He was from Bagdad, and emigrated to Tiflis. Vid. about him, Qirqisâni, ed. Harkavy, pp. 285, 315 (Hadassi, Alphab. 98, letter צ, has, incorrectly, אבועמרן). His theory, according to which the day of the conjunction belongs alone to the new month, and which is refuted here, is briefly mentioned by Qirqisâni: באנה כאן יתכׄר ראס אלשהר מנד אול ... אליום אלדׄי תקע פיה אלמפארקהׄ; and more fully by Jefeth to Gen. i. 14. He first makes some remarks which are of general interest: אני וגׄדת אלאמהׄ ואן אכׄתלפת עלי וגׄוה שתי פאנהא לא תכׄרג מן וגׄהין אחד אלחסאב ואלבׄ אלרויהׄ ואלקאילין בחסאב אנקסמו עלי קסמין פמנהם מן גׄעל חסאבה עלי אלאגׄהמאע [אי אגׄתמאע אלקמר מע אלשמס יום אבתדאה] והו אבו עמראן אלתפליסי ואצחאבה יאלבׄ חסאב אלרבאנין והו חסאב

This is easily refuted. For [he bases his assertion] upon arguments, and not upon tradition. To the question 'Whence has he got this opinion?' he and his adherents can only answer that they compared [the month] with a boy born only a minute before the end of the day. That day counts for a whole day, and his circumcision takes place [1 b] on the corresponding [eighth] day. In the same way, if a woman at the time of her menstruation, sees [symptoms] at the end of the day, that day counts for a whole day; the same rule applies to other cases of uncleanliness. But his opponents can reply: Before you conclude such analogies, tell us first, what proof you have in regard to the time of the end [of the month], and what do you know about the duration of the month, which is 29½ days and a certain number of parts [of an hour] [1]? No artifice remains him wherewith to defend himself, except one of

אלמבני עלי אלמילאד פאמא אלקאילין באלרויה̈ פהו כל פריק כ̇אלף אלרבאנין גירה אבו עמראן והדה ואמא אצחאב אלבדר ואלצדוקיה̈ לם יבק אחד מנהם נלהמס אלרד עליה ואו̇א כאן ליס ת̇ם קסם מוגוד פי זמאננא הד̇א והד̇א (r. אלא הדא) אלג̇ לא הכ̇רג̇ ען אן יכון אלקמר דליל עלי רווס אלשהור אלך̇. In reference to Tiflîsi, he continues: . . . פנחן נמנע אן יכון אלחסאב מנקולא פאן כאן [כ̇דלך] מ̇והב אבו עמראן אלתפליסי פמן אלמעלום אן חסאבה מחדת̇ ואנה ג̇מע ד̇ זיגאת ואכ̇ד̇ מן אלוסט הסאב עמל עליה ואחתג̇ למ̇והבה בנצוץ ליס תתעלק בשי ממא ד̇כרה והו מא תעלק בקול אלכתאב בכסה ליום חגנו והד̇א אלנץ ירחמך אללה הו לכ̇צומה ולא לה לאן קולה בכסה ימשי עלי מ̇והב אלקאילין ברויה̈ אלהלאל אלד̇' אבדא כל ראס שהר מגטא ענהם מערפתה מן קבל אנ̇ ליס יעלמו הל אלשהר יכ̇רג̇ חסר או מלא הד̇א או̇א פסרנא בכסה אלגטא וקד פסרוה יום אלרביחה̈ יגעלוה מן לגה̈ אלתרגום והו תרגום ושחט פבנא אלרגל אצלה עלי הד̇א אלנץ ואלתמס לה חסאב מן זיגאת אלמנגמין לם יכן ביר אחר מן אלאמה̈ ולא נץ ד̇כרה פקד בטל אן יכון חסאבה מנקולא. Qirqisâni and Jefeth inform us that, in their time, followers of this sectarian still existed. Thus the former says of him: פאקאם בהא (אי בתפלים) ותאבעה עלי מ̇והבה גמאעה̈ והם אלי הדה אלגאיה̈ בהא; and the latter, besides the passage mentioned, also to Lev. xxiii. 5: ולים פי זמאננא הד̇א גיר ת̇לת̇ מ̇ואהב והי מ̇והב אלרבאנין ומ̇והב אלתפליסי ומ̇והב אלקאילין באלרויה̈. The author of the חלוק הקראים והרבנים (Pinsker, p. 100) also says that, at his time, only four sects were still extant, of the fourteen which existed previously: namely, Rabbanites, Karaites, Tiflisites, and Meswites (i.e. followers of Meswi al-Okbari). Cf. *Revue des Études Juives*, XXXIV, 163.

[1] It is known that the month in the Jewish Calendar has 29½ days and $\frac{793}{1080}$ of an hour, or, as the formula is, כט̇ יב̇ הת̇שצג̇.

the following three. Either he appeals to the Bible, but there he finds nothing on the subject[1]; or he appeals to observation [of the moon] and the consideration [of that which was observed], as the astronomers do. But this calculation [of his] has nothing in common with the astronomers, for it is in harmony, neither with the mean nor with the corrected circuit of the moon; he must therefore leave astronomy alone. Only a third alternative remains him, namely, when he says: 'Thus it was delivered to the Israelites by the Messenger [Moses].' Should he resort to this argument, the answer would be this. The bearers of the tradition maintain on the contrary that the Messenger commanded that we should take care to terminate the whole year at the commencement of Tishri, in order that we utilize here these conditions for the purpose of analogy (?). He has, therefore, made it clear to us, that we need not be concerned about anything [else], in reference to the months which either precede or follow [Tishri]. If you are a Jew, and adhere to these bearers of the tradition, [know] that such is their opinion; but if you have others who transmit a different transmission, quote them to us in order that we may respect them. This he cannot do. But if he can adduce no proof for his assertion, it falls to the ground, and we have enough of his analogies and we need not refute him any further.

"We have in our midst yet another class of people, who regulate their festivals according to the [first appearance of the] new moon, and believe nevertheless that they proceed after the methods of the Rabbanites. [They say] that the first teachers among the Rabbanites proceeded in the same way, that they convened an assembly of the people, and caused witnesses to come, whom they cross-examined. If they approved of the evidence, they sanctified [the new month], and proclaimed: 'Sanctified!' In the same way

[1] We know from Jefeth that Tiflîsi quotes Ps. lxxxi. 4 for his theory.

they kindled, when they were certain of the first appearance of the moon . . .[1]

". . . [2 a] but if he belongs neither to this, nor to the other class, but keeps [only] to the Bible, in that case the [present] exposition applies to him more than to all others. For we have in the Bible many similar phrases; for instance, the word of the prophet [David]: 'If I ascend to heaven, thou art there,' &c. (Ps. cxxxix. 8), but it is impossible for anybody to ascend to the heaven; similarly, the word of God: 'Though they dig into grave,' &c. (Am. ix. 2), but it is impossible to hide in the damp; also, the word of God to Esau: 'Though thou mount on high as an eagle and fix thy nest among the stars,' &c. (Obad. 4); also the word to Jechoniah: 'Though Coniahu the son of Jehoiakim were the signet upon my right hand' (Jer. xxii. 24); also, 'Were Moses and Samuel to place themselves before me' (ib. xv. 1), but they could place themselves before God only by his permission. In the same way the leprosy of buildings and clothes is described, although it does not occur at all. All such phrases must be taken as hyperbolical expressions, and thus must the dicta of the sages of blessed memory in the Mishna be understood[2]. Namely, the latter wanted only to give [theoretical] decisions in case people would wish [to know them]. In proof I also adduce here the opinions of the logicians and dialecticians, in order to show that there are many who express themselves in an hyperbolical manner on things which have no existence in reality. Thus is the man, who slandered our sages, refuted, and his opinions rejected.

[1] The passages in Rosh Hashana, II, are alluded to. Thus, this class, which kept to the Tradition, believed nevertheless, that the first appearance of the new moon ought still to be observed, and that the months and festivals ought to be fixed accordingly. They also rejected the constantly fixed Calendar. Nothing else is known of that class, but vid. infra, p. 273, note 1.

[2] On the expressions used here to denote "hyperbolical," תגאי' and תגאהי', which are not found in the Arabic dictionaries, I hope to treat shortly in another place.

"The same sect also often puts the question, why it should be impossible for Nissan to fall on a Monday, or a Wednesday, or a Friday? We should like, in the first place, to adduce [in reply to that question] something from tradition, which thou [O reader!] wilt find correct, if thou wilt bring into thy recollection. God has made manifest his will in reference to the Marcheshvan and Kislev and [consequently] the whole year by this, that he made the number of days of the week an uneven number, and fixed for every [week?] that which we mentioned already. Through this the months . . . reciprocally, and they follow each other, as they should (?)[1]. Namely, once something was fixed in regard to these two months by the fixed norm [of the Calendar(?)], there is no possibility either to add to or to detract anything from the other months, for by it the other ten are already fixed. If this be so, it is also correct to assume that Nissan or Tishri . . .[2] Now it has been computed, that Nissan is never to fall on an even number but on an uneven number of days, namely, on the first, the third, the fifth, and the seventh [day of the week]. As little as it is possible to divide 50 by 7 in even portions, or 25 by 4, this being against the rules of arithmetic, as impossible it is for the computation [of the Calendar] to bring it about that Nissan fall on an even number of the days of the week.

"I will also adduce something from the Bible, and point first the following premises which are in accordance with

[1] This sentence is not quite intelligible, and the word תמרד makes no sense. Prof. Steinschneider thinks that some form of the verb מר׳ is concealed here. At all events, the author means to say, that by means of the fixing on every occasion of Marcheshvan and Kislev—the only months that have no uniform number of days—the other ten months follow each other in turns, and by a fixed law, alternately defective (חסר) and plene (מלא).

[2] The word ירחיאן makes no sense either. We must perhaps read ידחיאן, "Nissan or Tishri are extended," i. e. somebody thought that these two months, and not Marcheshvan and Kislev, could alter their number of days. But the word דחא in the sense of "stretching" is in Arabic used in a different sense. Or is, perhaps, the Hebrew word ירח concealed in ירחיאן, and the text not quite correct.

the Law, viz. whenever God reveals one commandment before another, the second can never annul the first; the second can apply only to cases which are not included in the first. Thus, for instance, circumcision was [revealed] before the Sabbath, and God commanded us to perform the circumcision on any day. When, afterwards, the commandment was given to observe the Sabbath, it cannot be applied to circumcision so as to annul it. In the same way, burnt-offerings were commanded to be brought on the Sabbath, therefore the offerings were brought on every day and the Sabbath did not interfere with them. In the same way, the Paschal offering was ordained before the observance of the Sabbath, therefore it could be brought also on the Sabbath. But such commandments as were revealed after the commandment of the Sabbath may not be fulfilled on the Sabbath. We therefore say, since we see that God (he is mighty and strong!) gave us commandments for the festivals, which must necessarily be observed on them, he fixed them for those days only for this reason, that he knew, that they should not fall on a Sabbath; for, in that case, we should be unable to fulfil them, as having been ordained after the Sabbath. From this we can infer that the reckoning of the Calendar, revealed to us by his Messenger . . ."

The reasons that induce me to attribute this fragment to Saadiah are as follows:—

1. The tenor of the whole fragment points to a defence of the Calendar and its authority. We know that Saadiah all along maintained, in opposition to the Karaites, that the Jewish Calendar, with all its laws and regulations, was of remote antiquity, a point on which he was not only contradicted by the Karaites, but also by the Rabbanites (Hai Gaon, Isaac b. Baruch, Abraham Ibn Ezra, Maimonides, &c.)[1]. His opinion was only followed by Chananel b. Chushiel[2],

[1] Vid. *Responses of the Geonim*, ed. Lyck, No. 1; Abraham b. Chija's ספר העבור, 59, 94; Ibn Ezra on Lev. xxiii. 3; Maimuni, הלכות קד"ח, V, 3; Israeli, *Jesod Olam*, IV, 6.

[2] *Migdal Chananel*, p. 32.

Meshullam b. Kalonymos[1], and Obadiah b. David[2]. But not one of these latter can have been the author of our fragment, even only for the reason that they wrote nothing but Hebrew.

2. Saadiah, in consequence of this theory of his, was also compelled to maintain, that all the Postponements (דחיות) were also of the same ancient origin, and that, therefore, the Passover, for instance, never could have fallen on Monday, Wednesday, or Friday, in accordance with the well-known rule לא בד״ו פסח. And on this point also he was contradicted, not only by all Karaites, but also by many Rabbanites. When it was objected, that many passages in the Talmud showed nevertheless, that the Passover fell on one of these days, e.g. the Mishna Sabbath, xv, 3; Pesachim, viii, 10; Chagiga, ii, 4; Menachot, xi, 7, &c., Saadiah answered, that, in these passages, the question was discussed only theoretically, namely, what was to be done, suppose the Passover fell on one of these days. For, Saadiah said, it is nowhere written that Passover actually fell on one of those days. But here also his opponents could show him the passage: פעם אחת חל שביעי של ערבה להיות בשבת (Tosefta, Sukka, III, Babli, 43 b)[3]. Of all Karaites, it was Salmon b. Jerucham, who had collected the greatest number of arguments against Saadiah, having devoted chaps. 4–6 of his controversial writing to this subject[4]. He uses several passages to show that Saadiah had not only gone against the Karaites, but also against his own authorities, and there says of him (chap. 5): ״גועל בדרכי אבותיו · בוזה בדבור רבותיו · בוחר ברוע מחשבותיו · הורו והוגו מלב שקרותיו · · · ״הפך תורת אדון האדונים · וחבל דברי שושנים · עם תלמוד ותורת כהנים · וסדר עולם וכל ענינים[5]. I add some characteristic Talmudic passages quoted by him: ״והלא[6] כתוב חל

[1] Vid. סמ״ג, Commandments, No. 47.

[2] Comm. to הלכות קה״ח, VII.

[3] Vid. particularly Abr. b. Chija, l. c.

[4] Cf. Jewish Quarterly Review, VIII, 685.

[5] Cf. Pinsker, p. 16.

[6] From chap. 5 I used the Leyden MS. (Cod. Warner, 41) and Pinsker's copy (in the Vienna *Beth Hamidrash*), on the margin of which various

להיות יום כפור בשבת הקדושה · החלות מתחלקות לערב לה מקודשה ·
חל להיות ערב שבת השעיר של יום הכפורים נאכל בערב ביראה ונעשה ·
והבבליין אוכלין אותו חי מפני שדעתן יפה ומאוששה · "זאת ראיה גדולה ·
כי יום כפורים נפל ערב שבת בתחלה · כידוע לכל קהלה · והיום למה שנו
דרכם להתחבלה ·

"סח ר' עקיבא וקולו הרים · לא חלבי שבת מקריבין ביום הכפורים · ולא
של יום כפור קרבין בשבת בחבורים · והוא לכם ראש הסופרים · "ענו בני
מקרא · זאת לכם ראיה גמורה · כי בערב שבת יום הכפורים קרה · והם אמרו
לא אָגוֹ יום כפור שלא כתורה · · ·

"רבותיך [1] כתבו בפרק באי זה צד צולין · העצמות והגידין ישרפו בששה
עשר בימי חולין · חל שבעה עשר להיות בשבת כלולין · שרופים בשבעה עשר
ומבוטלין · "קרב עתה ושמע דברים נכוחים · אם ששה עשר יפול בשבת
מנוחים · הלא חמשה עשר בניסן יום ששי צורחים · ואתה תאמר כי הם
לא בָדוֹ פסח שוחחים · · · "סמך פיתומי ידו על משענת קנה · אמר חל ששה
עשר להיות בשבת מן השבת פונה · ופתרונו אם חל ככת' אם תגביה כנשר
ואם בין כוכבים תחנה · אשיבנו על זה הדבר ואל אדם לא אכנה · · ·

We see, therefore, that to Saadiah all these passages of the Talmud have only an hypothetical meaning (as we know already from Isaac b. Baruch), and that they must be taken in the same way as Obad. 4. Now, we find at the beginning of the second leaf of our fragment that the author, to prove an hyperbolical interpretation of Talmudic passages, quotes, *inter alia*, also Obad. 4, and we may assume from the whole, that such passages from the Talmud are here alluded to, as were quoted by Salmon b. Jerucham, and Isaac b. Baruch.

3. At the end of the first leaf we read, that the class of persons who still fixed their months by the first appearance of the moon maintained that they stood, notwithstanding, on Rabbinical ground, their first teachers having proceeded in the same way, &c. It would appear from this, as if the author of the fragment doubted these facts, as mentioned in

readings from other MSS. are also recorded. I consider it unnecessary for our present purpose to give here all those variations.

[1] From chap. 6.

the Mishnah! But we know that Saadiah asserted, that the new moons had always been fixed by calculation, and that they commenced summoning witnesses, &c., only after Zadok and Boethos and others had maintained that the Torah enjoined to fix the new moons by observation; and that they did so for the purpose of showing that calculation and observation coincided[1]. The above cited passage becomes only thus intelligible.

4. We read further in the fragment that a divine precept cannot be annulled by another and subsequent one, and that circumcision must take place, and the two daily burnt-offerings be brought on the Sabbath, because these commandments were anterior to that of the Sabbath. We find the same idea in Saadiah's philosophical work. The Gaon speaks there of the impossibility of abrogating the Law (נסך אלשרע) and says, that there is much which apparently admits of abrogation, but that it is not really the case. Thus are the offerings and the circumcision on the Sabbath no abrogation, because they were commanded before the Sabbath: ואלד̇ תקריב אלקרבאן פי אלסבת בעד תחטיר אלעמל פיה הד̇א איצ̇א ליס בנסך̇ בל הו ממא יו״ד דפע אלנסך̇ לאן שריעה̈ אלקרבאן כאנת קבל אלסבת פלם יג̇ז אן יחט̇רה שריעה̈ אלסבת פיכון ד̇לך נסכ̇א פחט̇רת סאיר אלאעמאל אלא אלקרבאן ואלכ̇תאנה̈ אלמתקד̈מין קבלהא.[2]

5. Our fragment further shows that such work as was prohibited the Sabbath, may under no circumstance be done on the Sabbath. If, then, God commanded several things to be done on the festivals that were prohibited to be done on the Sabbath, he must have intended that these festivals should not fall on the Sabbath. Here, unfor-

[1] Vid. my Miscellanies on Saadiah, II (l. c., 209). May not the assertion that the new moon should be observed, in spite of the tradition, be connected with the action taken by Ben Meir, who, at the time of Saadiah, wanted to re-establish the authority of Palestine in regard to the fixing of the festivals? (vid. JEWISH QUARTERLY REVIEW, IX, 36–38). In that case, another proof could be found for Saadiah's authorship of our fragment.

[2] *Kitâb al-'amanât*, ed. Landauer, 136 (ed. Slucki, 70).

tunately, the fragment stops; the author alluded probably to some such case as the bringing of offerings of rejoicing on the Feast of Weeks. And this case is really adduced by Isaac b. Baruch, in the name of Saadiah, as an argument for his theory, vid. ספר העבור, p. 60: ... וכן אנו אומרים על פסח שאינו ביום ששי ... ועוד מפני עצרת שלא יהיה בשבת ואין מקריבין שלמים בשבת והקב"ה חייב בעצרת הקרבת שלמים ככתוב ושני כבשים בני שנה לזבח שלמים וכו'.

The parallel passages quoted here, which may perhaps be added to in course of time, raise the assumption of Saadiah's authorship to a degree of probability, approaching certainty. The question then arises, to which of his works does it belong? If my above-mentioned conjecture be correct, that Isaac b. Baruch's writing was based on Saadiah's כתאב אלעבור, it would be obvious to suggest that work, for such questions as solar and lunar months are also treated there; further, several theories of the Calendar, such as those of 'Abû 'Imrân at-Tiflîsi, and others, are dealt with. But it is also possible that it was part of an anti-Karaite book of Saadiah's, and, in that case, the כתאב אלתמייז would suggest itself, in which the question of the age of the Calendar and its rules are dwelt on at length. We submit our conjecture for the approval of experts; if they consider it to be correct, it would be an important gain for the history of Jewish literature.

. . . .

We have seen that Saadiah was the first great teacher of Judaism, who opposed the Karaites by special writings, but he was also the last. Of the Geonim that came after him, it was only Samuel b. Chofni who casually combats the Karaites, but he has written no special work on the subject[1]. Nothing anti-Karaite is, as far as I know, found in the works of the last two celebrated Geonim, Sherira and Hai[2]. Nor was any one found among the

[1] Vid. Harkavy, *Stud. u. Mittheil.*, III, 6, 7; 44-47.

[2] The *responsum*, שערי תשובה, No. 34, is not of Hai, as Weiss (l. c., IV, 189) assumes, for Chananel is quoted there.

great teachers of the East who defended the "dead lion" against the attacks and slights of the Karaites. A pupil of Saadiah who had undertaken the task, Jacob b. Samuel, would almost have been forgotten, if the Karaites who controverted him had not preserved his name. The controversy did not cease on account of a peace concluded by the parties, but from exhaustion. It is true, a small anti-Karaite pamphlet appeared at the beginning of the twelfth century in the East, probably in Egypt, but it does not touch at all upon points of the Law on which the Rabbanites and Karaites differ; in fact, it is no more than a literary curiosity [1]. In Europe, the controversy with the Karaites never assumed important dimensions. A great teacher of the West, Meshullam b. Kalonymos, combats the views of the Karaites towards the end of the tenth, or the beginning of the eleventh century, but we do not know the motives that called forth the controversy, nor does it seem that he has written a separate book against them [2]. The scholars in Spain were contented, either with a defence of the Tradition only, without taking the offensive (Jehuda Hallevi), or they corroborated their truth from the never ceasing source of Tradition, and by the distinguished achievements of its adherents (Abraham ben David), or they appealed to the secular power (Jehuda Ibn Ezra).

But the Karaites themselves also seem to have lost vitality and productiveness, by the absence of a strenuous controversy against them. Not regarding a few sporadic followers, the independent creative power of the Karaites ceases with Jeshua b. Jehuda (Abulfaraǵ Furqân ibn ʿAsad), who wrote some twenty years after Samuel b. Chofni. For the im-

[1] Vid. Jewish Quarterly Review, VIII, 700, 701, where I communicated the epigraph and some lines from this little pamphlet. I hope shortly to give more of it.

[2] On Meshullam's polemic against the Karaites cf. Rapoport, *Biography of Nathan b. Jechiel*, note 36; Müller, *Responsen des R. Meschullam*, p. 8; Epstein, *Revue des Études Juives*, XXVII, 84, 85. The latter says that a leaf of the MS. of the Vatican, No. 32, contains the words: אלו תשובות שהשיב למינין רבנא משלם הרב בחכמה, but, unfortunately, the leaf is illegible.

portance of his pupil, Tobia b. Mose, lies really in his translations, from which he is called "ha-ma'atîq." The brilliant period of Karaite literature ends with Jehuda Hadassi, but he was after all only a compiler, although his work, *Eshkol Hakkofer*, is invaluable to us, because it contains the results of the Karaite learning before him. The Karaite authors from the twelfth century, except, perhaps, the two Aarons, produced hardly anything new, especially in the field of the knowledge of the Law. They all depend on their predecessors, and "enrich themselves by their writings[1]." They all, even to their last teacher, Abraham Firkowitsch, draw inspiration from the repetition of the most virulent attacks against the Rabbanites in general, and the Fajjûmite, "that man there" (הדא אלרג׳ל)[2] in particular. But a literature cannot live on chewing the cud of older opinions and on controversy, and nothing more, especially when these are not even fertilized by any new thoughts. Thus it is that the Karaite literature vanished silently. A new Saadiah would be required to rouse it to fresh life, but our age is not such as to produce one, nor has Judaism any interest in calling forth new animosities.

SAMUEL POZNAŃSKI.

[1] Hadassi says, in reference to what he borrowed from previous authors (Alphab. 64, letter ק): כי מספריהם נתעשרנו. Cf. *Monatsschrift*, XL, 126.

[2] Thus most of the Karaites who wrote in Arabic designate him. It must, however, be observed, that his Rabbanite opponent, Mebasser Hallevi, designates him in the same way. Vid. *Zapiski*, l. c., p. 208.

The Karaite Literary Opponents of Saadiah Gaon

BY

SAMUEL POZNAŃSKI, Ph.D.

THE

KARAITE LITERARY OPPONENTS OF SAADIAH GAON

THE literary campaign that Saadiah, first among the Rabbanites, started against the Karaites, and whose external history I have on a former occasion attempted to trace [1], found the foe ready to join battle. There arose a complete array of Karaite scholars, who, either in special writings, or incidentally in the course of their works, repelled the attacks of Saadiah with energy. But they were not content to remain on the defensive. They speedily assumed an offensive attitude, and endeavoured, with varying degrees of success, to overthrow the arguments and proofs advanced by Saadiah in support of the Oral Law. A disagreeable element in the campaign is the personal abuse into which the controversy often degenerated: objective treatises are marred by regrettable recrimination. It must, however, be admitted that in this respect both parties sinned, although perhaps the Karaites sinned the more deeply.

The controversy initiated by Saadiah's activity did not cease with his death. It was not confined to the Gaon alone, but drew within its range the whole of Rabbinism. Henceforth polemics form a principal feature of Karaite

[1] *J. Q. R.*, X, 238-76. For Addenda and Corrigenda to that essay see end of the present dissertation (pp. 94-101).

literature: they inspire Karaism with fresh life, and stimulate the development of its literature in a very great measure. In truth, the polemical element existed in the very nature of Karaism. The latter was a product of opposition and revolt against the principles of Rabbinism, and hence its progress depended upon strife. Personal attacks were not unknown even in its very early days, for 'Anân is said to have prescribed the reading on every New Moon of Psalm lxxiv, because, in his opinion, there was an allusion, especially in verses 4 and 8, against the Rabbanites[1]. Still, polemics play a very small part in the oldest writings of the Karaites, which, by the way, are still accessible only to a very small extent. It was not till the advent of Saadiah that their polemics assumed a tone of bitterness and occupied the most prominent place in their literary activity, and in the centre of the controversial medley was the figure of the Gaon. I now propose giving a bibliographical survey of this literature down to modern times. In the first place, it must be observed that the practice of the Karaites to repeat one another consciously, and often to copy one another verbally, is pursued to a still greater degree in their polemical treatises. The controversy carried on against the Rabbanites in general and against Saadiah in particular was for them a necessary of life, upon which they continuously drew as their main resource. Hence, even at a time when all spiritual life in their midst had been stifled, they still roused themselves, and brought forth their rusty weapons to attack the execrated Fayyumite.

A brief survey of the earliest Karaite controversy directed against Saadiah is given by Sahl b. Maṣliaḥ in his polemical work תוכחת מגולה[2]. We there read: והספרים אשר כתב . . .

[1] Another statement of 'Anân, reported by Moses Taku, most probably belongs to the realm of legend. 'Anân is said to have wished that he could contain within himself all the learned Rabbis, so that by a single stroke of the sword he might be able to slay them all with himself. See *R. É. J.*, XLV, 201–2.

[2] Communicated by Steinschneider, *Catal. Lugd.*, p. 403, and Pinsker, לקוטי קדמוניות, p. 37. The variants are unimportant.

(ר״ל סעדיה) לא הוציאם בחייו מתחת ידו על בני מקרא ואחד מהם נפל ביד בן משיח והשיב עליו בחייו וכן שלמון בן ירוחם השיב עליו בלשון הקדש על אשר כתב אשא משלי וָאֹמַר ואחרי מותו נפלו ספריו ביד בני מקרא בכל מקום ומקום וישיבו עליהן תשובות בדברים נכוחים כמסמרות נטועים בספרים הרבה כמו שעשה אבו אלטייב הנודע אלגבלי וכן עלי בן חסון וכן בן משיח ובן ירוחם הנודע בן רוחים ואבו עלי חסן אלבצרי וזולתם וגם אני כתבתי תשובה לדבריו כאחד מהם וכו׳ "The writings that Saadiah composed against the Karaites did not leave his possession throughout his life. But one work fell into the hands of Ben Mashiaḥ, and he replied to it during Saadiah's lifetime. Similarly Salmon b. Jeroḥam wrote against him in Hebrew and refuted his statement, beginning with the words אשא משלי ואמר [1]. But not until the death of Saadiah did his writings fall into the hands of the Karaites in various places, and give rise to a multitude of convincing arguments in a number of works. Among the authors of the latter were Abu-l-Ṭajjib, known as al-Jebeli, ʿAli b. Ḥasan, Ben Mashiaḥ, Ben Jeroḥam, known as Ibn Ruḥeim, Abu ʿAli Ḥasan al-Baṣri, and others. I also have written a reply against his contentions," &c.

But this list is not complete. We miss, for example, of Saadiah's contemporaries, so important a writer as Qirqisâni; and even granting that Sahl mentions only those who composed special polemical treatises against the Gaon, we still miss Isaac b. ʿAli, &c. But what sense is there in the assertion that Saadiah throughout his life did not publish his polemical writings against the Karaites? He did not compose them for purely literary purposes, but wished by their means to counteract the increasing propaganda of the Karaites. Hence, had he suppressed his writings his intention would have been quite frustrated. The statements of Sahl are therefore to be treated with

[1] A chapter of Salmon's controversial work actually begins with the words (Pinsker, p. 18): אדרת סעדיה רבתי שדודה . . . וחכמה אבדה מן האומר אשא משלי ואחודה וכו׳. Perhaps we should read here also: על אשר כתב אשא משלי ואחודה.

caution. His order, too, I would rather not follow, but propose to give in chronological sequence all the Karaite literary opponents of Saadiah known to me, including also those who only indulged in occasional controversy against him. In any case, this sequence cannot be quite exact, inasmuch as there are no data respecting the lives of many Karaite authors, or the data extant are much confused and mutually contradictory, or, finally, they are fabricated intentionally. In order to make this survey clear, therefore, I shall enumerate these authors according to the centuries in which they lived.

TENTH CENTURY.

1. **Ben Zuṭa** (or **Ziṭa**). This otherwise little known Karaite, whose full name was Abu-l-Surri[1] b. Z., probably lived in Egypt, and disputed with Saadiah only by word of mouth, so that, strictly speaking, he does not belong to the *literary* opponents. If he did live in Egypt, he must have disputed with Saadiah whilst the latter was still very young. The substance of his polemical utterances, which are only known from references in Ibn Ezra, has already been fully dealt with in my *Miscellen über Saadja*, II[2], to which the reader may be referred.

2. **Ibn Sâqaweihi** (or **Saqûje**), one of the oldest Karaite authors, about whose personality we likewise know nothing[3]. He composed an anti-rabbinical work bearing the title כתאב אלפצׄאיח, "Book of Shameful Things" (i. e. of the Rabbanites), which consisted of the following ten sections:

[1] As Steinschneider rightly remarks (*Z. f. H. B.*, VI, 184), אלסרי can only correspond to the Arabic السرى. But then it must be transcribed al-Surri (and not, as hitherto, al-Sari), see Sujuti, "De nominibus relativis ed. Veth.," p. 136: السرى بالضم والتشديد الى سُرّ قرية بالرّىّ. In *Jew. Encycl.*, V, 105 a, ben Z. has the forename "Eleazar"!

[2] *Monatsschrift*, XLI, 203-12. Cf. also *J. Q. R.*, X, 256, and *R. É. J.*, loc. cit., 193-4.

[3] See Steinschneider, *Die arab. Liter. d. Juden*, pp. 45 and 281, no. 56 (also my *Zur jüdisch-arabischen Litteratur*, Berlin, 1904, p. 40).

(1) on the unity of God[1]; (2) on a branch of the Sabbath laws, viz. the kindling of lights; (3) on another branch of these laws, viz. on presents (or, on irrigation on Sabbath); (4) on the determination of the New Moon; (5) on the rule לא בד״ו פסח (hence on the validity of *Deḥijot*); (6) on leap-year; (7) on the prescriptions respecting forbidden fat; (8) on forbidden degrees of relationship; (9) on the prescriptions respecting menstruation; and (10) on pollution (בעל קרי). This work was preceded, by way of introduction, by a polemic against the Mishna, in which it was shown that the latter cannot be of divine origin. Ibn Sâqaweihi maintained therein, with regard to the subject-matter of the first four chapters, that the later Rabbis had erred in equal measure with the earlier ones; and with regard to the remaining six chapters, he was of opinion that here the later Rabbis had deviated from the earlier ones, and he sought to confirm this by proofs from the Talmud.

The work of Ibn Sâqaweihi thus comprised the entire scope of the controversy between Rabbanites and Karaites, dealing both with theological matters (anthropomorphism) as well as with matters of Halakha (Sabbath and festival laws, calendar science, and laws of diet, marriage, and cleanliness); and we should have had before us not a mere reply but an independent anti-rabbinical work (the oldest of its kind)[2]. It is probable, however, that this work was the result of Saadiah's activity, so that it rightly belongs to the category of works dealt with in this study.

[1] This section must be the source of Ibn Sâqaweihi's opinion, quoted by Moses ibn Ezra in his מקאלה אלחדיקה, that דמי in Ps. lxxxiii. 2 does not mean "to be silent" but "to be similar" (quoted by Harkavy in his *Notes to the Russian translation of Graetz*, vol. VI, p. ci): ... ולקר אפחש בעץ אלכֿוארג ענא פי שרח אלהים אל דמי לך פאנה מאל בה מן מעני אלסכות אלי מעני אלתשביה פכֿרג לה מן סו אלקיאס ואל תתנו דמי לו (Jes. lxii. 7) אן לא שבה לה תעאלי חתי הנבני ירושלם קיר בן סאקויה הדֿה אלכֿבאתֿ פי כתאב פצֿאיח לנפסה.

[2] Everything points to the positive inference that Ibn Sâqaweihi was a Karaite and not a sectarian *sui generis*, as Firkowitsch (see Gottlober, בקרת לתולדות הקראים, p. 149) asserts. Moses ibn Ezra (see Harkavy, ibid., p. c, and חורשים גם ישנים, VII, 33) places him in the same rank with Ḥivi al-Balkhi.

Express testimony to this effect is given by al-Hiti, who was intimately acquainted with Ibn Sâqaweihi's work, in the following words[1]: ובן סקויה רח את רד̈ עלי אלרבאנין ועלי אלפיומי פי אלהלאל ואלאביב ואלענצרה̈[2] ואלאליה ואלשחם ואלתקליד ואבטל נקלהם. This is the conclusion also to be derived from the fact that Saadiah, in his polemical work (about to be mentioned) against Ibn Sâqaweihi, already alludes to his principal work against the Karaites, the כתאב אלתמייז[3]. It is, therefore, probable that Ibn Sâqaweihi also had before him many polemical writings of Saadiah[4], which now provoked him to a counter-attack.

Of this polemical work of Saadiah, which bore the title כתאב אלרד̈ עלי אבן סאקויה, and of which only a few single quotations were known hitherto[5], some extensive fragments have now been discovered. One of these, belonging to the early part[6], contains the information about Ibn Sâqaweihi's work given above, as well as a part of the refutation of the first chapter, namely, the reproach that the Talmudists anthropomorphized the Deity[7]. A more extensive frag-

[1] *J. Q. R.*, IX, 435. Cf. ibid., X, 253, note 3, and *Z. f. H. B.*, II, 79.

[2] On the Feast of Weeks (i. e. on the controversy respecting ממחרת השבת) Ibn Sâqaweihi had no special section, but he doubtless dealt incidentally with this important theme in another section. Saadiah's views on this matter were preserved at the end of his כתאב אלתמייז. See *J. Q. R.*, XVI, 102–5.

[3] In the fragment soon to be mentioned, ed. Hirschfeld (*J. Q. R.*, XVI, 109). It is thus established anew that the controversial work against Ibn Sâqaweihi formed a separate work of Saadiah, and that therefore the correction is necessary in the words of Moses ibn Ezra: הגאון ז"ל כתב בספר המבחן [ו]בתשובותיו על בן סקויה האפיקורוס; resp. (in Arab. original): וקד ביין רבינו סעדיה גאון ז"ל פי כתאב אלתמייז [ו]פי רד̈ה עלי בן סאקויה צאחב כתאב אלפצאיח לנפסה, see ibid., p. 100, note 1.

[4] Above all his controversial work against 'Anân, which appeared in the year 915. See *J. Q. R.*, X, 241.

[5] Collected by me, ibid., 252 seq.

[6] Edited by Harkavy from the St. Petersburg Library, ibid., XIII, 662 seq. (partly also ibid., XVI, 112). Cf. also *R. É. J.*, XL, 88.

[7] It can therefore be assumed with Harkavy (p. 667, note 2) that the quotation from Saadiah in Judah b. Barzillai's Commentary on Jeṣira, p. 20, is perhaps likewise taken from the polemical work against Ibn Sâqaweihi (so that *J. Q. R.*, X, 255 should be corrected).

ment (consisting of six leaves)[1] contains the refutation of the sixth chapter (on leap-year; the beginning is missing of what seems to have been a very complete treatment of the subject), the seventh (on the fat tail, אליה, the use of which was forbidden by the Karaites, as opposed to the Rabbanites, see *Steinschneider-Festschrift*, p. 203, n. 3), and of the ninth chapter (on menstruation; the conclusion is missing). The refutation of the eighth chapter (on forbidden degrees of relationship) was thus not included in the work[2], probably because Saadiah composed a separate treatise on this subject[3]. Still another fragment[4], in which the objections against the Mishna are refuted, is perhaps likewise an offshoot of the work against Ibn Sâqaweihi, as the latter (as we saw above) attacked the Mishna in his own polemical writing, and Saadiah expressly states that he will follow up the refutation of the first four chapters with a defence of the Mishna[5]. In this fragment Saadiah does not address his words to a particular person, as in the other two, but speaks of "those people"[6].

The treatment that Saadiah accorded to Ibn Sâqaweihi in his work was not very generous. He usually calls him

[1] Edited by Hirschfeld from the Cambridge Geniza, *J. Q. R.*, XVI, 105–12. That this fragment belongs to the polemical work against Ibn Sâqaweihi is shown by the contents here presented, which correspond exactly to the order of the sections in the work of Ibn Sâqaweihi.

[2] This follows expressly from Saadiah's words (p. 110, l. 15): ואוׄ שרחנא אלגׄ אלאבואב מן אלו̇ אלאכׄידה̈ (r. אלאכׄירה̈) אלתי אדעא עלינא פיהא אנא כׄאלפנא קדמאנא וכשפנא מא קד תביין פינבגי אן נשרח אלג̇ [אל]באקיה̈ והי תמאם אלכתאב אלךׄ. On the division of the ten sections of Ibn Sâqaweihi into four and six, see above.

[3] Steinschneider's doubts (loc. cit., p. 49, no. 8) as to the existence of this work seem to me to be unfounded. Cf. my *Zur jüd.-arab. Litter.*, p. 42, and the Addenda at the end of the present dissertation, p. 99.

[4] Likewise edited by Harkavy, loc. cit., 656–7.

[5] See p. 663, l. 7 from bottom: ... וקדם (אי אבן סאקויה) קבל הוה אלי̇ אבואב אלטען עלי אלמשנה כיף יקאל אנהא ען משה רבינו ... פלדׄלך ארי אן אקד̈ם קבל ד̇כר אלו̇ אבואב אלאכׄירה̈ ד̇כר אלמשנה למוצׄע מא העלׄק פי הוׄה אלאבואב בשי מנהא ואמא אלד̇ אבואב אלאואיל פארד̈ עליהא פי מא שנע בה פיה קבל אחתגאגי לצחה̈ אלמשנה.

[6] See p. 656, l. 7 from bottom: ... ראית האולי אלקום יטענון בהא עלי אלמשנה אלךׄ.

"the ignoramus" (הדֿא אלגֿאהל), or "novice" (הדֿא אלגֿדיד), or "that fellow" (הדֿא אלאנסאן ,הדֿא אלרגֿל), applying to him the verses Psalm xxxi. 19, Prov. xviii. 3, and Job xiii. 5. He says that he has rightly called his work כתאב אלפצֿאיח, because he has revealed in it only his own shame and confusion.

Besides being mentioned in the special polemical work, Ibn Sâqaweihi is referred to in another fragment, the author of which, according to Harkavy, must also have been Saadiah. We there read[1]: ולא קאל בן סאק[ויה] באן אלצֿאים יגֿוז לה שרב אלסכנגֿבין אדֿא א . . א צ . . . מן אלדוא, i.e. "did not Ibn Sâqaweihi maintain that one who is fasting may drink *sakanjabin* (a sort of syrup prepared from sour wine), as it is to be regarded as medicine?"

3. **Abû Jûsuf Ja'qûb [b. Isaac b. Shemaja?] al-Qirqisâni** is rightly regarded as one of the foremost Karaite authorities, but the full extent of his literary importance has only become known in recent times[2]. His chief work was a complete commentary about the passages of the Pentateuch not bearing on law (פי שרח מעאני אלתוריה̈ אלתי הי גיר אלפראיץֿ), entitled כתאב אלריאץֿ ואלחדאיק "Book of Beds and Gardens," which had as introduction a complete compendium of law, entitled כתאב אלאנואר ואלמראקב "Book of Lights and Watch-towers." In the former work the date of composition, Rabia' II, 326 of the Hegira = Adar 1249 contr. (= 938), is expressly given[3]; and the second work, too, which claims our chief interest, was composed, according to Ibn al-Hiti, a year earlier, i.e. 325 of the Hegira (= 937)[4]. Qirqisâni was accordingly

[1] *Voskhod*, January, 1900, p. 83.

[2] Steinschneider details the literature on him, loc. cit., § 43 (supplemented in my *Zur jüd.-arab. Litter.*, p. 48). In these places everything is enumerated that has hitherto been edited of the works of Qirqisâni.

[3] See Neubauer, *Med. Jew. Chron.*, II, 249, l. 7 from bottom: ... פארֿא אצֿיף עלי דֿלך סני אלאסכנדר והי סני אלשטרות וגֿמלתה אלי סנה̈ שכֿו מן סני אלערב צאר אלף רמֿטֿ . . . ופיהא תם̈ תאליף הדֿא אלכתאב ודֿלך פי שהר אדר והו שהר רביע אלאכֿר. Cf. also Firkowitsch, בני רשף, p. 21.

[4] *J. Q. R.*, IX, 432: אלשיךֿ אלעאלם יעקב בן יצחק אלקרקסאני רח̇ את̇ תאריךֿ תצניפה

a contemporary of Saadiah, but, so far as is yet known, his name has not been found mentioned in the writings of the Gaon. Harkavy, indeed, conjectures [1] that the quotations from Saadiah found in Jehuda b. Barzillai's *Jeṣira* commentary are taken from a work directed against Qirqisâni. But it is much more probable that Jehuda b. Barzillai had before him the polemical work against Ibn Sâqaweihi [2], especially as only one of the *Agadot*, but not the second [3], defended by Saadiah, is cited by Qirqisâni. Moreover, it cannot yet be proved that Saadiah may have known the writings of his younger Karaite contemporary. On the other hand, Qirqisâni often quotes Saadiah and controverts him [4]; but unfortunately only a single long passage [5] from the "Book of Beds" and a few chapters from the "Book of Lights" have hitherto been published. Still, I shall adduce here all the passages known to me.

The Pentateuch commentary exists in a longer and a shorter version, and there are fragments of both in St. Petersburg and in the British Museum. In the published passage from the longer version, which deals with chronology, there is an anonymous rejoinder to Saadiah. After stating that the Bible in dealing with large numbers of years often omits smaller ones, e. g. one or two years, the writer concludes: ופי הד̇א כלה הדם אלעבור ופציחה̈ מן ידעי אנה קדים מנד̇ אול כ̇לק אלעאלם יג̇רי עלי סנן ואחד אלי הד̇ה אלגאיה̈ "From all this may be inferred the futility of the *'Ibbur* (i. e. of the permanent calendar) and the confusion of the one who has maintained that the calendar is very ancient, and that its rules have remained the same since the creation

אלאנואר סנה̈ אלף ומאיתין ת̇מאניה̈ וסבעין ללשטרות פיכון ד̇לך פי סנה̈ ٣١٥ ללהג̇רה̈. Both these dates do not agree, and we must correct וסבעין into וארבעין and ٣١٥ into ٣٢٥ (hence p. 437, note 1 must be rectified; in בני רשף, loc. cit., we rightly have 1248, Era of Contracts, but equally wrongly 315 of the Hegira).

[1] Introduction to Qirqisâni, p. 248.

[2] See above, p. 6.

[3] Cf. *J. Q. R.*, X, 255.

[4] Harkavy, loc. cit.

[5] See Neubauer, loc. cit. Cf. also my *Miscellen über Saadja*, III, p. 9, note 1 (= *Monatsschrift*, XLIV, 408, note 2).

of the world." As is well known, this was the theory of Saadiah.

In the *Kitâb al-'Anwâr*, of which I possess several excerpts in manuscript besides those printed, there are a few chapters exclusively devoted to the refutation of Saadiah, e.g. section xi, chap. 29, on forbidden degrees of relationship, and section xii, chaps. 15–16, on the use of the fat tail (אליה)[1]. Again, in other passages Saadiah is controverted incidentally (often anonymously), or he is the chief object of controversy: e.g. section ii, chap. 13, on Saadiah's theory about the age of the permanent calendar[2]; ibid., chaps. 14–15 (partly edited in *Z.f.H.B.*, III, 175), on the divinity and the necessity of the oral law; section xi, chap. 30 (edited in the *Kaufmann-Gedenkbuch*, p. 182; reprint, p. xiv), on the prohibition to marry a niece; section xii, chap. 7, on the wrenching off of a fowl's head (מליקה)[3]; ibid., chap. 10, on the eating of dead fish (Saadiah's name is not mentioned here, cf. *Z.f.H.B.*, IV, 74); ibid., chaps. 20–1 (edited loc. cit., p. 184; reprint, p. xvi) on the use of an embryo, &c. Similarly, according to Harkavy, Saadiah and his polemical work against 'Anân are meant in the following passage of the *Kitâb al-'Anwâr*, the section and chapter of which cannot be ascertained for the present[4]: וקד זעם בעץ מן יחתג ללרבאנין וירד̈ עלי מן זעם אן אלצלאה̈ מן אלתהלים אלך̇, i.e. "A Rabbanite has refuted the view that the prayers are to consist only of psalms," &c. As a matter of fact, this was a prescription of 'Anân, who endeavoured by this means to annul the hitherto prevalent order of prayer, because the latter went back upon tradition[5].

[1] See the headings of these chapters in *Steinschneider-Festschrift*, pp. 201, 203.

[2] *J. Q. R.*, XIII, 661: וקד כאן אלפיומי יקול אן אלעבור מן מוסי ת̇ם צאר אלאן יקול אנה מן אדם; hence the same as in the passage just mentioned from the Pentateuch commentary.

[3] See *Steinschneider-Festschrift*, p. 203, note 1, and *R. É. J.*, XLV, 196–7.

[4] See Harkavy, *Stud. u. Mitt.*, V, 107. The continuation in his *Otcherki*, I, 52, note 3.

[5] See, e.g., *Gan Eden*, fol. 71 a; *Adderet Elijahu*, ענין הפלה, chap. 5 (cf.

There is also a compendium of the *Kitâb al-'Anwâr* (Brit. Mus. MS., Or. 2525, Catalogue II, no. 588, cf. *Steinschneider-Festschrift*, p. 211), containing many controversial rejoinders to Saadiah, which had not yet been discovered in the main work: e. g. on the science of the calendar, where Saadiah's name is not expressly mentioned (fol. 44 a, seqq.; see *J. Q. R.*, VIII, 686); on incest (fol. 101 b, similar to section xi, chap. 29, of the main work; the passage may perhaps be taken from Saadiah's treatise on this subject, see above, p. 7, n. 3); on the idea of מים חיים (fol. 137 b; cf. *Z. f. H. B.*, IV, 17 seq.), &c.

We thus see that Qirqisâni also touches on all the points of difference between Rabbanites and Karaites. It must be observed, moreover, that of all the older Karaite authors Qirqisâni is most deeply versed in the Talmudic literature, and that his polemics are calm in tone and objective in character.

[4. **Menaḥem b. Michael b. Joseph** is the author of a poem with commentary on the laws of slaughtering[1], in which a controversy is directed quite clearly against a Rabbanite opponent. The superscription of this poem reads: זאת האגרת ששלח רבנו מנחם הקראי לעקלם הגר אצל ר׳ סעדיה הרבן על אדות הלכות שחיטה. Pinsker identifies the latter with Saadiah Gaon, makes Menaḥem his contemporary, and maintains that Menahem indulged in polemics against the

also Harkavy, *Stud. u. Mitt.*, VIII, 1, 203). In another passage Qirqisâni reproaches the Rabbanites for not taking prayers [exclusively?] from the Psalms (sect. 1, chap. 3; ed. Harkavy, p. 286: ומן ד̇לך אנהם אסקטו אלצלאה̈ מן ספר תהלות וג̇עלוהא ממא אלפוה הם אלך̇). A sectarian, Malik al-Ramli, prescribed that Ps. xxix should take the place of the Eighteen Benedictions, probably in agreement with the dictum of Hillel, the son of Samuel b. Naḥmani, in *Berachot*, 28 b. See Harkavy, *Voskhod*, Jan., 1900, p. 79. Similarly Petaḥia relates of the heretics in the land of Kedar: ואינם מתפללין אלא מזמורים וכשספר להם הר"ר פתחיה התפלה שלנו וברכת המזון היה טוב בעיניהם (cf. Harkavy, *Altjüd. Denkmäler*, p. 106). Cf. also the Responsa of Levi b. Ḥabib, no. 79: שהמינים בישראל אין להם ברכות מסודרות ומתוקנות אלא .. כל תפלתן היא זמירות ופסוקים וכו׳.

[1] Edited from a Leyden MS. (Cat. Steinschneider, no. 41[6]) by Pinsker, p. 55 seq.

Gaon[1]. But this identification can hardly be considered correct, because the language of Menaḥem points clearly to a Byzantine Karaite, e. g. גבול for "definition" (p. 59, l. 7), יענה in the sense of "i. e." (= Arab. يعنى; ibid., l. 28), expressions that the ancient Karaites in the East do not know. Consequently our poem cannot have been directed against Saadiah. Menaḥem belongs to a much later time, and is adduced here only for the purpose of showing that he does not belong to the category of the Karaite authors dealt with here by us. The lifetime of Menaḥem can, in any case, be determined with a certain probability. On the one hand, he is doubtless identical with the Karaite liturgical poet, Menaḥem b. Michael, of whose writings we possess (among others) a Zion Ode[2], so that he could not have composed any poetry before Jehuda Halevi. On the other hand, he is already cited by Aaron b. Joseph in the *Mibḥar* (composed 1294) on Gen. xxvii. 3 (ed. fol. 50 b). We shall therefore not go wrong if we assume that he flourished somewhere in the second half of the twelfth century. For other proofs of a later date, see Geiger (אוצר נחמד, IV, 31) and Schorr (החלוץ, VI, 76).]

It is thus established that only three Karaites disputed with Saadiah during his lifetime. The other two, who, according to Sahl, likewise refuted the Fayyumite during his life, certainly developed their main literary activity after the demise of the Gaon. This is also true of

5. **Salmon b. Jeroḥam** (Arab. **Sulejmân b. Ruḥeim**), about the circumstances of whose life we possess hardly

[1] It is superfluous to enter into the other identifications of Pinsker (such as that of Menaḥem b. Michael with Menaḥem ha-Giṣni, &c.), as their impossibility has long been proved.

[2] Begins ציון תקונן עלי בנים יקרים מפז ("Karaite Prayer Book," ed. Wilna, 1890, I, 134; cf. Landshut, *Amude ha-Aboda*, p. 76). Other liturgical poems of Menaḥem are: two Kinnot, כנור ועוגב לקול בוכים and משכנותי חצרותי הציתו קרח ויעלם (ibid., I, 127 and 135), and a Seliḥa, beginning אלהי אצוק נגדך שיחתי (ibid., III, 316; cf. Pinsker, p. 139, no. 25; lacking in Luzzatto, נחלת שד"ל, in אוצר טוב, 1884, p. 4).

any authentic information [1]. His Hebrew polemical work against Saadiah, written in wretched rhymes, is the only one that has been preserved from remote times, and this has been only partly edited. It was possibly composed while Saadiah was yet alive, about 940. I have already analysed its contents thoroughly in another connexion, and referred there especially to its snarling tone [2]. Salmon wanted to render this work into Arabic too for the people, but we do not know whether this was carried out. In any case no Arabic version has been preserved.

Besides this polemical work Salmon also composed a series of Biblical commentaries, which were probably all issued in the sixth decade of the tenth century (i.e. after Saadiah's death), and which have been preserved partly in the original Arabic, partly in a Hebrew translation. Here, too, aggressive war is waged against Saadiah [3], especially in the Commentary on Psalms (MS. in St. Petersburg). Salmon speaks here of Saadiah as of a completely unknown man (ושאהדת פי עצרי רגלא יוערף באלפיומי), and refutes his view that the Psalms might be recited as prayers only in the Temple and only with musical accompaniment [4]. Then he also controverts another view of Saadiah, that entire psalms are prophecies of David, and that the royal minstrel had assigned many of them to the sons of Moses and to other Levites, to be sung [5].

[1] See in particular Steinschneider, loc. cit., § 40 (also ibid., p. 340).

[2] *J. Q. R.*, VIII, 684 seq. I have since published many more passages from it, thus ibid., X, 271; *Z. f. H. B.*, III, 172; and *Kaufmann-Gedenkbuch*, p. 186.

[3] Sahl's statement, quoted above, is thus confirmed, that Salmon conducted his campaign against Saadiah in his lifetime as well as after his death.

[4] See the passage in question in Neubauer, *Studia Biblica*, III, 18. It is not difficult to see that Saadiah with this assertion aimed at an ordinance of 'Anân. See above, p. 10, n. 5.

[5] Ibid., p. 19. According to Saadiah, e.g., the heading למשה in Ps. xc means as much as לבני משה (he points to Judges i. 3, where יהודה and שמעון likewise stand for בני יהודה and בני שמעון), the heading לשלמה, in Ps. lxxii,

On Psalm cii. 14 there is a rather long excursus on the reckoning of the year of redemption, where likewise a vigorous attack is made on Saadiah. I have edited in full and thoroughly discussed this excursus [1], which Salmon again repeats almost verbally on Canticles ii. 11. On Psalm civ. 19 Salmon quotes his כתאב אלרד̈ עלי אלפיומי, but it is doubtful whether he means here the Hebrew or the Arabic work [2]. In connexion with cxl. 6 is related the often discussed fact that Saadiah denied that the Talmud speaks of physical struggles between the followers of Shammai and those of Hillel. This passage has also been thoroughly examined by me [3].

In the commentaries on Echa and Kohelet, the only ones that I saw complete in the original Arabic, I found nothing polemical against Saadiah and especially nothing objectionable against the Rabbanites, who are elsewhere so violently attacked by Salmon [4]. Perhaps, therefore, Steinschneider is right in doubting their genuineness [5], which has yet, in any case, to be established.

Finally, it may be mentioned that, according to Ibn al-Hiti, Salmon died in Aleppo during Saadiah's lifetime. The latter is said to have followed the funeral procession and to have pronounced a eulogy on the departed. All this naturally belongs to the realm of fiction (from mere chronological considerations), but still it is possible that Salmon indeed died in Aleppo [6]. We now know that Saadiah stayed in this town, even before his appointment as Gaon (about 921) [7], but at that time Salmon was just a new-born babe.

is equal to "on Solomon," &c. Even David's authorship of any psalm is not to be disputed.

[1] "Miscellen über Saadja," III, Berlin, 1901 (reprint from *Monatsschrift*, XLIV, 400–16 and 508–29).

[2] See Pinsker, p. 133.

[3] *Kaufmann-Gedenkbuch*, pp. 169 seq. (For a correction see my תהלה לדוד, Warsaw, 1902, p. 16; cf. also *Monatsschrift*, XLVI, 376.)

[4] See *J. Q. R.*, VIII, 689; XIII, 337.

[5] *Hebr. Bibliog.*, XIII, 103 (cf. *R. É. J.*, XLI, 305).

[6] See *Z. f. H. B.*, II, 79.

[7] In a letter to his pupils, dated 922, on the dispute about the Calendar

6. **Ḥasan** (or **Ḥusein**) **ben Mashiaḥ**[1], according to the above-cited account of Sahl, wrote polemics against Saadiah both in his lifetime and after his death. He is also said to have tried to hold a dispute with the Gaon verbally, but the latter roughly repulsed him. He succeeded, however, in obtaining one of Saadiah's anti-Karaite writings (which the author is said never to have allowed to leave his possession), and refuted it immediately (in a separate work?)[2]. It is, of course, difficult to establish how much truth is contained in this report, but in any case Ben Mashiaḥ ought to be a contemporary of Saadiah, although a considerably younger one. According to Ibn al-Hiti, who often had good information at his disposal, Ben Mashiaḥ, who lived in Bagdad, disputed with his fellow-townsman, the Christian physician, Abû 'Ali 'Isa b. Zar'a. The latter wrote his polemical work against the Jews in the year 387 of the Hegira (=997), and if we assume that this disputation took place before the appearance of this work, that is, about a few years before 997, and that Ben Mashiaḥ was already an old man then, he can hardly have been engaged in literary activity before 940. Hence al-Hiti is quite right in coupling him with Salmon b. Jeroḥam, as they were of about the same age[3].

with Ben Meir, Saadiah says : דע כי בעודני בחלב באו מקצת התלמידים מבעל גד וכו׳ (*Saadyana*, ed. Schechter, p. 25, l. 12 ; cf. *J. Q. R.*, IX, 37, and *R. É. J.*, XLVIII, 149, note 3).

[1] For the literature about him refer to my article in *Jew. Encycl.*, s. v. (VI, 247 ; where, however, the determination of the period of his life must be modified in accordance with the present conclusions), and *Zur jüd.-arab. Litter.*, p. 47.

[2] Pinsker, p. 37 : ... וגם לא היה (ר״ל סעדיה) מביא אליו כי אם את אשר הוא חפץ . . . ובן משיח הקציר נפשו מביניהם (?) והביא אותו חדר בחדר עד שצעק ואמר מה לי ולך מעלי. והספרים אשר כתב לא הוציאם בחייו מתחת ידו על בני מקרא ואחד מהם נפל ביד בן משיח והשיב עליו בחייו וכו׳. For continuation see above, p. 3.

[3] See *J. Q. R.*, IX, 434 : ... אלשיכ֗ין אבו אלחסן (sic) בן משיח וסלמון בן ירוחם כאנא פי זמאן אלפיומי וכאן בן משיח נאקצ֗ה מנאקצ֗את כת֗ירה֗ פי בגדאד ובן ירוחם נאקצ֗ה פי חלב . . . ואבו [עלי] עיסי בן סרעה֗ (l. זרעה֗) פי רסאל֗ה֗ אלת[א]ם סבעין(?) רד֗ פיהא עלי אליהוד ת֗ם אנה באבן משיח אלמד֗כור ותנאדרא (l. ותנאט֗רא) הו והו ואלרסאלה֗ אלמד֗כורה֗ תאריכ֗ה עמלהא סנה֗ ٣٨٧. The date 387 is confirmed by Ibn abi Oṣeibia (ed. Müller, I, 236, l. 10 from bottom). Ibn Zar'a was born in August, 943,

Of Ben Mashiaḥ's polemics against Saadiah, we are principally acquainted with a passage directed against the Gaon's defence of the antiquity of the present calendar-system, in which Ben Mashiaḥ refers to "Sadducean writings (כתבי צדוקים, כתב אלצדוקיה), which are known among the people." This passage has been preserved in Arabic, in a commentary on Exodus, of which Sahl or perhaps even Ben Mashiaḥ himself is the author, and in Hebrew in a fragment that originates from Hadassi[1]. Besides this, a MS. has been recently published, in which Ben Mashiaḥ reproduces a complete Hebrew treatise on the calendar of an otherwise unknown Rabbanite, Joshua b. 'Alân[2], and which writing perhaps originally formed the constituent part of a polemical work by Ben Mashiaḥ.

7. **'Abû 'Anân Isaac b. 'Ali b. Isaac** was, according to Ibn al-Hiti, an important Karaite scholar, who in a special work, entitled כתאב אלסראג (?), tilted his controversial pen against Saadiah among others. I have already compiled in another place the little that is known about him, and there shown that he probably flourished about the middle of the tenth century[3].

8. **Abu-l-Ṭajjib al-Jebeli** (Hebr. **Samuel b. Asher b. Manṣûr**)[4] is also mentioned by Sahl among the Karaites who wrote polemical works against Saadiah after his death. According to Ibn al-Hiti, he is said to have been a contemporary of Abu-l-Faraj Harûn; but as the latter flourished about 1026, al-Jebeli could hardly have been cited by Sahl. According to a further account of Ibn al-Hiti, al-Jebeli disputed with the head of a school, Menaḥem, after he became acquainted with a work of a son of Menaḥem

and died at the beginning of May, 1008; see *Fihrist*, I, 264; II, 121. Cf. also Steinschneider, *Polem. u. apolog. Literatur*, pp. 146-7.

[1] Both versions are published and discussed by me in *R. É. J.*, XLV, 176-7, where all particulars may be found.

[2] Edited in הצפירה, 1899, nos. 141-2, and again in הגרן, IV, 75 (cf. *Zur jüd.-arab. Litter.*, l. c.).

[3] See ibid., pp. 15, 16.

[4] See on him my short article in *Jew. Encycl.*, VII, 16a.

addressed to a certain Abû Ṯâbit[1]. If this Menaḥem, as I conjecture, is identical with another of the same name, who addressed inquiries in Arabic to Saadiah (see הגרן, I, 91)[2], then al-Jebeli could likewise have composed his polemical work about the middle of the tenth century.

9. **'Ali b. Ḥasan** (or **Ḥusein**) likewise figures in Sahl's list among Saadiah's disputants, but there are no particulars known about him. Pinsker (p. קיא) identifies him with the grandfather of Levi b. Jefet, who, in his *Muqaddima* (ibid., p. 64, where 'Ali b. אלחסן), mentions a commentary on the Pentateuch by him. Accordingly, 'Ali, as he was the father of Jefet, would have flourished about 960–70. But there is a lack of sufficient proof for this, and, besides, the authenticity of the *Muqaddima* is not quite free from doubt[3].

10. **David b. Abraham al-Fâsi** is the author of a comprehensive and voluminous Hebrew dictionary in Arabic, bearing the title אגרון or כתאב גאמע אלאלפאט. Pinsker and Neubauer have published detailed specimens from it, and placed the author in the second half of the tenth century, soon after Saadiah. On the other hand, there was no lack of attempts, especially on the part of Schorr, to place him in the twelfth century, after Ibn Ezra. But one will have to decide for the first date[4]. In this lexicon Saadiah is

[1] *J. Q. R.*, IX, 435: ואלשיך שמואל בן אשר בן מנצור אלמערוף באבו אלטייב אלגבלי כאן פי זמאן אלשיך אבר (אבי .l) אלפרג̇ הארון ותנאצ̇רא (=והנאט̇רא) פי אלאביב ואלסנה̈ אלשרעיה̈ וכאן עלי ראי אלמולי אבו עלי רח̇ את̇ ולה מקאלה̈ פי אפסאד אלמחזור וחסאב אלמולד ורד̈ עלי מנחם ראש מתיבא ענד וקופה עלי רקעה̈ בן מנחם אלי אבי ת̇אבת אידה את̇. Al-Jebeli's work against the Maḥzor-cycle and the calculation of the Molad must be identical with the polemical treatise against Saadiah, as these subjects form the principle theme of polemics. When Ibn al-Hiti says further, that al-Jebeli was of the opinion of Abu 'Ali, i. e. Jefet, one need not yet conclude from this that he followed him, but that their opinions on this point were in agreement.

[2] Cf. Steinschneider, *Arab. Liter. d. Juden*, § 30 (and also ibid., p. 339).

[3] Cf. also Steinschneider, *J. Q. R.*, X, 539, and my *Zür jüd.-arab. Litter.*, p. 49, l. ult.

[4] See the literature dealing with the matter in Steinschneider, pp. 86 and 341, and in Bacher, *Jew. Encycl.*, s. v. (IV, 459, 460).

quoted twice s.v. דש (Pinsker, p. 108), and his interpretation of the verses Gen. i. 11, 12, is refuted. In these verses the yielding of fruit-bearing trees only is mentioned, not of ordinary trees (see Naḥmanides on the passage). Now Saadiah must have explained ver. 11 in such a way, that the latter are to be understood by עץ פרי, i.e. trees that are a fruit of the earth, as opposed to fruit-bearing trees, which are עשה פרי. Ver. 12 is shortened, and should also read here עץ [פרי] עשה פרי. This explanation of Saadiah, which is combated by David b. Abraham, is, however, in contradiction to the Gaon's translation of the particular two verses.

11. **Abu Sa'id (?) David b. Boaz**, the Prince (אלרייס, הנשיא), according to a genealogical list of Solomon the Prince (Pinsker, p. 53), was in the fifth generation of descent from 'Anân. Hence David would have flourished about 910 (approximately 5×30=150 years after 'Anân), and have been a contemporary of Saadiah. On the other hand, according to Ibn al-Hiti, David composed his commentary on Kohelet in the year 383 of the Hegira (=993), and was mentioned even after Levi b. Jefet by the Solomon referred to[1], so that David would belong to the last quarter of the tenth century. This date seems to me also to be the more correct, principally because David, so far as is yet known, is first quoted by Joseph al-Baṣîr in the ספר המועדים[2]. Hadassi also mentions him between Jefet and his son[3], though this may be accidental.

Of David's works Ibn al-Hiti mentions, besides the commentary on Kohelet, still another on the Pentateuch and a book on the principles of religion (כתאב אלאצול)[4].

[1] *J. Q. R.*, IX, 432: ואלסייד דוד בן בועז רח̈ את̈ תצניפה קהלת פי סנה̈ שפ״ג ללהג̈רה . . . . לאנה (אי שלמה הנשיא) ד̈כר אולא : and ibid. ; ולה תפסיר אלתורה וכתאב אלאצול ענן ת̈ם בנימין ת̈ם דניאל ת̈ם אלקרקסאני ת̈ם אבו אלסרי ה̈ם אבו ע̈לי אלבצרי וולדה ת̈ם דוד בן בועז אלנשיא ת̈ם אלמ̈עלם אבו עלי (?) רחמה̈ את̈ ע̈ליהם אג̈מעין.

[2] See the passage in Pinsker, p. 199 (cf. also ibid., p. קיא).

[3] *Eshkol*, 241, ם: . . . . פשרונם תמצא בספר אוצר הנחמד ובספר הורת כהנים [של] המלמדים סהל ויפת ודוד הנשיא וכן (ובן .l) יפ̈ת נ״ע יחד וכו׳

[4] The composition of such a work also points rather to a post-Saadyanic Karaite than to a contemporary.

Of the Pentateuch commentary there have been preserved only considerable parts in MS., namely, on Leviticus and on the second half of Deuteronomy in St. Petersburg; on Exod. xxv. 1–xxxiii. 13 in the British Museum (Catalogue Margoliouth, Vol. I, No. 384), and, in addition, on the whole of Exodus in a modern copy in the Karaite synagogue in Jerusalem[1]. According to Harkavy (*Z. A. T. W.*, I, 157), David, in the St. Petersburg MS., frequently controverted Saadiah, not expressly naming him, however, but only designating him as הדׄא אלרגׄל. In the London MS. there are two such passages (fol. 19 a on xxv. 32 and fol. 31 b on xxvii. 4), and in both the discussion is about the construction of appurtenances of the tabernacle[2].

Besides this MS. of the British Museum, Margoliouth has been trying to show that some other MSS. of the same collection also have David as their author, but the demonstration is not everywhere quite convincing[3]. We have to consider only two of them here. The one (MS. Or. 2494[1]; Cat. No. 318[1]) contains a commentary on the first pericope of Leviticus (the beginning and end are missing), and in two passages (ff. 1b, 4b) there is a hit at the הדׄא אלרגׄל. The second is much more important (Or. 2495; Cat. No. 306). This MS., of which I have a copy of a few excerpts, contains a very detailed commentary on Lev. xi. 1–xv. 25. Of authors mentioned here besides the Talmudists (designated אלאולון and אלרבאנין) and 'Anân, only Saadiah is very often cited[4], sometimes as אלפיומי, sometimes also as הדׄא אלרגׄל, his name being accompanied by the formula רחׄ אללה. The points on which Saadiah's views are combated naturally concern the laws of purity, but they are mostly questions of subordinate

[1] See Steinschneider, § 39 (also ibid., p. 340).

[2] See the beginning of both passages in Margoliouth's Catalogue, where Saadiah is referred to in the one as ודׄלך אלרגׄל, and in the other as הדׄא אלרגׄל. In this MS. David is also called אבו סעיד דוד בן בועז קרא (the entire MS. is otherwise, without exception, written with Arabic letters).

[3] Cf. *R. É. J.*, XLI, 305, 306.

[4] See the list of passages in Margoliouth's Catalogue.

importance. Once (fol. 181 a, on xv. 25; see further, p. 25) the prescriptions about menstruous women are also discussed. The controversy is conducted calmly and pertinently. Different expressions are adduced, e.g.: אד טאהר אלנץ לם יקתצי דלך (fol. 47 a)[1]; והדא איצא פאסד (ibid.); בטל מא אורדה (fol. 78 a); פקד רדנא עליה מא יסקט קולה (fol. 179 b); גמלה מא קאלה . . . לא יצחחה אלנטר ולא אלכתאב (fol. 182 a), &c. Thus, unlike the Karaite custom elsewhere observed, only views but not personalities are combated. In one passage the author refutes an opinion of Saadiah, which is really that of the Talmud (viz., the well-known explanation of בין דם לדם in Deut. xvii. 8, that what is intended here is a decision respecting the pure and impure blood of a menstruous woman, see Sifre, ad loc., and parallel passages), and he refers to his own commentary on this verse (fol. 165 a): . . . אעלם אן גמיע מא קאלה (אי אלפיומי) לא יצח מנה שי ודלך באן קולה בין דם לדם הו פי דם נדה דעוי ולכצמה אן יקול הו פי דם נפשות אלדי תקע בין שוגג אלי מזיד פיחתאג אלי פקה כהן גדול אד הו מעלק בה ואיצא קולה דבר למשפט ידל אן דלך כורג מנה ואנמא אלקצאץ אלדי יקתל ען אמר אלחאכם וליס דם נדה וזבה מן דברי המשפט ולא דברי ריב בל הו מן אלמצות אלדי תערפהא אלנסא כמא יערפו אלרגאל שכבת זרע וליס פיה טאהר וקד בינא פי תפסיר הדא אלפסוק מא ידל עלי אן הדא פאסד אלך[2]. The Karaite author doubtless used as his source in every case Saadiah's commentary on the Pentateuch, and we should thus possess here important fragments of this vanished work.

12. **Jefet b. 'Ali ha-Levi** (Arab. **Abû 'Ali Hasan b. 'Ali al-Baṣri**) must have flourished in the last quarter of the tenth century[3]. He is the most prolific Karaite exegete of

[1] See the whole passage in *R. É. J.*, XLV, 56.

[2] Perhaps the Samaritan Munajja b. Ṣedâqa also disputes with Saadiah on this point; see Wreschner, *Samarit. Traditionen*, p. 33. Cf. also *Keter Tora*, ad loc. (fol. 20 b).

[3] His commentary on Daniel, which is apparently one of his latest commentaries (perhaps even the latest), appeared about the year 1000. See D. S. Margoliouth's preface to his edition of this commentary (Oxford, 1889), p. v.

the Bible, for he has translated the entire twenty-four books of Scripture into Arabic and commented upon them very fully, partly at least in two recensions (Pentateuch, Psalms ?; see *R.É.J.*, XLI, 306). The commentaries of Jefet, especially that on the Pentateuch, afford very much valuable material for the history of the older Karaite literature and theology; but of the many MSS. extant in St. Petersburg, London, Oxford, Paris, Berlin, &c., unfortunately only a comparatively small portion has been edited [1].

According to Sahl, Abû ʿAli Ḥasan al-Baṣri, i. e. Jefet, likewise combated Saadiah in a special work, which is further corroborated by Jefet's own statements. The composition of such a work is promised in the passage on Gen. i. 14. After Jefet advances controversial arguments about the calendar against Saadiah in very thorough fashion [2], he adds that he has entered into this dispute only incidentally, because his main purpose is to present here an exposition of Holy Writ. But should God vouchsafe him the time, then he will refute the views of Saadiah in a special treatise (. . . ויגב אן יעלם אלקאר פי הדֿא אלבאב אני לם אקצד אלתעד̈ץ בראס אלמתיבה או בגירה מן מכֿאלפי אלקראיין ואנמא למא כאן חרד אלכלאם פי באב אלמטאלבה ואסתקצֿא עליהם נֿהדה דֿכרת עיון מטאלבאתה ואלרד̈ עליהא באכֿתצאר לאנה כתאב תפסיר ולא יחתמל אלאתסאע ואן פסח אללה פי אלעמר פרדת להדֿא אלבאב כתאב יחתוי עלי גֿמיע מא אתֿבתה פי כתבה מן כתב אלתפאסיר וגירהא ואטֿהר מא עליה פי כל באב ובאב אן שא אללה תעֿ אלךֿ). On the other hand, in the passage on Exod. xxxv. 3 (published by Pinsker, p. 20), he quotes this controversial treatise as already in existence: . . . ודֿלך במא רדדת בה עלי מדעייה פי אלכתאב אלדֿי אלפת לה. Jefet's polemical work, like many others, is now lost,

[1] A review of the known and available MSS. and of the parts edited so far is given by Steinschneider in *Die arab. Liter. d. Juden*, § 44 (also ibid., p. 341, and *Zur jüd.-arab. Litter.*, p. 49; add the MS. no. 234 of the library of the Alliance isr. univ. in Paris, containing the comm. on Lev. xxvi. 38–xxvii, cf. *R. É. J.*, XLIX, 286, and the translation of Gen. viii. 1–22, and ix. 18–28, printed in Kahle, *Die arab. Bibelübersetzungen*, pp. 29–31).

[2] See *J. Q. R.*, X, 246.

and we do not know whether he composed it in Arabic, like all his other works, or in Hebrew, like a work directed against Jacob b. Samuel, to be mentioned below. But although Jefet maintains that he will not expand his commentary by a controversy with Saadiah or with other opponents of the Karaites, he does nevertheless indulge in polemics, especially in the Pentateuch commentary, very often and very thoroughly against the ראס אלמתיבה, and quotes rather long passages both from anti-Karaite works as well as from the Bible commentaries of Saadiah[1]. I now proceed to give a survey of the passages in question from Jefet's commentaries, so far as I have them before me either in printed form or in manuscript excerpts[2]. I arrange them according to subject-matter, and must observe that here especially Jefet very often repeats himself verbally.

1. On the justification of the Oral Law in general, its divinity and necessity: Exod. xxi. 33 (here Jefet defends very thoroughly especially the method of analogy, היקש, קיאס, applied by the Karaites) and Dan. xii. 4 (ed. D. S. Margoliouth, p. 141). Contrary to his usual custom, Jefet uses, in the last passage, very harsh words, and says that Saadiah and his party, in maintaining that one must, without personal investigation, follow the representatives of the prophets, that is, the teachers of the Mishna and Talmud, have thereby led Israel into ruin, and so forth[3]. Jefet treats

[1] See ibid., 241 seq., the passages from Saadiah's anti-Karaite writings preserved by Jefet. Saadiah's commentary on the Pentateuch, e.g., is expressly mentioned by Jefet on Gen i. 14: . . . כמא קלת פי תפסיר הדה אלקצה פי בראשית והו קולך וקולה ולהבדיל בין היום ובין הלילה ישיר אלך; Exod. xxi. 33: . . . תם מע דלך פאנא וגדנא לה פי הפסיר ואלה שמות פי ושמתי לך מקום אשר ינוס יקול אלך; xxiii. 15: . . . ולך אנה חכי ענהם אלפיומי פי פצל מכת צפרדעים מא הודא נחכיה חרף בחרף והו קולה אלך; xxiv. 4: ואמא אלפיומי פקד אבדע עלי כתאב אללה תע . . . כמק פי תפסיר הדא אלמוצע חרף בחרף אלך; Lev. xviii. 6: . . . פהדה חכאיה מא דהב אליה אלפיומי פי תפסיר הדה אלפסוק וזעם אלך.

[2] I use copies from the most varied libraries.

[3] . . . פהדה אלאקאויל ונטראוהא הדל עלי בטלאן קול אצחאב אלתקליד מתל קול אלפיומי יגירה אלדין אהלכו ישראל במא דונו וקאלו ליס יגוז אן הערף פראיץ אללה תע מן אלבחת . . . ויגב אלתקליד לכלפא אלאנביא והם אצחאב אלמשנה ואלתלמוד . . . פאמגי אלנאס בכתבה אלמזכרפה אלך. Cf. also my conclusions in *R. É. J.*, XLI, 183 seq.

this subject also in some other passages of his commentaries, and disputes here with the Rabbanites in general. He clearly hints at Saadiah in the passage on Deut. xxxiii. 14, and there employs similar expressions to those used in the Daniel passage: ויمכן אן יכון מעתמד ללקול אלבאטל ליצ̈ל אלנאס ען אלחק̈ במא ילבס עליהם באקאויל מזכרפה̈ נשאהא פי כתבה אלך.

2. Questions of calendar-science: hence the rise and age of the present calendar, validity of the *Deḥijot*, fixing of leap-years, &c.—questions that are known to have been in the very centre of the controversy between Rabbanites and Karaites. The chief passage is Gen. i. 14 (partly edited *J. Q. R.*, X, 246 seq.; cf. also above), where Saadiah's theory about the great age of the calendar-system is quoted from his *Kitâb al-tamjiz* and the Pentateuch commentary and very thoroughly refuted. There further belong to this section: Gen. viii. 3 (the chronology of the Flood is here considered, and various questions of calendar-lore are discussed; cf. *J. Q. R.*, X, 241); xlix. 14 (partly the same as on i. 14; cf. ibid., 248, n. 2; Saadiah's proof from 1 Chron. xii. 33 is chiefly refuted here)[1]; Exod. xii. 2 (see ibid., 248, n. 3, and 253); xxiii. 15 (on the determination of the אביב, hence on the question of the intercalary month; in two versions); xxxiv. 18 (on the same subject; Jefet refers here to the second version of his commentary on xii. 2 וקד רדינא עליה פי החדש הזה לכם פי אלנסכה̈ אלאכרה̈ במא פיה כפאיה̈); Lev. xxiii. 3 (partly the same as on Gen. i. 14); xxiii. 5 (likewise in two versions; see *J. Q. R.*, X, 249 and 253); Deut. xvi. 1 (see ibid., 250 and 253); xxxiii. 18 (likewise on the proof from 1 Chron. xii. 33); and 1 Sam. xx. 27 (see ibid., 251). In many of these passages Jefet affords interesting material also about the history of the calendar among various sectarians and kindred matter (see e.g., ibid., 265, n. 2).

[1] The same thing is again repeated by Sahl (in Pinsker, p. 37; cf. further *infra*, p. 39), Levi b. Jefet in his ספר המצות (see כרם חמד, VIII, 56), Jeshua b. Jehuda (בראשית רבא, MS. Leyden, 41[2], f. 89 b), and Aaron b. Elias (גן עדן, f. 4 c; the latter two without mentioning Saadiah).

3. The kindling of fire on the Sabbath, a question likewise often discussed in Karaite polemics. The Karaites, as is well known, not only prohibit the kindling of fire on the Sabbath, but even the continued burning of anything—a severity derived, as I have shown (*R. É. J.*, XLIV, 174 seq.), from the expanded meaning of the word מלאכה. Jefet often deals with this subject, viz. Exod. iii. 2; xx. 10 (Saadiah is mentioned here only cursorily at the end: ... ונחן נתכלם פי תחרים סראג אלסבת כלאם אוסע מן הדֹא פי לא תבערו אש אלדֹי הו מוצֹע אלחאגה וננקץ גמיע מא דֹכרה ראס אלמתיבה בעון אללה); xxxv. 3 (this is the detailed passage to which Jefet previously refers; Saadiah's entire proofs are here adduced and thoroughly refuted; cf. Pinsker, pp. 18, 90); Lev. xxiii. 3 (completely the same as on Exod. xxxv. 3); Deut. v. 13 (here Saadiah is adduced only anonymously: ... פאן קאל קאיל אן וַיְּבַעֵר הו מנעטף עלי אלנאר תגדהא פי אלעבראני מונתה קיל לה אלך; this conception of the word in Judges xv. 5 is that of Saadiah); xxv. 4 (see *J. Q. R.*, X, 251).

4. On the time of sacrificing the Paschal offering: Exod. xii. 6. This question is notably linked together with the Karaite interpretation of the concept בין הערבים, which deviates essentially from the Rabbinical: see my remarks in *R. É. J.*, XLV, 176 seq.

5. The fixing of the time of Pentecost, i.e. the interpretation of ממחרת השבת, one of the differences that the Karaites have taken from the Boethusians (see *Monatsschrift*, XLI, 206, and *J. Q. R.*, XVI, 407): Lev. xxiii. 15 (edited by Hirschfeld, *Arabic Chrestomathy*, p. 109 seq., Jefet's most detailed passage on this subject; cf. also *J. Q. R.*, X, 250, n. 2); Num. xxxiii. 3 (here Jefet refers to the former passage: ... וקד כנא אוסענא אלכלאם פי אלרד עלי ראס אלמתיבה פי מא אחתאג ללרבוניין פי אתבאת מדאהבהם פי וספרתם לכם ממחרת השבת אלך); Deut. xvi. 9 (very detailed; Saadiah is not expressly mentioned here, but is designated as הדֹא אלרגל, once also as בעץֹ אלנאם ללרבאנין); Joshua v. 11 (here also Saadiah is cited only anonymously: פקד גלט מן טןֹ אן ממחרת הפסח הו

יום סתה עשר אלך); Ezek. xlvi. 12 (here also שבת signifies not festival, but Sabbath; cf. further below).

6. Laws of Purity. Of the differences existing between Rabbanites and Karaites on this point, the prescriptions about menstruous women come in specially for consideration. There are two points in particular, one concerning the interpretation of דמי טהרה in Lev. xii. 5, where the Karaites follow the severe view of the Sadducees (see Geiger, *Jüd. Zeitschrift,* II, 27; cf. also below), and the other dealing with the determination of the colours in the impure blood of a menstruous woman, which, according to the Talmud, is five-fold (see, e.g., Aaron b. Elia, גן עדן, fol. 110 a seqq.; cf. also *Z. f. H. B.*, IV, 20). Jefet combats Saadiah on the first point, on Lev. xii. 7 (Saadiah says here, among other things, one must, according to Prov. xxii. 28, follow the wise: וזעם אן אלחכמים אוגבו דלך וקד וגב קבול דלך מנהם לקול אלכתאב אל תסג גבול עולם אשר עשו אבותיך אלך, and this leads Jefet to a short digression on the Oral Law); and on the second point, on Lev. xv. 19.

7. Marriage laws, notably one of the most difficult and complicated chapters in the legal lore of the Karaites, especially in regard to the forbidden degrees of relationship. Nevertheless, in his controversy with Saadiah, Jefet mostly touches only subordinate points, which are besides more of an exegetical nature. Thus, on Lev. xviii. 6, concerning the expression שאר בשר (cf. *Kaufmann-Gedenkbuch*, p. 175; Jefet also considers here the interpretation of Ezra x. 3, on which further below); on xviii. 15, on the expression כלתך, which, according to Saadiah, includes also the son's betrothed, so that the words אשת בנך had to be added here. Much more detailed is the controversy about Levirate marriage, on xviii. 18. Here Jefet follows the opinion of 'Anân, according to which אחים, in Deut. xxv. 5, means not "brethren" but "kindred" (cf. *R. É. J.*, XLV, 61 seq.), and among other things very thoroughly refutes Saadiah's proof, that just as the prohibition of Lev. xviii. 16 is limited by the command of Deut. xxv. 5, so also a

biblical prohibition can be liable to limitation by another command (or, in other words, עשה דוחה ל״ת, cf. *R. É. J.*, XXXIV, 169), as e.g. the prohibition of Exod. xx. 10 by the command of Num. xxviii. 9 [1].

8. Civil law: Exod. xxi. 24 (published and discussed in *Monatsschrift*, XLI, 205), where Jefet upholds the literal interpretation of the *jus talionis*, and at the same time disputes with Saadiah, without mentioning his name.

9. Exegetical and miscellaneous matters: Gen. i. 2 (communicated by Munk, *Notice sur Abou 'l-Walid*, p. 40, n. 1: ...וקד גלט מן געל אשתקאק תהו מן תהום אלך; Saadiah is meant, see Ibn Ezra, ad loc.); xv. 9 (a refutation of Saadiah's allegorical interpretation of the kinds of beasts mentioned here, where the Gaon partly follows the Midrash [2]; especially interesting are Jefet's concluding words: ...פלו כשא (אי ראם אלמתיבה) עלי טאהרה כעאדתה פי כתיר מן אלמואצע אלדי ירד עלי מן אכרג אלנצוץ מן טאהרה אלי אלתאויל בגיר מאנע לכאן קד סלם מן הדה אלזלקה אלכבירה); xix. 11 (Saadiah is said to have maintained that ויאכלו in xviii. 8 referred to Ishmael and the servants of Abraham! In the translation there is no trace of this); Exod. iii. 2 (communicated by Pinsker, p. 72; on the explanation of לבת אש) [3]; xi. 4 (? see Munk, l. c., p. 41); xxiv. 4 (according to Saadiah what is related here happened on Sivan 9, soon after the Revelation); xxx. 12 (on כסף כפורים [4]; Saadiah is quoted here anonymously: ...פאלדי

[1] The words of Jefet in question are: ...וליס סביל אלאסתתני אן ירד בלפט מחתמל ואנמא ירד בלפט מחכם מתל וביום השבת שני כבשים בני שנה אלדי אורדה אלפיומי פאנה מחכם פהדא אלפרק בין כי ישבו אחים ובין וביום השבת שני כבשים אלך. These words of Jefet must be the basis of Aaron b. Elias' conclusions, which are interesting though tinged with a philosophical tendency (*Gan Eden*, f. 159). Cf. also Pinsker, p. 66.

[2] This interpretation of Saadiah is also criticized by Dunash b. Labraṭ (no. 7), cf. Ibn Ezra's שפת יתר, no. 7, and Lippmann's notes on it, as well as Geiger's *Wiss. Zeitschr.*, V, 311, and כרם חמד, V, 101. On the Agadic interpretation of the Vision of Beasts especially see Steinschneider, *Polem. u. apolog. Liter.*, p. 266 seq., and on Saadiah's principles in his allegories, see the passages quoted *Monatsschrift*, XLI, 208, n. 3.

[3] For the original of Saadiah's commentary on this verse, see *Z.A.T.W.*, I, 152.

[4] The particular passage from Saadiah's commentary on this verse in

(טֿן אן כסף כפורים כאן יעטא פי כל סנה אלף); Isa. lii. 13 (published by Neubauer, *The 53rd Chapter of Isaiah*, &c.; on the Servant of God); Jer. xxxvi. 1 (see my פתרוני רבי מנחם בר חלבו לכתבי הקדש, p. 31, n. 9; the Megillah mentioned here cannot possibly mean Echa, as Saadiah following the Talmud maintains); Ezek. xlviii. 12 (according to Saadiah the form תרומיה would point to a duplication); and Dan. xii. 13 (ed. D. S. Margoliouth, p. 151; on the calculation of the year of Redemption, see my *Miscellen über Saadja*, III, 11 = *Monatsschrift*, XLIV, 410).

The tone is mostly calm and agreeable; but the demonstration is not always fortunate. But it must be remembered that the arguments of Saadiah too are very often superficial. The commentaries of Jefet, however, are also in this respect of great importance.

Nothing has yet been discovered of Jefet's polemical work against Saadiah, as has already been observed. On the other hand, a work of this kind in Hebrew, directed against a pupil of the Gaon, Jacob b. Samuel, has been preserved[1]; and I have expressed the conjecture, which still needs verification, that this pupil is identical with the Jacob ibn Ephraim mentioned by Qirqisâni as his interlocutor (so that his full name must have been Jacob ben Samuel ibn Ephraim)[2]. But as the Karaites, and especially Jefet, repeat themselves very often, and inasmuch as particularly in their anti-rabbinical campaign they almost always advance with the same arguments, it is therefore more than probable that the polemical work against Jacob contains much that Jefet also adduced against

German translation: Bacher, *Die jüd. Bibelexegese*, &c. (Treves, 1892), p. 13 seq.

[1] The heading here reads: ואלה התשובות שהשיב החכם השלם הרב רבנו יפת הלוי המלמד הגדול בן רב עלי הלוי נ"ע ליעקב בן שמואל העקש. See corrections thereto in Geiger, אוצר נחמד, IV, 19 seq.

[2] See *Kaufmann-Gedenkbuch*, p. 169 seq. On Jefet's controversial work, ibid., p. 180 (reprint, p. xii). It is, at any rate, remarkable that the name of Jacob, as far as hitherto known, does not occur even in Jefet's commentaries.

Saadiah. One would therefore be justified in briefly analysing this polemical work, more especially as Saadiah also is expressly mentioned here, in the second poem: צמדת למלמדך סעדיה הנופי (i.e. from נף in Egypt), אשר דבריו מלאים דופי, והם חושבים שהם כליל יופי . . . רבך סעדיה בא מיפיפיה (i.e. out of Egypt, cf. Jer. xlvi. 20), אל ארץ דשא אכזריה, להטעות שוגים ולחבל סמדרי פוריה, כזאת עשה בן צר[ו]עה.

This polemical work consists of three sections in doggerel verses of four members, in which, after the manner of the Arabic Muwashshaḥ songs, three members of each strophe rhyme with one another, whilst the fourth members have one common rhyme. The acrostic in all three is alphabetical[1]. That they all three belong together may be inferred from the superscription of the third: אשלש אל"ף בי"ת. Possibly these were originally followed by replies in prose. Their contents are as follows:—

In the first section Jefet combats the view that there exists an Oral Law revealed by God to Moses, and employs the following four proofs: (1) Moses commands Joshua (Deut. xxxi. 11?) in the presence of all Israel to read the Torah; there is no mention of an Oral Law. (2) To all questions that the son should put to his father, the Torah gives (Exod. xiii. 8, 14 &c.) such answers as can be derived from itself, but not out of any Oral Law existing beside it. (3) Moses, in his last exhortation (Deut. xxxii. 7), enjoins that questions should be asked of the ancestors, the answers to which are contained in the same address: so that here also there is no need of an oral supplement. (4) God promised the scattered members of his people he would turn to them again when they would abandon the work of man (cf. Isa. xxix. 13), among which are to be understood Mishna, Talmud, and Agada, which men invented[2].

[1] The fourth, with the acrostic מקצת החרדים חוק, belongs, as Geiger, l. c., rightly recognizes, to Sahl's polemical work.

[2] To be sure, we cannot regard this point as an argument against tradition. In the last strophe the first two members must be reversed: הופשי הורת

In section II the same theme is treated, and two proofs of Jacob b. Samuel for the authenticity of the Oral Law are refuted. From Jer. xvii. 21, 22 Jacob seems to have urged that the Pentateuchal laws need a supplementary Oral Law, because it does not follow from the Torah that one may not carry a burden on the Sabbath, as the prophet here insists. Jefet replies that this prohibition is to be derived from Num. iv. 13, because here the carrying of a burden is called work (לעשות מלאכה; and the sons of Kehat had only parts of the tabernacle to carry). The second proof, which Jacob repeated after Saadiah, was that from 1 Chron. xxiv. 19. Here the words כאשר צוהו, which refer to the twenty-four priestly divisions, must necessarily refer to the command of an Oral Law, as there is nothing of it contained in the Written Law. Whereupon Jefet again replies, that כאשר צוהו particularly refers to the service of the priests (hence to Num. xviii. 7); but the twenty-four divisions were indeed first introduced by David[1].

In section III various ordinances and institutions are discussed: on the one hand, it is shown that the data of Scripture for these completely suffice, contrary to the view of the Rabbis; and on the other hand again, that a part of them are not of biblical origin, as the Rabbis maintain, and hence they cannot have any validity whatsoever. For example, the Priestly Blessing[2] is expressly enjoined in the Torah (Num. vi. 23); but its details, as in many similar commandments, are to be derived by means of the thirteen

ה׳ הכתובה, המיד הונים בה בחשק ובאהבה, תמורהה וחלופה (i.e. the Oral Law) ישימו להועבה, מלים לא יועילו ולא יצילו כי ההו המה. (1 Sam. xii. 21)

[1] Saadiah can only have asserted that the priests were already grouped into divisions in the time of Moses, but not into twenty-four, for this number is ascribed to David in the Talmud also (Taanit Babli, 27 a; "Tosefta," IV, 2, ed. Zuckermandel, p. 219). Cf. also *Commentary on Chronicles*, ed. Kirchheim, p. 36 seq.; Hai's "Responsum" in קהלת שלמה, ed. Wertheimer, no. 20, as well as Maimonides and Naḥmanides, "Precepts," no. 26. See also Zunz, *Literaturg. d. syn. Poesie*, p. 206.

[2] This and the following points must, therefore, have been advanced by Jacob as arguments for the necessity of an Oral Law.

Rules of Interpretation (which, as is known, the Karaites also accepted)[1]. The libation at sacrifices is biblical, but the water-libation is a capricious addition to the words of God (for 2 Sam. xxiii. 16, e. g. has nothing to do with sacrifices), and hence to be avoided. Again, the singing of the Levites belongs to the nature of their service, and had no need to be enjoined; and if at the offering of firstfruits a hymn of thanksgiving was sung, a similar hymn with instruments must have accompanied sacrifices.—In Ezra x. 3 the Rabbis refer מהם to the children, that is to say, these were also expelled from Judaism. But this is revolting; the word rather refers only to the mothers[2].—The different שעורים were devised by the Talmudists, and it was particularly the Rabbis rather than the Karaites (however the latter can determine without an Oral Law what kinds of work are permitted on the Sabbath and what forbidden), who had to ask themselves how it came about that in this law, which claims to be of Divine origin, there should be so many differences of opinion. This last reproach is notably repeated by all Karaite controversialists.

13. **Sahl b. Maṣliaḥ ha-Kohen (Abu-'l-Surri)** is one of the most prominent, but also of the most fanatical Karaites of the older period[3]. He is generally considered very

[1] The thirteen Rules are also used by 'Anân and the earliest Karaites, see *Steinschneider-Festschrift*, p. 208. Cf. also Harkavy, *Stud. u. Mitt.*, VIII, 1, p. xi.

[2] Cf. Pinsker, p. 23, n. 12, and Geiger, l. c., 21.

[3] For the literature on him see Steinschneider, *Cat. Lugd.*, p. 294; *Die hebr. Übers.*, p. 964, n. 306; and *Z. f. H. B.*, VI, 184. The short article on Sahl in the *Jewish Encyclopaedia*, s. v. (X, 636; by Ochser), is written without any special knowledge of the subject and is not without a comic touch, for Sahl is said to have been one of the Rechabites! The Maṣliaḥ ha-Kohen (Alphab. 47 ו), or Maṣliaḥ Abu 'l-Surri (Alphab. 62 י) quoted twice by Hadassi, was perhaps the son of Sahl also cited by the author of the Ḥilluk (cf. Pinsker, p. 106, l. 10; Pinsker, p. 87. n. 2, considers him to be the father of Sahl). On the other hand, the Maṣliaḥ b. Sahl ha-Kohen and Sahl b. Ṣalaḥ (see *J. Q. R.*, XVII, 632), mentioned in a Pentateuch Codex of the Karaite Synagogue, might have been descendants of our Sahl b. Maṣliaḥ. These two are brought into connexion with the Massorete, Mishael b. Uzziel, who probably lived in the twelfth century (see Steinschneider, *Arab. Liter. d. Juden*, § 167).

much older than Jefet, but the fact was overlooked that in the oft-mentioned list of Saadiah's disputants he also mentions Abû Ali Ḥasan al-Baṣri, i. e. Jefet. On the other hand, Aaron b. Joseph, in his commentary on Lev. xv. 25, expressly states that Jefet combats a view of Ṣahl (fol. 25 a: ... ודעת הכהן רבינו סהל ידועה שאם תהיה בסוף יום השביעי טהורה ותטבול ואחר שטבלה ראתה דם בתחלת יום השמיני היא נדה ולא זבה ... ודעת הלוי ז״ל להפך וטען לכהן במאמר על נדתה שלא יצא משלשה דברים וכו׳), which indeed occurs in the commentary of the former, although anonymous (see Munk, *Notice sur Abou 'l-Walid*, p. 6, n. 2). In any case, such anonymous citations are no convincing proofs, for the view represented by Sahl could be that of a much older Karaite exegete [1]. But another circumstance must be considered. In his polemical work (soon to be mentioned) against Jacob b. Samuel, Sahl speaks of letters and various questions which this Jacob addressed to him (see Pinsker, p. 26: עוד כתבת אלי באגרת שלך; and p. 36: ואתה עתה אם למען בקש חכמה ובינה שאלת השאלות ממני טוב עשית ... ואם למען תואנה שאלת לא טוב עשית &c.), and as Jacob was a pupil of Saadiah [2], Sahl can have written his work at the latest *circa* 960. He was thus most probably a contemporary of Jefet, of the same age [3], and wrote about 960–1000. In agreement with this are the statements of Ibn al-Hiti that Sahl in his commentary on Leviticus controverted Joseph b. Noaḥ, and that he was probably his contemporary, and further, that Levi b. Jefet controverted Sahl in his law-book [4]. Joseph b.

[1] Thus Munk concluded (l. c., p. 12), on the ground of such anonymous quotations, that Jefet is later than Jeshua b. Jehuda.

[2] See above, p. 27.

[3] In Karaite literature now Sahl, now Jefet is put forward. See, e. g., Hadassi, 178 כ and מ, 213 ל and ט, 236 ח (where והכהן והלוי), 241 פ, 257 מ and ז; Aaron b. Joseph on Num., f. 29 b; Aaron b. Elias, גן ערן, f. 52 d, 167 c, 168 b, 170 a, and כתר תורה on Num., f. 45 b, &c. The name of Ṣahl does not seem to have yet been found in Jefet.

[4] *J. Q. R.*, IX, 433, l. 2: ... ואלאקרב אנה (אי אבו אלסרי) כאן מעאצר אלשיך אבו יעקב יוסף בן נח; ibid., l. 12: ... וכאן לאנה נאקצ̇ה פי אלאביב מנאקצ̇ה טוילה̈ אלך (אי אלמעלם אבו סעיד בן אלמעלם אבו עלי) פ׳ ומאן אלמעלם אבו אלסרי לאנה (ms. עלי ולאנה)

Noaḥ flourished (according to Ibn al-Hiti) about 393 of the Hegira (=1002–3), and Levi wrote at the beginning of the eleventh century[1]. That Sahl speaks of the period of Saadiah as of that of his predecessors, agrees with these facts (see Pinsker, p. 36: ולפני מזה בימי הפיתומי).

Sahl also composed a special controversial work against Saadiah, which he mentions in the same list, and which is likewise lost. But he must have disputed violently with the Gaon in his other works also, of which two, both in Arabic, deserve particular consideration. In the first place, there is a commentary on the Pentateuch, of which a fragment on Deuteronomy is said to exist in a MS. in St. Petersburg (*Z. A. T. W.*, I, 157). The part on Deuteronomy was also used in an anonymous Karaite compilation of the year 1351 (MS. Brit. Mus. Or. 2498, Cat. Margol., I, no. 334, cf. also below No. 38). But another MS. fragment on Exodus, at St. Petersburg, is said to belong perhaps also to Sahl, and here there are two passages against Saadiah. In the one (communicated by Harkavy, *Stud. u. Mitt.*, V, 225) Saadiah's contention, that 'Anân taught that the new month should be fixed by observation of the moon only in order that the Mahommedans (whose custom was the same) should appoint him head of the Jews, is rebutted with great indignation. The reproach is levelled against himself, that in his attempt to succeed to the leadership he relied upon the Mahommedans and desecrated the Sabbath, and that during the strife with David b. Zakkai, his opponents turned to every community with a ban against the man who wanted to attain office in such a manner. In another passage (communicated by the same in his edition of Qirqisâni, p. 254, n. 4, and *Otcherki*, I, 11, n. 3) Saadiah's assumption, that the

אלהצר תפסירה ור״ד עליה (ms. עלי) פי ספר מצות אלוי לה [לאנה can only refer to Abu Said, i. e. to Levi; see Steinschneider, *Z. f. H. B.*, l. c.]; ibid., l. 19: פי כניסת אלקראיין בדמשק ראו (l. ראית) גזו מן הספיר ספר ויקרא רקא ומן גמלה. מא קאל אלמעלם אבו אלסרי פי מנאקצתה לבן נח לה ג׳ סנה פי אלקדס אלשריף אלך

[1] See my *Zür jüd.-arab. Litter.*, p. 6.

calculation of the calendar was first introduced in consequence of the advent of Sadok and Boethos, is disputed. But I have already expressed the conjecture that the author of this fragment is perhaps Ḥasan b. Mashiaḥ (see p. 16).

A second important work of Sahl was a ספר המצות in Arabic (of which there are fragments in St. Petersburg), with a Hebrew introduction (edited by Harkavy in מאסף נדחים, I, no. 13=המליץ, 1879, cols. 639–43), which contains much valuable information about the Jews in Jerusalem in the time of the author (see *R. É. J.*, XLVIII, 154), and is also otherwise very interesting. According to Steinschneider (*Z.f.H.B.*, VI, 185), this work is perhaps identical with the ספר דינים of Sahl cited by Samuel al-Magribi (Pinsker, p. 144). But it is more probable that Sahl treated ritual and civil law matters in two works, like Benjamin al-Nahawendi before him, of whose ספר המצות some fragments have recently become known (collected by Harkavy, *Stud. u. Mitt.*, VIII, 1, pp. 175–84), and whose ספר דינים on Civil Law is printed under the title (probably invented later) of משאת בנימין. In his law-book also, as a matter of course, Sahl disputed with Saadiah, and perhaps this book is the origin of a passage (communicated by Harkavy in Saadiah's *Œuvres*, IX, p. xlii) in which the Fayyumite is reproached with not recognizing analogy as a legal noun, contrary to the Thirteen Rules instituted by the Talmudists: ויקול (אי אלפיומי) אן סדר עולם אלדׄי פיה קאל רבי יוסי בעשרים ובחמשה באלול נברא העולם הדׄה אגדה ואין סומכין על דברי אגדה אלךׄ[1]. ואסקט אלקיאס פי אלשרע ותרך מא קאלוה פי צדר תורת כהנים מן שלש עשרה מדות התורה נדרשת ולפטׄה נדרשת פהי

[1] That Saadiah did not hold the Agada as a standard authority follows also from the above-mentioned fragment of his polemical work against Ibn Sâqaweihi (No. 2), where he reproaches the latter with having derived arguments for his assertions not from Mishna, Mekhilta, and Targum, but from Agadot, from unauthenticated writings, and from Piyutim (*J. Q. R.*, XIII, 664: ולם יסתשהד עלי קולה בשי ממא פי אלמשנה ולא אלמכׄילאת ולא אלתרגום ואנמא אתי בה̇ שעב בעצׄהא מן אלאגאדאת ובעצׄהא מן כתב לא שהאדה̈ עליהא ובעצׄהא מן אלחזאנה̈ אלךׄ). It is also interesting to establish the fact that the expression ואין סומכין על דברי אגדה, which also occurs in Sherira

תד״ל עלי אלאסתכ̇ראג ואלקיאס לאנהם לם יקולו נמצאת פכאן יקול קאיל אנהא מוגודה̈ פי אלנקל[1].

Moreover, according to a conjecture of Harkavy, Sahl is perhaps the author of an Arabic lampoon against Saadiah, in which is included a similar Hebrew lampoon of one of Saadiah's most ardent opponents, namely, of the Gaon Aaron (or Khalaf, cf. *R.É.J.*, XLIX, 300) ibn Sarjâdo, as well as the libellous document of the deposition of David b. Zakkai (edited as far as extant, and completely discussed last, by Harkavy, *Stud. u. Mitt.*, V, 222 seq.). In any case Sahl's authorship is very doubtful, for in the first place the previously mentioned fragment on Exodus, which offers some parallels to this lampoon, originates rather from Ben Mashiaḥ than from Sahl; and in the second place, Harkavy himself admits that everything seems to point to the Karaite author of this work having been a contemporary of Saadiah, and having lived in Irâq. But we know that Sahl probably wrote in the last third of the tenth century, and that he sojourned in Jerusalem[2]. Besides, as this work is purely personal, and does not touch on any legal or other points of difference between Rabbanites and Karaites, it does not exactly fall within the scope of this dissertation, and it is only mentioned here incidentally.

Sahl, like Jefet, composed a polemical work, not only against Saadiah, but also against his pupil, Jacob b.

(see *Eshkol*, ed. Auerbach, II, 47) and Hai (*Responsa*, ed. Lyck, no. 98), is already found in Saadiah, and was perhaps coined by him.

[1] Harkavy wavers between Sahl and Jeshua b. Jehuda, but the authorship of the first should be more probable: see his polemical work (soon to be mentioned) against Jacob b. Samuel (in Pinsker, p. 26): הוי ס[ו]תרי דבריהם ולא ידעו בושת, האומרים יש תורה בפה עם המשת, והלא כתוב בתורת כהנים שלהם מפורשת, משלש עשרה מדות התורה נדרשת. [It may be remarked, by the way, that the passage cited in *Œuvres*, l. c., from a commentary on Exodus, is actually derived from Jefet's commentary, on xxi. 33; see above, p. 22.]

[2] This follows not only from the preface to the ס׳ המצות mentioned above, but also from many passages of the polemical work against Jacob b. Samuel; see, e. g., Pinsker, p. 27 below: אני מבית המקדש באתי להזהיר את בני עמי, and so forth (בית המקדש here in the sense of the Arabic بيت المقدس, i. e. Jerusalem).

Samuel, which has now been edited from a copy of Elias b. Baruch Jerushalmi (Pinsker, p. 25 seq.)[1]. Elias is probably also the author of the title תוכחת מגלה or אגרת התוכחת. It is written in Hebrew, but Sahl also intended to publish it eventually also in Arabic, so that those ignorant of Hebrew could also read it (p. 25: ... ואולי אכתוב פתשגן הכתב הזה בלשון ישמעאל למען שיקרא בו מי שלא ידע לשון יהודית וכו'), but we do not know whether he carried out this project. Sahl's work has more the character of a reply, as it was preceded by letters of Jacob to Sahl, both in Hebrew and in Arabic[2]. In any case the assertion of a controversialist so passionate and relentless as Sahl was, seems rather comical, that he took up his pen against Jacob only because the latter in his polemics indulged in irony and sarcasm (p. 31: ולולי כי דבריך כמתלהלה היורה זקים לא הייתי כותב אלה הדברים). The style is lively, but too pathetic and too propagandist[3]. Here and there one also meets various Arabisms[4].

The polemical work in its existing condition is not a uniform composition. At the beginning there is a poem with the acrostic סהל בן מצליח הכהן הקרא מקצת החרדים חזק[5],

[1] Corrections and variants in Geiger, אוצר נחמד, IV, 22 seq. Cf. also *Kaufmann-Gedenkbuch*, pp. 180, 181.

[2] Cf. above, p. 31, then the passage (in Pinsker, p. 239): כי כתבת אלי אגרת בלשון ישמעאל.

[3] Many expressions are verbally repeated here and in the above-mentioned Hebrew preface to the ס' המצות, thus, e. g., ואם ערלת פנימה לא נמול, מילת חוצה מה תגמול (המליץ, col. 639, l. 34, and Pinsker, p. 43, l. 16); ... ומאכילת בשר ושתות יין נואשו, ובתורת ה' דבקו, ועל דלתותיו שקדו ושמרו (ibid., l. 2, from bottom; Pinsker, p. 31, l. 10). Pinsker, p. 31, l. 1 seq., is a complete Kinna. Sahl could not free himself, too, from Talmudical turns of expression, see Pinsker, 24, l. 3 from bottom: וראיתיך מבקש גדולה לעצמך (from the Boraita קנין תורה). Also interesting is the phrase (p. 26, l. 22): מאבותינו סבלנו חקי המצות כלם, which reminds one of the well-known סבל הירושה.

[4] Thus בית המקדש for Jerusalem (see p. 34, n. 2), then the expression מקצת החרדים (= בעץׂ אלנשיטין? see following note), &c.

[5] Divided in Pinsker by mistake into two (pp. 26 and 24), and the other half ascribed to Jefet, see Geiger, l. c., p. 20. That the poem forms a rounded-off whole is shown by the conclusion (p. 25); on the other hand, in the poem as well as in the epistle and in the actual polemical work, one and the same phrase of Jacob b. Samuel, in which the word הרדה occurs, is alluded to: see p. 24, l. 4 from bottom; p. 27, l. 16, and

in which it is particularly and emphatically shown that the Oral Law cannot be of divine origin, as the teachers of the Mishna themselves were of divided opinion on many questions. Probably to this poem was attached an epistle, the beginning of which is missing[1], and in which grammatical and even orthographical errors of Jacob are pointed out, Sahl remarking that he found nearly sixty such errors in the letters of his opponent (p. 72: ועד הנה קרוב לששים שגגות מצאתי באגרותיך). But as a matter of fact, the errors branded by Sahl (where, e.g. כסידרי, מסילה, קידה, &c., are written *plene*) are not errors at all, for this mode of writing was usual in the time of the Geonim in order to facilitate the reading of words without vowels.

The actual controversy begins with the words (p. 27): אני מבית המקדש באתי להזהיר את בני עמי, and is addressed to Jacob b. Samuel; but it is really directed principally against the Rabbanites, as it is more in the nature of an admonitory and missionary pamphlet, in which Sahl appeals incessantly to the followers of the Talmud to abandon their former conduct and to walk in the only right way, the way of the Karaites: "Have mercy, O Israelites," he exclaims in one passage (p. 34), "upon your souls and your children! Behold, the light is burning, and the sun shines forth (i.e. Karaism). Choose for yourselves the good path, where there is living water, and walk not in a waste and waterless land (i.e. Talmudism)," &c. "Brethren!" he exclaims in another passage (p. 43),

p. 30, l. 14 from bottom. By חרדים Sahl understands his rather strict co-religionists, see p. 36, l. 17: עתה אחינו הלא טוב ללכת אחרי החרדים (cf. also p. 26, l. 1: כי הוא אלהינו ואנחנו עם מרעיהו כי לקולו אנחנו חרדים . . .).

[1] This follows from the opening words (p. 27, l. 16): עוד כתבת אלי באגרת שלך. The piece, p. 25, l. 26—p. 26, l. 5, seems to be the continuation of p. 27, l. 3 from bottom (if the words of Elias Jerushalmi, p. 25, l. 24, refer to it: ומפני שיש לו ז"ל תשובות כתובות לפני זאת האגרת כתב הנה בזה הלשון?); and here also the conclusion shows that this epistle forms an independent whole. According to Elias (p. 25, l. 12), Sahl is said to have written besides this epistle ten further replies (i.e. letters most likely) to Jacob. But is this based on reality?

"hearken not unto those who say that the Karaites (בני מקרא) wish you evil. God forbid! Verily we pray unto God, that he should have mercy upon his people, the remnant of Israel, and be mindful of the love for our forefathers. We write all this only out of love for you: circumcise the foreskin of your heart, for the time has come to awake from the sleep of the exile." In a similar strain he goes on reproving the Rabbanites repeatedly for their numerous sins, and accuses them of transgressing many prescriptions of the law respecting diet, purity, marriage, and the Sabbath (pp. 28–30, 32)[1], of being devoted to superstition (p. 32)[2], &c. And if many of the Rabbanites of Palestine have entered upon a better course, that is due to the influence of the Karaites (p. 33), whose ascetic mode of life Sahl describes in eloquent words (p. 31). The allegorical allusions of many verses are also interesting, as, e.g. Canticles i. 8 (p. 34), and iii. 7 (p. 36; cf. Geiger, l. c., p. 24); Zech. xi. 12 (ibid.) and 14 (p. 42). In the last verse he makes the staff נעם symbolize the empire of the heathen nations, which is styled "grace," because these nations have not destroyed the religion of Israel; by the staff חבלים is meant the yoke of the two women (Zech. v. 9), i. e. of the two *Jeshiboth* in Sura and Pumbaditha, which by means of Talmud and Agada "have destroyed the vineyard of the Lord" (מחבלים כרם ה׳ צבאות). This staff will now be broken, i. e. the traditional writings

[1] They are mostly such prescriptions in which the Karaites differ from the Rabbanites, and are inclined to the severer view; thus, with regard to the enjoyment of an embryo (שליל or קבוט) and of the fat tail (אליה), the adoption of a minimum (שעורים) in the mixing of clean and unclean food, the marrying of a step-sister (בת אשת אב) and a childless sister-in-law (יבמה), &c. Almost all Karaites, from Qirqisâni and Salmon to Firkowitsch, are not tired of repeating these complaints.

[2] This passage is of especial interest for the history of culture: ... ואיך אחריש ודרכי עובדי עבודה זרה בין מקצת בני ישראל יושבים בקברים ולנים בנצורים ודורשים אל המתים ואומרים ר׳ יוסי הגלילי רפאני הבשינני ומדליקים הנרות על קברי הצדיקים ומקטירים לפניהם על הלבנים וקושרים עקדים על התמר של הצדיק לכל מיני חלאים וחוגגים (= ويحجّون) על קברי הצדיקים המתים וכו׳ (partly repeated in Hadassi, Alphab. 104; cf. also Bacher, *Agada d. Tann.*, I[2], 354, n. 5).

will be given over to destruction, and thus their declaration (אחוה in the sense of אחוך, Job xv. 17!) will be suppressed[1].

As can be seen, there is hardly anything of a personal controversy here with Jacob b. Samuel, but the attack is all the more violent against his teacher, Saadiah, whose name is accompanied by abusive epithets (p. 40: הזד הרשע האיש הרע התועה והמתעה המסית ומדיח את עם [ישראל] מדרך הטוב ואת הישרה עקש, also: [pun on הפיתומי] סעדיה הפיתומי העקש הפותי). Besides the passage already quoted in this dissertation, where Sahl relates that Saadiah avoided disputing with Karaites, and did not publish his anti-Karaite writings during his lifetime, whereupon there follows a list of the Karaite controversialists (Pinsker, p. 37); it is also related of the Fayyumite that in consequence of his persuasive arts[2] a dispute about the festivals broke out between the Palestineans and the Babylonians, so that they observed the festivals on different days, and hurled the ban against one another. I have shown (*J. Q. R.*, X, 154) that what is meant here is Saadiah's campaign against Ben Meir, in the year 921, which is now pretty well explained, and that Sahl's statements rest upon facts throughout.

Much more detailed is a complete excursus in which Saadiah's well-known theory of the great age of the calculation of the calendar is refuted (Pinsker, p. 37, l. 7 from bottom—p. 42, l. 25)[3]. Only one of the Gaon's proofs is there combated, namely, that from 1 Chron. xii. 33: ומבני יששכר יודעי בינה לעתים לדעת מה יעשה ישראל.

[1] Jefet interprets this word similarly in Cant. iii. 2 (ed. Bargès, p. 41), although he gives a different allegorical explanation to the entire verse. In his MS. commentary, ad loc., he refers to the vision of the two women to the Talmudic colleges of both countries, Palestine and Babylon (ואמא שתים נשים פהי אלמתׄיבתין אלתי אלואחדהׄ באלשאם ואלאכׄרי באלעראק . . .; and further: ואמא שתים נשים והם רוסא אלמתׄאיב אלקאילין באלמשנה ואלתלמוד אלדׄי . . . דפעוהא פי אלשואהק אלאעלא). Cf. also Hadassi, f. 10 a infra (letters ש and ת).

[2] Pinsker, p. 28: ולפני מזה בימי הפיתומי אשר פתה אנשים, a play on words.

[3] This excursus is not free from errors and repetitions, which cannot well be removed here. Whether Saadiah is meant by the מהעה (p. 28, l. 14), as Geiger (l. c., p. 23) presumes, is uncertain.

The sons of Issachar had, according to Gaon, understanding of the times (i. e. of the principles of the calendar), and let Israel know when they should "make," i. e. observe, the festivals. The verb עשה is also used of the observance of festivals, see Deut. xvi. 1, 10, 13. Sahl replies, not without humour, that the sons of Issachar fixed only the time of the paschal offering (for Deut. xvi. 1 refers only to this), of Pentecost, and of Tabernacles, but not that of the remaining festivals, in connexion with which that verb is not used. On the other hand, they must have taught the order of the festival offerings, the recurrence of the Sabbath, &c., because here תעשו (Num. xxix. 39) and לעשות (Deut. v. 15) are used respectively. In the same way the counsellors of Ahasuerus must have calculated the calendar, because they are called יודעי העתים (Esther i. 13). Finally, Saadiah contradicts himself, as he elsewhere maintains that the fixing of the calendar lay in the hands of the Sanhedrim, and he contradicts the Talmud, which speaks of torches used as signals on the determination of the new month, and of witnesses who were questioned about the new moon, and who, on that account, might desecrate the Sabbath (see Mishna, *Rosh ha-Shanah*, II)[1]. Indeed, Sahl continues, the command for the observation of the calendar follows from Gen. i. 14, Ps. lxxxix. 38 and civ. 19, and calculation is strictly forbidden according to Deut. xviii. 10[2]. Sahl also

[1] These objections are repeated, partly in the same words, by Jefet and his son Levi, then by Jeshua b. Jehuda and Aaron b. Elias, see above, p. 23. The words of the last but one (MS. Leyden, 41², f. 89 b) are as follows: ומהם אמר ומבני יששכר יודעי בינה לעתים אשר החפץ בזו הבינה דעת החשבון ואמר ולעתים החפץ בהם עתות המועדים אמר וכל אחיהם על פיהם יורה על היות ישראל כלם שבים אליהם בזה השער וגם זה מושחת מאופנים הא׳ כי הסמיכה על דבר איש באין ראיה רע והוא אלתקליד (cf. *R. É. J.*, XLIV, 183, n. 4) והב׳ כי זה לא יורה [f. 90 a] על אשר אמרו אבל הקרוב בו היות אלה יודעי בינה לעתות המלחמה והג׳ כי אם היה ישוב אל החשבון השוב הָשיב אותו אל הכהנים אשר הם טוב יותר מבני יששכר והד׳ כי היה כבר אמר בגלל חירם (2 Chr. ii. 12) יודע בינה לחורם אבי ואם היה אמר פה יודעי בינה לעתים יגוש אשר אמר אותו כן יתחייב [גם כן] זה והוא אליל (i. e. null) והה׳ כי מצאנו אותו ויאמר המלך לחכמים יודעי העתים (Esther i. 13) ואין החפץ בו כמו אשר אמרו ויש שם אופנים הרבה להשחית אלה הראיות כלם ואולם קצרתי אותם.

[2] That is to say, the calculation of the calendar system is to be regarded

does not miss the opportunity of dealing a blow at the Talmud. He says that Saadiah's strange interpretation of the verse in question is not to be wondered at, as he only follows his teachers (i. e. the Talmudists), who have made assertions that are not less comical, e. g. when they deduce the commandment about Kiddush on Sabbath and festivals from Exod. xx. 8[1], or when they order the trumpet to be blown to confound Satan (see *Rosh ha-Shanah*, 16 b supra), &c. Finally, in support of the statement that the Talmudists also speak of an observation of the moon, Sahl (p. 41, l. 19 seq.) quotes a story that is said to be derived from the Talmud, but which has quite the character of the biblical stories of the Koran. Here also are truth and fiction interwoven, and the most diverse passages of the Talmud are welded together[2]. But it is not impossible that Sahl had before him some apocryphal *Boraithoth*. Hadassi, who

as sorcery and astrology. This strange assertion is first found in Daniel al-Qumisi (9th cent.), and must have been advanced already by 'Anân, see Harkavy, *Stud. u. Mitt.*, VIII, 1, 189: וקול דניאל אלקומסי נ"ע פי ספר מצוות אסור לנו לדרוש ולחשוב את חשבון הקוסמים ככתוב לא ימצא בך מעביר בנו ובתו באש קוסם קסמים וג'. ואין מוהר לנו לדרוש חדשי יוי ומועדיו בחשבון הקוסמים והוברי שמים וכו'.

[1] P. 40, l. 26: ... ואל יפלא בעיניכם פתרונותיו כי התלמיד ילך בדרך רביו ומעשה אבות יעשו בנים וכן אמרו בפתרון זכור את יום השבת לקדשו תנו רבנן זכור את יום השבת לקדשו זכרהו על היין בכניסתו (צל היין) מכאן סמכו הכמים על קדוש (לקדוש .l) היום מן התורה. ואין לי אלא שבת וחג המצות מנין ת"ל למען תזכר את יום צאתך מא"מ. חג השבועות מנין ה"ל וזכרת כי עבד היית במצרים [ושמרת ועשית]. חג הסכות מנין [ת"ל] וזכרת כי עבד היית במצרים (בארץ מצרים ויפדך ה' אלהיך .l). ומנלן דבחג הסכות קאים דכתיב מעיל אליה (דיליה .l) הענק העניק לו וגו' וסמיך ליה חג הסכות תעשה לך שבעת ימים. ואע"ג דמדבר (דמדכר .l) בקידושא צריך לאדכורי בצלותא ובברכת המזון מ"ט זכור וזכרת בו ב' פעמים פסוקים כתובים ואתו מועדות וילכו (וילפינן .l) משבת לשבת (מה שבת .l) בתפלה ועל הכוס אף (על פי) יום בהפלה ועל הכוס וכו'. This Boraitha agrees neither with the passage in the Mekhilta, ad loc., nor with *Pesahim*, 106 a, but is taken from the *Halakhot Gedolot*, beginning of הלכות קדוש והבדלה, cf. also אור זרוע, II, no. 25.

[2] Cf. e. g. *Rosh ha-Shana*, 25 a, *Menahot*, 29 a, *Shebuot*, 31 a, *Berakhot*, 63 b, &c. In consequence of the conflict that broke out between Gamliel II and Joshua b. Ḥanania, the former, in conjunction with Akiba and Tarfon, is said to have introduced the nineteen-year cycle, and to have abolished the observation of the moon: ... וישבו הם (ר"ל רבן גמליאל ור' עקיבא ור' טרפון) והשבו חשבון לבנה ועשו מחזור ג' כ"ט כ"ג (גה"ח אדז"ט = ג' בגג"ג ב"ג .i.e ,ג'ב"ט ב"ג .l) כדי שיעשו ז' עבורין בי"ט שנים ובטלו את הראייה וכו'.

adopted the same story, with a few unimportant deviations (*Eshkol*, Alphab., 192 ח–194 ז), probably drew from Sahl.

14. An anonymous Karaite author, whose work (in Arabic) is partly extant in a St. Petersburg MS., and who (among other things) controverted a passage from Saadiah's Arabic commentary on the ספר הגלוי (edited by Harkavy, *Stud. u. Mitt.*, V, 195), must likewise belong to the tenth century. Evidence of his antiquity is afforded by the fact that he quotes nobody but 'Anân, Benjamin al-Nahawendi, and Saadiah. This Karaite quotes from the work of Saadiah just mentioned, that the compilation of the Mishna began forty years after the restoration of the second Temple and was closed 130 years after its destruction, thus amounting (as the second Temple stood 420 years, according to tradition) to 510 years[1]; secondly, that there were eleven generations of Mishna-doctors (see ibid. 196, n. 11); and thirdly, that the latter generation fixed the Mishna in writing because they feared, in consequence of the cessation of prophecy and the increasing dispersion, that the tradition might fall into oblivion. The anonymous Karaite replies (see ibid. 196, n. 13), that if the Mishna rests on true tradition, why was such a long period necessary for its compilation, whence the many differences of opinion, &c. They are the usual objections that all the older Karaites advance in their controversy upon these points: e. g. Qirqisâni, section ii, chap. 13 seq.[2]; Salmon b. Jeroḥam (cf. *J. Q. R.*, VIII,

[1] In the original it reads: ... אן אלאבא אבתדו בהדוין אלמשנה מן ארבעין סנה כלה מן בנא אלבית אלת֗אני ועלי מאיה וכ֗מסין סנה בעד כ֗ראב אלבית וד֗לך כ֗מס מאיה ועשר סנין. These numbers do not agree with one another (for 420 − 40 + 150 = 530), and Harkavy (p. 195, n. 6) therefore emends כ֗מס מאיה ועשר into כ׳ מ׳ ות֗לת֗ין, but it must be corrected reversely מאיה וכ֗מסין into מאיה ות֗לת֗ין. The last date is given by Saadiah himself in his polemical work against Ibn Sâqaweihi (*J. Q. R.*, XVI, 108, l. 4 from bottom): ... ואלי אכ֗ר וקת את֗באת אלמשנה וד֗לך בעד כ֗ראב אלבית אלת֗אני ק֗ל סנה.

[2] Only a part of chaps. 14 and 15 (see above, p. 10) is preserved, where in chap. 14 Saadiah's arguments for the authenticity of the Oral Law are advanced, and in chap. 15 they are refuted (partly edited in *Z. f. H. B.*, III, 175, 176). Yet Qirqisâni says here expressly that he will deal with this theme again in further chapters, and that he has already dealt with it in chap. 13 (MS. Brit. Mus. Or. 2580, f. 49 a): ואמא מא אכ֗ברה (אי אלפיומי) בה

687 seq.); Jefet b. 'Ali on Exod. xxi. 33 (see ibid. n. 6, and above, p. 22), &c. It may here be observed that both, Qirqisâni and Jefet, make verbal quotations from Saadiah on the questions dealt with here, and it is therefore possible that both used the Arabic commentary on the ספר הגלוי.

Eleventh Century.

15. **Levi b. Jefet ha-Levi,** a son of the famous Bible exegete, is also designated "the teacher (אלמעלם) 'Abû Saîd[1]." The name Abu Hâshim, on the other hand, is based on a confusion with a Mahommedan philosopher of the same name, whose father was also called Abu 'Ali [al-Jubbai]. Levi has composed in Arabic commentaries on the Bible, which, unlike those of his father, were merely short glosses, and hence bear the name נכת. There remains of them a part on Genesis (MS. at St. Petersburg), but Levi's authorship is doubtful (see *Z. A. T. W.*, I, 158); and the British Museum possesses fragments on Joshua (Cat. Margoliouth, I, no. 308^1 and 330^{11})[2], Judges (no. 330^{12}), and perhaps also on Psalms (no. 336^1). I have also already expressed the conjecture (*R. É. J.*, XLI, 307), that the ר' לוי, quoted by Ibn Ezra in three passages (Gen. i. 11, long commentary, ed. Friedländer, p. 28; Ps. vii. 10 and xxxv. 13), is perhaps ours.

More important than this commentary is a Book of Precepts, ספר המצות, composed by Levi, which contains the date of composition (Pinsker, p. 90) 397 of the Hegira (=1006–7). Fragments of the Arabic original are also extant in the British Museum (Cat., no. 309^2 and probably also

מן כיפיה̈ אלנקל וקולה באן אלתוראה̈ כתבת פי סנה̈ אלארבעין ומא אתבעה מן אלכלאם . . . וסנשרחה פימא בעד . ואמא מא אדעאה מן אן אלעלמא עמדו אלי אלעלם אלתקלידי̈ פדו̈נוה וסמ̈וה משנה ובקו פרועה ואן אלתלאמיד דו̈נו מא בקי מן אלפרוע וסמ̈ו ד̇לך תלמוד פקד תקד̈ם אספארנא לו̇לך פי אלבאב אלת̇לת̇ עשר ובי̈נא ד̇לך מן וג̇וה עדה̈ וליסת בנא חאג̈ה̈ אלי עאדתהא אלך.

[1] See on him finally Steinschneider, *Die arab. Liter. d. Juden*, § 46, also my *Zur jüd.-arab. Litter.*, p. 49, and *Jew. Encycl.*, s. v. (VIII, 33).

[2] The first of these two MSS. originally contained Levi's commentary on all the earlier prophets, as is evident from the superscription given in the Catalogue.

no. 308[2]). A Hebrew translation is at Oxford (Cat. Neub. 857), Leyden (Cat. Steinschneider, 22), and St. Petersburg (Firk. 613, and in the Asiatic Museum, cf. *Z. f. H. B.*, X, 26), and many passages from it have been communicated by Schorr (כרם חמד, VIII, 56), Pinsker (pp. 89–92), and Harkavy (*Stud. u. Mitt.*, VIII, 1, 132–135). It is from this work that the various quotations among the later Karaites must be derived, and it is evident from them that Levi was inclined to mitigation and was also in other respects of a gentle nature[1]. Cf. the quotations in Hadassi (*Eshkol*, 187 י, 201 מ, 241 פ, and 257 ד); Aaron b. Joseph (*Mibḥar* on Exod., fol. 17 b, and on Lev., fol. 15 b; he calls him both times אבו השם); Aaron b. Elias (גן עדן, fol. 7 b, 17 a, 18 b, 31 b and c, 33 d, 39 a, 49 a, 67 c, 113 a, 114 a, 123 b and c, 148 c [where בן יפת], 163 d, 167 c, 169 a, and 178 b; כתר תורה, on Exod. fol. 71 b and 72 a, and on Num. fol. 26 b); Elias Bashiatchi (*Adderet* preface; ענין קדוש החדש c. 5, 14, 15, 34, and 37; ע׳ שבת pref. and c. 4, 7, 12, 17, 19, and 20; ע׳ חג המצות c. 2, 6; ע׳ חג השבועות pref. and c. 3, 6, and 9; ע׳ הנהגת האדם c. 5; ע׳ שחיטה c. 7, 13; ע׳ טמאה וטהרה c. 10, 19; סדר העריות c. 3; סדר נשים c. 1, 5; ס׳ ירושה c. 2, 3) and Caleb Afendopolo (additions to *Adderet*, ע׳ שמטה ויובל c. 6, 13, 15, 17 and 18; ע׳ כלאי בהמה c. 2; ע׳ כלאי זריעה c. 2 and 6; ע׳ כלאי בגדים c. 3; ע׳ שבועה c. 5, 6, 7, and 12).

Levi did not compose any special work against Saadiah, as he expressly states in his "Book of Precepts" (see Steinschneider, *Cat. Bodl.*, 2164, and Pinsker, p. 89): ואם באנו שנדבר על כל טענותיו (ר״ל של סעדיא הפיתומי) על ההעתקה וכל אשר עליו מן הקושיות נצטרך לספר מופרד. Hence he indulges in pretty frequent polemics against the Gaon in the book mentioned, and touches upon most of the usual points of dispute[2]. He naturally deals most frequently and most circumstantially with the questions referring to the

[1] Cf. also P. Frankl's article, "Karaiten," in Ersch u. Gruber, II, 33, p. 20, n. 56.

[2] Besides the excerpts printed, I have also at my disposal copies of many passages from the Oxford MS.

calendar, but he only repeats the arguments of his predecessors. Thus, he too refutes Saadiah's proof of the great age of the calendar-system, derived from 1 Chron. xii. 33, almost with the same arguments as Sahl used before him and Jeshua after him (כרם חמד, l. c., and MS. Bodl., fol. 4 a). He likewise tries to invalidate Saadiah's assertion, that the observation of the moon cannot have been commanded by God as a precept, as its fulfilment cannot always be carried out, in consequence of the moon not being always visible (MS., fol. 6 b; in *Gan Eden*, fol. 6 a, cited as קושיא רביעית and refuted). He also combats Saadiah's view, that והיו in Gen. i. 14 refers to day and night (*J. Q. R.*, XVII, 170), and, with particular violence, the Gaon's rather strange interpretation, that those passages of the Talmud testifying against the validity of the *Deḥijot* are to be conceived figuratively (MS., fol. 13 b)[1]. In another passage again (Pinsker, p. 20; MS., fol. 18 a), he mentions that Saadiah reproachfully asked the Karaites, whence they knew that אביב means "ripe corn" and not the name of the month, just as there is a place תל אביב (Ezra iii. 15). Levi does not name Saadiah here expressly, but designates him rather remarkably as one of the modern Rabbanites (ודבר מי אמר מן הרבנים החדשים); but we know from Aaron b. Elias (fol. 16 d), that Saadiah is meant by this (cf. also Hadassi, Alphab., 190 ס seq., who likewise quotes Saadiah only anonymously). In addition to questions of

[1] ... ועוד נזכיר אחר זה קצת מדבריהם בנפול המועדים בימים אשר אינם כשרים היום מן המסורת אשר תקנו אותם אחר שעשו על החשבון והם לא בד"ו פסח ... אמרו בתוספתא לולב דוחה את השבת [בתחלתו וערבה בסופו] (see *Tos. Sukka*, III, 1) ... ואשר אמר הפיתומי כי אמרם חל הוא על דרך רדיפה וכן היה אומ' לו היה יום ערבה בשבת איך יהיה חיב שיעשה יהיה אומר לו זכרתם מעשה שוכר אותו וכו'. All the Karaites attack this weak position of Saadiah, which they storm with success, selecting their weapons from the Talmudic arsenal, especially Salmon (cap. iv–vi; cf. *J. Q. R.*, X, 271), Hadassi (Alphab. 185), and Aaron b. Elias (*Gan Eden*, קדוש החדש 'צ, cap. v). Levi also returns to the subject in another passage (see Pinsker, p. קיב, n. 1). Saadiah's contentions in the matter, which were hitherto known only from Abraham b. Ḥija's ספר העבור (ed. Filipowski, pp. 59, 60), are now partly also accessible in the form of fragments from the Gaon's original writings. See *J. Q. R.*, l. c., p. 263.

calendar-science, Levi also deals particularly with the Oral Law (MS., fol. 14 a), cites the passage from *Jerushalmi Berakhot* (והוא שאמר בתלמוד ברכות ארץ כנען) on the attitude towards the differences of the Shammaites and Hillelites (*Jer.* ed. Venice, fol. 3b, l. 6 from bottom), and mentions Saadiah's objection to the application of the method of analogy (כי הראיה והדרישה ישחית[ו] ההעתקה כי כן אמר . . . הפיתומי כי התורות לא יעשה בה ההקשה כי הפרחים הם רודפות אחרי העיקרים וכי יהיו העיקרים מן התורות יתכן להיות פרחיהם כן וכו'), &c.

Other points touched on by Levi are: the burning of fire on the Sabbath (Pinsker, p. 90), where Saadiah's attack upon the proof from Jud. xv. 5, advanced by all Karaites since Salmon b. Jeroḥam, is refuted[1]; the meaning of ממחרת השבת (see Pinsker, p. 92); the enjoyment of an embryo (MS., fol. 80 a), where Saadiah's argument from Lev. xxvii. 32 is controverted anonymously (ואשר אמר . . . הלא אם יעבר השה או זולתו מן הבהמות במספר תחת השבטים תחשב כא' מן העשור לא כשנים לא כן הדבר וכו': cf. *Kaufmann-Gedenkbuch*, p. 178, n. 2), as well as the enjoyment of the fat tail forbidden by the Karaites (אליה, MS., fol. 88 b). Here also Levi disputes the views of Saadiah anonymously, and contrary to his usual custom employs an insulting expression: (וזה הממרה שבקש ממנו פתרונה אמר לנו כי אם תפתרו אותה תרבא והוא שם המכסה את הקרב בלשון ישמעאל יתחייב עליכם להתיר אשר איננו תרבא מפני כי האליה יקרא תׄרב בלשון ישמעאל וכו'; cf. Bashiatchi's *Adderet*, ענין שחיטה, c. 18: ראיה . . .

[1] In this verse the first ויבער means "to kindle," and the other "to cause to be consumed," because in both the subject is Samson: hence the kindling and the maintaining of fire on the Sabbath are forbidden from לא תבערו. Salmon has this argument first (in his polemical work, cap. xii), and most of the Karaites repeat it (see Hadassi, Alphab. 145 צ; Aaron b. Elias' *Gan Eden*, f. 29 b, &c.). Our Levi especially, who elsewhere holds all Karaite arguments for the prohibition of fire-burning on the Sabbath as not sound enough, admits the validity of this one alone; see *Adderet*, ענין שבת, 18: סוף דבר כונת החכם רבינו לוי שכל הראיות שהביאו חכמינו באסור הדלקת הנר הן בטלות זולת הראיה שהביא מפסוק הנאמר בשמשון ויבער מגדיש ועד קמה.

שנית טען מר סעדיה הפיתומי ואמר . . . איך יתורגם בלשון ערבי ואם תתרגמנו תרבא . . . יתחייב להתיר זולתו וכו׳).

16. **Joseph b. Abraham ha-Kohen,** known under the name of הרואה (Arab. **al-Baṣîr**), is the most important Karaite philosopher of the older period [1]. He was confused quite early with Qirqisâni, and was regarded as older than the latter; but it is now established that he belongs to the first half of the eleventh century, as he already disputes with Samuel b. Ḥofni. Of his numerous philosophical and religio-legal works, which have only been partly preserved, chief consideration is here due to his "Book of Precepts," כתאב אלאסתבצאר (composed 428 of the Hegira=1036/7)[2]. Al-Baṣîr probably controverts Saadiah often here, but so far only a single passage from a compendium of this work (MS. in St. Petersburg) is known, in which the *Mekhilta* on XII, 2 a is used against Saadiah [and Samuel b. Ḥofni] to show that the present calendar cannot be so old [3]. One section of the *al-Istibṣâr* on the Festivals (מקאלה אלמועדים)[4] was translated by Tobias b. Moses as a separate work under the title ספר המועדים (also MS. in St. Petersburg), and here also, at the very beginning, is mentioned that Saadiah's view, that אביב can also signify the name of the month (and not ripe corn), has already been sufficiently refuted by earlier Karaites: ... ודע כי בארנו בספר האביב מהו ומה דמותו (של חדש האביב) על מה אתה תמצא

[1] See on him Steinschneider, l.c., § 50 (also my *Zur jüd.-arab. Litter.*, p. 50 and Goldziher, *R. É. J.*, XLIX, 224). According to Firkowitsch (בני רשף, p. 21) he was not a *Kohen*.

[2] See Ibn al-Hiti (*J. Q. R.*, IX, 434, l. 2): ... ווגדת שי מן אלאסתבצאר אלדי לה תאריכה פי סנה ٤٢٨. Cf. also Firkowitsch, l. c., p. 22. One section of the *al-Istibṣâr* on the law of inheritance (MS. Brit. Mus. 2576[1]; Catalogue, vol. II, no. 591[1]) is dated Dhu-l-Qa'da 409 of the Hegira=March, 1019. (Another fragment of the al-Baṣîr on the 'Omer, contained in the MS. Brit. Mus. 2570, Cat., no. 596, is probably also taken from the *al-Istibṣâr*, cf. *R. É. J.*, LI, 158.)

[3] Published by Harkavy, *Stud. u. Mitt.*, III, n. 120. Another passage, given there also, on Gen. i. 14, is perhaps also directed against Saadiah.

[4] This section is cited under this title by al-Baṣîr in *Muḥtawi*, see Frankl, *Beitr. z. Literaturgesch. d. Karäer*, p. 7.

אותו שמה ועם צחות דבור הפיומי כי אמר זה יבוא כמו ירח בול וחדש זו ותל אביב כאשר הוא די מן אשר דברו אליו חכמים בעלי מקרא עם דלות דבורו ובארנו כי דבור שמואל (i. e. Samuel b. Ḥofni) יש לו חוזק על דבורו והשחתנו אותו וכו׳[1].

From the *Kitab al-Istibṣâr* must also have come certain chapters that are extant in an Oxford MS. (MS. Heb. f. 12, fols. 9 b–44b; Cat., Vol. II, no. 2789), and from which I have already published many things (*J. Q. R.*, VIII, 701 seq.). This MS. is dated Sivan 5344 (1584), gives the impression of a commonplace book, and also contains something by Joseph al-Baṣîr, including polemical remarks against Saadiah. In the first place (fol. 9 a), there is a piece taken, not direct from al-Baṣîr, but from a controversial work of Natan [b. Jehuda] against Saadiah[2]. Here some of Saadiah's proofs for the great age of the calendar-system are refuted, e. g., that based on the Talmudic sayings (*Rosh ha-Shana*, 19 b): מימות עזרא ואילך לא מצינו אלול מעובר and אדר הסמוך לניסן לעולם חסר. Then Saadiah's assertion that והיו in Gen. i. 14 refers not to the luminaries of heaven but to day and night—a point that often recurs in Karaite polemics[3]. Saadiah is further controverted in a section on ממחרת השבת (fol. 17 a), and especially is his attack on the Karaite argument from Josh. v. 11 rebutted[4], and his interpretation of Ezek. xlvi. 12 overthrown. From this verse Saadiah wanted to deduce that שבת can also signify Festival, as on Sabbath one may not bring any peace-offerings (שלמים), which are here in question (hence ממחרת השבת can also signify "on the morrow of the Festival").

[1] Cf. this passage also in Pinsker, p. מד, who did not recognize who is meant here by this Samuel, and therefore deduced false conclusions.

[2] In this MS. there is another piece given from this Natan b. Judah, which I have also (l. c., p. 703) published, only I overlooked the fact that this piece [and similarly the passage אמר יהי מאורות הוא דבור למלאכים וכו׳] are also quoted in Moses Miṣorudi's מצות משה (written 1602): see Steinschneider, *Cat. Lugd.*, p. 246. Cf. also below, No. 35.

[3] Cf. the text, l. c., p. 702, with the necessary explanations there.

[4] Ben Zuṭa also did this already; see *Monatsschrift*, XLI, 205 seq.

Joseph al-Baṣir replies that one may not bring any private offering, either whole burnt-offering or peace-offering, on the Festival day also, and that hence כאשר יעשה ביום השבת refers most probably to the opening of the gate (see xlvi. 1)[1] or to burnt-offerings; but that שבת never signifies a Festival day.

Whether al-Baṣîr controverted Saadiah in his philosophical writings too, I do not know. I should only like to call attention to the fact, that he too was of a gentle nature and inclined to leniency. Thus notably, he successfully combated the well-known *Rikkub* theory in the Karaite marriage laws, which made it almost impossible for the Karaites to marry among themselves.

17. **Jeshua b. Jehuda** (Arab. **Abu-l-Faraj Furqân b. 'Asad**, abbreviated פֿפֿ) was a pupil of the preceding writer, and probably lived in Jerusalem[2]. According to al-Hiti (*J. Q. R.*, IX, 433, 434), he was also a pupil of Levi b. Jefet and Abu-l-Faraj Harûn. Jeshua developed a very fruitful literary activity, and wrote works of exegetic, religio-legal, and philosophical character, which we shall deal with in order.

As a Bible exegete Jeshua was very important; hence he is mentioned by Ibn Ezra (Introd. to Commentary on the Pentateuch) as a representative of Karaite Bible exegesis, together with 'Anân, Benjamin al-Nahawendi, and ben Mashiaḥ. He composed an Arabic translation of the Pentateuch, together with a detailed and a shorter commentary (the second composed later). I pass over the translation (MS. Brit. Mus., Cat., Vol. I, no. 93) which is unimportant for our purpose, and come first of all to the short commentary, the compilation of which, according to Ibn al-Hiti, was begun Rabi' I, 446 of the Hegira (=June, 1054)

[1] Jefet already disputes with Saadiah in his Commentary, ad loc., see p. 25. It is remarkable that Rashi also refers the words of the text to the opening of the gate.

[2] Cf. on him finally Steinschneider, § 51 (also my *Zur jüd.-arab. Litter.*, pp. 50, 51).

(l.c., 434, l. 7: (sic!) ואבתדי בתפסיר אלתורה יג׳ ויא׳ אלדׄי הו גיר מבצוט כמׄה בידה אלכרימהׄ פי שהר רביע אוול סנהׄ ٤٤٢ ומן גׄמלהׄ דׄלך תפסיר ואלה שמות פי גׄזויין בכמׄה מדהׄ תצניף כמא ינקלהם פי סבעהׄ אשהר). A great part of this commentary is at the British Museum [1], viz. MS. nos. 310–312 (fragments on all five books), 313 (fragments on בשלח, יתרו, and משפטים), 314[1.2] (on Exod. xxiv. 12–17, and Num. xxxv. 9–34), and 330[10] (on part of Num. xxxii). In all these MSS. Saadiah is not mentioned, but he is in others that doubtless belong to this commentary also. They are as follows: MS. no. 315[1] (fragments on אמור, here the detailed commentary, אלתפסיר אלמבסוט, is also cited), 316 (on Num. xix. 4—xxiii. 16), 317[1-3] (fragments on Lev.-Deut.; here also the detailed commentary is quoted as אלתפסיר אלמסתופא or אלתצניף אלמבסוט, as distinguished from the shorter one, which he styles הדׄא אלמכׄתצר), and 329[1] (on Lev. xxiv. 9–23). Saadiah is mentioned several times, firstly in 315[1], whether as סעדיא אלפיומי (on xxii. 5, fol. 6 b), or as ראס אלמתיבהׄ (on xxii. 10, fol. 10 b, in connexion with Sahl b. Maṣliaḥ; xxii. 11, fol. 11 b, and xxiii. 12, fol. 24 a), or then in 317[2], fol. 59 a (on Lev. xiii. 30). Unfortunately, only the first of all these quotations lies before me. Here Saadiah's opinion, that שרץ in Lev. xxii. 5 includes also the carcass of a beast, because it is said of the latter ושרצו בארץ (Gen. viii. 17), is quoted and refuted. The expression ושרצו proves nothing, as it also occurs in connexion with the sons of Noah (ibid. ix. 7), though it is impossible that the latter could be designated as שרץ. Here Saadiah follows the Talmudists, but the latter deduce the prohibition from כל (see *Sifrâ*, ad loc.), which is likewise wrong [2].

[1] Parts of Jeshua's Commentary are also in MS. in St. Petersburg, see *Z. A. T. W.*, I, 158.

[2] To the short commentary belong perhaps also the compendious explanation of the Decalogue translated by Tobias (Cat. Leyden, 26[1]); see Steinschneider, l. c., no. 2. Of the comprehensive commentary the part on Leviticus was perhaps in the hands of Hadassi, who designates it (Alphab. 33, ח) as ויקרא הגדול. In any case, we cannot take it to be Jefet's

Much more interesting than the short commentary is the detailed one, of which a fragment on Lev. xi. 37–44 has likewise been preserved in the British Museum (no. 318[2], fol. 31–80), and of which I have already edited many passages (see *J. Q. R.*, VIII, 682 seq.; *R. É. J.*, XLV, 54 seq.). Here also occurs (fol. 75 b) the date, the 5 Rajab, 442 of the Hegira (=Nov. 23, 1050), so that G. Margoliouth's view that Jeshua is the author also agrees chronologically, apart from various internal grounds[1] (cf. also Harkavy, *Stud. u. Mitt.*, VIII, 1, 192, n. 1). In this fragment polemics are several times indulged in against Saadiah, whether under the name of אלפיומי or הד׳א אלרגל (once, fol. 59 a, also as הד׳א אלמתעצ̃ב, and another time, fol. 59 b, as הד׳א אלאנסאן), viz. on xi. 37 (fol. 35 b–36 a; unfortunately I do not possess this passage), 38 (fol. 44 a–47 a), 40 (fol. 53 a–60 b), and 43 (fol. 70 a–77 b). In all these passages there is a discussion about the explanation of the verses in question, hence about various questions from the province of the purity laws. Jeshua quotes the views of Saadiah from his commentary on these verses (see fol. 72 b: . . . וקד ד׳כר אלפיומי מא לא יצ̃ח מעהא ינסב אלי אלאואיל שיא חכאה פי תפסיר הד׳א אלפסוק), whereat he abridged the words of the Gaon (see fol. 44 a: . . . ובעד הד׳א אלביאן פאד׳כר לך קול אלפיומי לא בלפט̇ה הד׳א מכ̇תצר: fol. 46 a; בל אוגד אגראצ̃ה פי מא יתעל̃ק בהד׳ין אלפסוקין כלאמה פי הד׳א אלמוצ̃ע; fol. 55 b: ת̇ם קאל בעד שי אכ̇תצרתה, &c.). As the abbreviated statement of Saadiah occupies sufficient

commentary on Leviticus, nor can ויקרא הגדול אוצר נחמד be regarded as one book (so Bacher, *Monatsschrift*, XL, 122, n. 4), as the אוצר נחמד is a work of Tobias (see below No. 27), and Alphab. 98, ז is separately mentioned.—ויקרא הגדול would therefore form an analogy to the בראשית רבא soon to be mentioned.

[1] See *J. Q. R.*, XI, 209 seq. Another argument of Margoliouth for the authorship of Jeshua, namely, the citing of a מסל̈ה מפרד̈ה, is, however, of no importance. In the first place, the title of a work is hardly to be understood by it, and secondly, that portion of the Leyden MS. 41[1], in which is also cited a שאלה מופרדה (see Steinschneider, *Cat. Lugd.*, p. 172), belongs not to Jeshua but to Joseph al-Baṣîr or Tobias. See Frankl, *Beitr. z. Literaturgesch. d. Karäer*, p. 7; Steinschneider, *Hebr. Übersetz.*, p. 454.

space, it follows that his detailed commentary was used here[1]. The refutation of Jeshua is also fairly circumstantial, but without any passion. He twice quotes the explanation of the *Sifrâ in extenso*[2] (fol. 53 a: והאוכל מנבלתה יכבס בג וג׳ קאל אלאולון יכול תהי נבלת בהמה [מ]טמאה בגדים בבית הבליעה . . . מה האוכל כזית אף הנוגע והנושא כזית, see *Sifrâ*, ed. Weiss, fol. 57 a; then fol. 70 a: וכל השרץ השורץ על הארץ להוציא את שבכליסים . . . הא מה אני מקיים לא יאכלו [לחייב] את המאכיל כאוכל, see ibid.), translates and explains it, adds the explanation of the Saadiah based on that of the *Sifrâ*, and shows that the Gaon does not follow the *Sifrâ* correctly. He likewise reproaches Saadiah with the habit of accusing 'Anân of ignorance and the lack of insight (fol. 46 b: ומן שאנה הו אן יתעקב עאנאן רח׳ אללה ויסמיה גאהלא וינסבה אלי קלה׳ אלעקל אלך)[3]. In connexion with the explanation of verse 43 (fol. 75 b), general canons of Bible exegesis are also discussed, and Saadiah's principles are combated. But here Jeshua already borders on the province of dogmatics.

[1] This MS. may thus also contribute to the knowledge of this lost commentary of Saadiah. I should like to call particular attention to a specially interesting passage on v. 40 (fol. 54). Here Saadiah tries to show that בהמה very often means all beasts, hence birds also. This is the case also in Exod. xx. 10, whence it is forbidden to send forth carrier pigeons on the Sabbath: . . . פמנהא שריעה׳ אלסבת אלמקול פיהא אתה ובנך ובתך עבדך ואמתך ובהמתך ואנה לא בד׳ מן דכול אלטאיר פיהא ולולך הרמת בעה׳ אלחמאם באלכתאב יום אלסבת.

[2] In both these places the *Sifrâ* is not named, but the opinion contained in it is designated as that of the אלאולון. On the other hand, we read in another passage (fol. 73 a): . . . פהו אלדי קלנא אנה (אי אלפיומי) יכאלף מא דכרתה תורת כהנים אלך.

[3] In another passage (fol. 55 a) Jeshua relates how Saadiah drives to an absurdity 'Anân's opinion that a new-born animal causes impurity only after its eighth birthday (cf. *R. É. J.*, XLV, 57 seq.), and asserts that the founder of Karaism probably misunderstood the words of the Talmudists (*Sifrâ*, ad loc.; *Sabbath*, 136 a), which he thought to turn into the opposite: תם חכי (אי אלפיומי) מדהב ענן וסמאה כארגיא ואטנב פי אלתנקץ בה. ופי אלרד עליה פי קולה מן ולד אלבהימה׳ אלצגיר לא ינגס אלי אן המצי עליה המאניה׳ איאם . . . הם קאל בעד שי אכתצרתה ואחסב אן אלאמר אלדי אגלטה חתי ארעא הדא הו אנה כמע אלחכמים יקולון להביא בן שמונה פתוהם הו אנהם ארדו אבן המאניה׳ איאם פעכס הו וקאל להוציא בן שמונה ולם יעלם אנהם אנמא קצדו אלי בן שמונה חדשים אלך.

A part of this long commentary of Jeshua consists perhaps of the work בראשית רבא, known only in Hebrew translation, the beginning of which (on the pericope Bereshit and beginning of Noaḥ) has been preserved in a Leyden MS. (no. 41[2]). In any case, this MS. has more the character of philosophical and theological homilies on the pericopes mentioned than that of a commentary. The philosophic-dogmatic part has been thoroughly analysed by Schreiner (*Studien über Jeschua b. Jehuda*, Berlin, 1900, pp. 25 seq.), and here Saadiah is not mentioned. On the other hand, in those passages in which Jeshua treats of the calendar (especially fols. 86–92) the Gaon is often controverted. Thus, the Karaite proof for the duty of the observation of the moon, from Gen. i. 14, is especially treated at length, and then Saadiah's view, repeatedly quoted here too, that והיו in this verse refers to "day and night," is refuted on four grounds (fol. 88 a, b). On fol. 89 b, Saadiah's proof for the great age of the calendar system, derived from 1 Chron. xii. 33, is likewise refuted on various grounds (see the text, *supra*, p. 39, n. 1). In a section on the *Molad* (fol. 90 a: שער א״א [= אם אמר] בארו דרכי הרבנים ודתותיהם האומ׳ במולד) is quoted Saadiah's assertion that the permanent calendar comes quite near to the *Molad*, but does not quite agree with it (ואולם הפיתומי אמר בעבורם כי חשבונם קרוב במולד ואיננו באמת על המולד). Further, several proofs for the great age of the calendar are quoted anonymously, and combated (fol. 91 a). But they are all derived from Saadiah, e.g. the proof from 1 Sam. xx. 18 (פונה אחרת דבר יהונתן מחר חדש יורה על היותם יודעים בו קודם ראיית הירח, cf. *Gan Eden*, fol. 5 c), then the objection why God did not expressly command the observation of the moon (פונה אחרת אלו צוה אותנו הקב״ה בירח היה חוב לפצוח [= فصح] בו בתורה באש׳ יאמ׳ הבדילו בין חדשיכם בירח, cf. ibid. 6 a), &c.

Not less important than as a Bible exegete and dogmatic philosopher is Jeshua as a teacher of the law. But the only thing preserved is the Hebrew translation of a work on incest, ספר העריות (MS. in Leyden, Cod. Warner 41[16], and in St. Petersburg) which, according to Steinschneider, probably forms part of a comprehensive work on all the precepts, bearing the title ספר הישר. It is most likely the same work that Jeshua himself quotes in his short commentary (MS. Brit. Mus. 2544, Cat., no. 310, fol. 165 a; cf. *J. Q. R.*, XI, 197) as (read אלעריות) גואבאת אלמסאיל פי אלערוות, and which Samuel al-Magribi (see Neubauer, *Aus d. Petersb. Bibl.*, p. 114) quotes as כת' אלמסמי באלמסאיל ואלגואבאת[1]. In this ספר העריות there is quoted a rather long passage from Saadiah, perhaps out of his treatise on the same subject (see *supra*, p. 7, n. 3, edited by Steinschneider in מגד ירחים III, 76, and partly in *Cat. Bodl.*, 2163; then by Müller in Saadiah's *Œuvres*, IX, 171), but without any polemics. This passage bears the superscription שער אחר שנויות, and is introduced by the words: וכבר נראה לי אחר זה לזכור אשר אמר אותו סעדיא ראש הישיבה בפתרון העריות מן ספור הנשים האסורות משום היותו יודע בחפץ הראשונים בדברים ויתר ועדוף להבין ממנו אשר לא יבין אותו זולתו ממי לא נתעשק בו מי קרא דבריהם[2]. If these words emanate from Jeshua himself (and not from the translator) they would show that he also knew how to treat his opponents with esteem. In other places also Jeshua's mode of expression in his polemics, apart from a few exceptions, is free from animosity and personality.

18. **Sahl b. Faḍl al-Tustari** (or **al-Dustari,** Heb. **Jashar b. Ḥesed**) is a fertile Karaite author, who has hitherto been little known. He is quoted, so far as we are at present

[1] Cf. on the ס' העריות, Steinschneider, *Cat. Lugd.*, pp. 190 seq., and *Die arab. Liter. d. Juden*, pp. 92, 93, as well as Schreiner, l. c., pp. 68 seq. The latter has also edited the introduction to the ס' העריות (after Cod. Leyden) as an appendix to his work. Other excerpts have been published by Harkavy, *Stud. u. Mitt.*, VIII, 1, 90 seq., and a full edition appeared by Markon. The fragment, MS. Brit. Mus. Or. 2497[3], which, according to Margoliouth (*J. Q. R.*, XI, 213 seq.; Cat. I, no. 314[3]), should form a part of the Arabic original of Jeshua's work, is actually a remnant of Solomon ha-Nasi's כתאב אלעריות. See my *Zur jüd.-arab. Litter.*, pp. 51 seq.

[2] The excerpt from Saadiah forms the conclusion of such a one from another Rabbanite work in Hebrew, which, according to Neubauer (*Israel. Letterbode*, IV, 55 seq.), is taken from the הלכות ראו.

aware, by Melammed Fâḍil in his Siddur as ישר בן חסד אל בן ישר אלתסתרי, and by the author of the חלוק הקראים והרבנים as ישר בן חסד (see *Monatsschrift*, XLI, 189). His period cannot easily be determined, but, according to Steinschneider (*Arab. Lit. d. Juden*, § 69; also ibid., p. 342), his place of birth (Tustar in Persia)[1], and the contents of his works, soon to be mentioned, appear to show that he belongs to the older Karaites. This is confirmed by the statement of al-Hiti, who follows Jashar with Solomon b. Mubârak b. Ṣagîr, the author of a lexicon כ׳ אלתייסיר (MS. in St. Petersburg, see *Z. A. T. W.*, I, 158), and the latter with ʿAli b. Sulejmân (*J. Q. R.*, IX, 435: ...תֹּם אלשיךְ שלמה בן מברך בן צעיר צאבח או צאחב אלתייסיר תֹּם אלשיךְ עלי בן שלמה צאחב אלאגרון אלמכֿתצר). As the last named probably flourished at the beginning of the twelfth century [2], Sahl must have written about the middle of the eleventh century, and have been a contemporary of Jeshua. Of his writings there have been preserved fragments of a commentary on the Pentateuch in St. Petersburg (see *Z. A. T. W.*, l. c.), and extracts of two philosophical works—אלתלויח עלי אלתוחיד ואלעדל (Glosses on monotheism and justice) and אלתחריד לכתאב אריסטו פי מא בעד אלטביע (Critical remodelling of the *Metaphysics* of Aristotle)—in a Brit. Mus. MS. (Or. 2572). According to Ibn al-Hiti (l. c.) Jashar b. Ḥesed also composed other works, and wrote polemics against Saadiah: ואלשיךְ ישר בן חסד בן ישר אלדסתרי רחֹ אתֹ כאן מן אלעלמא אלכבאר ולה כתאב אלתלויח פי עלם אלכלאם פי אלפאצֿהם ובראהינהם ורדّ עלי אלפיומי איצֿא ולה כתאב פי אלאעתדאל

[1] Our Jashar b. Ḥesed is probably also meant by the al-Dustari who is cited in an Arabic compilation on Deuteronomy of the year 1351 (see below, No. 38, and *Semitic Studies in Memory of Dr. Kohut*, p. 436, n. 3).

[2] According to Steinschneider (l. c., § 180), Ali hardly lived before the middle of the twelfth century. On the other hand, it must be observed that in his commentary on the Pentateuch (of which there are fragments on Numbers and Deuteronomy in MS. Brit. Mus., Cat., no. 309[1]), he compiles only from Karaite authors of the tenth and eleventh centuries. Hence he most probably belongs to the end of the eleventh and beginning of the twelfth century.

וכתב כתירא מן אלפקה אלמדכל[1]. At any rate, it cannot be clearly ascertained from these words whether the controversy with Saadiah was contained in כ׳ אלתלויח or in a separate work. Should the former be the case (and perhaps the extracts in the British Museum could confirm this), then Sahl would have combated Saadiah's philosophical views.

With Jeshua (and possibly Jashar b. Ḥesed) there closes the specific Arabic period of the older Karaite literature, and I therefore here append a few anonymous authors who wrote in Arabic, and whose period cannot be determined without difficulty, owing to the fragmentary character of the pieces preserved. But they probably all belong to the first half of the eleventh century, which does not exclude the possibility of many being identical with those already mentioned. These *anonyma* are as follows:

19. The Geniza-fragment, *Saadyana*, ed. Schechter, No. X, forms a remnant of **a Karaite polemic treatise against Saadiah** (אלפיומי). It deals with the observation of the moon and the calculation of the calendar; and from facts that have been handed down in the Talmud (*Rosh ha-Shanah*, 21 b: התקינו שלא יהיו מחללין אילא על ניסן ועל תשרי בלבד) and in the Tosefta (ibid., II, 1: ... ודלך אנהם קאלו פי אלתוספה מעשה ברבי נהוראי וכו׳), it is shown that they cannot possibly be regarded as purely theoretical cases, as Saadiah asserts[2]. Similarly, the Gaon's well-known statement is combated that the observation of the moon was introduced only with the advent of Sadok and Boethos, in order to fortify the calculation that generally prevailed hitherto. This statement, he declares, has no basis whatever in the writings of the Rabbis (fol. 1 v°, l. 6: פאדעא קול לא אצל לה פי סאיר כתב

[1] These titles are difficult to identify exactly, see Steinschneider, p. 342, and on אלתלויח and אלאעהדאל my *Zur jüd.-arab. Litter.*, pp. 15 and 59 *infra*.

[2] *Saadyana*, p. 35, fol. 1r°, l. 7: ... פהו֗ה ואשבאהה יבטל קול מן יקול אנה מבאלגה֞ לאן מא יקאל פיה מעשה פהו כ֗בר שי כאן פ֗עַל פקד בטל בהו֗ה אל֗מעשים קול מן יקול אן הו֗ה אלאכ֗באר מבאלגה֞. As a matter of fact, in the discussion of such cases Saadiah uses the expression מבאלגה֞. See *J. Q. R.*, X, 263, 271.

והדׄא כׄבר כדׄב לאנה לא יוגד הדׄא אלכׄבר פי אלרבאנין ; fol. 2 r°, l. 9 : סאיר כתב אלרבאנין ואדׄא כאן אלאמר עלי הדׄא בטל אן יכון לה אצל).

20. A Geniza-fragment in Cambridge, belonging to the Taylor-Schechter Collection (Ar. T-S. 30), six leaves [1], 18 × 13 cm., contains a remnant of **an old Karaite Law-book**. The book was apparently divided up into sections (מַקאלאת), and each section into chapters (פצול). The superscription of such a chapter has been preserved (fol. 2 r° : אלפצל אלכׄאמס עשר פי קולה תעאלי ואת אלה תשקצו מן העוף), and then the following sections are incidentally quoted: on the Sabbath (מקאלה̈ אלסבת ; fol. 3 v°, 5 v°), on the ripening of spring (מקאלה̈ אלאביב, fol. 3 v°), and on [the enjoyment of] hens (מקאלה̈ אלדגׄאג, fol. 5 v°) [2]. In addition, the author cites his work כתאב אלשכוך (fol. 4 r°), which is otherwise also unknown. In another passage (fol. 6 r°), ʿAnân's views (known from another source too) about the characteristics of permitted fowls, which differ entirely from those given in the Talmud (*Ḥullin*, 61 a), is cited. Our author states that Saadiah combated this view of ʿAnân, and remarks that the refutation of the Fayyumite is directed against him personally, i. e. against the Rabbanite characteristics : ולאן חאלתהם (אי חאלה̈ אלרבאניין) תגרי מגרי חאלה̈ ענן פי קו׳ אן אלטאהר הו מא יזֶק̈ וימֶג̈ . . . . וקד רד̈ עליה אלפיומי במא לא מעני לה והו קולה אן פי אלזק̈ ואלמג̈ ירגע אלי אלפעל ואנה לא יגוז אן יכון עלאמה אלמטלק אלא מא ירגע אלי גסדה אלך. I reserve a full consideration of the subject-matter treated of here till I have an opportunity of publishing the whole fragment, but cf. Harkavy, l. c., 154.

21. Another fragment of the same collection (so far without any press-mark), two small leaves, paper, deals with **questions of calendar-science**, holding that if the

[1] There is a gap between leaves 3 and 4.

[2] ʿAnân is known to have forbidden their enjoyment, maintaining that the hen is identical with the biblical דוכיפת (see Harkavy, *Stud. u. Mitt.*, VIII, 1, 145, n. 5). In our fragment (fol. 3 v°) this view of ʿAnân is also quoted and likewise that of the sectarian Mâlik al-Ramli (see ibid.).

new moon is invisible through some cause or other, the 31st day must be adopted as the day of new moon [1]. The unknown Karaite author adduces as examples the cities of Tiberias and Ramla [2]: he must therefore have been a Palestinean. He furthermore cites the following argument of the Karaites for the above view: Just as even a death-sentence follows upon the declaration of witnesses, although the certainty is never present that these witnesses have not lied, so the 31st day can hold good as the day of New Moon, even though it is quite possible this actually occurred already on the 30th. He then says that Saadiah tried to refute this analogy (זעם אלפיומי אנה גיר קיאס צחיח פקאל וגׄדת אלךׄ בינא פרקא בין התין), and shows that this analogy holds true nevertheless (זעם אלפיומי אן בינהמא פרק בדעוי אדעאה לא אלךׄ בינהמא אלתופיק נורי ונחן לה אצל).

22. MS. Bodl. Heb. e 32, fols. 9–18 (Cat., Vol. II, no. 2631[2]), contains a fragment of **an Arabic commentary on Gen.** iv and vi, mostly in the form of questions and answers. Its Karaite character is evident from the following passage (fol. 13): וראינא ראס אלמתיבה קד אלזם אלנדה ז נקיים נקיים ז אליולדת ילזם לם (l. פמא באלה) פאאבאלה[3]. It is well known that the duration and the degree of the impurity of a woman with child forms a subject of dispute between Rabbanites and Karaites, inasmuch as the latter also forbid any sexual intercourse during the thirty-three days after the birth of a boy and the sixty-six days after the birth of a girl (see

[1] This question is also discussed elsewhere in Karaite literature, most fully by Jefet in his *Comm. on Gen.*, VIII, 3; see *J. Q. R.*, X, 241.

[2] The interesting passage reads as follows, *in extenso:* וכמא אנה קד . . . יתפק גים פי מדינהׄ טבריה ענד גיבובהׄ אלשמס ויכון צׄחו פי מדינה אלרמלה פי דׄלך אלוקת בעינה פיכׄתנון אהל אלרמלהׄ אליום ויכׄתנון אהל טבריה פי גד ואלכׄל תחת נץׄ אלכתאב (Lev. xii. 3) וביום השמיני ימול כדׄאך נקול איצׄא אנה אן רׄיׄ אלהׄלאל באלׄרמלה ולא יורא בטבריה יגׄב עלי אהל אלרמלה אן יעתקדון דׄלך אליום ואהל טבריה יעתקדו פי אליום אלתׄאני ואלכׄל תחת נץׄ (Num. xxviii. 11) ובראשי חדשיכם פלים בינהם פרק פי אלבׄאב והדׄא ואצׄח הדׄא. On Ramla see *R. É. J.*, XLVIII, 156, n. 2.

[3] Cf. my *Zur jüd.-arab. Litter.*, p. 31.

the various Karaite views in Aaron b. Elias, *Gan Eden*, fol. 114 b seq.; cf. also *supra*, p. 25).

23. Another MS. of the same library (MS. Bodl. Heb. d 44, fols. 60–3; Cat., Vol. II, no. 2624[11]) contains the fragment of **a commentary on passages from Lev.** i. 15–xii. 3. This commentary belongs in any case to the older period of Karaite literature, as the Karaite author Abu Sulejmân [David] al-Qumisi is quoted here, who is otherwise almost quite unknown, and is only mentioned by Jefet besides (see *J. Q. R.*, VIII, 681, n. 1; cf. also *R. É. J.*, XLV, 178, 179, and *Jew. Encycl.*, IV, 465)[1]. On iii. 9 (fol. 60 b) Saadiah's interpretation of the words חלבו האליה is cited and thoroughly refuted: ואלפיומי קאל קולה חלבו האליה מעניה חלבו והאליה ואלאליה הו גיר אלחלב וליס אלאמר כמא זעם וקאל אן לנא אדם שת אנוש והמא אגיאר בלא וו עלי ראס אלכלמה̈ פכדלך קולה חלבו האליה מענאה חלבו והאליה אלך.
The enjoyment of the fat tail is known to be forbidden by Karaite law, and Saadiah's explanation, taken from his commentary on the passage[2], is mentioned by many other Karaites, e. g. by Tobias b. Moses (אוצר נחמד, MS. Bodl. 290, fol. 91 a), Hadassi (Alphab. 233, ק; Saadiah's name is not mentioned here), Jacob Tamâni (Pinsker, p. 87), Aaron b. Joseph (*Mibḥar*, fol. 5 b; here also Saadiah's name is not mentioned; cf. further, *infra*, Nos. 36 and 48), Aaron b. Elias (*Gan Eden*, fol. 96 c; cf. also his *Keter Torah*, on Leviticus, fol. 8 a), and Elias Bashiatchi (*Adderet*, ענין שחיטה c. 18: here the presentation of reasons and counter-reasons is especially the most complete).

24. MS. Brit. Mus. 2580[2] (Cat. II, no. 587[2]) contains a fragment of **an old Karaite Book of Precepts** (written throughout in Arabic characters). In one passage (fol. 13 a) is quoted an objection of Saadiah against ʿAnân and Benjamin al-Nahawendi with regard to the prescriptions

[1] I have published and translated another passage from this commentary on X, 19 (fol. 62 a) in *J. Q. R.*, VIII, 695, 696.

[2] This follows explicitly from Tobias' words to be mentioned further on. In the section in question of the polemical work against Ibn Sâqaweihi (*J. Q. R.*, XVI, 110, 111), this explanation is not to be found.

about menstruating women, which reads as follows [1]: واعلم ان الفيومى طعن على عانان وبنيامين وقال انهما جذف (l. جذفا) احد الشرطين وانهما ذكرا ان الנדה اذا اتصل دمها حصلا (l. حصلت) זבה فالغياها (l. فاليها ?) اقتضاء قوله בלא עת נדתה (Lev. xv. 25) وشنع عليهما بذلك ثم عوّل على بيان المراد بقوله בלא עת נדתה الخ. The question here discussed is that, according to the Talmudists, ימים רבים in this verse mean "three days," and they refer this verse to the י״א יום שבין נדה לנדה (see *Sifrâ*, ad loc., and *Nidda*, 72). But 'Anân explains the verse thus: if a woman, whether within or without the period of menstruation, has a flow of blood more than seven days she must then (in contradistinction to a menstruating woman) count another seven days after her purification, see his words in the original by Harkavy, *Stud. u. Mitt.*, VIII, 1, 42: ... אבל אי חאזיא טפי משבעת ימים מחיבי למספר שבעה בתר דדכיא דכתיב ואשה כי יזוב זוב דמה ימים רבים בלא עת נדתה או כי תזוב על נדתה כל ימ זוב טומאתה כי מי (l. כימי) נדתה תהיה טמאה [הוא] קא אמא ימים רבים בלא עת נדתה משום דנדה קביע לה שבעה ימי טהרה קא אמא גבי בלא עת נדתה ימים רבים לאודעך דבלא עת נדתה נמי כי חאזיא טפי משבעת ימים הוא דצריכה ספירת שבעה וכו׳ (cf. also *Mibḥar* and *Keter Tora*, ad loc.). That Saadiah (probably in the Commentary) combats this view of 'Anân, we also see from the commentary [of David b. Boaz ?] on the passage in question (MS. Brit. Mus. Or. 2495, Cat., no. 306, fol. 181 seq.): ... וקאל ימים רבים קאלו אלרבאנין ימים ... רבים שלשה ... וקאל אלפיומי׳ אן הדֿא אלקול מן אלנבי עֿל אלסֿ לקנהם איאה והו אן ימים רבים גֿ ועת נדתה פהו בעד אלטהר יֿא כמא קאלו אחד עשר יום שבין נדה לנדה . . . ואעלם אנה חכא ען ענן אן אלנדה אדֿא נטֿרת דם אכתֿרֿ מן זֿ והי זבה וקֿ אנה לם יאת בשי אלךֿ.

25. MS. Brit. Mus. Or. 2573 and 2574 (Cat. II, nos. 589, 590) contains a work on the differences and agreements in the exposition of the laws between Abu 'Ali and Abu-l-

[1] I owe the communication of this passage to the kindness of the Rev. G. Margoliouth. The Hebrew words are here transcribed in square letters.

Surri, i. e. between Jefet b. ʿAli and Sahl b. Maṣliaḥ: כתאב פיה עיון מא בין אלשיכ֗ין אבי עלי ואבי אלסרי רצ֗י אללה ענהמא מן אלכ֗לף פי אלמצות ומא אתפקא עליה. Here also, according to Margoliouth (*Cat.*, II, p. 180 a), Saadiah is rather often cited, but I have not a single passage before me[1].

26. **Israel b. Daniel**[2], according to Firkowitsch, composed in 1062, at the age of twenty-six, a Book of Precepts, ספר המצות (Arab. or Heb.?), which was preserved in the Karaite synagogue in Damascus. He is mentioned without any further epithet by Jefet b. Ṣagir; on the other hand, in an alleged book-list of the synagogue named (see Pinsker, p. 174; cf. also p. 94, n. 1), he is designated as ר׳ ישראל הדיין האסכנדרי בכ״ר דניאל רי״ת, and is said to have

[1] It should, however, be observed that a leaf of this work, which is added to the Catalogue as a facsimile (Plate V), contains a passage that seems to have been directed against Saadiah. Here the argument derived from 1 Chron. xii. 33 for the antiquity of the calculation of the calendar is combated; the same argument is cited and refuted by many Karaite authors (see above, p. 23, n. 1), but in the present instance the Gaon is not expressly named but referred to as belonging to the "men of calculation" (אצחאב̇ אלחסאב). I give the passage here, as far as it is contained in the facsimile page of the MS. (fol. 7 a), while adding the diacritical points and other signs:—

وقد احتجّ بعض اصحاب لحساب بقوله ומבני יששכר יודעי בינה לעתים
وتمامه قالوا لما اخبر عنهم انهم علماء بالاوقات وبالنظر فيما يعملونه ישראל وان
اخوتهم تتبعونهم لم نجد ذلك الا فى الاعياد ولما كان الهلال ليس يحتاج الى
تمييز وانما يحتاج الى حدّة بصر ولم يذكر فى هذا الموضع ما يقتضى غير
العلم وجب انه قصد حساب الاعياد، واعلم انه اذا استمرّ ان يكون لهذا القول
وجه اخر بطل الاستدلال به وقد ندرى ان القدماء كانوا يعملون على الهلال
على ما هو مفصوح به فى الמשנה وان لحساب محدث .... من اصحاب אלתלמוד
واذا كان كذلك فيجب ان يكون هذا القول انما قصد به الى ضرب اخر من
العلوم وهو فى تدبير العساكر وحوائج الامة مثل ויאמר המלך לחכמים
יודעי . . . .

[2] See on him Steinschneider, *Die arab. Liter. d. Juden*, § 70 (also ibid., p. 342).

lived in Hebron. Moses Bashiatchi calls him ר׳ ישראל בן הח׳ (read תסתר) רבי׳ דניאל הקמסי מחכמי הסתרה, and quotes his Book of Precepts under the title מצות ה׳ ברה (Steinschneider, *Cat. Lugd.*, p. 14). He thus regards him as a son of Daniel al-Qumisi (who wrote in the ninth century), and assigns his domicile to Tustar (where Jashar b. Ḥesed also had his home). But all these statements, especially that of his home, are very doubtful, and those of Firkowitsch seem to have been specially concocted[1]. If Israel b. Daniel flourished in the second half of the eleventh century, then he might be identical with an Israel b. Daniel al-Ramli, who is mentioned in an anti-Karaite work (composed or copied 1112) as a contemporary (see the passage in question, *J. Q. R.*, VIII, 700: ...אלי אסראיל בן דניאל הדא אלרמלי). At the top of the Firkowitsch MS. (now in St. Petersburg) of David b. Abraham al-Fâsi's Lexicon there are a few poems with the superscription למר׳ ורב׳ ישראל הדיין זצ״ל, which may have been composed by Israel b. Daniel (cf. Pinsker, pp. 174 seq.; Firkowitsch, בני רשף, p. 3, and Harkavy, *Stud. u. Mitt.*, III, notes 94 and 122). The first of these poems is directed against Saadiah, "the erring Fayyumite" (השוגה הפיתומי), and Samuel b. Ḥofni (שמואל ילד חפני), who thought to uproot the creed of the Karaites. From the clumsy form of the poems we might assume an earlier writer; but it is also possible that they originate from Israel ha-Maarabi, who is also called הדיין (see further *infra*, No. 37).

27. **Tobias b. Moses**, called העובד, הבקי, and also המעתיק, "the translator," as his chief importance consists in his

[1] The communication from the catalogue of books in Damascus seems to have undergone various changes, for the statements that Israel b. Daniel was twenty-six years old at the time the list was made, and that he sojourned in Hebron, occur only in the בני רשף, p. 4, but not in Pinsker [here also there have been added the dates 202 of the Hegira and 745 (of the Creation ?), which, however, do not agree with the year 1373, Era of Contracts]. In Ibn al-Hiti (*J. Q. R.*, IX, 432, l. 4 from bottom) it seems that we must really read דניאל instead of ישראל בן דניאל, see ibid., p. 438, n. 1.

numerous translations from the Arabic of works by co-religionists [1]. He is said to have been a pupil of Jeshua b. Jehuda, and lived in the second half of the eleventh century in Constantinople, where the first traces of Karaite literature show themselves in his time. Besides the translations, which he partly curtailed and revised, Tobias also compiled complete works from earlier authors. For example, there is a sort of commentary on the Pentateuch, entitled אוצר נחמד [2], which is compiled chiefly from David b. Boaz (הנשיא) and Jefet b. Ali (המלמד), and to which Tobias made some additions, especially in the form of questions. All that has been preserved, in a Bodleian MS. (Cat. Neub. 290), is the part on Leviticus i–x, from which I have communicated several small and long passages (see *J. Q. R.*, VIII, 697; *R. É. J.*, XXXIV, 167, 181; XLIV, 186).

In the אוצר נחמד Saadiah is controverted pretty often, and the name of the Gaon, who is mostly called הפיתומי, is accompanied with nasty expressions (cf. Steinschneider, *Cat. Bodl.*, 2168), e.g. הבער (MS. fol. 14 b), הזד (90 b, 101 b), הלץ (101 b), התועה (90 a), התועה והמתעה (91 b), הנער המצרי (90 b, 93 b), זה האיש (=הדא אלרגל, 95 b), &c. The questions on which Tobias disputes with Saadiah in the portion preserved are naturally such as are connected with explanations and prescriptions of the Third Book [3], but in one place (fol. 96 a) there is a controversy especially about the Oral Law, where Saadiah's commentary on Exod. xxiv. 12 is cited: ... והירושה אשר תזכור אותה היא אצלך המשנה והתלמוד וזולתם מן ספרי הרבנים והדומ׳ להם כאשר זכר[ת]ו בפתר׳ פסוק עלה אלי ההרה והיה שם וכו׳ (cf. *J. Q. R.*, X, 257, n. 3). The whole of the passage is of a personal character throughout, and we read

[1] See on him lastly Steinschneider, *Die hebr. Übersetz.*, pp. 454 seq., 940 seq., and *Jew. Encycl.*, s. v. (XII, 166).

[2] That this work extended to the entire Pentateuch I gather from the words of Tobias: אני טוביה ... כתבתי זה הספר שהוא א׳ מספרי אוצר הנחמד והוא סדר כהנים וכו׳.

[3] The polemical passages also Tobias doubtless took for the most part from his sources, but unfortunately the sources bearing on this particular part of Leviticus are not accessible to me.

here: "If thou (Saadiah) and thy followers maintain that Mishna and Talmud were dictated word by word by God to Moses, then do I say that thou liest and deniest what is manifest (דע כי זה שקר אתה מתנבא אי נבל וכפרת ושכחת לדברים הגלויים והברורים אש׳ הם ודאי), as these works contain the dicta of individuals and events from the time of the second temple and still later."

In the province of ritual law, Tobias discusses very often and very thoroughly two questions especially. In the first place, that on the operation of מליקה (ff. 6 a–7 b and 37 a–39 b)[1]; according to Saadiah this took place before the slaying of the sacrificial bird, and its process does not rest upon scriptural demonstrations, but upon continuous statements of eye-witnesses (fol. 7 a: ... ואמ׳ סעדיה הפיתומי כי המליקה מעשה יעשהו הכהן בעוף קודם השחיטה ... ואמ׳ סעדיה הפיתומי כי אש׳ אמרו זה הדבר אין להם ראיה על זה הדבר בדבר מן הכת׳ אבל הם מדרך ההעתקה מן המספרים ומגידים מה שראו בעיניהם מן המעשה וכו׳...; similarly fol. 37 b). Tobias then proves from Sifrâ on i. 15 (fol. 37 b: כי הרבנים אמ׳ בתו׳ כהנים בפתרון והקריבו הכהן אל המזבח יכול ימלקנו בסכין הדק [l. ודין] הוא וכו׳, see ed. Weiss, fol. 8 d) and from Tosefta, *Zebaḥim*, cap. VI (ibid.: ...כי כן אמ׳ בפרק הששי מן מסכתא הראשונה בתוספת קדשים והיה מולק בצפורן ממול ערפה, see ed. Zuckermandel, p. 489, where our passage is VII, 4), that the Talmudists seek a support in the Scriptures for their opinion, and that Saadiah deviates from them and contradicts them. In any case, the argument of the Talmudists is also not valid. Tobias also cites on this occasion Saadiah's commentary on Leviticus (fol. 38 a: ואמ׳ זה פיתומי בחלק הג׳ מן חלקי הקרבנות אשר זכר בפתרון שלו בספר ויקרא).

The second question is that on the enjoyment of the fat tail (אליה), which forms a constant theme in Karaite polemics. Tobias also devotes much space to it (ff. 90 a–94 a, 95 b, and 99 a–99 b). Saadiah's reasons and the counter-reasons of the Karaites are the same here as in the

[1] For the various Karaite opinions on this subject, see the passages quoted in *R. É. J.*, XLV, 196, 197.

other sources hitherto known elsewhere (see above, No. 23), but expressed much more passionately and often more thoroughly. It is interesting to establish that all Saadiah's reasons and objections are taken from his commentary on Leviticus, and that here also is mentioned the explanation of חלבו האליה mentioned above (fol. 90 a: ואמר מקצת יע׳ מקצת הרבנים [= בעץ׳ אלרבאנין] בפתרונו לס׳ ויקרא נבאר בזה המקום אש׳ בדא מלבו מקצ׳ הקושרים בדורנו זה והם כי אמ׳ כי האליה אסור אכילתם [אכילתה .l] . . . אמ׳ הפיתומי ואני אגלה שבושם ושגיונם בזה הפרק . . . ואם יאמרו כי התורה אמרה חלבו האליה תמימה יש לנו יכולת למנעם ממנו מב׳ פנים הראש׳ שנ׳ להם יתכן להיות שאמ׳ חלבו האליה חלבו והאליה תמימה בתוספת אות וי״ו . . . לאש׳ מצאנו העמרניים[?] יע׳ כתבי הקדש כי יחברו בלא ו״ו כמו שכת׳ אדם שת אנוש ומענהו . . . . . . ודעו כי זה האיש [=הדׄא אלרגל] then fol. 95 b: אדם ושת ואנ׳ וכו׳ א׳ בחלק הי״ז [מ]חלקי הקרבנות אשר זכר אותם בפתרון הפרק הראשון מן פרש׳ ויקרא כאשר חלק הקרבנות לשריפה ג׳ חלקי׳ וכו׳). Tobias also quotes from Saadiah the well-known opinion of Meswi al-Okbari, that only the fat of offerings was forbidden, and he spurns in indignant and abusive terms the insinuation of the "frivolous Fayyumite" (זה הפיתומי הלץ), as if the Karaites also follow the opinion of Meswi (ff. 101 b–102 a)[1].

Finally, Tobias controverts the following explanations of Saadiah of single passages in Leviticus: (1) on ii. 1 (fol. 8 b), on the amount of oil to be used with a meat-offering; (2) on ii. 14 (fol. 14 b). The offering of firstfruits mentioned here is not the obligatory offering of barley-sheaves, but a private and free-will offering that everybody can bring from the firstfruits of his field products. Tobias cites here Saadiah's interpretation, and the refutation in the name of Jefet: ואמ׳ יפת המלמד ז״ל ואם תקריב מנחת בכורים לי״י

[1] Cf. detailed treatment in *R. É. J.*, XXXIV, 164. Saadiah does not give the name of Meswi here, but says: . . . ושמענו כי אנשים היו בתוך האומה מתירים החלבים בדורנו ואמ׳ כי ײ׳ ית׳ אמ׳ כי כל אכל חלב מן הבהמה אש׳ יקריב ממנה ואלה הבהמות נקרב מהם דבר אמרו וכן היה הדרך בזמן שהמקדש קיים כי הראש אש׳ היה יקריב ליײ חלבו אסור ואש׳ איננו נקרב חלבו מותר וכו׳.

זכר מנחת בכורים מופרדה מן המנחות המוקדמי׳ לב׳ דברים הא׳ כי
היא מן זרע החדש ואם [l. ואלה] יהיו מן הישן ומן החדש והב׳ כי היא
מובא מן אלבכור לבד . . . ובזה המע׳ טעות גדול מי שאמ׳ כי זאת המנחה
תעשה מעומר התנופה . . . כי לא תצא זאת המנחה מג׳ פנים . . . אמ׳
המלמד ז״ל לו היה יודע הפיתומי הבער כי הבכורים לא יהיו לכל א׳ וא׳
וכי יבכר זרע של זה [היום] ומחר לאחר . . . לא היה מחלק זה החלק וכו׳.
Both Karaites overlooked the fact that Saadiah here follows the explanation of the Talmudists (see *Sifrâ*, ad loc.). (3) On iv. 13 (ff. 22 b, 29 a, and 29 b; in the MS. the leaves are here wrongly bound), respecting the question, who is to be understood here by the "congregation of Israel," Tobias indulges in exclamations against the shepherds, i. e. against the leaders of the Rabbanites, who allow what is forbidden and forbid what is allowed. (4) On vii. 12 (fol. 117 b), against the assertion that both the shewbread and the loaves brought with a thank-offering and a Nazarite offering and the Omer—all belong to meat-offerings. The source is here also Saadiah's commentary on Leviticus:
ודע כי מקצ׳ הרבנים הזכיר בפת׳ ספר ויקרא שלו והוא סעיד הפיתומי כי
לחם הפנים והלחם אשר יוקרב עם התורה ואשר יוקרב עם שלמי נזיר
והעומר הוא מן המנחות וכו׳.

28. **A Karaite compilation on Exodus and Leviticus** in Hebrew exists in a Leyden MS. (Cod. Warn. 3), and is identical with the St. Petersburg MS. (No. 588), described by Pinsker (pp. 71 seq.) and Harkavy (*Stud. u. Mitt.*, VIII, 1, 136). It doubtless originated in Byzantium, because it contains Greek words (see e. g. Pinsker, p. 73, l. 2 from bottom); as date of compilation is given 1020 since the destruction of the second temple and 480 of the Hegira, i. e. 1088[1]. The latest Karaite author mentioned by name is Abu Jaqûb, probably Joseph al-Baṣir, but the compiler used

[1] So rightly in Pinsker, p. 75: ואחריהם קמו אדומים . . . ומולכים עד עתה אלף וכ׳ שנים . . . ומן התחברות מלכות ישמעאל מלכה עד עתה ה״פ שנה (see also p. 76, l. 3). In the Leyden MS. (cf. Cat. Steinschneider, p. 7) erroneously 1000 and 380, which together does not at all agree (1000 from the Destruction = 1068, and 380 of the Hegira = 990). Cf. also Geiger, אוצר נחמד, IV, 26.

Jeshua and Tobias also[1]. It is also not impossible that the above date (and the Greek words too) was simply taken from some older source, and thus our compilation is possibly of later origin. Saadiah is cited here a few times and controverted, and among other well-known questions (e.g. on לבת אש in Exod. iii. 2, see above, p. 26; on the rejection of the היקש[2], see above, p. 22) are mentioned also such explanations of Saadiah as are not known from other sources, e.g. that on Exod. xix. 2 (see Pinsker, p. 72, l. 4), then that a sin-offering must be brought for all involuntary transgressions for which extermination is threatened (ibid., p. 73, l. 10: כי אמר פיומי דבר שחייב בזדונו כרת יהיה בשגגתו חטאת ולא כן הוא וכו׳). A Karaite opinion is falsely given as that of Saadiah, namely, that it is forbidden to enjoy meat in the Diaspora (Pinsker, p. 74, l. 19; Harkavy, p. 138, l. 16: לכן פיומי אמר חייב על ישראל להנזר מאכילת בשר בקר וצאן עד עת הקבוץ שישובו הכהנים על עבודתם וכו׳; cf. my remarks in *Monatsschrift*, XXXIX, 443, and הגרן, II, 96, 97).

Twelfth Century.

29. **Jacob b. Reuben** is the author of a Hebrew compilation on the Bible, entitled ספר העשר, which exists in manuscript in several libraries (Leyden, Paris, St. Petersburg), and a part of which (from Jeremiah to the end, excluding Psalms) is also in print (Eupatoria, 1836). He lived in Byzantium, and as he already uses 'Ali b. Sulejmân

[1] For parallels to Jeshua see Pinsker, pp. 76 seq. (who, however, wrongly concluded that Jeshua was the author; cf. also Steinschneider, *Polem. u. apolog. Liter.*, p. 347). From Tobias, e.g., is taken the passage on מליקה (p. 73), where the compiler has combined conclusions found in two widely-separated passages in Tobias (אוצר נחמד, ff. 7 a and 37 a).

[2] In Pinsker, p. 75, l. 6: ואמר פיומי כי אין מקישין בכל דבר ומצאנו י״ח דברים מבוארים בתורה וכו׳, but in the Leyden MS., f. 343 (Steinschneider, p. 8): ואמר פיומי כי אני מקיש בכל דבר וכו׳.

(see Harkavy in *Jew. Encycl.*, VII, 442 b *supra*), he probably belongs to the first half of the twelfth century[1]. Jacob's chief source was the commentary of Jefet b. 'Ali, whom he reproduces mostly in a very abbreviated form, and the passages having reference to Saadiah must have been taken for the most part from this commentary. All these passages (with the exception of a single one) occur only in the portion on the Pentateuch, and have been communicated by Pinsker (pp. 83 seq.) and Steinschneider (*Cat. Lugd.*, p. 25). They are (1) Gen. i. 1: ופתר פיתומי בראשית בי"ת טפל ולא כן הוא, this agrees with Saadiah's translation: אול מא כלק אלך; cf. also Ibn Ezra, ad loc.: וי"א שהבית נושא ומוסיפין אותו [נוסף ?] בלי טעם, and Parḥon's *Maḥberet*, fol. 2 c: [ר"ל את הבי"ת] בלי צורך כמו בראשית ברא כלומר תחלה ברא אלהים; (2) Exod. iii. 2 on לבת אש (from Jefet, see above, p. 26); (3) ibid., xxi. 1: לפניהם means before the Sanhedrin; (4) ibid., xxiii. 19, on Lev. xxvii. 32, from which Saadiah proved that the enjoyment of a שליל is permitted: ופיומי אמר אם הקרה להיות מְעֻבֶּרֶת מה משפטו אם יקחנו הכהן הלא הם שנים ואם תאמר א׳ בטל פתרוניהם על המְעֻבֶּרֶת (cf. above, p. 45); (5) Lev. xi (והשומרים [probably the Samaritans] כן אומרים וגם פיומי אומר כן, but it is not clear what the question is here); (6) ibid., xi. 29 on צב; (7) ibid., on grasshoppers, which may be eaten without ritual slaughter (cf. *Z. f. H. B.*, IV, 73, and the passage cited there); (8) ibid., xx. 13, on the various degrees of punishment for committing the crime mentioned in this verse; (9) ibid., xxii. 8, on Ezek. xliv. 31; (10) ibid., xxiii. 15 on ממחרת השבת (extract from Jefet, cf. above, p. 24). In addition there are two passages, which neither Pinsker nor Steinschneider quotes,

[1] On the conjectured period of the life of 'Ali b. Sulejmân, see *supra*, p. 54, n. 2. That he is used by Jacob b. Reuben was unknown to me when I wrote an article on the latter in the *Jew. Encycl.*, s.v. (VII, 41). To the literature there given must be added: Geiger, אוצר נחמד, IV, 25; Harkavy, *Altjüd. Denkmäler aus d. Krim*, p. 62; Steinschneider, *Polem. u. apolog. Liter.*, p. 347; Adolf Posnanski, *Schiloh*, I, 273. Cf. also the passages on 'Anân, communicated by Harkavy, *Stud. u. Mitt.*, VIII, 1, 152–155.

and which I take direct from the Leyden manuscript (Cod. Warn. 8); (11) Gen. i. 2 ואמ׳ פיומי תהו מן תהום ולא כן כי המי״ם אמר הגאון תהו שהוא מתהום וזה לא עקר (cf. Ibn Ezra, ad loc. יתכן כי מ״ם תהום שרש כמ״ם המים); and (12) Lev. xix. 27: וההולכים אחרי הרבנ׳ אמ׳ כמו סעיד כי השער אשר בזקן [ובראש] יש לו ז׳ פיאות ג׳ בצד הימיני וג׳ בצד השמאלי והא׳ פי אלענפקה ואם יוציא א׳ מהם בתער יחייב עליו (עוד) ארבעים ואם ב׳ ב׳ ארבעים כי אמר פאת ולא פאות (cf. *Mishna Makkoth*, III, 5, where we read: ר״א אומר אם ניטלו כלן כאחת אינו חייב אלא אחת). In the printed portion Saadiah is cited only at the end of Daniel, with regard to the year of Redemption (fol. 20 b: וכן פיומי פתר כי הם שנים וגם בטל פתרונו), but this passage also is curtailed from Jefet (see my *Miscellen über Saadja*, III, 12 = *Monatsschrift*, XLIV, 411).

30. **An Arabic Commentary on Exodus,** of which a fragment is extant at the British Museum (MS. Or. 2493; Cat., I, no. 332), must likewise belong to the first half of the twelfth century, for here also ʿAli b. Sulejmân is the last author quoted[1]. On xxx. 24 (fol. 73 a) Saadiah (אלפיומי) is also quoted, but the substance of the quotation is unknown to me.

31. **Jehuda b. Elias Hadassi,** of Constantinople, in his work אשכל הכפר (Eupatoria, 1836), composed in 1148, brought the science of Karaite law and dogma to a certain close[2]. His encyclopaedic work is, as Jost rightly expresses himself (*Gesch. des Judenthums*, II, 352), a vast sea into which all the rivulets of Karaite lore empty themselves, and hence, despite its inelegance in outer form, which makes reading pretty difficult, it is of extraordinary value. In his polemics against Rabbinism he follows in the foot-

[1] Other authors cited in this commentary are: אלריים נׄעׄ (David b. Boaz), עׄ נׄעׄ (doubtless Abu ʿAli, i. e. Jefet b. ʿAli) and פׄפׄ נׄעׄ (Abu-l-Faraj Furqân, with whose translation the one in our commentary also often agrees). On the explanation mentioned here of Exod. xx. 26 from a book נכת, by which are perhaps to be understood the glosses of Levi b. Jefet, see *R. É. J.*, XLI, 306, n. 2, and *Z. f. H. B.*, V, 17.

[2] For the literature on him see *Jew. Encycl.*, s. v. (VI, 132, 133).

steps of Salmon b. Jeroḥam, Sahl b. Maṣliaḥ, and Tobias b. Moses, and sometimes surpasses them in harshness and want of consideration. All the more remarkable is it that he names Saadiah only seldom (altogether six times), and treats him with comparative indulgence. In three places (Alphab. 168 ה, 174 ק and ש) the question is about the application of the method of analogy, which was employed by the Karaites in considerable measure, and was energetically opposed by Saadiah. Hadassi urges that without analogy one would not know, for example, that the father inherits from a son, or that the damage done by a goring ox, by crouching, trampling, or devouring, must be made good (Alphab. 168 ה: הפיתומי סעדיה אמר בחכמתו כי אין הקש בתורה וכדבריו אם אין הקש לא יירש האב לבן . . . כי לא אמ׳ והעברתם את נחלתו לאביו ובזה בטלו דבריו ודברי רבותיו להתברדה . . . וכן בשור נגח אמר נזק וחצי נזק ולא זכר לשור לא רביצה ולא בעיטה ולא נשיכה כשורה וכו׳; on the latter cf. *Baba Kamma*, 2 b)[1]. Much more interesting is another passage, where the sources of our cognition, according to Saadiah, are given, and it is stated, that his words can serve as a support to the Karaites (169 ג: גלה סעדיה הפיתומי בזה דוק [דיוק?] התורה: ומאמריו יעזרו לבעלי מקרא: משכילי נ״ע ויחיי׳ האל הנאזר בגבורה: באמור ככה כי שרש השכל ועקר החכמה ועין המליצות שלשה מדעים כשורה: מדע המראה ומדע השכל ומדע הכרחי והוסיף אלהינו ית״ש לנו להתגברה ד׳ והוא המשמע מדע גם עליה׳). They are the same four sources of information that Saadiah discusses in the introduction to his religio-philosophical work, and Hadassi also drew from them without doubt[2]. The other two

[1] The second passage (Alphab. 174 ק seq.) reads: ופיתומי רב סעדיא אמר במלולו והלולו כי אני מקיש בכל דבר ומצאתי י״ה דברי׳ מפורשי׳ בתורה ואם לא היו מפורשי׳ וגלויים הייתי אומר אני בזו העלה שזכרה התורה וכו׳. Hence here too the reading is like that in the Leyden MS. of the anonymous compilation on Exod. and Lev. (see above, p. 66, n. 2. Could Hadassi perhaps have drawn from it, or the reverse?). — הלולו here most probably means "his wantonness" (see Ps. lxxv. 5).

[2] See *Amanât*, ed. Landauer, p. 12 infra: . . . ונקול אנהא (אי מואד̈ אלחק) ת̇לת̇ה̇ מואד̈ אלאולי עלם אלשאהד (=מדע המראה) ואלת̇אניה̇ עלם אלעקול (=מדע השכל)

passages deal with the argument from Josh. v. 11 for the correctness of the Karaite interpretation of ממחרת השבת (Alphab. 224 ג), and with Saadiah's argument from Lev. xxvii. 32, that the enjoyment of an embryo is permitted (Alphab. 240 מ: ... והפיתומי אמר באמור הכתוב העשירי יהיה קדש לה׳ אם הקרה מעובר היה לוקחו כאחד ומזה מותר לנו המעובר כי הוא כאחד בחשבונימו: ובטל פתרוניכ׳ שאסרתם אותו לעם אלהיך: ״נאמו לו משכילי נ״ע אי גונב הלבבות מאין לך כי נהיו [מ]עשרים מעוברות ... והרבו עליו משכילי נ״ע תשובות אך מקצת הרמזתי לך ולכל חרדי אלהיך)[1].

But besides these few passages, Hadassi now and again controverts the views of Saadiah without naming him, e. g. the assertion that אביב can signify the name of the month (Alphab. 190 ס: ... ומי שאמר שמור את חדש האביב הוא שם לחדשך ... עות המשפט והדרך כי לקחו ודמהו ממה שאמר תל אביב והוא שם מקום וכו׳; see above, p. 44), or the explanation of חלבו והאליה as חלבו האליה (Alphab. 233 ק; cf. *supra*, No. 23), and so forth. It must be against Saadiah also that those passages are directed in which Hadassi shows that in the Talmudical period the rule לא בד״ו פסח had not any validity yet (Alphab. 185 ש seq.), or that 1 Sam. xx. 18 is no argument for the great age of the calendar-system (Alphab. 197 ש seq.),

ואלתֿאלתֿה עלם מא דפעת אלצֿרורהֿ אליה (=מדע הכרחי) ... ואמא נחן גמאעהֿ אלמוחֿדין ... ינצֿיף אליהא מאדֿהֿ ראבעהֿ ... והי צחֿהֿ אלכֿבר אלצאדק (=מדע המשמע) אלךֿ. But it seems that Hadassi, in the fourth source, chose משמע not without intention (instead of, e. g., ההגדה הנאמנת in Ibn Tibbon), because this word among the Karaites signifies the Scriptures. Hadassi further adds: ועוד אמר (ר״ל סעדיה) כי התורו׳ מתקיימות בשכל ובשמע ובקבלה ואמנ׳ דבריו השכל והקבלה אשר אינ׳ הורסות מה שכתו׳ בס׳ תורת אלהיך. Here again is Saadiah's division of the commandments into precepts of reason (שכל=מצות שכליות, אלשראיע אלעקליהֿ) and precepts of revelation (שמע=מצות שמעיות, אלשראיע אלסמעיהֿ), to which is also added truthful tradition (קבלה=כֿבר צחיח); see *Amanât*, § iii. Cf. also Kaufmann, *Geschichte d. Attributenlehre*, pp. 1 seq.; Guttmann, *Die Religionsphilosophie d. Saadia*, pp. 22 seq., 134 seq.

[1] This argument, as already remarked, is also advanced by Qirqisâni, Levi b. Jefet and Jacob b. Reuben (see *Kaufmann-Gedenkbuch*, p. 178, n. 2, and also above, pp. 45 and 67), but Saadiah's name is mentioned only by the last of these. As Jacob b. Reuben draws especially from Jefet, it may be presumed that the latter also handed down the name of the Gaon and has used to Hadassi as a source. But unfortunately I have not before me Jefet's commentary on this passage of Leviticus.

or that one cannot conclude from Dan. x. 3 that the eating of meat was permitted in the Diaspora (see above, p. 66), &c.

Besides the *Eshkol*, another fragment of Hadassi has been preserved, which Pinsker (pp. 94 seq.) has edited. The latter holds Tobias to be the author, but this time Firkowitsch, who ascribes it to Hadassi, has exceptionally hit upon the truth, as we find at the end quite explicitly (p. 97, l. 5): ואני יהודה בן אליה קטון התלמידים[1]. This fragment is not a remnant of a Book of Precepts, but *collectanea* which Hadassi probably compiled as material for his *Eshkol*. Saadiah is mentioned a few times here also, and the matter at issue is that eternal question about the age of the calendar-system. According to Saadiah it is no argument against the great age of this system that there is nothing about it in the Bible, for reason does not forbid us to assume that God revealed, e.g. 100 precepts to his prophet, and commanded him to write down only fifty of them, but to hand down the other fifty only orally, or not to fix any of them at all in writing. The precepts were indeed already known to the patriarchs, although they were not written down; similarly Mishna and Talmud already existed before, and were only later made into a record by the sages[2]. Further, Saadiah maintains that the calendar with all its rules originates from Moses, and only when Ṣadok and Boethos, the two heretical disciples of Antigonus, also opposed the system, was the observation of the moon also made known [in order to show that both

[1] Cf. also Frankl, *Monatsschrift*, XXXI, 77 seq. and השחר, VII, 50; Buber's introduction to the לקח טוב of Tobia b. Eliezer, p. 47.

[2] Saadiah had this argument in his commentary on the Pentateuch (p. 94, l. 23: דע כי פיתומי השיב על בעלי המקרא בפתרון שלו בענין החדש בעבור החשבון והעבור וכו'; l. 25, for שיכתוב כ' read שיכתוב נ'). By the assertion that the patriarchs already knew the commandments, Saadiah means such sayings as קיים אברהם אבינו כל התורה כלה and the like. In Karaite literature also it is discussed whether the Biblical precepts were binding before the Sinaitic legislation. I intend dealing fully with this problem, described as קדם אלפראיץ, in another connexion.

coincide][1]. The generally prevalent rules were again used as a guide, until ʿAnân and Benjamin al-Nahawendi arose and again abolished the system that is of Sinaitic origin. Hadassi further reports in Saadiah's name about the wonders displayed by R. Eliezer in his dispute with R. Joshua (see *Baba Meṣia*, 59 a), about the sacrifice brought with the Omer, the amount of meal to be used with the Omer, and finally about the argument from Josh. v. 11 for the Karaite interpretation of ממחרת השבת and its refutation. This refutation agrees verbally with that by Jefet on Lev. xxiii. 15 in the *Kitab al-tamjiz* (Hirschfeld, *Arabic Chrestomathy*, p. 113, l. 24 seq.), and Hadassi also drew from this indirectly[2].

With Hadassi the older period of Karaite literature closes, and henceforth all independence is stifled. With the exception of the two Aarons (and, in many respects, of Elias Bashiatchi and Caleb Afendopolo), the later authors only repeat what the earlier ones have said, and "enrich themselves by their works." On this ground the Fayyumite still continues to be the object of controversy (but naturally without any new factor in the campaign), although this controversy has long become an anachronism. But, in accordance with our task, we will follow the traces of this controversy, so far as it is present to our view, still further, till the most recent times.

To the twelfth century, and perhaps even to the first half of it, must most probably also belong

32. **Elias b. Abraham,** the author of the חלוק הקראים עם הרבנים (ed. Pinsker, pp. 99 seq.)[3]. This follows from the

[1] With this is connected the answer of Ben Mashiaḥ mentioned previously (cf. above, p. 16).

[2] This follows from the fact that the words of Hadassi following upon the conclusions of Saadiah (p. 96, l. 17): דע כי דברי בעל הפיתומי באשר הביאו ראיה מן ויאכלו מעבור הארץ כי הם ב׳ לולאות שריין אין הדבר כאשר זכר, are simply translated from Jefet (Hirschfeld, p. 114, l. 20): אמא קול אלפיומי פי מא אחתג׳ מן ויאכלו מעבור הארץ אנהא ערותין מנחלתין פליס אלאמר כמא ד׳כר.

[3] The view of Pinsker (p. יט), Schorr (החלוץ, VI, 77), and Gottlober (בקרת להולדות הקראים, p. 157), that Elias b. Abraham is not the author, seems

fact that Elias speaks of the sects of the Tiflisites and the Meswites (i. e. the adherents of Abu Imrân al-Tiflisi and Meswi al-Okbari) as still existing in his time (p. 100, l. 13 from bottom: והיום אין בזמננו כ"א ד' דתות דת רבנים ודת קראים ודת תפליסיים ודת משוי)[1], and that, as will soon have to be mentioned, Saadiah's polemical work against 'Anân (כתאב אלרד̈ עלי ענן) was probably still in his hands. But the traces of this work can only be followed up to the twelfth century (cf. *R. É. J.*, XLV, 192). His home cannot be determined, but as Karaite literature in this century has its centre in Byzantium, he should most probably belong to this century[2]. The work of Elias has the form of an epistle to a Rabbanite (Jehuda b. Sabbatai?), and serves the double purpose of defending Karaism and attacking Rabbanism. Saadiah is not mentioned here explicitly, but Pinsker's conjecture seems to be right, that it is he who is meant by "the co-religionist of the receiver, who insulted 'Anân, the teacher of the Diaspora" (p. 103, l. 14: ולבן דתכם אשר חרף לענן משכיל הגולה כנואם הנואם ודובר תמים יתעבו למה לו תאמינו). There then follows in the "lying story" of this Rabbanite, as Elias expresses himself (וכתב בספור שקרותיו), the well-known account about the advent

to me to be unfounded. Just as little ground is there for the view of Schorr, that the actual work begins with the words אמרו בני [מ]קרא (p. 100, l. 27), for a few lines before (l. 23) the author expressly says: ולכן השתי ולא התמהמהתי מלכתוב בדלתות שורותי אלה עסקי דתי וכו', then a scriptural passage is here introduced with הנאם (l. 20: ויתקיים הנואם הורוני ואני אחריש וכו'), just as in p. 103, l. 15. Cf. also conclusions of Steinschneider, *Hebr. Bibliogr.*, V, 49 seq.

[1] Pinsker (p. 98) also calls attention to this. With regard to the Meswites, I have shown (*R. É. J.*, XXXIV, 163) that they still existed in the twelfth century, and that will certainly have been the case with the Tiflisites. It is thus unnecessary to presume with Harkavy (*Voskhod*, Feb. 1900, p. 77), that here the author of the חלוק simply copied from older sources. The context is also against such a presumption.

[2] See Pinsker, p. 98. In the list of Karaite scholars at the end of the חלוק (p. 106) only Tobias is mentioned of the well-known Byzantine Karaites; the citation of Hadassi, however, is not certain. See Steinschneider, l. c., 54.

of 'Anân[1]. His injured ambition, following upon his removal from the Exilarchate in favour of his younger brother Ḥanania, drove him to Schisma. 'Anân was in mortal danger owing to the interference of the Arabian government. But following the advice of a Moslem scholar (Abu Ḥanifa?) imprisoned with him, he was able to win the favour of the Chalif by declaring that he represented a different religion from his brother, to wit, that in opposition to the latter he taught the fixing of the months on the basis of the observation of the moon and the consideration of the ripeness of the corn. The Chalif saw therein a concession to Islam, and showed him favour. Pinsker must also be right in saying that this report was preserved in Saadiah's above-mentioned polemical work.

Thirteenth Century.

33. **Jacob b. Moses Tamâni** (of Taman in the Crimea), according to a tombstone inscription (Firkowitsch, אבני זכרון, no. 98), was the head of a Karaite school, and the author of a work ספר הפתרון, and he was buried in 958 in Tschufut-Kalé. It goes without saying that the date of this inscription, on which the word Tamâni does not occur, was fabricated by Firkowitsch, as there were not yet in the tenth century in the Crimea any Karaite heads of schools, who had many pupils (המעמיד תלמידי' רבי'). It does not at all follow from the work mentioned (the beginning of which is missing) that it bore the title ספר הפתרון, and that its author was called Jacob b. Moses. It is more likely to have been, according to Harkavy (*Altjüd. Denkmäler*, p. 268), the work of an anonymous Byzantine Karaite of the twelfth or thirteenth century. In the few lines that Pinsker (p. 68) has published from this work, "the heretic" (אלמכאלף=המחליף) Saadiah is also mentioned a few times. We have, e.g. his explanation of Exod. iii. 2 (on the burning of fire on the Sabbath; cf. above, p. 24),

[1] Cf. *R. É. J.*, XLIV, 166 seq.

then the assertion that analogy is not to be applied in the case of incest, and hence that it is not forbidden, as the Karaites maintain, to marry a niece[1]; and lastly, Saadiah's explanation, mentioned often already, that interprets חלבו האליה as חלבו והאליה.

34. **Jefet, called Ibn abi-l-Ḥasan al-Barqamâni,** was a Karaite physician and author in Alexandria. A *terminus a quo* for his life is afforded by the fact that he quotes no later author than Moses Maimonides (מוסי אלקרטבי); a *terminus ad quem* is supplied by the mention of his name in a Karaite compilation on Deuteronomy of the year 1351 (see *infra*, No. 38). He must therefore be assigned, with Steinschneider (*Arab. Liter. d. Juden*, § 172), to the middle of the thirteenth century. Apart from a medical work, אלמקאלה̈ אלמחסניה̈ פי חפט̇ אלצחה̈ אלבדניה̈ (MS. in Berlin and Oxford), Jefet also composed a polemical work in Arabic against the Rabbanites, under the title ספר תשובה (MS. in St. Petersburg), which consists of seven sections (וגוה), and is said to be very violent (see *Monatsschrift*, XLII, 189). Here also Maimonides is quoted very often, and designated as אלריים מוסי, אלריים (also אלמולי אלריים). A passage about Saadiah has been published by Gurland (גנזי ישראל, III, Russian part, p. 91): ... ואדעו (אי אלרבאנין) פי אלעבור אלנקל כמא אדעו בעץ̇ אלחכמים מת̇ל רב סעדיה אלפיומי אן אלעבור הלכה למשה מסיני ואן אדם הראשון עבר עליה אלשהר ואלסנין אלך̇ (cf. above, p. 10, n. 2).

35. **Natan b. Jehuda** is an otherwise quite unknown Karaite author. A passage in his name on the subject of calendar-lore is quoted in a Bodleian MS. of the year 1584 (Cat., vol. II, no. 2789, fol. 45 a; published *J.Q.R.*, VIII, 703) and in Moses Miṣorudi's מצות משה, which was written in 1602 (MS. Leyden, p. 52[7], fol. 247; see above, p. 47, n. 2). The beginning of this passage reads: אני נתן בן

[1] ורב פיומי עם חבריו התירו אותו מענה בת אחות ובת אח ואמרו אין מקישין בעריות וכו'. 'Anân already derives the prohibition to marry a niece from the analogy respecting the aunt: see *Kaufmann-Gedenkbuch*, p. 173.

יהודה נשאלתי שאלה זאת מן אלופי הקראים אשר הם יושבים בעיר אדום כי מאין לנו מן התורה שני ימים כסוי הירח וכו'. From these words we may infer that Natan did not live in Constantinople (עיר אדום) and that this city was still under Christian dominion. We are, therefore, perhaps not wrong in assigning him to the Crimea in the thirteenth century[1]. From the same Bodleian MS. another passage from this Natan is communicated, which is directed against Saadiah's well-known explanation of the verse Gen. i. 14 (והיו לאותות; see above, l. c.), and here we read towards the end: וזה הטעם כתבתיו אני נתן בספרי אשר עשיתי תשובה על פיומי וכו'. Thus Natan also composed a polemical work against Saadiah. This fact also testifies to an earlier date for our author, for, as the present essay shows, the Karaites did not cease indulging in polemics against Saadiah till modern times, though they do so only incidentally. None of them, however, composed a special work of controversy. Other traces of Natan's polemics are hitherto unknown.

36. **Aaron b. Joseph**, or Aaron the Elder, the famous physician of philosophical training, Bible exegete, and liturgical poet, is one of the most prominent representatives of the later period of Karaite literature. Of special importance is his commentary on the Pentateuch, ספר המבחר (ed. Koslow, 1835), which he composed according to his own statement in 1292/3 (on Exod. xii. 2; fol. 14 b: . . . זה לי ארבע עשרה שנה קודם זה הפירוש שנת ל"ט בפרט והיה לרבנים מולד תשרי ואנחנו ראינו הישן קרוב בזריחת השמש והראינו אותו לרבנים

[1] Simḥa Isaac Lutzki (ארח צדיקים, f. 21 b, l. 22) mentions a הר"ר נתן הקוסריני, who was perhaps a brother of the Aaron b. Judah קוסריני, to whom Solomon ha-Nasi sent his epistle on incest (see Steinschneider, *Cat. Lugd.*, p. 234), and who accordingly had lived at the beginning of the twelfth century. But it is impossible to identify him with our Natan, as the latter, in my opinion, did not live in Constantinople. Further on Simḥa Isaac (l. c., f. 22 a, l. 17) mentions among the Karaite scholars of Lithuania a Judah b. Daniel, together with his two sons, Daniel and Natan. But the latter also cannot possibly be our Natan b. Judah, as the literary activity of the Karaites in Lithuania only began in the sixteenth century, hence at the time when Byzantium was no longer Christian.

(הנמצאים שם באותו מקום הנקרא סולכאט וכו׳)[1]. Saadiah is mentioned here only twice: (1) on Exod. xiii. 4 (fol. 19 b), on אביב. According to Saadiah's declaration, this verse speaks against the Karaite interpretation of אביב as ripeness of corn, for here the question is about the ripeness in Egypt, which takes place one month earlier than that in Palestine, and therefore cannot serve for the fixing of the months. Aaron replies that this verse would then also point against the Rabbanites, who likewise pay regard to the אביב (והפיתומי חשב כי טען לקראים בשמור את חדש האביב באמרו כי אביב מצרים כבר הושחת ולא ידע כי בנפשו הוא). (2) On Lev. iv. 35 (fol. 7 a), on the use of the fat tail (אליה). Contrary to his custom elsewhere, Aaron deals with this subject rather fully. In this passage he already reverts to it a second time, and mentions the name of Saadiah only in connexion with an argument. In Lev. ix. 19–20, where אליה is included in the general concept of חלבים, the Karaites find a support for their prohibition of this fat tail. Saadiah refutes this argument by showing from Exod. xx. 8–10 and similar verses, that when two groups of things are enumerated, of which the one is much less than the other quantitatively, then only the larger group is mentioned, whilst the other is included in it (thus in ver. 20 only חלב is repeated, as this is greater quantitatively in comparison with כליות and יותרת הכבד of ver. 19). This view is opposed by Aaron in the following words: ... ואין טענת הפיתומי טענה שאמר מנהג העברי להזכיר הרוב ולהניח המעט הנה כי יתן איש אל רעהו חמור או שור או שה ושם כתוב וכל בהמה לשמור ואם נשבע השומר לשקר ישלם על כל דבר פשע על שור על חמור על שה ועל שלמה ולא יתכן שהבגדים נקראו בהמה . . . כן הנה מזכיר החלב ומניח הכליות והיותרת ושמע תשובתו כבר האיש ר׳ סעדיא שכח בין פרשת שומר חנם לפרשת שומר שכר ודי בזה וכו׳[2]. But Saadiah is also meant in the passage

[1] For the literature on him see *Jew. Encycl.*, s. v. (I, 14). On the Mibḥar cf. especially Jost, *Gesch. d. Judenthums*, II, 356 seq. It is not quite certain that Aaron lived in Constantinople.

[2] Both these conclusions of Saadiah have hitherto not been known from older sources, so far as I am aware. Could Aaron perhaps have drawn them immediately from Saadiah?

on iii. 9 (fol. 56), where several of his arguments are refuted: ... הנה· אלית הכבש קרבה למזבח וטעו המתירים אותה לאכילה עד שקצתם הוסיפו וי״ו ואמרו חלבו והאליה ... ועוד טען כי חלבו שם כלל לחמשה הנזכרים .... ועוד טען כי חלבו הוא כמו חלב יצהר וכו׳ (cf. *Gan Eden*, fol. 9 b; *Adderet*, ענין שחיטה, cap. 18). Apart from these passages Aaron must hint at Saadiah many times without mentioning his name.

Fourteenth Century.

37. **Israel [b. Samuel?] ha-Dajjan** (also called **ha-Maʿarabi**) lived in Cairo at the beginning of the fourteenth century, and is the author of several works in Arabic[1]. I have made the conjecture above (No. 26), that the poems preserved at the top of a MS. of David b. Abraham's Lexicon, and which are aimed against Saadiah and Samuel b. Ḥofni, were perhaps composed, not by Israel b. Daniel, but by our Israel ha-Maʿarabi.

38. The MS. of the British Museum, Or. 2498 (Cat., I, no. 334) contains **an Arabic commentary on Deuteronomy**, the beginning of which is missing, and which originally extended perhaps over the whole Pentateuch. This commentary, as the colophon states, is compiled from Qirqisâni, Jefet b. ʿAli, Sahl b. Maṣliaḥ [Abu-l-Surri], Abu-l-

[1] Enumerated in Steinschneider, *Arab. Liter. d. Juden*, § 184. The name of his father Samuel only rests upon a combination of Pinsker (p. 176) that has yet to be confirmed. On the other hand, the Karaite authors call him only רבי ישראל הדיין or המערבי; e.g., his pupil, Jefet b. Ṣagir (in Pinsker, ibid.); Aaron b. Elias (*Gan Eden*, f. 22 b; *Keter Tora* on Exod. xii. 2, f. 28 a); Samuel al-Magribi (*Murshid*, Section vii, chap. xiii, ed. Lorge, p. 14); Ibn al-Hiti (*J. Q. R.*, IX, 435, l. 8 from bottom); Elias Bashiatchi (*Adderet*, ענין קה״ח, cap. XL); Moses Bashiatchi (in the ספר עריות, see Steinschneider, *Cat. Lugd.*, p. 12); Judah Meir Taurizi (in Pinsker, p. 144), and Simḥa Isaac Lutzki (ארח צדיקים, f. 21 b, l. 22).—In the Arabic compilation on Deuteronomy about to be mentioned, the author cited as ר׳ יש׳ [=ישראל] פי אלרד̈ עלי אלר̇ [=אלרייס] צאחב אלעריות (see Margoliouth, *Catalogue*, I, p. 268 b) must likewise be our Israel.

Faraj Harûn, Abu-l-Faraj Furqân b. 'Asad [i. e. Jeshua b. Jehuda], and others, of whom Jefet seems to have been used the most, and it was finished in the first ten days of the month Nisan, 1663 (Era of Contracts) or the end of Muharram, 752, of the Hegira (=March, 1351)[1]. On xvii. 8 (fol. 49 a) a vigorous controversy is waged against Saadiah, who (according to the precedent of the Talmudists) refers the words בין דם לדם to the difference between pure and impure blood (וקד קאל אלפ̇ ותבֿאעה אן קו׳ תע׳ בין דם לדם הוא דם נדות ודם זיבות והדֿא ידל̈ עלי פסאד מדהבהם ועדם עקלהם ודינהם פהל יכון נקל אקבח מן הדֿא אלך̇). As mentioned already (cf. above, p. 20), David b. Boaz (?) also controverted this explanation of Saadiah, and it is therefore possible that he was the source whence our compiler drew.

39. **Aaron b. Elias**, or Aaron the Younger, is also important as a Bible exegete, a teacher of the Law, and a religious philosopher, on which account his co-religionists place him by the side of Maimonides. His place of origin was Nikomedia, in Asia Minor, and he died 1369[2]. For our purpose we have first to consider his Book of Precepts, entitled גן עדן (composed 1354, ed. Koslow, 1866). Here also Saadiah is the subject of rather frequent controversy. Aaron deals most fully with the subject of the calendar, and is uncommonly incensed against Saadiah's theory of the great age of the permanent calendar with all its rules. He says that Saadiah, in this assertion, scoffs at his own teachers, the Talmudists, who all firmly maintained the method of observation (fol. 5 b: ... מכלל האיש ר׳ סעדיא התל לרבותיו אשר היו מתנהגים בראיית הירח כרבן גמליאל ור׳ יהושע ור׳ עקיבא וחבריהם ואמר שהם תפשו דת שלא כדין תורה וכו׳), then

[1] Cf. my *Aboul-Faradj Haroun ben al-Faradj*, p. 37 (=*R. É. J.*, XXXIII, 216). That Jefet was the principal source follows from the remark on Deut. xxxiii. 4 (published in *Semitic Studies in Memory of Dr. Kohut*, p. 436, n. 3). See also Margoliouth, *Catalogue*, l. c., and Steinschneider, *Arab. Liter. d. Juden*, §§ 132, 235 (also my *Zur jüd.-arab. Litter.*, p. 79).

[2] Cf. on him finally *Jew. Encycl.*, s.v. (I, 9, 10), and אוצר ישראל, s.v. (I, 161).

advances his arguments and objections against observation (ואלו הם פוגותיו וקושיותיו ושבושיו, altogether ten in number), and refutes it. Then Aaron opposes Saadiah's assertion that all the data in the Talmud from which it is inferred the *Deḥijot* had no validity, are to be understood only theoretically (fol. 6 d: ... והואיל והביאו זה מצד המעשה בטלו דברי הפיתומי שאמר כי כל מקום שיאמרו חל טעמו ע״ד רדיפה וכו׳). Incidentally we learn that Saadiah's opinion of those data, which could not in any case be taken theoretically, was that they contain only the view of individuals but not the generally accepted view (fol. 7 b: ... כשעיין באלו הענינים זה האיש סעדיא הפיתומי אמר כי זה היה דת לקצת אנשים אך לא לכלל האומה ודבריו גלויי הסתירה לפי הנראה ומכחיש האמת בידוע וכו׳). He further attacks the theory of the great age of intercalation, which he refutes with arguments from the Talmud itself (fol. 15 b); and he also mentions his objection, that אביב can also signify the name of the month (fol. 16 d, where he calls Saadiah המהתל בנפשו). The other passages concern the problem of ממחרת השבת (fol. 53 a), the process of מליקה (fol. 89 d), the use of the fat tail (fol. 96 d: וראש החולקים הוא סעדיא הפיתומי אשר עמד לחלוק כנגד דעת הקראים וחכמינו ע״ה כבר שברו מלתעותיו; rather thorough and complete), and the theory of the Levirate marriage (fol. 159 b: the name of Saadiah is not mentioned here, though he is the author of the view, introduced by ואם יטעון, that Lev. xviii. 16 suffers limitation through Deut. xxv. 5, just as, e. g. Lev. xxiii. 3 through Num. xxviii. 9, see *supra*, p. 26).

All the views of Saadiah mentioned here are already known from earlier sources, from which Aaron also must have obtained them. On the other hand, the refutations often contain new points, especially with regard to the last matter, where logical categories are introduced. The manner of treatment is mostly pertinent and calm, as befits a serious scholar, though we have seen that the tone is not always distinguished.

In the commentary on the Pentateuch, כתר תורה (composed 1362; ed. Koslow, 1866–7), in which rabbinical authors are very often mentioned[1], Saadiah, remarkably enough, is not quoted a single time, and just as little in the religio-philosophical work עץ חיים (composed 1346; ed. Leipzig, 1841; Koslow, 1847).

Fifteenth Century.

40. **Samuel b. Moses al-Magribi**, a Karaite physician and author in Cairo, composed among other things a Book of Precepts in Arabic, entitled אלמרשד (finished July 2, 1434), which consists of twelve sections, and is extant in MS. in London, Berlin, and (partly) in St. Petersburg[2]. It is distinguished by lucidity and orderly arrangement. The parts edited are: Section II, on Sabbath, ed. N. Weisz (Pressburg, 1907); Section III, on the calendar, ed. F. Kauffmann (Frankfurt a. M., 1903; see my critical notice, *J. Q. R.*, XVI, 405 seq.); Section IV, chap. i–xviii, on the fast- and feast-days, ed. Junowicz (Berlin, 1904; cf. ibid., XVII, 594); Section VI, chap. i–xxii, on the laws contained in the section *Mishpâtîm*, ed. Gitelsohn (Berlin, 1904; cf. ibid., XVIII, 560), and Section VII, on the dietary-

[1] They are as follows: David (al-Muqammeṣ? I, f. 15 b); Ḥayyûj (I, 39 b, 45 b; II, 69 b); Abulwalîd (I, 39 b, 64 a, 68 a, 69 a, 80 b; II, 4 b, 22 a, 49 a); Moses ibn Chiquitilla (II, 101 b); Rashi (I, 6 a; II, 93 a, 95 a): Abraham ibn Ezra (very often); Maimonides (I, 7 a, 25 b; III, 63 b); Naḥmanides (I, 7 a); David Kimḥi (I, 45 b; II, 4 b; III, 16 b); Judah (b. Solomon ibn Matqa) of Toledo (I, 7 b, 8 a) and Shemariah Ikriti (I, 6 b).

[2] Cf. Steinschneider, § 199 (also my remarks in *Monatsschrift*, XLII, 189, and in my *Zur jüd.-arab. Litter.*, pp. 76, 77). According to Steinschneider, Samuel b. Moses [b. Jeshûa] al-Magribi [the physician, הרופא] was already identified or confused by the Karaites with Samuel (so read for Solomon) b. Moses b. Ḥesed El ibn al-סני [the teacher, המלמד] (cf. especially Catalogue of Heb. MSS. in Berlin, II, no. 202), and hence a work entitled מקדמאת is ascribed first to the one, then to the other. It is interesting to point out that in a Karaite prayer-book written by Daniel Firuz (MS. Brit. Mus. Or. 2531; Cat., II, no. 725) we read as follows (f. 90 b, cited in the *Catalogue*, p. 462 b): ויקום יקף אלדי ביקרא אלדרש אלדי רהבוה אלחכמים עלי כל פרשה מן אול אלסנה לאכרהא והם מרי ורבי שמואל המלמד ושמואל הרופא תנצבה ואסמוהם אלמקדמאת אלך. Thus both Samuels have composed such a work, and hence the confusion. Or, on the other hand, is this confusion reflected also in our notice? Cf. also *R. É. J.*, LI, 155.

laws, ed. Lorge (Berlin, 1907). No rabbinical author is mentioned in this work by name, but Saadiah is anonymously made the subject of controversy. Thus, in Section III, chap. 1 (ed. Kauffmann, p. 4*, l. 7), Saadiah's interpretation of Gen. i. 14, already mentioned a few times in this study, is characterized as that of a heretic (וקו׳ והיו לאותות הו ראנע אלי אלמאורות אלמדכורה לא [אלי] אליום ואללילה כמא זעם בעץ אלמכאלפין; cf. also *J. Q. R.*, XVI, 406).

41. **David b. Saad'el [=Saadiah] ibn al-Hiti** (of Hit on the Euphrates) is the author of a register of Karaite scholars, among whom the Samuel al-Magribi just mentioned is the latest. It thus appeared probably about the middle of the fifteenth century, but in spite of his comparative youth and in spite of his lack of critical power, it is not altogether without value, as the author apparently often had at his disposal good older sources. We have also made use of it here rather frequently, not without profit. This register is edited, with an English translation, by G. Margoliouth (*J. Q. R.*, IX, 429–43, also separately; cf. my notice in *Z.f.H.B.*, II, 79), under the title "Ibn al-Hiti's Arabic Chronicle of Karaite Doctors." Saadiah is mentioned here a few times in conjunction with various Karaite authors (see p. 432, l. 19; p. 433, l. 11; p. 435, ll. 8, 10, 19), but the only thing of interest is the statement that Salmon b. Jeroḥam died in Aleppo, that Saadiah followed the bier in rent garments and barefooted, and that, when he was reproached about it, he is said to have replied: "We have both derived great profit from our mutual controversy. There is not the slightest doubt about his [Salmon's] knowledge; and hence I did what I did" (p. 434, l. 20 seq.). Probably Ibn al-Hiti did not invent this fable, but took it from an older Karaite author. —Cf. also Steinschneider, *Arab. Liter. d. Juden*, § 200, and *infra*, No. 49.

42. **Elias b. Moses Bashiatchi**, who is distinguished "by conspicuous knowledge of the older literature, by complete mastery over the rich material, and who presents

the clearest and plainest method among the Karaite codifiers[1]," died in Constantinople, 23 Sivan, 1490, without completing his Book of Precepts אדרת אליהו (ed. Constantinople, 1531; Koslow, 1834; Odessa, 1870)[2]. In this work, which attained predominant authority among the later Karaites, Bashiatchi records the older opinions and hence mentions also the opinions of Saadiah. In the introduction, for example, he disputes Saadiah's explanation of Exod. xxiv. 12 (ובזה הפסוק נדחקו קצת מבעלי הקבלה עד שהגאון ... הפיתומי אמר כי מה שאמר כתבתי דבק עם לוחות האבן לא עם התורה והמצוה כי השם יתעלה לא כתב רק עשרת הדברים ופירש התורה תורה שבכתב והמצוה תורה שבעל פה ... והתשובה עליו מה שאמר כתבתי דבק עם לוחות האבן לא עם התורה והמצוה זה צריך אהוב שיאמין בו כי כתבתי הוא אחר התורה והמצוה והיה ראוי שיהיה קודם מהם וכו׳)[3]. Then he discusses the themes touched on most often in the controversy with Saadiah, viz. the questions of calendar-lore (ענין קדוש החדש, chap. 6, 9, 15, and 36), fire-burning on the Sabbath (ע׳ שבת, chap. 4, 18), and the forbidden pieces of fat (ע׳ שחיטה, chap. 18). Moreover, he also controverts Saadiah without mentioning his name, e. g. in reference to ממחרת השבת (ע׳ חג השבועות; chap. 3), &c. In all these questions Bashiatchi follows earlier protagonists, especially Aaron b. Elias, but by his clear and systematic classification of the material he throws a brighter light upon many a matter that had till then received scant consideration.

43. **Kaleb b. Elias Afendopolo** (or **Efendopulo**). He was a pupil and brother-in-law of the preceding. He is justly called the last Karaite polyhistor, for he represents

[1] Frankl in his article "Karaiten" (in Ersch u. Gruber, II, vol. XXXIII, p. 21).

[2] The work was then completed by Kaleb b. Elias Afendopolo, the well-known pupil and brother-in-law of Bashiatchi; but he was also overtaken by death before he was able to bring his work to a complete conclusion. Cf. the following number.

[3] This explanation of Saadiah is already controverted by Tobias b. Moses, who, however, does not quote it fully: see above, p. 62. Cf. also Wolf, *Bibl. Hebr.*, IV, 1093.

in his own personality the entire learning of his age[1]. Among his numerous writings, which deal with the most diverse scientific subjects, there is also an incomplete supplement to the אדרת אליהו, which has just been mentioned. This work mentions the date, 1497, in several places. In the supplement to ענין טומאה וטהרה (ed. Odessa, 136 c, at foot), he discusses the commandment of the red heifer, the ashes of which possessed the well-known property of defiling the pure and cleansing the unclean. He quotes Saadiah's view[2], but he is as little satisfied with it as with the exegesis of the other Rabbanite and Karaite authorities, whom he quotes previously.

Sixteenth Century.

44. **Moses b. Elias Bashiatchi**, a great-grandson of Elias b. Moses Bashiatchi (no. 42 above), is generally represented as a prodigy. Born in 1554, at Constantinople, he is said by his sixteenth year to have already acquired many languages (Greek, Arabic, Spanish) and to have composed many works. He then started on his travels, but died two years after, 26 Iyar, 1572, as a young man of eighteen (Mordecai b. Nisan, דד מרדכי, ed. Vienna, fol. 9 b). How much of this is true it is hard to ascertain[3]; but it is a fact that he understood Arabic, and that he had before him many

[1] For the literature about him, see my article in the *Hebrew Encyclopedia*, אוצר ישראל, vol. II, pp. 172-4, s. v. אפנדופולו, where I have endeavoured to determine the time when he lived.

[2] ואמר רב סעדיה הגאון שהפרה דומה לדבש שמזיק לבעל המרה האדומה ויועיל לבעל הליחה גם דומה לשמש שמלבין הדבר המכובס ומשחיר פני הכובס: It appears from the examples quoted here, which do not agree with those given in *Emunoth* (section iii, end), that Afendopolo must presumably have used an intermediary source—i. e. ibn Ezra on Numbers xix. 2. It must, however, be remarked that the first instance only is adduced there.

[3] Much more probable is another statement contained in the St. Petersburg MS. of his מטה אלהים (in Neubauer, *Aus d. Petersb. Bibl.*, p. 121), that Moses B. died in 1555, at the age of twenty-eight. Cf. also Steinschneider, *Die Geschichtsliteratur der Juden*, I, p. 106, no. 124, and *J. Q. R.*, XVIII, 188.

monuments of the oldest Karaite literature. In Egypt he found fragments of 'Anân's Book of Precepts in the original Aramaic, which he included in his זבח פסח (cf. *R. É. J.*, XLV, 176 seq.). The Pentateuch commentary of Abu-l-Faraj Harûn was also known to him (see ibid., XXXIII, 217; reprint, p. 38), &c. In his מטה אלהים he gives a chain of tradition of the Karaite teachers (reproduced by Mordecai b. Nisan, l. c., fol. 11 b). Here we read, among other things, that Saadiah flourished at the time of Salmon b. Jeroḥam, Joseph b. Noaḥ, Jacob b. Isaac Qirqisâni, Ḥasan b. Mashiaḥ, and Abraham b. Isaac al-Baṣri; that he was a disciple of Salmon; and that Joseph disputed with him in his ספר המאור, composed in 930 (. . . והם העתיקוה לרב נח והוא העתיק לרב שלמה בן ירוחם ולרב יוסף בן נח ולרב יעקב בן יצחק הקרקסאני ולרב חסור [*sic!*] בן משיח ולרב אברהם בן יצחק הבוצרי ובזמניהם היה רב סעדיה גאון ז״ל הפיתומי והוא היה תלמידו של רב שלמון בן ירוחם ורב יוסף השיגו ונמצאו יחד שניהם בזמן אחד והקשה עליו ר׳ יוסף והכריח לו בטענותיו כאשר מזכיר בספרו בספר המאור וחבר בשנת ארבעת אלפים שש מאות וצ׳ ליצירה). Here we have, so far as is known, the oldest source for the information, often repeated by later Karaites, that Saadiah was a pupil of Salmon[1], and this information caused Firkowitsch to fabricate the *Muqaddima* named after Salmon (Pinsker, p. 61 seq.). By the Joseph who disputed with Saadiah we have likewise to understand Qirqisâni, whom Moses Bashiatchi mostly calls רבי׳ יוסף הקרקסאני, but whom he also styles once as Joseph b. Isaac b. Jacob Q. and another time as Joseph b. Jacob Q. Hence we should probably read in the chain of tradition: ולרב [יוסף בן] יעקב בן יצחק הקרקסאני. He always entitles his work as המאור הגדול, and only once as ספר האורים, so that here also המאור is to be given the full form of המאור הגדול[2].

[1] Another of the recent writers on the Talmud (Bernfeld, *Der Talmud*, Berlin, 1900, p. 83) asserts that this is a fact, and that it is admitted by both sides, Karaite and Rabbinical!

[2] Cf. the passages in question from the works of B. in *Steinschneider-Festschrift*, pp. 214 seq., where I also point out that Qirqisâni was

Seventeenth Century.

45. **Elias b. Baruch Jerushalmi** belongs to the second half of the seventeenth century. We find him in Elul, 1654, in Constantinople, where he hospitably entertained the Karaite travellers from the Crimea, Moses Jerushalmi b. Elias ha-Levi and Elias b. David, in his house[1]. But he must have migrated later to the Crimea, for Simḥa Isaac Lutzki mentions him among the scholars of this country (ארח צדיקים, fol. 21 b, l. 3 from bottom). Elias composed certain works (enumerated by Fürst, III, 67), which, however, exist only as manuscripts. He was also a scribe and particularly copied old polemical works of the Karaites, which he provided with prefatory remarks and postscripts, e.g. the polemical treatise of Sahl b. Maṣliaḥ against Jacob b. Samuel (Pinsker, pp. 25, 27, 43). In a concluding note on a copy of Salmon b. Jeroḥam's controversial work, which has been preserved from Pinsker's literary remains in the Vienna *Beth ha-Midrash* (No. 27[3]; cf. Pinsker, p. 35), Elias indulges in such violent abuse of Saadiah that the pen refuses to repeat the words[2]. We there read that many Karaites engaged in a polemical campaign against the godless Fayyumite, e.g. David b. Boaz (מר דוד הנשיא בן בועז הזכאי הנשיא ע"ה)[3], "his teacher" Salmon b. Jeroḥam (סלמון

confused with al-Baṣir (but perhaps this confusion originates with the copyists; cf. also the following number). The designation of Qirqisâni's כהאב אלאנואר as המאור הגדול ought to serve as a sufficient distinction from Baṣir's כתאב אלאסתבצאר (= ספר המאור).

[1] See the account of the travels of this Moses, ed. Gurland (גנזי ישראל, part I, p. 31): ... וביום ה׳ [י"א אלול התי"ד] באנו לקוסטינא וחנינו בליל יום ששי בבית כה"ר אליהו ירושלמי יצ"ו בכ"ר ברוך ירושלמי יצ"ו ואכלנו ושתינו משלחנו עמהם ממה שזמן הקב"ה. Cf. also Neubauer, *Aus d. Petersb. Bibl.*, pp. 47, 67.—The surname Jerushalmi, which both Elias and his father Baruch bear, and which is also to be met with among other Karaites of the later time, does not signify absolutely that its bearers came from Jerusalem, but that they had made a pilgrimage to the holy city (hence analogous to the Moslem Ḥajji) or had sojourned there some time.

[2] Published by Bardach, מזכיר לבני רשף (Vienna, 1869), p. 27.

[3] Elias has here a hovering notion of the name of the Exilarch David b. Zakkai, the opponent of Saadiah.

בן ירוחם רבו המשיב לו תשובות כהלכה ומוכיחו על פניו על חלומותיו ועל דבריו), and his colleague, Joseph al-Baṣir, also a disciple of Salmon, in his work *ha-Maor*, composed in the year 910 (וגם חברו של פיומי רבנו יוסף הרואה תלמידו של רבינו סלמון רבו בספרו המאור המחובר בשנת ד"א שש"ע). The ban which Salmon, according to right and custom, hurled against his rebellious pupil, provoked Saadiah to such a degree of agitation and fear that he fell into a melancholy, died of it in 942, and was denied an honourable burial in Sura. Elias seems to have taken these various chronological snippets partly from Moses Bashiatchi[1].

46. **Mordecai b. Nisan** composed among other things, as is well known, in the form of an answer to the questions of Trigland, the little work דד מרדכי, which pretends to be a history of Karaism. He finished it July 18, 1699, in Krasni Ostrow (or Kokizow), not far from Lemberg, and it first appeared in Wolf's *Notitia Karaeorum*, Hamburg, 1714. Saadiah is mentioned here only quite incidentally, e. g. in the above-mentioned chain of tradition of Moses Bashiatchi reproduced here. In another passage (ed. Vienna, fol. 13 a) Mordecai states that the Karaite chronology agrees with that of the Rabbanites. For example, of the latter, Gedaliah ibn Yaḥya, in his *Shalshelet*, gives 942 as the year of Saadiah's death (... וכמו כן כשנעיין במספר תאריכיהם שזכרו את רבי סעדיה גאון שלהם שכתב בעדו רבי גדליה אבן יחייא בשלשלת הקבלה שרבי סעדיה גאון נפטר בשנת ד' אלפים תש"ב ליצירה), and this agrees (?) with the assertion of the Karaites just mentioned, that Saadiah was a pupil of Salmon, and that he is the object of a polemical attack in the *Sefer ha-Maor*, composed in 930. In conclusion, he speaks (fol. 13 b) of the letter of Menaḥem, mentioned by Trigland, to עקילס הגר אצל ר' סעדיה הרבן (ed. Pinsker, p. 55 seq.; see *supra*, No. 4), and doubts whether this Saadiah is identical with the Gaon. He does not evince a trace of hatred against the Fayyumite.

[1] So for instance on the polemics against Saadiah in ספר המאור, only that he independently added after רב יוסף the word הרואה.

Eighteenth Century.

47. **Abraham b. Josiah Jerushalmi** is included among the scholars of the Crimea by Simḥa Isaac Lutzki (ארח צדיקים, fol. 21 b, l. 2 from bottom), and lived in Tschufut-Kalé, as he also bears the surname קלעי (ibid., fol. 26 a, s. v. שאול שאול). He is the author of a work entitled אמונה אמן (ed. Koslow, 1846), which is uncommonly interesting in many respects. In the first place the author manifests an unexampled extensive knowledge of the Rabbinical literature, extending not only to the halakhic but also to the theological and other branches, and he speaks of this and also of the Talmudical literature with an esteem that could hardly be surpassed by a Rabbanite. He especially reveres Maimonides, whose works he has studied with diligence [1]. Abraham composed this work whilst he was still young and lived a wandering life, and he finished it, according to the postscript, in the year 1712 [2]. The greatest part (ff. 4 b-44 b) is devoted to the demonstration whether the Karaite or the Rabbanite law is the true one, and here also he discusses the matter with the Rabbanites in the calmest tone and only occasionally uses a rather violent expression. For example, in the only passage in which Saadiah is mentioned (fol. 33 b), it is said that the Rabbanites in their controversy with the Karaites adopt as their support either the plain meaning of scripture (פשט) or tradition (קבלה). But they could not succeed with the *Peshat*, as this is against them. Thus Saadiah maintained that the Jewish religion does not teach the observation of the moon but the calculation of the calendar, and that this is based upon scripture itself. But this is wrong, as Maimonides in his commentary on the Mishna and Ibn Ezra, besides others, admits [3]. Similarly, his opinion that

[1] I hope to analyse this work shortly in a special notice.

[2] F. 49 b: ... ועוד כי הברתיו ואני נער גולה ונודד ממקומי ... ועוד חסרוני מהפירושים וספרי הגמרות ... וזכני להשלים מחברת זה הספר עצות מרחוק אמונה אמן ביום שני לשבוע בסדר ואת העם צו לאמר בשנת התע"ב ליצירה וכו'.

[3] ... בראשונה רב סעדיה גאון שהשיב ואמר כי לפי פשטי הכתובים אין דת ישראל בנויה

the fat tail (אליה) is not designated in scripture as fat is altogether wrong, and Ibn Ezra admitted here also that the Gaon was mistaken. Nay, even Alfasi expressly states in his *Halakhot* (*Ḥullin*, section VII), that the fat tail is indeed called fat, but that the Bible nevertheless permitted its enjoyment[1]. In fact, all Saadiah's objections against the Karaites were void and vain (ולא באלו בלבד אלא כל תשובות שהשיב לבעלי מקרא הם בנויות על קו תהו ואבני בהו), and even the greatest Rabbanite scholar could not offer any real reply, as what was false could not possibly be given out as truth (ולא הגאון סעדיה בלבד שלא יוכל להשיב תשובות אמתיות לבעלי מקרא אלא אפילו הגדול שבהם לא יוכל בזה כי אין בעולם מי שיאמת השקר כי לנמנע טבע קיים והמשכיל יבין). By the "greatest" scholar he doubtless means Maimonides, whom, as already mentioned, he places in the highest rank of Rabbinical learning.

על פי הראיה אלא על פי החשבון כמו שנוהגים היום ואין ספק כי זה שקר גמור וכבר העיר לשקרות זה הרב הגדול רבי׳ משה בר מיימון זצ״ל בפירושו במשנה וז״ל ואני המיה מאדם יכחיש הראות ויאמר כי דת היהודים איננה בנויה על ראית הלבנה אלא על פי החשבון בלבד ... וכן הראב״ע ז״ל אמר ובמשנה ראיות כאריות שנפל הפסח בבד״ו וכו׳. What is meant here is the passage in Maimonides' *Comm. on Rosh ha-Shana*, II, 6, and in Ibn Ezra on Lev. xxiii. 3 (but the latter passage is indirectly taken from Aaron b. Elias).

[1] ... וכבר ידוע שאפילו רבותיו מודים שהאליה תקרא חלב כמו שכתוב בהלכות רב אלפס בפרק גיד הנשה ז״ל ואליה גופא אף על גב דמקריא חלב רחמנא שריא דכתיב כל חלב שור וכשב ועז לא תאכלו דבר השוה בשור וכשב ועז הוא דאסור ואליה הואיל ואינה שוה בשור וכשב ועז דבכבש היא דקרבה ובשור ועז לא קרבה [שריא] ע״כ. But Abraham b. Josiah, who, according to his own statement, had no copy of the Talmud before him when composing his work (see above, p. 88, n. 2), was unable to know that Alfasi here simply paraphrases a Talmudical passage, see *Ḥullin*, 117a (cf. *Keritot*, 4a): א״ל רב מרי לרב זביד אי אליה איקראי חלב היתסר באכילה א״ל עליך אמר קרא כל חלב שור וכשב ועז דבר השוה בשור וכשב ועז רב אשי אמר חלבו האליה איקראי חלב סתמא לא איקראי וכו׳. Incidentally be it remarked that this Talmudical passage, in which only late Amoraim appear, and which in *Ḥullin* gives quite the impression of an editorial addition, was perhaps also intended to weaken the objections of many people to the permitted enjoyment of the fat tail. Thus the Karaites would in this case have only had to attach themselves to a pioneer opposition of earlier times.

Nineteenth Century.

48. **Joseph Solomon Lutzki b. Moses** (called היש״ר), Haham in Koslow in the first half of the nineteenth century (born 1769, died December 10, 1844; for his epitaph see Firkowitsch, אבני זכרון, pp. 241-2), composed a very thorough supercommentary on the *Mibḥar*, entitled טירת כסף (completed 17 Ab, 1825), which was published together with the *Mibḥar* in Koslow, 1835[1]. Here Joseph Solomon remarks, on Lev. iii. 9 (fol. 5 b, n. 136 seq.), that the arguments adduced by Aaron b. Joseph, that the fat tail is not comprised under חלב, are those of Saadiah: [וטעו המתירים אותה לאכילה] עד שקצתם הוסיפו וי״ו [ואמרו חלבו והאליה] זה ר׳ סעדיה גאון שפירש והאליה בתוספת וי״ו כדי שלא תוכלל בתוך פרטי החלבים הנזכרים אחריה . . . עוד טען הפיתומי כי אע״פ שיהיה חלבו שם כלל הוא כולל הה׳ חלבים הנזכרים אחר אמרו האליה אבל האליה אינה נכללת במלת חלבו וכו׳. He naturally obtained this information from Aaron b. Elias (*Gan Eden*, fol. 96) or Elias Bashiatchi (*Adderet*, ענין שחיטה, cap. 18).

49. **Abraham b. Samuel Firkowitsch** (born at Lutzk 21 Elul, 1788, died at Tschufut-Kalé 22 Sivan, 1874), a brother-in-law and pupil of the preceding, is at the same time the last noted Karaite scholar[2]. His epoch-making importance, which was the cause of much blessing as well as of much harm, is too well known that we should dilate upon it here. We shall therefore, in accordance with our object, merely examine his relations with Saadiah.

Firkowitsch began his literary career with abusive writings directed against Rabbanite Judaism. One of them (חותם תכנית) he added as an appendix to the מבחר ישרים

[1] See on him and his work also Jost, II, 374; Gottlober, p. 179, and Fürst, III, 131 seq.

[2] The day and year of his birth are given by Firkowitsch himself in הכרמל, II (1861, 1862), 169. The literature on him in *Jew. Encycl.*, s. v. (V, 394), is not complete. Cf., e. g., Geiger, *Jüd. Zeitschrift*, XI, 142 seq.; Frankl, *Monatsschrift*, XXV, 479; Steinschneider, *Vorlesungen über d. Kunde hebr. Handschriften*, p. 82, &c.

(Koslow, 1835) edited by him (fol. 49–58)[1]. The other (מסה ומריבה) appeared as an independent work (ibid., 1838). In outward form the author here follows the example of Hadassi, inasmuch as he takes the Ten Commandments as his text, and writes in rhymed prose, although the style is somewhat more fluent and pleasant than that of his predecessor. But in regard to matter also, he follows throughout those of the older Karaite authors who are lacking in every feeling of respect for their opponent. In this work Saadiah is occasionally made the object of a polemical attack, and is mentioned by name. The author also repeats the statement that the Gaon was a pupil of Salmon, and that in his religio-philosophical work he followed the footsteps of his teacher (fol. 134 b: וגם ראה [ר"ל הרמב"ם] ספרי קדמונינו ולמד מהמה כספר רבנו סלמון (*sic*) מאד מחברת נעמה שהיה רבו של סעדיה גאון משנאנו: בכן דרך בספר אמונות שלו בדרך רבו סלמון בן ירוחם אין לחכמתו ערך משלמות הפעולה שלמות הפועל נוכחת), nay, that he had learnt the philosophy of the Kalâm, upon which this work is built, from the Karaites, just as Maimonides himself admits that this philosophy first appeared among them (fol. 135 a: ... בכן הודה [ר"ל הרמב"ם] שאצל הקראים נמצאה חכמה [l. חכמת] הדברים בשם פילוסופיא נקראה וסעדיה החל באמונות אשר למד אצלמו; see *Moreh*, I, 71). In fact, all important Rabbanite scholars who, in accordance with the precept of 1 Chron. xxviii. 9, strove after a true knowledge, like Saadiah, Maimonides, and others, only followed the example of the Karaites, who first made this knowledge a duty (fol. 137 a: ...הראשונים בדבר זה החקירה חייבו היו הקראים . . . ותלו עצמם על פסוק דע את אלהי אביך . . . ואחריהם כל ישרי לב רבנים נמשכו גדולי חכמיהם בדרכי קראים הלכו סעדיה ורמב"ם וכל הנלוים האמת קבלו וכו'). In the controversy about single points of difference among Rabbanites and Karaites,

[1] Also in the supplement to Aaron b. Joseph's Isaiah commentary (from cap. lix), entitled קצור הכלית ישעיה, he continually disputes with the Rabbanites in a very abusive tone; see, e. g., on lix. 5; lx. 22; lxii. 11; lxv. 4, 7, 8, 11, &c. Cf. also Geiger, l. c., 147.

Saadiah is mentioned only in the discussion about the burning of fire on the Sabbath (fol. 51 a: גם פיתומי בהפכו תבערו לתבעירו לא הרויח כי שתיהן להדלקה נאמרו וכו').

But in proportion as Firkowitsch began to make his discoveries, his relation towards Rabbinism changed. Whether it was that in consequence of his scientific ardour his ideas had become enlarged[1], whether it was that he now needed the good will of the Rabbanite scholars[2], the fact is that from 1839 he no longer indulged in any objectionable remarks in his published works against the Rabbanites, and that he gave expression to this altered disposition in his famous letter to Bezalel Stern in the year 1841 (published in part in אוצר נחמד, I, 105)[3]. Now Saadiah also receives honour from his hands, especially in a treatise in which he communicates the discovery of fragments of two works of Saadiah, the ספר האגרון and the ספר הגלוי (in המליץ, VIII, 1868, no. 26–7; partly quoted by Harkavy, *Stud. u. Mitt.*, V, 12 seq., 135 seq.). He rejoices exceedingly at the discovery of his "great and wonderful work," the ספר האגרון, because here Saadiah, "our holy teacher," gave a positive date (... ומי יוכל לחות ולהופיע את גודל השעשוע אשר אני משתעשע בתאריך חבורו שהיה נעלם עד היום מכל חכמי לב אשר כתב רבנו הקדוש הזה בידו הקדושה במלות ברורות וכו'). All the Gaon's opponents were worthless fellows who invented godless libels against him (... כל הטענות אשר טענו על דבריו ... ר' דוד בן זכאי וכלף בן שרגאדו בעלילות רשע את אישים פועלי און הקושרים עליו). He regretted himself that he was once one of the foes of the Gaon (וגם קבלתו [של הראב"ד] על פטירת הגאון מן המרה השחורה .... לא העלוה על ספריהם רק קצת המאמינים לקבלתו או השונאים את הרס"ג מבני מקרא (כמוני, לפני זה) הביאוה בספריהם ... ועל חטאתי אבקש מכבוד מעלתו מחילה בעולם הבא). Firkowitsch also admits here that Saadiah was older

[1] So Geiger, l. c., 149.

[2] So Harkavy, *Altjüd. Denkmäler*, pp. 211 seq., whose judgment, however, is somewhat too one-sided.

[3] Cf. also his preface to Solomon b. Mubḥar's חוק יד (Odessa, 1866).

than Salmon, and hence that the statement of Ibn al-Hiti (see *supra*, No. 41) caused difficulties (ואולי יש שרש דבר ... בדברי בן אלהיתי שהיה הרס"ג בארם צובה בזמן פטירת הרסב"י והתאבל עליו אך לא אוכל לדעת איך אפשר להיות אחרי שהרסב"י חבר פי' תהלים בשנת תתפ"ז לחרבן ד"א תשי"ו והרס"ג נפטר בשנת ד"א תש"ב לפי המוסכם כהנ"ל וכו')[1], and so forth in the same tone. In another work, where he likewise has the opportunity of mentioning Saadiah (בני רשף, Vienna, 1871, p. 8 seq.), he does this quite objectively.

With Firkowitsch the fountains of Karaite learning dry up completely, for the extremely little that has flowed from a Karaite pen during the last thirty years is hardly worthy of mention; and so with him there closes the polemical campaign against Saadiah. But it is worth while now calling particular attention to a phenomenon. In this essay we have passed in review almost a full thousand years, and we have seen that we cannot speak of any development whatever in this controversy. The number of the controversialists is indeed not very great, but still it forms a distinguished host. The points in the dispute, however, are almost always the same, and we seldom meet any new factors or new points of view. The tone mostly depends not on internal but on external factors: it is calm or violent according to the temperament of each disputant. But throughout the course of centuries the argument proceeds along the same track. Our dissertation, therefore, is of interest not only as a bibliographical document but also as a chapter in the history of culture.

[1] Harkavy, *Stud. u. Mitt.*, V, 136, n. 2, did not yet know who is meant by this Ibn al-Hiti.

ADDENDA AND CORRIGENDA TO MY ESSAY ON "THE ANTI-KARAITE WRITINGS OF SAADIAH GAON"

(*J. Q. R.*, X, 238–76).

In general, cf. Steinschneider, *Arab. Liter. d. Juden*, pp. 50–1 and 65 (no. 10–13), also ibid., p. 339; my *Zur jüd.-arab. Litter.*, pp. 42–3, and Bacher, *Jewish Encycl.*, X, p. 582, as well as the passages quoted there. In particular, the following must also be added:

P. 242, l. 3 from bottom. Saadiah's work against ʻAnân was preserved longer than I originally assumed, for it is mentioned in a list of books at the end of the twelfth century. See *R. É. J.*, XLV, 192, No. 2, and the passages quoted there. Cf. also *supra*, No. 32, and Hirschfeld, *J. Q. R.*, XIX, 137.

P. 244, l. 23 seq. The conclusion of the כתאב אלתמייז has been found in the Geniza, and edited by Hirschfeld (*J. Q. R.*, XVI, 102–5)[1]. We learn from it that the whole work consisted perhaps of eight sections (see p. 103, l. 18: ... ושרח אלבאב אלח̇ אלדי הו מערפה̈ אליום אלי אלמתכ̇ד פי אלגלות), and that the penultimate seventh section (the conclusion of which is extant in this fragment) dealt with the problem of ממחרת השבת, whilst in the last the question about the two days' observance of festivals (except the Day of Atonement) in the Diaspora is discussed. This last section, which has been preserved in its entirety, occupies altogether two printed pages, and if we were to conclude from this with regard to the other sections, the כתאב אלתמייז must have been small in compass. But it is also possible that the work became split up into several

[1] The fragment edited by Harkavy (*J. Q. R.*, XIII, 656, 657) is probably rather a part of Saadiah's polemical work against Ibn Sâqaweihi, see above, No. 2.

parts (מקאלאת), and that we have before us only the seventh and eighth sections of the last part[1]. We know, as a matter of fact, that this work must have dealt with other subjects besides the calendar and the festivals (see my essay, p. 252).

We can enter only very briefly here into the contents of this fragment. In the seventh section it is shown, in the first place, that one and the same word (in our case שבת) in two neighbouring verses, or even in one and the same verse can very well have two different meanings (hence, in our case, festival-day and week); and secondly, that the Karaites are wrong in deducing an argument for their own interpretation from the non-mention of a fixed date for the Feast of Weeks in the Bible. Then the opinion of a יהודה אלאסכנדראני is advanced, that just as the harvest of wheat is fifty days distant from that of barley, so is that of the new wine from that of wheat, which thus falls at the end of Tammuz, and that a similar interval divides the harvest of oil from that of the new wine, so that on the 20th of Elul an oil offering had to be brought. Saadiah adds that the author had arguments in support of this (ואלדליל לה עלי דלך). That Philo is meant by this Judah the Alexandrian, as Hirschfeld supposes, is possible; these recent discoveries have shown that his works (in an oriental translation) were known in the ninth and tenth centuries in the East, and that he is also quoted, for example, by Qirqisâni as אלאסכנדראני (see all the details in my essay, "Philon dans l'ancienne littérature judéo-arabe," in *R. É. J.*, L, 10–31).—In the last or eighth section it is also stated that it is a tradition handed down by the prophets that outside Palestine two days were observed instead of one; and it is then shown that no offence is thus intended against Deut. xiii. 1, for we do not read here: "Whatsoever I *write* unto you . . . ye shall not add thereto, nor diminish from it," but "Whatsoever I *command* you," and that which is handed down by tradition must be regarded as having been

[1] This would become a certainty if the אלמקאלה אלאולי, mentioned in the next note, were really taken from the *Tamjiz*.

commanded just as well as that which is written (p. 103, l. 9 from bottom: ... פאלתמסת אלמקרא לעלי אן אגדה ינאקצׄהם בקול לא תוסף עליו ולא [ולם .MS] תגרע ממנו פתבינ״ת אול אלפסוק פאדׄא ליס פיה את כל הדבר אשר אנכי כותב לכם ואנמא הו מצוה אתכם ווגדת אלמנקול ענד אלנטׄר צווי כאלמכתוב). A principle is here expressed, of the range of which Saadiah himself was perhaps not conscious.

The fragment edited by Schechter (*Saadyana,* No. IX) must also belong to the *Kitab al-tamjiz*[1]. In this fragment Saadiah adduces various passages in *Rosh ha-Shanah* as a support for his theory of the great age of the calculation of the calendar, e. g. from Mishna, I, 9, which shows that often witnesses arrived after the lapse of a whole night and a whole day, so that their declaration could not be of influence any more on the fixing of the new month. The object of the observation, therefore, was only to support the calculation (see *Saadyana*, p. 33, l. 1: ... פהד״ה דלאיל ביינה ואצׄחה אן טלבתהם ללקמר ואשעאלהם וארסאלהם אנמא הו אלביאן [לביאן read] אלחקׄ וצחה אלדלאיל אלדי כאנ[ו] יעטוהא פי תחקיק אלחסאב אלךׄ), a well-known favourite hypothesis of Saadiah. The earlier Karaites, on the other hand, forged a weapon against the Fayyumite out of the data in *Rosh ha-Shanah*, I–II.

P. 245, n. 3. The passage from Moses b. Ezra is now known in the Arabic original, and here also we read: פי כתאב אלתמייז פי רד״ה עלי בן סאקויה, see *supra*, p. 6, n. 3.

P. 252, l. 22 seq. On the כתאב אלרד״ עלי אבן סאקויה (so read line 24 instead of סקויה), of which several fragments of the Arabic original have likewise now been discovered, see *supra*, No. 2. On the passage cited by Mebasser respecting the controversy between R. Meir and the sages, see also *Z.f.H.B.*, IV, 21 (where in n. 3 instead of *J. Q. R.*, X, 852, read 252).

[1] As I have observed subsequently, there is here a gap between leaf 2 and 3 of the MS. Natan b. Isaac al-Siqili seems to have compiled a work for the support of tradition in general and that of the great age of the 'Ibbur in particular, and for this object to have included the first chapter (אלמקאלה אלאולי) of the כתאב אלתמייז in his work or compilation (my *Schechter's Saadyana*, p. 16, s. v. Natan, is therefore to be corrected).

P. 254, l. 19 seq. This polemical work of Saadiah is mentioned in a list of books from the end of the twelfth century as כתאב אלרד̈ עלי מתחאמל, and in another of uncertain date as אלרד עלי אלמתחמ̈ל. In both places, therefore, the mysterious word היום is missing (see my *Schechter's Saadyana*, p. 23, no. 24). The passage from Nissim's מגלת סתרים is really taken from the anonymous ספר החיים, and is again printed in Jellinek's קונטרס תרי"ג, p. 46 (cf. also his קונטרס הרמב"ם, first edition, p. 29, and Steinschneider, l.c., p. 65, n. 13). The quotations in Jehuda b. Barzillai's Jeṣira commentary originate perhaps rather from the polemical work against Ibn Sâqaweihi, see *supra*, p. 6, n. 7.

P. 255, l. 27 seq. On Ben Zuta, see *supra*, No. 1.

P. 256, l. 4 from bottom. Verbal examples of Saadiah's anti-Karaite Polemic in his commentary on the Pentateuch have now been supplied by Harkavy (directed against 'Anân, see הגרן, VI, pp. 38–40), and by Hirschfeld. The latter has printed from the Geniza two fragments: on Exod. xxxv. 3, and on Lev. xi. 11–21 (*J. Q. R.*, XVIII, 600 seq.; XIX, 136 seq.). In the first fragment, which contains an extensive polemic on לא תבערו, the following passage is especially interesting (p. 607, l. 7): ומנהם מן תעלק עלינא בטריק אלקיאס פאתגה פי גהאת שתי פאלמקדם אולא אבטאל אלקיאס פי אלשראיע אלסמעיה̈ ודלך במא רדדת בה עלי מדעייה פי אלכתאב אלדי אלפת לה. Hirschfeld (p. 600, n. 3) sees here the title of a book composed by Saadiah against the application of Analogy in traditional laws, identifies it with an elsewhere cited כתאב אלקיאס עלי אלשראיע אלסמעיה̈, would here amend אלקיאס to אלקיאס (and also apparently עלי to פי), and would insert אבטאל. But all that Saadiah says is that a Karaite, in order to establish the prohibition (Exod. xxxv. 3) according to Karaite views, had relied on the method of Analogy, but that in a work which he had written against this Karaite (probably 'Anân) he had opposed the application of this method in traditional laws. There is thus no reference here to a special work against the method of Analogy. Anyhow, it follows from this passage that it has been wrongly ascribed to Jefet, and therefore my own conclusion (*supra*, p. 21) must be corrected. In the fragment on Leviticus, Saadiah is throughout controverting 'Anân, as Hirschfeld rightly says. Saadiah does not name him, but indicates him as בעץ׳ אלמחדתין (fol. 1vo, l. 16; fol. 4vo, l. 14), הדא אלרג׳ל (fol. 2ro, l. 15; ibid.vo, l. 3; fol. 5ro, l. 17), and also הדא אלמבדע (fol. 4vo, l, 18). All the opinions here opposed are from other sources known to be 'Anân's. Thus besides the prohibition against eating fish which one of another religion has caught (see the proof by Hirschfeld, XIX, 138), there are also the following prohibitions: (1) to touch dead fish and birds; see his ספר המצות, ed. Harkavy, p. 66; (2) to eat dead fish, see *Z.f.H.B.*, IV, p. 74, and above, p. 10; (3) to eat hens, see above, p. 56 (where the words of Saadiah entirely agree with the foregoing); and (4) to eat any birds except pigeons, with reference to Gen. viii. 20, see ספר המצות, p. 67.

P. 257, l. 19. Besides in the commentary on the Pentateuch, Saadiah also disputes with the Karaites in the commentary on Proverbs: for the passages see Heller, *R. É. J.*, XXXVII, 229–30 (the passage on xxx. 10–17 must also be added, which Saadiah likewise refers to the opponents of tradition, who "calumniate the servants," i. e. the prophets, and those who follow them, before "their Lord," i. e. God, inasmuch as they characterize their tradition as falsehood. Verse 10 is especially directed against these calumniators).

Ibid., l. 2 from bottom. That Saadiah with the קום ממן יתסמ̃ון באליהודי̈ה aims at the Karaites was doubted by Horovitz (*Die Psychologie des Saadia*, Breslau, 1898, pp. 69–70) and Schreiner (*Z.f.H.B.*, III, 90), but without justification; see ibid., p. 176, n. 22.

P. 259, l. 3. In his commentary on the thirteen rules of R. Ishmael perhaps Saadiah also followed, however, an anti-Karaite tendency; cf. *R. É. J.*, XLVII, 136.

Ibid., l. 8. Cf. my *Zur jüd.-arab. Litter.*, p. 42, where I conjectured, *inter alia*, that a passage from this work is quoted in the fragment *Saadyana*, ed. Schechter, no. XVI. We here find that the persons with whom cohabitation is subject to limitations are to be divided into seven ascending degrees (p. 44, l. 17: קאל רבינו סעדיה גאון מחס[י]ה נב״ע אלאנסאם אלמחטור גשיאנהא וכל ואחד אצעב מן אלאכר והי אלך [read סבעה] סכעה) as follows: (1) harlots; (2) those despoiled of virginity; (3) relatives (twenty-eight in number, twenty according to scripture, eight according to tradition); (4) married women; (5) women in menstruation; (6) heathen women; and (7) sodomites [1]. Similarly Hirschfeld edited a Geniza fragment (*J. Q. R.*, XVII, 713 seq.) and rightly proved that it belongs to Saadiah's work on "forbidden marriages." Here allusion is actually made to the "heretics" (אלכוארג), who stand in opposition to "us, the entire body of Rabbanites" (נחן גמיע אלרבונין, p. 717, ll. 15, 26). There ought, therefore, to be no doubt any longer about the existence of this work of the Gaon.

Ibid., l. 23. A כתאב תחציל is also mentioned in a book-list of the end of the twelfth century; it is probably Saadiah's work of the same name. See *J. Q. R.*, XIII, 328; *R. É. J.*, XL, 87. But the Geniza fragment edited by Hirschfeld (*J. Q. R.*, XVII, 721 seq.) belongs not to the כתאב אלשראיע of Saadiah, but consists of a portion of his *'Amanât*, cf. ibid., XVIII, 146.

P. 260, l. 7 seq. On the כתאב אלתאריך see also my *Schechter's Saadyana*, p. 23, no. 23, and Bacher, *R. É. J.*, XLIX, 298.

P. 261, l. 2 from bottom. Read MS. Heb. e 45 (Cat. Bodl., vol. II, No. 2787[1]).

Ibid., n. 2. On the נקוד רב סעדיה quoted by Rashi on Ps. xlv. 10, cf. also Bacher, *Die Anfänge d. hebr. Grammatik*, p. 60, n. 2, and Steinschneider, *Vorlesungen über d. Kunde hebr. Handschriften*, p. 15.

P. 263, l. 14. In the commentary on Job xii. 7 (*Œuvres*,

[1] Cf. an analogous classification with regard to the marriage law, of which Jacob b. Ephraim is the author, in my monograph on the latter, pp. vii, xviii (= *Kaufmann-Gedenkbuch*, pp. 175, 186).

V, p. 40), besides this verse Ps. cxxxix. 8 is also given as an example of a figure of speech: ולו אמכן אן תסאל אלבהאים לדל̈תך ··· הד̇א תבאלג פי אלכלאם ··· והד̇א מת̇ל קו׳ אם אסק שמים שם אתה אלך.

Ibid., l. 25. Instead of מא באלניסן we should read (as Herr Mag. Israelson points out to me in a letter) מא באל ניסן.

P. 265, n. 1. This passage of Saadiah is, as can now be established, directed not against Jehuda ha-Parsi, but against the noted Karaite author of the ninth century, Benjamin al-Nahawendi. The latter had maintained that there are two kinds of month, lunar and solar (חדשי ירח and חדשי תקופות); and even found a proof for his position in Haggai i. 15 and ii. 1, where an event is dated in two ways, by the 24th Elul and the 21st Tishri. The difference of twenty-seven days is, he holds, to be referred to the difference between the lunar and solar months. Compare my remarks in *R. É. J.*, L, 19.

P. 268, n. 2. The article I promised here on Arabic expressions for the figure of hyperbole among Jewish authors appeared in *Z. f. H. B.*, III, 93 seq. Cf. also ibid., p. 177, and the passage just cited from Saadiah's commentary on Job.

P. 275, l. 8. I published a rather long passage from this little anti-Karaite work on ʿAnân in *R. É. J.*, XLV, 194 seq., and discussed it in detail. Cf. also Steinschneider, l. c., p. 342 *infra*, and my *Zur jüd.-arab. Litter.*, p. 86. Naturally the polemical campaign against the Karaites did not cease after Saadiah, but continued till the most recent times. I need only mention, e. g. (besides those named in my essay, pp. 274–5) in the Orient, Samuel ibn Jâmiʿ (see *R. É. J.*, l. c., 201), David b. Zimra (*Responsa*, No. 796), and Levi b. Ḥabib (see above, p. 11, n. 5); in Byzantium, Tobias b. Eliezer, author of לקח טוב (see Buber's *Preface*, § 14); in Spain, Judah ibn Balʿâm (*R. É. J.*, l. c., 193), Moses ibn Ezra (ibid., 198), and Judah b. Barzillai (ספר העתים, ed. *Mekize Nirdamim*, p. 25); in Germany and France, Moses Taku (*R. É. J.*, l. c., 201), Zeraḥia ha-Levi (*Maor*,

Sabbath, § 3 beginning), and Simson of Sens (see *R. É. J.*, VII, 41); in Italy, Aaron Abulrabi (in his commentary on Deut. xxv. 4; cf. *R. É. J.*, XXI, 253), &c. The polemics of these writers, however, are only of an incidental character; with the exception of the author of the anonymous little work just mentioned, none of them composed a special controversial treatise, unless we are to consider as such the work of a Turkish Rabbi of last century, Solomon Ḳimḥi, entitled מלאכת שלמה (printed 1862). The author here endeavoured to show that the Karaites are to be considered as beasts, that it is forbidden to instruct them in the Torah, and that it is permitted to kill them. These statements were so monstrous that every copy of the work that could be seized was consigned to the flames by order of the Haham Bashi, Yakir Géron, in Constantinople. See Franco, *Essai sur l'histoire des Israélites de l'Empire Ottoman* (Paris, 1897), pp. 171, 172, and *Jew. Encycl.*, s.v. (VII, 497).

ADDITIONS AND CORRECTIONS.

Pages 6–7 (comp. p. 96). The anti-Karaite Fragments of Saadiah, edited by Harkavy (*J. Q. R.*, XIII, 656), which are nearly all directed against Ibn Sâqaweihi, have been printed for a second time, with a Hebrew translation, in הקדם, I, 65 seqq.

P. 14. On the struggle between the Shammaites and Hillelites, reported in the Yerushalmi, see my article in הקדם, I, 39. On Salmon's Commentary to Koheleth, see also *Monatsschrift*, LI, 718 seqq.

P. 21, foot (comp. p. 97). The citation from Jefet (on Exod. xxxv. 3) made by Pinsker may, it now appears, be a quotation from Saadiah.

P. 39, foot. The assumption of the older Karaites that Deut. xviii. 10, forbade the fixation of months and feasts perhaps arose under the influence of Islam. The Koran (ix. 37) makes intercalation a heresy. Compare Albirûni's *Chronology of the Ancient Nations*, ed. Sachau, p. 12 (translation, p. 14).

P. 42. To the Karaites who had connexion with Saadiah in the eleventh century must be added the Jerusalem Grammarian (המדקדק הירושלמי) Abu-l-Faraj Harûn b. al-Faraj, who unquestionably knew and used Saadiah's works. See my essay on him (Paris, 1896), p. 18, and my further citations from his writings in *R. É. J.*, April, 1908.

P. 48. Some parts of the chief philosophical work of Joseph al-Baṣîr (the כתאב אלמחתוי) have recently been published as Doctorate-Dissertations with a Hungarian translation. The parts published include chapter xxiii (with excerpts from chs. xix, xxii, and xxiv), ed. Goldberger (Buda Pesth, 1906); chs. xxv–xxix, ed. Bánde (Ráczkeve, 1906), and ch. xxxiv, ed. Horovitz (Buda Pesth, 1905). But Saadiah is not quoted in any of these. On al-Baṣîr compare further the article in *R. É. J.*, cited in preceding note.

P. 52. A part of Jeshu'a's long Commentary on Numbers, in a Hebrew recension, is perhaps contained in the Leyden MS., Warner 26[3] (Cat. Steinschneider, p. 111). Here, as in בראשית רבה, the paragraphs begin אם אמר and only the oldest Karaites are quoted: viz. 'Anân, Benjamin al-Nahawendi, Daniel al-Kumisi and Joseph al-Baṣîr.

P. 79, top. The citations from Abu-l-Faraj Harûn, which are contained in this compilation from Deuteronomy I have collected in my article, *R. É. J.*, l. c. Abu-l-Faraj is here described as פה.

P. 81. On Samuel al-Magribi's אלמרשד, section II, ed. Weisz, and section VII, ed. Lorge, see my review in *J. Q. R.*, April, 1908.

P. 86. I have now before me a modern copy of Elia b. Baruch's עשרה מאמרות. This copy belongs to Samuel Neeman (נאמן), a Karaite ḥazzan in Eupatoria. In the introduction he speaks of the prohibition לא תבערו and he has a long passage against Saadiah which I now quote in full:

... פירוש שני פירש הבודה סעדיא הפיתומי ואת הישר עקש והוא נגד דקדוק הלשון ומהות הענין כי אמר שמלת לא תבערו אש הוא מענין ובערת הרע מקרבך וירצה לומר לפי שיבוש דעתו שלא ישמידו האש ממושבותיהם ביום השבת אבל ישאירוהו בביתם ובמושבותם. והנה האיש הזה הוכה בסנורים ולא חשש מהמלות הסמוכות כי מהמלות הסמוכות יודע פירוש הענין ולא הקפיד לראות היטב שמלת בכל באה בבי"ת ואם הוא לפי דעתו המשובשת לשון השמדה היה לבוא מלת כל במ"ם והיה ראוי להיות ככה לא תבערו אש מכל מושבותיכם ביום השבת כאשר באו האחרים שהזכיר במ"ם תשביתו שאור מבתיכם וכן ובערת הרע מקרבך. ומלת אש תורה שהוא לשון בעור והדלקה וכן באו הכל בבי"ת והנה הסנה בוער באש וכן כפשתים אשר בערו באש. והנה הוא דבר פשוט ונגלה אצל בעלי הלשון ותינוקות של בית רבן יודעים זה אך זה בער מאיש רצה לשבש הלשון ולהחליף הענין כדי להיות לו סמך לתעתועיו ונפל במהמורות בל יקום כי כל רואה דברים זרים כהם ילעיגו לו. וככה פירש כמה ענינים בפירושים זרים כדי להשוות הדברים לפי מעשיו והכחיש דברים כתובים במשנה ובתלמוד ורצה לעַוֵּר עיני בני עמו וראוי לו לומר העיני האנשים ההם תנקר וחשב לחדש פירושים חדשים שבדה מלבו ולעמוד נגד דקדוק הלשון ולעלות בסלם החכמה ונגלתה ערותו עליו. וככה יקרה לכל יוצא מפשטי הכתובים יודע קלונו וישא עונו.

The explanation of לא תבערו "ye shall not destroy" is also combated, e g. by Aaron b. Elia (*Gan Eden*, fol. 28 c). In the last-mentioned place the author of this explanation is not given as Saadiah, but as "one who strays" (ומדברי תועה שאמר שהוא לשון השמדה וכו'). It is possible, however, that Saadiah is meant. The concluding words of Elia (ולעלות בסלם החכמה וכו') are modelled on Ibn Ezra's remark to Exodus xx. 23, though that remark is directed against the Karaite Ben Zuṭa. Mr. Neeman also possesses a copy of Elia b. Baruch's צרור המור; and the well-known עשרה מאמרות, as well as another writing of Elia, entitled ילקוט, are to be found in a MS. of Samuel Pigit, Karaite ḥazzan in Ekaterinoslav (see המליץ, 1888, no. 243).

KARAITE MISCELLANIES.

I. *From Daniel al-Qumisi's* ספר המצות.

DANIEL B. MOSES AL-QUMISI, or al-Damagâni, flourished at the end of the ninth or at the beginning of the tenth century. He seems to have been at first an admirer of Anan, whom he afterwards held in low esteem. He composed a ספר המצות in the Hebrew language, and, as is evident from Qirqisâni, also some other writings of which we do not know even the names[1]. Pinsker (*Lickute Kadmonioth*, Notes,

[1] We obtain some data about this Karaite in the first section of Qirqisâni's *Kitâb al-'Anwâr* (see Prof. Bacher in this Review, VII, 687–710), edited by Harkavy. We deduce his age from the fact that Qirqisâni, in the work here mentioned (written 937), considers him as the last sectarian. Qirqisâni mentions also other writings of Daniel, thus (ed. Harkavy), p. 316: וذلך מרו̈ן פי גיר מוצ̇ע מן כתבה ; on the other hand, p. 285, ודו̈ן כתאבא ; on p. 280, again, the singular as well as the plural occurs. From the name al-Damagâni it may be conjectured that Daniel was a native of the country Qumis in Tabaristan, and that he must therefore have been called al-Qumisi (Harkavy, l. c., p. 271, note 8). A David al-Qumisi, otherwise unknown, is mentioned by Mas'ûdi in his *Kitâb al-tanbîh*, ed. De Goeje, p. 113. He is said to have lived at Jerusalem, and to have died 945–946. That he was a Karaite, as Harkavy conjectures (לוח אחיאסף, II, 281), is to be proved from the following passage from a Karaite commentary in Arabic to Lev. iii. 9 (MS. Bodleian, Hebr. d. 44, f. 60 b): חלבו האליה תמימה אחת אג̇ אבו סלימאן אלקומסי בקולה חלבו האליה פקאל אן אלאליה סמי חלב קאל ואלדליל עלי ד̇לך הו אנ̇ כל כלמה̈ יכון פי אכ̇רהא וו משאר ואלכלמה̈ אלתי בעדהא יכון עלי ראסה הי גיר אצלי יג̇ב אן תכון אלכלמה אלת̇אניה̈ וצף̇ ללכלמה̈ אלאולה̈ ולא תכן גירהא וקאל אליס תרי בנו הבכור ידו החזקה זרועו הנטויה אלך̇. (See Hadassi, *Eshkol Hakkofer*, alphabet 233, letter ח; Aron b. Elia, *Gan Eden*, f. 96 c, and *Keter Tora* on this passage.) Subsequently I found this Karaite cited also in Jefeth's Comm. on Lev. xxiii. 5 (second recension? Brit. Mus. MS. Or. 2518, f. 72 a). Various opinions are here given for the circumstance, that the 15th of Nissân falls on a Sabbath. We read there, among others: ואלמד̇הב אלה' מד̇הב אבי סלימאן אלקומסי רחמה אללה ענדה אן אלפסח יג̇מל לילה̈ אלסבת שכ̇צא ואחדא ען אלאמה̈ באס̇רהא ולא יאכל בל יחרק.

pp. 188–189) cites from his code a long passage quoted by Jefeth b. Ṣagîr. Dr. Harkavy published (*Magazin für d. Wissensch. d. Judent.* XX, 227–228) three more passages from Petersburg manuscripts. Since Daniel's book is one of the oldest Karaite codes extant, and moreover, as it is written in the Hebrew language, it rouses special interest. It may therefore not be unwelcome if I now publish a further extract from the same book. The British Museum MS. Or. 2494, from which I take this extract, contains, ff. 31–80, a fragment of a Karaite commentary, in Arabic, on Lev. xi. 37–43. This commentary, composed 1050 E.C., is a compilation chiefly from Qirqisâni, 'Abu 'Ali (i.e. Jefeth b. 'Ali), 'Abu Saïd (i.e. Levi b. Jefeth, v. Pinsker, l. c., p. קי״ט), 'Abu-l Sari (i.e. Sahl b. Mazliach), Al-Raïs, and other authors. In addition to these, other Karaite authors are cited, such as 'Anan, Daniel and 'Abu Jaqûb, i.e. Josef al-Baṣîr[1].

The passage that follows is indeed not described as taken from the ספר המצות, nevertheless I believe this to be the fact on the evidence of its contents. As a convincing argument I may point out that, in the quotation in question Daniel deals with Lev. vii. 24, where it is said, that the fat of a beast that died by itself and that of an animal torn with beasts may be used for any other purpose except to be eaten. The Talmudists conclude from this, that the fat does not cause any uncleanness (v. Sifrâ to this passage). The Karaites, however, do not admit this conclusion, and accordingly they find the passage not free from difficulties. Daniel explains it by saying that if the body of the beast which died by itself, or was torn, is used in a manufacture, it is no more unclean. This opinion is cited by Jehuda Hadassi, *Eshkol Hakkofer*, alphabet 287, letter ג (f. 108 c):

״דברו שאמר וחלב נבלה וחלב טרפה יעשה לכל מלאכה וגו׳ הוא
למלאכת הטמאים עוד · · · · · ״גלה ושפט מזה דניאל בן משה משכילי
נ״ע כי נבלת בהמה טהורה אחר שנעשתה לפעולות אינה מטמאה לאדם
בנגיעתה להזהרה שנא׳ וחלב נבלה וחלב טרפה יעשה לכל מלאכה יען
כי יצא מקדושתו ואמר לא תאכלוהו אזהרה וכו׳.

The view quoted by Daniel, according to which by the term נבלה is here to be understood a sick beast which has been slain, was originally that of the Samaritans, with which, as it would seem, some Karaites concurred. By both sects the use of such

[1] See my description of Qirqisâni-MSS. in the British Museum in the *Steinschneider-Festschrift* (Leipzig, 1896), p. 215.

a beast was prohibited[1]. Compare further Geiger in *Hechaluẓ*, VI, 18–25, and *Jüdische Zeitschrift*, II, 21, 22.

The passage to which I have been referring runs as follows:

[f. 60 b] קול דניאל אלקומסי קאל ובהמה טהורה לא כתוב בהם טמאים הם לכם אחרי מותם למען כי אחרי אשר תעשה למלאכה לא תטמא כאשר לא כתוב בכלים בגד ועור ושק טמאים הם לכם למען כי גבול טמאתם עד הערב ורחיצה כן לא כתוב לבהמה טהורה טמאים הם לכם למען כי גבול טומאתה עד אשר תעשה למלאכה על כן כתוב וחלב נבלה וחלב טרפה יעשה לכל מלאכה [2] ועל כן כתוב וגם את המת יחצון [3]. וכתוב בה וכי ימות [4] כי לא כלם ימותו להודיע כי הנשחט לא מטמא. ויש שיאמר כי הכתיב וכי ימות היא הבהמה הנשחטת בחליה [5] [61 a] ולא כן הוא. וגם יאמרו וחלב נבלה היא הנשחטת בחליה ולא כן הוא כי אין בכל המקרא שם הנזבח נקרא נבלה וגם אם [6] נזבח לגלולים וכתוב וזבחו לאלהיהם [7] לבעלים יזבחו [8] זבח רשעים תועבה [9] קרא בשם זבח ולא בשם נבלה. והנזבח בחליו אם אסור לאכול ואסור לנגוע הלא הוא במשפט המת כאחד ובמה להפריד בינו ובין המת ואם מותר לאכול

[1] The following etymology of the word נבלה, which Hadassi quotes a few lines before (letter כ, f. 108 b), in the name of the Philosophers (חכמי הרעת, comp. Bacher in the *Monatsschr. f. Gesch. und Wissensch. d. Judent.* XL, 26, note 4), is interesting: "כי חכמי הרעת אפילו השחוט בכושר נבילה קוראים אותו יען [כך] אמתת המלה · כי אמתת מלת נבלה היא שנפלה מחיותה ונבלה · מגזרת ועליהו לא יבול כנבול עלה מגפן וכנובלת מתאנתך · "יושר המלה אמנם כזאת היא · אבל האלהים מן הנבולים ונופלים מחיותם התיר לנו · השחוט בכושר ביד בשר החיה החיא · ושאר הנבולים אסרם לנו שנא' לא תאכלו כל נבלה וכו'.

[2] Lev. vii. 24. [3] Exod. xxi. 35. [4] Lev. xi. 39.

[5] The representative of this opinion is ʿAnân, see the passage communicated by Harkavy from the former's ספר המצות (*Magazin*, l. c., p. 225; Graetz's *Geschichte*, V[3], p. 424; לקורות הכתות בישראל, p. 13): וכי ימות מן הבהמה דאי שחיט לה לבהמה בעיון דקריבה למות כנבלה היא וכו'. ʿAnân's opinion is also refuted by Qirqisâni in his *Kitâb al-'Anwâr*, ch. x, § 24 (Brit. Mus. MS. Or. 2580, f. 31 a). His words, for a copy of which I am indebted to the courtesy of the Rev. G. Margoliouth, Assistant Librarian of the British Museum, run as follows: · · · הד̇א איצ̇א ממא קד ד̇כרנא כ̇טא ענה א̇ד̇ ג̇על קולה וכי ימות ליס הו מותא טביעיא ואנמא הו ד̇ביחה̈ אלבהימה̈ אלמריצ̇ה̈ והד̇א מא לם יוג̇ד פי אלכתאב אן שיא מן אלבהאים אלטאהרה̈ א̇ד̇ ד̇בח סמי מיתא ותאכיד ד̇לך במא קאל בעדה וכל הנוגע בנבלתה והד̇א איצ̇א ממא יבטל קולה א̇ד̇ כאן אלמד̇בוח מן אלבהאים לא יקע עליה אסם נבלה.

[6] MS. אין.

[7] Exod. xxxiv. 15, MS. לאלהיהן.

[8] Hos. xi. 12.

[9] Prov. xxi. 27.

ומותר לנגוע הלא הוא כמשפט החי מְתֹם הגוף ולמה קרא אותו נבלה ובמה תפריד בינו ובין החי מְתֹם הגוף. ואם מותר לאכול [ואסור לנגוע] ושכן כתוב הנוגע בנבלתה [1] למה אסור לנגוע. ואם תאמר הוא האוכל בשגגה או לאונס ולמה גם כן לא יגיע שגגה ואונס גם על הבהמה המתה ולא נפלא זה מן הכתוב ונבשל את בני ונאכלהו [2]. בזאת תדע כי הנוגע בבהמה טהורה המתה אחרי אשר נעשה למלאכה לא יטמא והנוגע בבהמה וחיה טמאה ושרץ טמא אם נשחט למלאכה יטמא על כן כתוב או בנבלת חיה טמאה או בנבלת שרץ טמא [3] ולא הזכיר הנה בהמה טהורה.

II. *Saadja and Salmon b. Jerucham.*

Sahl b. Mazliach in his תוכחת מגולה, as his controversial tract against Jacob b. Samuel, the disciple of Saadja, is styled, gives a list of those Karaite authors who opposed Saadja's views. Of these, Ben-Mashiach and Salmon b. Jerucham must have written against the Gaon even during his lifetime; others again, such as 'Abul-Tajjib al-Jebeli, 'Ali b. Ḥasan, 'Abu 'Ali Ḥasan al-Baṣri (i. e. Jefeth b. 'Ali), Sahl himself, and several more, did not attack him till after his death [4]. It is not known whether all the Karaites here mentioned wrote whole treatises against Saadja, or whether, as is more probable, they only occasionally controverted his opinions. We only know with certainty that Salmon and Jefeth belong to the first class. The latter mentions his polemic against Saadja in his commentary to Exod. xxxv. 3 [5]; this treatise, however, has not yet been discovered, and we do not know whether Jefeth wrote it in Arabic, like most of his works, or in Hebrew, the language he selected for his controversy with Jacob b. Samuel. Salmon's book, however, is extant in MS. in some libraries [6].

[1] Lev. xi. 39, MS. בנבלתם.

[2] 2 Kings vi. 29. The sense is, if it can even happen that men should eat human flesh, how much more possible is it that they should consume that of an animal that had died of itself.

[3] Lev. v. 2.

[4] See Steinschneider, *Catal. Lugd.*, p. 403; Pinsker, *Lickute Kadmonioth*, Notes, p. 37.

[5] וֹלך כמא רדדת בה (אי באלפיומי) עלי מדעייה פי אלכתאב אלדׄי אלפת לה (Pinsker, l. c., p. 20).

[6] This appears in the Univ. Bibl. at Leyden, Cod. Warner 41, ff. 277 b–288 a, and in the Beth Ha-Midrash in Vienna (Pinsker's Collection), Cod. 27, ff. 26–38. My quotation follows the Leyden MS.

This treatise, entitled by the later Karaites מלחמות י״י[1], is written in Hebrew. The author also intended to translate it into Arabic[2], but it is not known whether he carried out his intention or not. Sahl distinctly says that Salmon entered the lists against Saadja with a Hebrew treatise. The book, which is written in a wretched rhymed-prose, has a scarcely intelligible introduction, which is only partly preserved, and has no connexion with the real contents of the work. The work contains, further, nineteen chapters, which are alternately written with the acrostic אבג״ד and תשר״ק; with the exception of chapters 11 and 19, in which the acrostic is סלמון בן ירוחם. The fragment of the introduction, which has been preserved, and the first two chapters are published in the *Litteraturblatt d. Orients*, VII, 23, 163, 311. Pinsker, pp. 16–19, gives a summary of the contents of the whole book, but he accounts only for thirteen chapters; in his copy chaps. 3, 4, 16–19 were lacking[3]. I will therefore supplement his account by giving the contents of these six chapters.

Chapter 3 is connected with the first two, and endeavours to refute the arguments for the inspiration and necessity of the oral law. Saadja's seven arguments for the necessity of tradition, as given in his Commentary to Genesis, are here specially cited and refuted[4].

Salmon's arguments against the alterations in the date of the Passover לא בד״ו פסח are given in chap. 4. He quotes in evidence Ezra vii. 9 and viii. 31–33, and maintains that at that time the Passover festival must necessarily have begun on one of the days which Rabbinical tradition excludes. This argument is also to be found in Qirqisâni, with whom probably it had its origin[5]. Hadassi

[1] This name is first mentioned by the author of the ארח צדיקים (ed. Vienna, f. 24 a), see Geiger, in אוצר נחמד, IV, 13, comp. also *Litteratbl. d. Orients*, VII, 17.

[2] See Pinsker, p. 15.

[3] See ib., p. 133, note 1.

[4] Saadja's arguments, without the refutations of Salmon, are given by Geiger, *Wissenschaft. Zeitschr. für jüdische Theologie*, V, 133. These seven arguments are also quoted and refuted in a fragment of a Karaite work in the British Museum, MS. Or. 2580, f. 46, entitled אלבאב אלכ׳אמס עשר. This fragment belongs (see *Steinschneider-Festschrift*, p. 209) to the second section (אלמקאלה אלת׳אניה) of Qirqisâni's *Kitâb al-'Anwâr*. Among other things there we find it stated: ואמא מא ד׳כרה מן אלסבב׳ה אלאצול מן אלשרע אלכ׳ברי אלתי זעם אנהא תצ׳טרנא אלי אלרג׳וע אלי אלנקל ומא ד׳כרה מן כיפיה׳ אלציצית ואלסכה ומא אשבהמא פאן אלתי קאל אצהאבה פי אלסכה [הו] בכ׳לאף מא אכ׳ברתה אלכתאב ומא שרח מן ד׳לך פי קצה׳ עזרא עליה אלג׳לאם אלך.

[5] Qirqisâni composed his work 937 (see ed. Harkavy, p. 247, and

also, in his *Eshkol Hakkofer*, alphabet 185 (comp. also *Gan Eden*, ענין קדוש החדש, § 5), quotes this argument, and I cannot say which of these two earlier Karaites was his authority.

In chapters 16–18 nearly the whole of the שעור קומה is paraphrased[1].

In the 19th and last chapter, Salmon expresses the hope that the temple will be erected again, and the truth established. He writes against Saadja also in this chapter.

The tone of this book is outrageously personal. He insults the Rabbanites in general, and Saadja in particular, in the rudest manner; in this respect he is scarcely surpassed by Jehuda Hadassi. It seems as if he himself felt that he had considerably overstepped the bounds of courtesy, for he urges the excuse that he was piqued and irritated by Saadja's attack on the Karaites[2]. His phraseology is awkward in the extreme, and makes everybody sensible of the deficiency of the book as regards a lofty ideal. At all events the work is worthy of notice as it is unique in its kind, and of so early a period.

We will now try to fix the time when this book was composed. We have in Sahl's statement a *terminus ad quem*, that Salmon wrote against Saadja during the Gaon's life. And indeed the whole tone of

Neubauer, *Mediaeval Jewish Chronicles*, II, 249). whilst Salmon wrote his polemic, if my conjecture be correct, not before 940. I have found the passage in a compendium (מכ׳תצר) of Qirqisâni (British Museum MS. Or. 2525, see *Steinschneider-Festschrift*, p. 211). The chapter referred to is headed : פצל פימא קאלה (אי צאחב אלאנואר) פי אלשהור ; and is also taken from the seventh section of the *Kitâb al-'Anwâr*. I give this passage in extenso: ומן ד׳לך [f. 46 b] מא קאלה פי עזרא פי באחד לחדש הראשון הוא יסד המעלה מבבל (Ezra vii. 9) פאכ׳בר מן צעודהם יום כאן פיה ולא יג׳וז אן יכון ד׳לך פי יום אלסבת ת׳ם קאל ובאחד לחדש החמישי בא [אל] ירושלם (ib.) ולא יג׳וז אן יכון ד׳לך איצ׳א יום אלסבת ואד׳א כאן ראס שהר אב לם יכן אלסבת ולם יכן ניסן א׳אחד וד׳לך אן ניסן ענדהם אבדא תאמא פאד׳א כאן אלאחד יכון ראס איר אלג׳ ואייר אבדא כ׳ט יומא פאד׳א כאן ראסה אלג׳ יכון ראס סיון אלד׳ וסיון תאמא פיכון אול תמוז יום אלג׳מעה ותמוז אבדא כ׳ט יומא פיכון אול אב אלסבת פעלם מן הד׳א אלפסוק [47 a] אן ניסן לם יכן פי תלך אלסנה לא אלסבת ולא אלאחד ת׳ם קאל ונסעה מנהר אהוא בשנים עשר לחדש הראשון (ib. viii. 31) ולא יג׳וז אן יכון ד׳לך יום אלסבת ואד׳א כאן כד׳לך לם יכן ראסה אלג׳ פת׳בת מן הד׳ין אלפסוקין אן ניסן פי תלך אלסנה לם יכן אלסבת ולא אלאחד ולא אלג׳ ת׳ם קיל פי אכ׳ר אלקצה ונבוא ירושלם ונשב שם ימים שלשה וביום הרביעי נשקל הכסף והזהב (ib. 32, 33) ולא יג׳וז אן יכון ד׳לך יום אלסבת ואד׳א כאן ד׳לך כד׳לך פלא יכון ראסה אלד׳ ואד׳א כאן ראס אב לא יכון אלד׳ לא יכון ראס ניסן אלה׳ פת׳בת מן הד׳ה אלקצה אן ניסן פי תלך אלסנה לם יכן לא אלסבת ולא אלאחד ולא אלג׳ ולא אלה׳ ובקי אן יכון יום אלב׳ ויום אלד׳ או יום אלו׳ בכ׳לאף לא בד׳ו.

[1] See Graetz, *Monatsschr.*, 1859, p. 67 ff.

[2] See Chapter II, letter צ (*Litteratbl. d. Orients*, l. c., 213).

the attack would suggest, that it was directed against a person who was still living. Note for instance the challenge thrown out to Saadja to be consistent with himself, and either to concur with the opinions of the Rabbanites, or to adopt the view of the Karaites[1]; to openly oppose him (Salmon) and to reply to his objections[2]; mark also the observation, that whatever Saadja might have to say would only be weak and inconclusive[3]. Where, however, can we place the *terminus a quo?* I think I shall be able to fix it from a passage taken from this polemical treatise itself. In the second chapter, Salmon cites one of Saadja's arguments for the necessity of committing the oral law to writing. The passage runs as follows (*Litteratbl. d. Orients*, l. c., 215):

״טפש מחלב אמרו וניבו · אשר חקר במגילה בכתבו ·

. . . .

״חקוק חקק כי ששה סדרים תורת משה · ולמען זה חקקוה למען לא תנשה

In other words, Saadja maintains, in one of his works, that the Mishnah was written down because it was feared it might otherwise be forgotten. Now Saadja gives this reason for writing the Mishnah in his ספר הגלוי, or rather in the Arabic commentary to it, as is distinctly mentioned in a fragment of a Karaite polemic against its author[4]. This will explain the term מגלה which Salmon uses. Saadja's opponents named this work thus, because of its being divided into verses and accented like a book of the Bible, and they reproached him by sneeringly asking whether he would pass for a prophet[5]. Consequently no other treatise of Saadja's could be meant, although this argument anent the compilation of the Mishnah may perhaps be mentioned elsewhere[6]. As therefore the ספר הגלוי

[1] Chapter VI, letter ב: ״בחר לך אחת משני פנים וכו׳ (quoted by Pinsker, p. 16).

[2] Chapter VII, letter ג: ״גשה אלי התיצבה · ואכפי עליך אל תעצבה · עת המערכה לקרבה · למה בחרר תשבה · ״דבר אנה צוה שוכן מעונה · לשמור תולדות הלבנה וכו׳.

[3] Chapter XIX, letter ו: ״וסעדיה הפיתומי אם יכתוב בוה תשובות · יודע השובות המתועבות (כי תשובותיו מתועבות ?) · ואם העתיקו ממנו תשובות משולבות · ידע כי הכל יושר (כושר ?) ידיו וכי שנגותיו מרובות.

[4] See Harkavy, *Studien und Mittheilungen*, V, 195.

[5] See *ibid.* 229: ויכתב מגלה להדמות בנביאים כאחד נביאי השקר.

[6] Jefeth also cites this fact in his Commentary to Exodus xxi. 33 (British Museum MS. Or. 2468, f. 7a); the same argument is literally copied from a work of Saadja (חרף בחרף), it is possibly from the Arabic Commentary to his ספר הגלוי, but it may be from some other of his writings. Among other things it is said there: ... פלמא גלת אלגלוה אלאולי הכות אלעלמא אן הנסי הדא אלאמר אלהי כאן גמע אלשמל יחפטנוהא פעמד עליהא פכסוהא כלאמא ואתבתוה

was composed in 934[1], Salmon's work must have been written between the years 934–42. I would be inclined to fix the later years of this interval as the date of Salmon's attack, because most of Salmon's Bible Commentaries were written in the sixth decade of the tenth century. The Commentary to the Psalms he composed, according to his own statement, in 955[2], the Commentary to Lamentations in 956[3], the Commentary to the Song of Solomon is mentioned as contemplated in the former work, in the latter, however, it is already quoted, consequently this also was composed between 955–956[4]. But the remaining Commentaries, with the exception of that to Daniel, were probably written after this time[5]. We may therefore suppose, with a certain amount of probability, that Salmon composed his work about 940.

If my conjectures in this respect be correct, we can also obtain an inkling as to the year of Salmon's birth. According to his own

וסמוהא [משנה] פכל מן סבק מנהם אלי אלתדביר בשי אתבתה (l. אתבתוהא) באסמה ליחתג אלתלאמיד עלי אלהפט ובקי שעבא יסירא מא רגו חפטהא או קד אתבתו אצולהא פלמא גלת אלאמה אלגלוה אלתאניה כאף אלתלאמיד עלי אלפרוע אלבאקיה אן תנסא פכסוהא כלאמא ואתבתוהא איצא וסמוהא תלמוד.

[1] See Harkavy, *ibid.*, 142. If this date only refers to the first recension of the ספר הגלוי, and not to the other which Saadja provided with an Arabic commentary, and in which the origin as well as the committal to writing of the oral tradition was laid down, then it becomes all the more certain that Salmon composed his polemic much later than 934.

[2] In Commentary to Psalm cii. he gives the year 887 after the destruction of the second temple as the date. This is not 4717 of the era *anno mundi*, as Pinsker (p. 130) wrongly states, but 4715 (= 955 C.E.), for according to Jewish reckoning the destruction occurred in the year 68 C.E., not 70.

[3] In Pinsker, p. 132, we read תתפה; likewise in the Paris MS. 295, where we find: תמאן מאיה כמסה ותמאנין סנה, viz. 953. But this is impossible, because the Commentary to Psalms is already cited here. The British Museum MS. Or. 2516, f. 113 a, has the right date, viz. תתפח = 956, MS. Or. 2513, f. 129 a, has even תתכה.

[4] Of this Commentary I have found eight pages in the British Museum MS. Or. 2520, ff. 68–75, for the most part illegible. To Song of Songs ii. 11 there is a long excursus, in which Saadja's calculation of the year of redemption derived from Daniel is quoted and attacked. He then cites the eighth section of Saadja's *Emunoth Vedeoth* (פי כתיב אמאנ[א]תה פי אלמקאלה אלח). Salmon writes on the same theme in his Commentary to Psalm cii. 15. See Pinsker, p. 81.

[5] This is inferred from the fact that only the Commentary to Daniel is quoted in that to Echa, see Pinsker, p. 132.

statement, he was at the time he wrote his polemic a young man[1]. Supposing he was between twenty and twenty-five years old, it will be evident that he was born about 915 or 920. At all events he was considerably younger than Saadja, and the fable invented by the later Karaites that the Gaon was his disciple, is chronologically impossible, besides being incredible for many other reasons[2]. It is further evident from this, that the pretended *Muqaddima* of Salmon (Pinsker, Notes, p. 61), according to which he would have been born 1196 aer. contr. = 885 C. E., is a clumsy falsification, also the statement that he came from Egypt, a statement which was probably only invented (by Firkowitsch ?), to make it possible that Saadja was the disciple of Salmon in that country[3].

Besides this polemic, Salmon attacks Saadja in his Commentary to the Psalms[4]. He attacks him likewise in his Commentary to the Song of Solomon[5]. On the other hand, Salmon does not mention the name of Saadja in his Commentary to Echa and Koheleth. Neither does he attack him anonymously, so far as I can judge from a superficial reading of these works. It is quite possible that he quotes now and then Saadja's translation or explanation anonymously and rejects it, but at all events this is done without any animosity[6].

But did Saadja write a reply to Salmon's attacks? I scarcely think that he did. Four anti-Karaite works of Saadja are known[7]: (1) כתאב אלרד עלי ענן, A Refutation of Anan, written 915. (2) כתאב אלתמייז, Book of Distinction, written 926. Both these are out of the question owing to the date of their composition[8], apart from the

[1] Chapter II, letter צ: צעיר אנכי לימים ואהם ממני קדומים.

[2] See Pinsker, p. 135; Weiss, דור דור ודורשיו, IV, 95, 139; compare also the Epigraph of Elia b. Baruch in Bardach's מזכיר לבני רשף, p. 37.

[3] It follows from his Commentary to Psalm cxl. 6 (by Pinsker, p. 14), וגהת בה אלי אלעראק, that he did not live at Babylon, which is also evident from his polemic, Chapter I, letter ג (*Litteratbl. d. Orients*, l. c., 163), גר הייתי בארץ נכריה וגו׳, yet this does not prove that his home was Egypt, as Pinsker maintains. Probably he lived at Jerusalem.

[4] Compare p. 3, note 10 and the preceding note; also Neubauer, *Aus d. Petersb. Bibliothek*, p. 12.

[5] See p. 3, note 10.

[6] I have examined the Commentary to Echa, in the two MSS. of the British Museum (see above p. 3, note 11), that to Qoheleth after the MS. Or. 2517 in the same collection.

[7] Compare Dukes, *Beiträge z. Geschich. d. aeltesten Auslegungen und Spracherklärung d. A. T.*, II, 32–33; Steinschneider, *Cat. Bodleian.*, col. 2165–68.

[8] With this also falls Graetz's hypothesis (*Geschichte*, V, note 20, 3rd ed., p. 460), that this work was directed against Salmon. Graetz relied upon

fact that the former is distinctly directed against Anan. (3) כתאב אלרד עלי בן סאקויה, Confutation of Ibn Saqûje. This Karaite is not mentioned anywhere else. Geiger[1] therefore conjectures, that it is the Arabic name of our Salmon, but this is a mere hypothesis which is destitute of probability. In the same manner it seems very unlikely that this work is, as Geiger conjectures, identical with (4) The כתאב אלרד עלי מתחמל היום (?), Refutation of the Bold Opponent[2], cited by Nissim b. Jacob, and to understand by this "bold opponent" Salmon, i. e. Ibn Saqûje. Saadja's work against Ibn Saqûje deals mainly with the fixing of the Spring, מציאת האביב, by the intercalation of a month[3]. The work mentioned by Nissim, however, chiefly aims at defending the Anthropomorphic Agada, and is doubtless identical with that work of Saadja, from which Jehuda b. Barzilai, in his Commentary to *Sefer Jeẓira* (ed. Halberstam, pp. 20, 34), quotes two passages. From the contents of these we can clearly see the aim of the whole work[4]. Salmon has of course in his polemical treatise devoted a large space to the Anthropomorphic Agada (see above, p. 3), but it is difficult to comprehend why Saadja in a work directed against Salmon, should have singled out only this one point[5]. On the other hand if our supposition be correct, that Salmon composed his polemical work not much before 940, it is extremely doubtful whether Saadja could have seen it, or if he saw it, whether he found it necessary to write a reply to a young Karaite author, who wrote in so conceited a tone.

We may remark, in passing, that Saadja composed the last-men-

the above-mentioned *Muqaddima* as accurate. Steinschneider (l. c., 2165) suggests that Salmon specially attacked this work of Saadja's, but this is also improbable, for he merely cites it as he does other works of Saadja, as his ספר הגלוי, his Commentary to Genesis, and Esther (see Dukes, l. c., p. 100).

[1] נטעי נעמנים, German part, p. 46. Pinsker's assumption (p. מג) that this Karaite was named Samuel, depends on a mistranslation of a passage in Josef al-Baṣîr's כתאב אלאסתבצאר (see Harkavy, *Studien und Mittheilungen*, III, 45). This Samuel is no other than the Gaon Samuel ben Hofni.

[2] נטעי נעמנים, Hebrew part, f. 16 b.

[3] See Pinsker, l. c. But this question was not exclusively the object of this work of Saadja, as we shall soon have occasion to prove.

[4] P. 20: ומצינו בספר אחד מספרי רבינו סעדיה ז"ל שחיבר על טענות מין אחד שם רשע ירקב שאמר אותו הרשע על רז"ל חלילה וחלילה שהם היו נוהגים דמות ותמונה לבורא העולמים ··· וחבר עליו ר"ס ז"ל ספר בתשובות נכונות וכו'.

[5] In his edition of Qirqisâni, p. 248, Harkavy supposes that Saadja is here attacking this Karaite, but he does not prove this supposition. Perhaps he relies upon some materials in MS. which are in his possession.

tioned anti-Karaite work after 933. For he cites in it his ספר היחור, by which he doubtless meant the second section of his religio-philosophic work, as the following parallels show.

Emunoth, ed. Slucki, p. 55 (ed. Landauer, p. 106).

...וכבר בלבל דעת קצת בני אדם ענין משה רבינו איך שאל מאלהיו הראני נא את כבודך...ונכפל בלבולם באמרו וראית את אחורי ופני לא יראו ואומר בגלות כל זה כי יש לבורא אור בראהו והראהו לנביאים . . . וכאשר יראה אותו אחד מהם אומר ראיתי את ה׳ על דרך ההסתר וכבר ידעת כי משה אהרן ונדב ואביהוא ושבעים מזקני ישראל אמר עליהם בתחלה ויראו את אלהי ישראל ופרשו אחר כך ומראה כבוד ה׳ כאש אוכלת בראש ההר וכו׳

Jehuda b. Barzilai, ed. Halberstam, p. 20.

ואלו היה חוזר אל לבו ומעיין בתורה וקורא אותה לא היה תמה על זה לפי שהיה מוצא בתורה כי המקום הראה למשה אחרית כבודו כי לא היה יכול לראות ראשיתו . . . והיה מוצא בה כי משה ואהרן ונדב ואביהוא ושבעים מזקני ישראל אמרה התורה עליהם ויראו את אלהי ישראל ונפירוש הכתוב כי ראו אור גדול . . . והוא האור הברוי תחלת כל הבריאות והנוצרות . . . וכן כל נביא וחוזה שראה זה האור הבהיר אומר ראיתי את ה׳ . . . כמו שפרשתי כל זה פירוש רחב בספר היחוד וכו׳

Now as Saadja composed his *Emunoth* in the year 933, this polemical work of the Gaon must have been written after that date[1]. Otherwise we must suppose that the reference to the ספר היחוד is a later interpolation[2].

III. *From Jefeth's Commentary to Genesis* xv. 3.

The Commentary of Jefeth to this verse is interesting in so far as it brings before us some Karaite opinions concerning the law of inheritance[3]. First of all, he says, some ask how could Abraham

[1] Luzzatto (הליכות קדם, ed. Pollak, p. 70) suggested that by the title ספר היחוד is probably to be understood the second section of the *Emunoth*. He merely says briefly: אולי הכוונה על המאמר השני מס׳ האמונות והדעות.

[2] Compare Kaufmann, *Gesch. d. Attributenlehre*, p. 87, note 146.

[3] There exist differences between Rabbanites and Karaites concerning the right of inheritance which would be out of place to give fully here; I will therefore note only one point, viz. that concerning the

utter the complaint: "Behold, I am childless," when God had twice promised him that he would bestow the land upon his descendants? (see xii. 7 and xiii. 15). To this Jefeth replies, that as the promise was not accompanied by oath or bond, Abraham was afraid that it might perhaps be dependent on certain conditions, and that its fulfilment might be uncertain. He was therefore anxious to assure himself[1]. The second question is, if Abraham had even remained childless how could Eliezer have become his heir? What became of his nearest relations, such as brothers and sisters, nephew, &c.[2]? To this Jefeth gives the following five answers. According to one supposition, as long as a man lives he can dispose of his fortune in accordance with his own pleasure, only after his death the heirs may step in to claim their right. Now as Eliezer was an excellent and obedient slave Abraham could present him with all his fortune during his lifetime. Others again maintain, that before the revelation of the Law a slave born in the house (יליד בית) was the privileged heir next to the children of the possessor, and had consequently the preference before the other relations. The supporters of this view rely upon the verse in question, Genesis xv. 3. On the other hand others suppose that the right of inheritance did not suffer any change through the revelation[3]. The sisters

daughter's share in the inheritance. One ר' יוסף הפקח, otherwise unknown, was of the opinion, that a daughter's share of the inheritance is equal to that of a son. The following words of this Karaite, which are given in his name by Aaron b. Elia (*Gan Eden*, f. 165 d; compare Bashiatchi, *Adereth*, f. 119 c), are worthy of notice: "I thought at first that I am alone in my opinion, but I found afterwards that David b. Boaz and many others also adopted this view," still he does not mention their names. But Aaron unveils this secret by quoting the passage of the Talmud, Baba Bathra, 115 b: כל האומר תירש בת עם בת הבן (עם הבן by Aaron) אפי' נשיא שבישראל אין שומעין לו שאינן אלא מעשה צדוקין וכו'. Accordingly we see here the close connexion between Sadducees and Karaites, and a further evidence for the well-known hypothesis of Geiger, according to which the later sect would be the spiritual successors of the former. The view of Daniel al-Qumisi, according to which one-third part of the heritage belongs to the daughter, is further to be noticed. This law is similar to that of the Qoran, see the quotation from the ספר העשר to Num. xxvii. by Pinsker, 85: ודניאל קומסי יתן לבת שלישית נחלה ויקח זה מן הערכים, also *Gan Eden*, f. 169 d.

[1] Compare Nachmanides (*ad loc.*), where this question is raised, and answered somewhat differently.

[2] In the Arabic original the passage runs אב ואכֿוה ואבן אך, "Father, sister and brother's son." But the word אב must be a slip, for Terah was already dead.

[3] The question whether at the revelation several divine ordinances were

and brothers of Abraham, however, cannot be taken into account because of their being disbelievers, and as such they were not allowed to become the heirs of a believer[1]. Lot, again, voluntarily departed from Abraham and assimilated with the inhabitants of Sodom. Therefore Abraham would rather bequeath his goods to a slave than to him. A fourth view is that the word יורש does not mean here "inherit" but "govern." Abraham complains then that he must, for want of a son, let his fortunes be governed by a slave. Lastly, many explain the text in the following way: Abraham had complained before God, that his fortune must necessarily fall into the hands of Eliezer because Lot had separated from him and he was at that time childless, nor could he appoint his relations of Haran as his heirs (because they were too remote from him?). So Eliezer thought: the fortune of my lord must needs come into my possession.

Of all these explanations Jefeth chose the second, and decided accordingly. His words run as follow[2]:—

. . . . וקד יסל אלנאס האהנא מסלתין אחדהמא יקאל אלים קד תקדם אליה קול אללה דפעתין באנה יכון לה זרע ירת̇ אלבלד כקו׳ לזרעך אתן וקאל לך אתננה ולזרעך פכיף קאל ואנכי הלך ערירי והנה בן ביתי יורש אתי אלגואב פי ד̇לך הו אן קול אללה לזרעך אתן יג̇וז אנה באסתת̇ני בעד מא לם יצ̇מנה אללה בשבועה וברית כמא סנשרח ד̇לך שרח שאפי פי והאלהים נסה את אברהם פג̈ו̈ז אב̇רהם ע̇אלס̇ אן יכון קול אללה לזרעך אתן לה אסתת̇ני מא פקאל הן לי לא נתתה [זרע] ליעלם מא ענד אללה הל הו קול באסתת̇ני אם הו חתם לא בד̈ מן כונה

modified was hotly discussed and variously answered by Karaites. Thus with regard to the Levirate marriage, which the Karaites mostly hold must be fulfilled not by the brother-in-law but by a more distant relative. But Genesis xxxviii. 8 proves that the brother-in-law was involved in the Levirate union. Karaites who deny that any change in the divine laws occurred at the Revelation, remove this difficulty by artificial assumptions.

[1] This law, also known to Islâm, was accepted by Rabbanites as well as Karaites. Thus Natronai ordered that a Jewish renegade was not to inherit his father's property (compare שערי צדק IV, iii. 25; *Resp. Geonim*, ed. Lyck, 24; *Resp. Geone Mizrach*, &c., ed. Müller, 11, where it is added: כי בדת ישמעאל דאינון לא מורתין למשומר נכסי אביו סמיכי רבנן למימנעיה מירושת אביו; *Pardes*, ed. Constant. f. 26 a, and Weiss, דור דור ודורשיו, IV, 117). Similarly with the Karaites, cf. e.g. *Adereth*, f. 120 d: והנה לפי זה הכפרן לא יירש למאמין.

[2] The passage from Jefeth I cite in accordance with the MS. Berlin or. qu. 828 a.

פלדׄלך קאל הדׄא אלקול ענד מא קאל לה שכרך הרבה מאד ואלמסלה אלבׄ
קיל אלים כאן לאברם פי הדׄא אלוקת אב (?) ואכׄוהׄ ואבן אךׄ פכיףׄ
קאל והנה בן ביתי ולם ירדׄ אלמיראתׄ אלי קראבתה אלגואב פי דׄלך
אוגׄה עלי חסב אכׄתלאףׄ אלנאס פי באב אלמיראתׄ פקאל בעצׄהם אן
אלמאל לצאחבה ויעטיה למן ישא פי חיותה פלמא כאן אקרבא אברם
בעידין מנה וכאן אליעזר עבד צאלח טאיע לה גׄאז לאברם יעטיה מאלה
בחיותה לאנה מאלך למאלה בעד אן לם תפות רוחה ואנמא יגׄב אלמיראתׄ
ללקראבהׄ דון אלעבד בעד אן ימות ואלמאל עלי גׄמלתה וקאל בעצׄהם אן
פי קדים אלזמאן קבל נזול אלתוריהׄ כאן ילידי בית אחקׄ באלמיראתׄ מן
גירה בעד אלולד והדׄא שרט אלעבד אלטאיע ועוׄלו עלי דׄלך עלי קול אברם
פקׄאלו אן למא ראינא לה קראבאת וקאל הן לי לא נתתה זרע ותמאמה
עלמנא אן כאן הדׄא שרט פי קדים אלזמאן אלי נזול אלתוריהׄ כאן ילידי
בית אחקׄ באלמיראתׄ מן גירה בעד אלולד וקאל בעצׄהם אן פרץׄ אלמיראתׄ
לם יכׄתלףׄ קט ואנמא קול אבר(ה)ם הנה בן ביתי יורש אותי עלי וגׄה והו
אן לם יגׄז לאברם יורתׄ אבוה (?) ואכׄוה לאנהם כפרהׄ ואלכאפר לא ירתׄ
מאל אלמומן ואמא לוט פקד רצׄי לנפסה יכׄרגׄ מן גׄמלהׄ עמה ומע דׄלך
פקד כׄאלט אהל סדום וצאהרהם פלם יר אברם אן יורתׄ מאלה ללוט מן
הדׄה אלגׄהׄה בל יורתׄ עבדה אלדׄי עלם אנה אחקׄ מן לוט לאנה הו
תחת טאעתה וכאן טאיע ללה בלא מחאלהׄ וקאל בעצׄהם אן ליס קולה
יורש אתי יריד בה אנה ירתׄ מאלה בעד אלמׄות ואנמא יריד בה אן מאלי
תחת ידה פי חיותי ולו כאן לי ולד כאן הו אלאחקׄ בה וקאל אכׄרון אנה
אראד בקולה יורש אתי אנה למא בעד לוט ענה ולם יכן ללוט ולד
פי אלוקת ולם יגׄז אן ירתׄ מאל אברם אהל ביתה בחראן קאל אליעזר אן
מאל מולאי ירגׄע אליׄׄ פכאן הדׄא יטׄן בה אליעזר מן טׄאהר אלקצׄהׄ פקאל
יא יוי הודׄא בן ביתי יומן אנה יכון וארתׄ מאלי ואלדׄי נדׄהב אליה מן
גׄמלהׄ אלאקאויל הו קול אצחאב קדם אלפרץׄ עלי מא משינאה:

IV. *The Karaite view of Leviticus* x. 19.

The second half of this verse is usually translated thus: "If I had eaten the sin-offering to day, would it have been acceptable in the sight of God?" This is its meaning according to the Talmud (Zebahim, 101 a), and almost all commentators agree with it. The verb ואכלתי would then have the force of an imperfect, and the ה in הייטב would be a sign of interrogation. Thus both words are irregular.

The first has the accent upon the penultimate syllable, and the ה has a patach with a dagesh following. The last circumstance especially forces itself upon the observation of Jewish grammarians, comp. e.g. Abulwalîd, *Kitâb al-luma'*, p. 357, l. 24: קיל הייטב בעיני ה׳ פחרכוא אלהא באלפתח ושדדוא אליא בעדהא וכאן אלוגׄה אן יכון אלהא בשבא ופתח ואן יכון מא בעדה מכׄפפא. An analogous instance is found in Amos v. 25, where the ה with a patach is followed by ז with a dagesh. See Ibn Ezra on this passage: הזבחים · יראה בדרך הפשט כי הא הזבחים הא התימה והנה הטעם שלא הגישו.

In order to avoid these two irregularities, there are some grammarians who consider ואכלתי as the perfect tense, and the ה of הייטב as an article. They explain the passage in the following manner: "Behold my sons have offered to-day their burnt-offerings and sin-offerings, and now this misfortune has happened to me. I ate therefore of the sin-offering (only so much) that was acceptable to God, that is I ate only a trifle in order to fulfil my duty, the remainder however was burnt." Ibn Ezra, commenting on this passage, cites this explanation in the name of some grammarians, יש מדקדקים שאמרו, but he adds, that in any case it remains an irregularity, as the ה in the sense of an article cannot be placed before an imperfect tense. From another passage we now gather that the grammarians here referred to were Karaites, see *Zahoth*, 18 a: והנה מלת הייטב בעיני ה׳ זרה על כן אמרו מכחישי תורתנו שהיא על פה כי טעמו בהא הדעת כמו אשר ייטב בעיני ה׳ וכל זה בעבור הדגשות וכו׳[1].

I will now give a longer passage from the Commentary to Leviticus mentioned above, p. 681, note 1, in which the Karaite view is quoted, as also is the opposed or rabbinical interpretation, the latter, however, is refuted. The passage runs:

[62 a] . . . פאלאקרב אן יפסר ואכלתי חטאת היום אלדׄי יחסן בעיני י״י
יעני ואן כאן פי יום אלמציבה̈ מא כאן ירידו אן יאכלו אלקראבין עלי אלרסם
פמא בדׄ להם מן אן ידוקו מנה לאדׄא אלפרץׄ ולו אלא לקמה̈ ואחדה̈ ומן
כׄאלפנא פי הדׄא אלבאב יקול אן מא כאן ידוקו מן אלחטאת פי יום אלמציבה̈
שי פקלנא להם אדׄא כאן משה עארף אן אלאכל מנה לא יגׄוז וחרקה ואגׄב
וקד סאל ען כׄבר הדׄא אלחטאת וקיל לה אנה אחרק פלאיש ויקצוף

[1] Compare *Safa Berura*, ed. Lippmann, f. 45 a: ויש מלה זרה והיא הייטב בעיני ה׳ ודעת קדמונינו ז״ל שהוא הא לתימה ודעת המורים שהוא הא הדעת. Cf. Bacher, *Abr. Ibn Esra als Grammatiker*, p. 42, note 9. David b. Abraham Alfâsi also considers the ה as article, see Neubauer, *Notice sur la lexicogr. hébr.*, p. 49.

על אלעזר ועל איתמר פגאובונא וקאלו אראד אן יגרבהם פזגר בהם
כמא אלאסתאד יציח עלי גלאמה חתי יסתפהם מנה פאראד אן יסתפהם
מנהם אן אלדי לם יאכלו מנה כאן בעלם אם כאן בגזאף וקאלו אן למא כאן
נדב ואביהוא גלטו והלכו אראד משה אן יסכת עלי האולי ליסתפהם עלי אי
וגה לם יאכלו פקלנא להם אלחכים לא יסכת עלי מתל הדה אלאשיא אלא עלי
צבי [62 b] או עלי אנסאן אכלה יסתפהם דלך[1] ואמא אהרן ובניו פלים
מחלהם הדא אלמחל ואדא כאן אלאמר כדלך פצחה[2] תפסרתי ואכלתי ואכלת
אקרב מן גירה :

. . . "The best explanation is as follows, and I ate to-day of the sin-offering, which is pleasing to God. That is, although they would not on this day, the day of his calamity[3], eat the sin-offering in the usual manner, yet they were bound at least to taste something of it. For according to the law, even a morsel is sufficient. Our antagonists interpret this passage as meaning that they did not eat any portion of the sin-offering on the day of their calamity. To which we reply: If Moses knew that the sin-offering ought to be burnt, and not eaten, why was he so angry with Eliezer and Ithamar, when on his asking as to what had become of the sin-offering, he was told that it had been burnt? They on their part contend that Moses wished to try them, and therefore he blamed them as a teacher declaims against his disciple, till he ascertains from him just what he would like to know. Moreover Moses was anxious to find out whether they had refrained from eating the sin-offering because they knew that it was prohibited, or whether their action was the result of an accident, more especially as Nadab and Abihu had already met with death through their ignorance. He was therefore angry with the other two in order to know why they did not eat it. In reply, we observe further: A wise man would not be angry about such a thing except with a child, or with a man, who has eaten without cognizance of the law (?). Aaron and his sons, however, do not belong to this class. If this should be true, it follows that my interpretation of the meaning is the better, and that the word ואכלתי is a perfect tense."

Still the fact remains, that not all Rabbanite grammarians support the view of the Talmud, nor are the Karaites unanimous on the other side. Of the former, a certain grammarian at the beginning of the twelfth century, is astonished at Abu-l-Fahm (Levi) Ibn at-Tabân for

[1] Probably the reading should be לא עלי אנסאן אלך, or או עלי אנסאן אכלה ולם יסתפהם ד'לך.

[2] MS. פצחר.

[3] I.e. on the day of אנינות.

maintaining that the ה in הייטב and in הזבחים is a sign of interrogation[1]. He seems to have been of the opposite view. Among the Karaites, Aaron b. Josef was the first to interpret the verse in the sense of the Rabbanites, and he refutes the common Karaite view with the same arguments as Ibn Ezra uses. But even Tobia b. Mose, as early as the second half of the eleventh century, says in his אוצר נחמד (Cod. Bodleian, Opp. fol. MS. 26) on this passage, that the interpretation of ואכלתי as a perfect is grammatically impossible, although in the end he inclined to the usual Karaite interpretation. His words run:

[149 b] ודע כי אשר פתר ואכלתי חטאת וכבר אכלתי חטאת שגה מדרך
הלשון כי אכלתי לשון עבר ובא עם אות ו״ו והעתיק המלה מן העבר אל
העתיד כמו עשיתי שהוא עבר ועשיתי עתיד ולו היה כאשר אמר היה
יתכן להיות ואכלתי חטאת כי הוא עבר במע׳ וכבר אכלתי חטאת היה יהיה
ואכלתי[2] וכאשר אינו כן בטל להיות פתרונו כבר אכלתי חטאת ואצל בעלי
הדקדוק כי זה הפותר שגה[3] כאשר שגה[4] ולו אכלתי חטאת הייטב בעיני ה׳
במע׳ עתיד כי לו אכלתי חטאת היה יכשר לפני ה׳ ויהיה הטוב שיפתר
אותו ואכלתי חטאת וכבר אכלתי חטאת היום כמדת אשר ראוי[5] מפני כי
אכלתי למען כי הקדים הטעם בו נהיה מעשה עבר ואם יתאחר הטעם יהיה
עתיד כמו ודברתי על הנביאים[6] ודברתי על לבם[7] · ודע כי ההא אשר הוא
במקום אשר יבוא על המעשה מודגש אשר אחריו כמו שבא הא הייטב כמו
השמה מעקי ים[8] השבה עם נעמי[9] אשר אלה ב׳ ההין יהיו במקום אשר למען

[1] ועגבני מן אבן אלפהם בן אלתבאן רחמה אללה אד קאל ואלהא אלתי פי הזבחים ומנחה הי הא אלאסתפהאם ואן כאן מא בעדהא משדדא ומתלה הייטב בעיני ה׳ הוא נץ קולה (cited by Kokowzow in his work on Ibn Barun, Russian part, p. 7, note 9). Derenbourg gives larger extracts from this Grammar in *Opuscules et traités d'Aboulwalid*, pp. xx–xxi, from a Petersburg MS. Another passage is quoted in my work, *Mose b. Samuel Hakkohen Ibn Chiquitilla*, &c. (Leipzig, 1895), pp. 135, 136. Since he mentions Ibn at-Tabân as deceased, it is clear that the author must have lived at the beginning of the twelfth century at the earliest, and cannot therefore possibly be identified with the כתאב אלתצאריף of Isaak b. Jashush, as Neubauer supposed. Compare further my above-mentioned work, p. 54.

[2] The meaning of these words is not perfectly clear to me.

[3] The reading should possibly be לא שגה.

[4] Here the word הפותר is probably missing.

[5] MS. ראו, i. e. "I ate as much as was necessary," see Ibn Ezra on the passage: רק אכלתי ממנה (מן החטאת) מה שייטב בעיני ה׳ והטעם מה שיוציאני לידי חובה.

[6] Hos. xii. 11. [7] Ibid. ii. 16. [8] Isa. li. 10. [9] Ruth ii. 6.

כי הם ב׳ מעשים לשון עבר על הנקבה לביאת הטעם בתחלתם ולא יכשר[1] על זה היותם בהם במע׳ הי המיודע ויכשר היות ההא במלת הייטב במקום אשר [מפני כי] הוא דגש ולא יהיה תופס[2] בזה היות הייטב לשון עתיד והיות השמה לשון עבר · וזה הפתרון יתר ועדוף מן הראשון לאשר זכר מדרך הלשון זולת מאשר יחזיק אותו גם מדרך המעני כמו שאמר בפסוק וזבחת מבקרך [150 a] ומצאנך אשר נתן י״י לך כאשר ציויתיך[3] אשר השיב מקצתם הצווי אל [האכילה] לא אל הזביחה ויהיה היתר והעדוף להשיבו אל הזביחה למען כי הוא . . .[4] במלת לך יע׳ כי הוא סמוך בו ולו היה מוכרת ממנו כאשר אמר הפותר . . . אותו אל האכילה היה יבא לך הלא תראה אל אשר אמר הלא שלח שלחתי לקרא לך[5] הוא מוכרת מאשר אמר אחריו למה לא הלכת אלי[5] ואל אשר אמר וקרא לך[6] שהוא מחובר באשר אחריו ואכלת מזבחו[6] וזולתו מאשר ידמה לזה · זה הדבר הוא אשר נגלה לנו מדרך הלשון והדקדוק כאשר בארנו והוא הטוב מב׳ הדרכים.

V. *Some hitherto unknown Karaites.*

1. *Said Shirân.* The manuscript of the British Museum, Or. 2523, ff. 47–88, contains a fragment of a Karaite polemic in Arabic, in which special prominence is given to the question of the consideration of the ripening of the wheat (אביב) as a means of fixing the intercalary month[7]. The book is especially directed against a Rabbanite author whose name I could not gather from the fragment that has been preserved. In fol. 58 a the author says:

ואמא אללגהֹ פליסת לך בל אלכתאב פיהא כאן לסעיד שיראן רחמה אללה אלדׄי סעיד שיראן כאן תלמיד פיהא לאבי יעקוב יוסף בן בכׄתוי מעלם אלנאליהֹ רצׄי אללה ענה.

"Now concerning the science of language[8], it is not thy province[9].

[1] The reading perhaps should be ויכשר. [2] MS. טופס. [3] Deut. xii. 21.

[4] There is a lacuna here in the MS. The next words deal with the passage Exod. xxxiv. 15.

[5] Num. xxii. 15. [6] Exod. xxxiv. 15.

[7] The first half of this MS., ff. 1–46, contains a polemic in the Arabic language by a Samaritan on the "chosen place" המקום אשר יבחר, which, however, is of no interest.

[8] Shortly before the following subjects are dealt with אלתוחיד ואלקיאס ואללגהֹ ואלאביב, i. e. the problems of the divine unity, the application of analogy to interpretation, the science of language, and the question of the ripening of the wheat harvest.

[9] For this reason it is improbable that this book is directed against Saadja.

However, Said Shirân (may God have mercy upon him) composed a book on this subject. He was in this science a pupil of 'Abu Ja'qûb Jûsuf Ibn Bachtawi, the teacher of the Diaspora (may God be gracious to him)."

This Said is otherwise quite unknown, nor do I know any other instance in which the name of Shirân occurs either in Jewish or Arabic writers. Perhaps it should be סעיד שירואני, which means Said of Shirwan in Buchara, or שיריני of Shirin near Qarmisin in Media[1], though it is hard to suppose that the name has been twice corrupted. Ibn Bachtawi is known through citations by David b. Abraham Alfâsi and Jefeth b. 'Ali[2]; here, however, we are informed that he was chiefly known as a grammarian, as he is also styled המדקדק in the pretended *Muqaddima* of Salmon b. Jerucham (Pinsker, Notes, p. 62). But whether he is therefore to be identified with Abu Jaqûb Jûsuf b. Nuḥ, cited by the author of the Mushtamil as the writer of an אלדקדוק, as Prof. Bacher supposes[3], is yet to be decided. There is preserved at St. Petersburg a commentary to the Pentateuch by the latter[4], and he is doubtless identical with that Josef b. Noah, who is mentioned by Hadassi (*Eshkol Hakkofer*, alphabet 168, letter ה) as having rejected the use of the analogy (קיאס, היקש): דרך בזו הדרך גם יוסף בן נח נ״ע ואמר כי לא יקיש בתורה

Our manuscript contains a further passage concerning Ibn Bachtawi, which I will also quote in this connexion[5]. It runs (f. 65 b): וסמעתך יום תצ׳ע מן אלמעלם אבו (l. אבי) יעקוב יוסף בן בכ׳תוי רצ׳י אללה ענה ותקול אנה כאן רגל מפסר (l. מפסד) וענד אלנאס אנה כאן סראג׳ מניר ופ״ר אללה נציבה פלקד כשף אלאבצאר ומא כאן לא נסור ולא מגזף.

"I heard that thou hast been endeavouring to disparage the learned Abu Jaqûb Jûsuf b. Bachtawi (may God be gracious to him), and hast said of him that he is a dangerous man; by the people, however, he is esteemed as a brilliant luminary, may God increase his lot. He opened men's eyes, was neither presumptuous nor an unmeasured talker (?)."

2. *Abu Ḥatim al-Rahabi* (?) and 3. *'Isra'il b. Danial al-Ramli.*

[1] See Sujjûti, *De nominibus relativis*, ed. Veth, p. 159. The Pseudo Messias שיריני (see Graetz, *Gesch.*, Bd. V, note 14) was probably a native of Shirin.

[2] See Pinsker, p. קי, compare also Geiger, *Jüd. Zeitschr.*, V, 177.

[3] *Revue des Études Juives*, XXX, 251.

[4] See Harkavy in Stade's *Zeitschr. f. Alttest. Wissensch.*, I, 156.

[5] For a copy of these two passages I am again indebted to the kindness of the Rev. G. Margoliouth.

The Bodleian MS., Hebr. f. 18, ff. 1–33 a, contains a small anti-Karaite work in the Arabic language. Its conclusion runs as follows: נגמר הספר הזה בעזרת שדי יום אחד בירח אלול שנת ארבעת אלפים ושמונה מאות ושתים ושבעים שנה ליצירה לכבוד יקר הדר מרנ׳ ורבנ׳ יוסף בן כבוד ג״ק מ׳ ור׳ רביעה הכהן ס״ט האלהים יעימהו עליו סימן טוב לחזות בנים ובני בנים לנגדו הוגים בתורת ה׳ ובכל המצות לקיים עליו וראה בנים לבניך שלום על ישראל אמן ואמן סלה.

It was therefore composed in the year 1112.

It seems that two leaves at the beginning are missing[1], as is also page 8. On the first page, as the MS. now stands, we meet with this sentence:

פקד וחלנא פי קום אקל̃ עדדא ואשד̃ לדדא ואפחש תאוילא ואשנע ג̇הלא ואקבח אעתזאלא לאנהם יתעלקון בזעמהם במא יג̇מע כלמתהם עלי תורה אחת ומשפט אחד וידפעון לכל כתאב מכתת (l. מכתוב ?) עלי תאויל אלסנ̃ה̈ גיר אלתורה אלמכתובה̈ ואד̇א הם יצנעון כתבא שתא ותאוילאת מכ̇תלפה̈ ותפאסיר מתנאקצ̇ה̈ מן ענן אלי בנימין אלי מאלך אלי ואחד בעד ואחד אלי אבי חאתם אלרהבי אלי אסראיל בן דניאל הד̇א אלרמלי.

"We have quarrelled with people who are smaller in number than we, but more powerful in disputation, who are detestable in their interpretation, repellent through ignorance, abominable in their schismatic attitude. They assert that all their words harmonize with one doctrine and one law and therefore reject every work which is based on the interpretation of tradition, and not on the written Torah. They themselves, however, have the most varied writings, and interpretations which differ from one another, and explanations which contradict one another. [This continues with them] from Anan to Benjamin [Nahavendi], to Malik [al-Ramli], and so in the course of time to Abu Ḥatim al-Rahabi to this Israil b. Danial al-Ramli."

The two Karaites last mentioned have also been hitherto unknown. The name of Abu Ḥatim is not mentioned, to my knowledge, by any previous Jewish writer. What is signified by אלרהבי I do not know, perhaps it ought to be אלדהבי. The expression הד̇א used by Israil b. Danial may perhaps indicate that he was a contemporary of the author. This Karaite is probably also referred

[1] Every sheet has ten leaves, leaf 9 forms the beginning of the second sheet, therefore not only leaf 8 is wanting but two other leaves besides.

to in a second passage of this work (f. 26), I do not however clearly apprehend the connexion of this latter passage. The text runs as follows: פקד וגב לנא אן נתענב מן תכלפך ען מפארקתנא איאהם ולא סימא אלא אנך תכאף מן שמאתה אלרבאניך פי חמלך דלך עלי סתר עיוב תפסיר אלרמלי ואלצבר עלי דעאויה אלכארבה ונסבה אלחכמה אלי נפסה ותרכת קול שלמה ענה כסיל כאולתו פן יהיה חכם בעיניו אלך. A certain Israil ha-Dajjan b. Daniel Iskenderi is known, who might be identical with our Israil if Firkowitch's statement be correct, that he wrote a ספר המצות in the year 1062[1], and it may be supposed that he emigrated from Alexandria to Ramle, or vice versa, but, as is well known, we dare not rely upon Firkowitsch's statements unless they are otherwise confirmed.

4. *Nathan b. Jehuda.* Another MS. of the Bodleian, Heb. f. 12, contains *inter alia* in ff. 9 b–44 b some chapters in the Hebrew language by the well-known Karaite religious philosopher of the eleventh century, viz. Josef al-Basîr, which are possibly translated from his כתאב אלאסתבצאר, Heb. ספר המאור[2]; fol. 9 b begins thus: הדבור בראיית הירח לזקן יוסף בן אברהם הרואה ז״ל · שאלה אמר יהי מאורות הוא דיבור למלאכים ואם היה כן מה המצוה אשר תתחייב עלינו מדבורו עליהם? תשובה · אמר הזקן יוסף בן אברהם נ״ע כי דבורו ויאמר אלהים יהי מאורות אין הוא עם המלאכים בלבד כי אם עמם ועם זולתם וכו׳[3]. This chapter concludes, fol. 12 a, with the words: זה מדברי יוסף בן אברהם נ״ע וזה המעט מאשר דברו החכמים בעבורו. Further on the MS. continues: בחדש סיון השמ״ד מצאתי בספר ישן ענין האביב של החכם

[1] See Pinsker, pp. 94, 174; Harkavy, *Studien und Mittheilungen*, III, 35, 46.

[2] See Harkavy, *ibid.*, 44–46.

[3] The sense of these words is as follows: The verb אמר can only be applied if there is a person present who is addressed; before the creation of man, however, there was none to whom this word could be directed. For this reason Saadja translates ויאמר in Gen. i. to ver. 26 always by ושא "and he willed," others again are of opinion that the divine word was spoken to the angels (for a full examination of this question see my work, *Mose Ibn Chiquitilla*, p. 124), the view last mentioned is also shared by al-Basîr. Now the Karaites cite Gen. i. 14 as a proof that the beginning of the month must be fixed by observation of the moon and not by computing the calendar (see e. g. *Gan Eden* ענין קידוש החדש, § 1). Therefore al-Basîr asks if this passage be directed to the angels how can a command for man be deduced from it? The obvious reply would be that the passage is directed to angels and to others besides.

רבי׳ יוסף ב״א ובו דבוק לענין זה ולא יש מקום לכתבו פה וכתבתיהו בסוף הספר הזה ושם תמצאנו. Fol. 12 b begins: מדבור הזקן יוסף בן אברהם נ״נ · דע כל האמה יאמרו כי יום הנפת העומר הוא משבעת ימי המצה וכו׳: Fol. 15 a: הדבור במחרת השבת, here he attacks Saadja. Fol. 21 a begins: הפרקים אשר מדבור הזקן יוסף בן אברהם נ״נ בעניני השבת מספרם י״ז, and these chapters conclude fol. 44 b.

Before the beginning of these chapters on fol. 9 a, the following occurs: זה הלשון מצאתיו בספר ישן בתחלת הספר הכתוב בדף הבא · הדבור לזקן יוסף בן אברהם הסומא · שאלה לבעלי החשבון אמר יהי מאורות דבור למלאכים ואם [כן] מה המצוה אשר תתחייב עלינו מדבורו עליהם? תשובה יאמר כמו[1] אלפיומי כי הראשונים היו יעשו על החשבון במאמ׳ מימות עזרא ואילך לא מצאנו אלול מעובר[2] בעבור כי הוא דבר יחיד והוא ר׳ חנניה ופיומי אמר לא יזכרו מאמר ביחיד אלא להבטלתו ואיך יעשה הוא דבר היחיד ראיה · ומאמרם אדר הסמוך לניסן לעולם חסר זה אמר אותו אחר עשיתם החשבון הלא תראה אם יאמר כי החשבון הוא מזמן אדם אמרו לא היה אדר לעולם מעובר ועל זה איך יהיה לו ראיה בו · ועוד אמר פיומי כי אמרו והיו לאותות ולמועדים לא יסמוך אל המאורות כי אם אל היום ואל הלילה[3] והוא אמר בו זה הפתרון הוציאו מנפשו וזה לא יצא משני דברים האחד אם ישיב והיו לאותות על המאורות הוא מאמרינו ומאמר הראשונים ואם יהיה הוא לבדו המעתיק די לו זה ואמר הכתוב כי הירח עשה אותו למועדים שנ׳ עשה ירח למועדים והירח הוא אחד מן המאורות ועל זה היה

[1] The answer seems to have fallen out. Perhaps the reading should be: יאמר כמו שכתוב למעלה ואמר אלפיומי וכו׳.

[2] Here, too, some words seem to be missing. The sense is, Saadja had assumed that the Calendar is very ancient (*Responsa Geonim*, ed. Lyck, 1), and used as an argument the Talmudical phrases (*Rosh Hashana*, 19): אמר ר׳ חנינא מימות עזרא ואילך לא מצאנו אלול מעובר and אדר הסמוך לניסן לעולם חסר. If, then, general rules can be subsequently formulated, the Calendar was obviously fixed. To this al-Baṣîr replies: The remark of R. Chanina is a דעת יחיד and therefore is indecisive; while the second passage dates from the time when the Calendar was already fixed. Compare *Gan Eden*, l. c., § iv, where the same controversy is reported.

[3] Cf. *Gan Eden*, § i: ולא השמע לדברי חולם הלום להיות מלת והיו חוזר אל היום והלילה הסמוכים וכו׳. Saadja is mentioned in Jeshua ben Jehuda's בראשית רבא (MS. Leyden, Cod. Warner, 41, f. 88 a): ואין אופן לאשר אמר אותו הפיתומי מן חיוב השיב והיו לאותות אל היום ואל הלילה ואלצמיר (l. ואלצ̇מיר) אנמא יעוד אל הקרוב לבד מן הרחוק אם יהיה הדבר מורבק בו וכו׳.

מאמרו והיו לאותות ישוב אל המאורות[1] ודבר גלוי מאד כי הזמן לא יהיה מבדיל לזמן ולא סימן לו וזה הטעם כתבתיו אני נתן בספרי אשר עשיתי תשובה על פיומי ויוצרי ידע כי לא עיינתיו (? שמעתיו) עד עתה [? מפי] רבי וכראותי זה לצורי וגואלי שבחתי שנתן לי דעת להכיר מכתביו.

The whole of this passage is copied from an old book, and the superscription referring it to Josef al-Basîr is unquestionable, as is clearly proved from parallel passages. Even the words beginning with וזה הטעם כתבתיו the copyist must have found in the old book referred to, and they cannot possibly have emanated from him himself, as is indeed evident from the two following reasons. First, it is very unlikely that a Karaite should, as late as the sixteenth century, still feel induced to write a polemic against Saadja. It is true indeed, that even the later Karaites controverted Saadja in their writings, as for instance, Aaron the second and Elia Bashiatchi, but this happens only occasionally, and the polemical passages are for the most part borrowed from their predecessors[2]. Secondly, after the end of the chapters by Josef al-Baṣîr, a further passage by one Nathan b. Jehuda is found, also headed העתקתיו מספר ישן, and no doubt attaches to the identity of these two Nathans. This passage (f. 45 a) runs thus: אני נתן בן יהודה נשאלתי שאלה זאת מן אלופי הקראים אשר הם יושבים בעיר אדום כי מאין לנו מן התורה שני ימים כסוי הירח השיבותי להם מן ספר בראשית שנאמר יהי מאורות ברקיע השמים וגו׳ וביום ששי ברא אלהים את האדם ומעת ברוא אדם על פני האדמה התחילו ימינו וחדשינו ושנותינו שנאמר ויהי אדם כן ויולד את קין והגיד הסדר הזה כי ראש חדש לא יהיה אלא בראשית השנה ולא נוכל לומר כי ראשית חדשיו ביום רביעי וראשית שנותיו וימיו ביום ששי כי הדעת והכרעת תורתו יהדוף זה ועוד לא נוכל לומר כי מיום רביעי היה רואה ומושל הירח ולא נחשבו לו אלא ביום שלישי שלו עשה האדם ראש החדש אלא כי מכוסה היה וכסויו אינו חשוב מראשיתו ובזה מנהגים של ימים האלה מגיד כסויו שאין כל חדש תחת השמש · ואמרו לי והנה היום כסוי הירח מן הישן ואם כדבריכם כסוי הירח מן החדש · אמרתי לא אלא גם אז כסויו מן הישן נחשב ונפלו שני הימים מן תחלת ימינו חדשינו ושנותינו כמו שנפלו שלשת הימים הראשונים מן חשבונינו כי כסוי הירח ידמה לולד אשר במעי אמו.

[1] Compare Ibn Ezra to Gen. i. 14 (first recension, ed. Friedländer, p. 29), and *Gan Eden*, l. c.

[2] *Gan Eden*, ff. 4 c, 5 b, 6 d, 7 b, 9 d, 15 b, 16 d, 53 a, 89 b, 96 b, 97 a; *Adereth*, ff. 8 a, 31 c, 67 c.

This Nathan is also unknown so far as I am aware. Perhaps the learned Librarian in Petersburg, Dr. A. Harkavy, who has at his command such rich Karaite treasures, might be able to communicate some further particulars as to the four Karaite authors here mentioned.

SAMUEL POZNAŃSKI.

QIRQISANI, THE KARAITE, AND HIS WORK ON JEWISH SECTS.

FOUR years after Saadyah had published his fundamental *Book of Beliefs and Doctrines* (933 C.E.), a Karaite savant wrote a work which had a similar tendency, namely, to offer some safe guidance amid the numerous religious opinions which were then put forth, and some justification for the application of speculative reasoning to things religious. The name of this Karaite scholar has long been known, Abû Jûsuf Jaʿqûb Al-Qirqisânî; but with regard to his work, we now for the first time receive reliable and precise information. For this we are indebted to the scholar who has already done so much towards elucidating obscure points in the domain of older Jewish literature, viz., Abraham Harkavy, of St. Petersburg. There recently appeared in the eighth volume of the transactions of the Imperial Russian Archæological Society a larger work, in the course of which Harkavy published a part of Qirqisânî's treatise in the Arabic original (pp. 279-319), introduced by an exposition and review in Russian (pp. 247-278) of the contents of this text published for the first time. Although I am only partially able to master this introduction, written, as it is, in Russian, I yet undertake to give wider publicity to Harkavy's work, and to reproduce new and important particulars derived from the text of Qirqisânî itself.

Abû Jûsuf Jaʿqûb Al-Qirqisânî—so called after Qirqisân or Qurqusân, the ancient Circesium, Karkemish—wrote the said work, as Harkavy pointed out before, in the year 937. He named it *The Book of Lights and the high beacons*

(Kitâb al-anwâr wal-marâqib).[1] It consists of thirteen parts (מקאלה̈), the contents of which we become acquainted with through Harkavy's Introduction (p. 249). The first part is the portion edited by Harkavy, and will be further discussed later on. The second part, consisting of twenty-eight chapters, demonstrates the duty of Speculative Enquiry with regard to religious matters, and establishes its conclusive power. The third part, in twenty-five chapters, deals with the various adverse religious sects and their views. In sixty-eight chapters the fourth part contains the fundamental principles, leading to the understanding of particular religious statutes. The following parts treat of the religious institutions or precepts themselves in systematic order:—

5th. Concerning Circumcision and the Sabbath (40 chapters);

6th. The nine other Commandments of the Decalogue (104 chapters);

7th. Concerning the New Moon and the First-fruits (21 chapters);

8th. Concerning the Feast of Weeks (15 chapters);

9th. Concerning the Remaining Festivals (24 chapters);

10th. The Laws of Levitical Uncleanliness in man and beast (66 chapters);

11th. On Forbidden Marriages and the Law of the Levirate (31 chapters);

12th. On Forbidden Meats, Dress, and Seeds, and the fringes (42 chapters);

13th. On the Laws of Inheritance (14 chapters).

The above shows that the last nine parts of Qirqisânî's work, to which the first four are a sort of general introduc-

---

[1] Hadassi mentions a ס' הנצנים of Qirqisânî (*vide* Pinsker, *Lik kadm.* I. 169), but הנצנים is only an erroneous rendering of כתאב אלאנואר, as אנואר in Arabic means "lights" as well as "flowers." The proper rendering would be ס' האורים, as Levi b. Jepheth names the work (*v.* Pinsker, II. 90, 193). The book was briefly quoted as כתאב אלאנואר (without ואלמראקב), *vide* Neubauer, *Aus der Petersburger Bibliothek* (1866), p. 114.

tion, form collectively a *Book of Precepts*, and this may probably be the ספר המצות, attributed to our author. The MS., Or. 2526 of the British Museum, contains the twelfth Maqâla (Part) and portions of the fifth and ninth Maqâla of the ספר המצות (*vide* Margoliouth *Descriptive List*, etc., p. 42); Or. 2578 contain portions of the eleventh and twelfth; Or. 2579 portions of the fifth and sixth parts. Or. 2525 of the British Museum contains "an abstract of the ספר מצוות of Abû Jûsuf Jakûb Al-Kirkisânî" (*v.* Margoliouth, p. 42).

According to information received from Professor Büchler, the MS. contains an explanation of the commandments of the Decalogue; and this would, accordingly be the sixth part of the Kitâb âl-Anwâr. Finally, in Margoliouth's *Catalogue*, we find the contents of Or. 2524 thus: "Two fragments of a ספר מצוות, probably by Jakûb al-Kirkisâni, containing refutations of the Christians, Mohammedans, and of several individual writers." The contents contradict the title *Book of Precepts*. As a matter of fact the title ס׳ המצוות never appears, as I was informed by Professor Büchler (Vide *Revue des Etudes Juives*, XXVI., 311). It contains a number of chapters (באב), marked as those from the seventh to the twenty-third. Also the end of the sixth chapter is preserved. The sixteenth chapter (אלבאב אל״יו) finds a place in H. Hirschfeld's *Arabic Chrestomathy* (London, 1892), pp. 116-121; and when Dr. Hirschfeld styles the MS. as the *Sefer Hammizvoth of Jaqûb Qirqisânî*, he but follows the designation adopted in the official Catalogue of the British Museum: this was unknown to me at the time I reviewed the said Chrestomathy (*Revue des Etudes Juives*, XXV. 155). M. Hartwig Derenbourg styles the contents of the MS., "Fragments of a כתאב אצול אלדין Karaite en arabe" (*Revue des Etudes Juives*, XXIII. 284), without mentioning Qirqisânî as the author. Now, as we have a means of learning through Harkavy the divisions of Qirqisânî's work, we are in a position to make the statement beyond doubt, that the MS. Or. 2524 of the British Museum contains the greater portion of the third part of the Kitâb al-anwâr (*i.e.*, of the twenty-five chapters of this part, the sixth to the twenty-third). This part is of a polemic nature, and can therefore not properly be styled כתאב אצול אלדין; and yet this description even would be more appropriate for it than that of ספר המצוות. Really, if any part of Qirqisânî's work might be called dogmatic (כ' אצול אלדין), it would rather be the second part, or even the fourth, according to the division given above.

In addition to the Kitâb al-anwâr wal-marâqib, the Imperial Library of St. Petersburg possesses also an exegetic work by Qirqisânî, viz., Kitâb ar-riyâd wal-hadâiq" (כתאב אלריאץ̇ ואלחדאיק), "The Book of Fields and Gardens." It is a commentary upon those portions of the Pentateuch not devoted to the laws, and is consequently supplementary to those portions of the chief work dealing with the laws of the Pentateuch. Harkavy cites (p. 250, note 1) an interesting passage from this work, bearing upon Gen. ix. 27. Qirqisânî there gives an explanation to the words וישכן באהלי שם, which makes them refer to the conversion of the Chazars to Judaism (...דלך ראגע אלי אלכזר אלדין תהודו). The MS., Or. 2492, of the British Museum contains the said portion of this work upon the first two pericopes (*v.* Margoliouth, p. 24; Derenbourg, *Revue des Etudes Juives*, XXIII. 282).

As Harkavy deduces from quotations occurring in the two works which have been preserved, Qirqisânî was also the author of the following works:—Commentaries to Job and Ecclesiastes; a book on the Unity of God (כתאב אלתוחיד); a work on the translation of the Bible (כתאב פי אלקול עלי אלתרגמה).

In the introductory part of his chief work, Qirqisânî gives a survey of the Jewish sects as they existed in ancient times, and also in his own times. This knowledge is now made available to all those acquainted with Arabic by the excellent edition of Harkavy. Much of that which we read here concerning the various sects and their doctrines has long been known; but even these data acquire a new charm, and further corroboration, when read in the context of an original work devoted exclusively to the subject in question, composed by one who spoke from experience, or who was in a position to obtain his materials from ancient documents now lost. Add to this that Qirqisânî, notwithstanding his Karaite proclivities and consequent prejudice against the Rabbis, makes upon us the impression of an objective compiler and chronicler, who devotes to the subjects he represents a lively interest, and conceals nothing which might be of importance. At the end of the first chapter, (which, by the way, serves as an introduction to the entire work,) he makes the assertion that he has drawn his materials, not alone from the works of his predecessors, but also from his personal experience among the learned societies in which he moved, and, in the case of such meetings as he did not attend, from the verbal reports of its proceedings (ממא בעצ̇ה מדון פי כתב מן תקדם ובעצ̇ה ממא ג̇רי פי אלמג̇אלס אלתי חצ̇רתהא ומא אנתהי אליי ממא לם אחצ̇רהא, p. 280, *l.* 23-25).

It is specially interesting to hear what Qirqisânî has to say regarding the remnants of ancient sects extant in his days. The ʿAnanites, says he, are very few, and gradually decreasing. Only about twenty persons are living at Damascus of the adherents of Abû ʿIsâ Isfahânî. Of the Judgânites, only few are extant at Isfâhân (317, 4-7). Not one of the adherents of Ismaîl the ʿOkbarite remains at the present day (317, 3). On the other hand, some of the followers of Meshuje are to be found in ʿOkbara, named after their founder; but among them are no persons of culture or of speculative turn of mind in religious matters (285, 17). The followers of Malik of Ramla are still called Ramlites or Malikites (285, 13); while those of Abû ʿImrân Mûsa Tiflîsî are yet to be found in Tiflis, Armenia (285, 11).

More interesting, however, is the picture which Qirqisânî

unfolds of the conditions existing in his time within the folds of the Karaites themselves. In the last chapter he gives so vivid and drastic a picture of the dissensions reigning among them in matters of greater or minor importance, as regards doctrine and practice, that, did we not know the portraiture proceeded from the pen of Qirqisânî, so zealous a Karaite, we might be inclined to put it down as a lampoon directed by some opponent in the ranks of the Rabbins. He takes occasion to point out their doctrinal and ritual differences as he observed them at different places—in Bagdâd (317, 20; 318, 5; 319, 8); Tuster (317, 23, 26; 319, 10); Basra (318, 25, 34; 319, 10); Persia (318, 25); Chorâsân (319, 2); Gebâl (319, 4); and Syria (319, 1); and he closes the long list of examples illustrative of the differences and doubtfulness existing among Karaites with the following words:—"Things are becoming worse day by day" (ואלאמר כל יום פי זיאדה̈, 319, 24). In another passage (285, 23) he says in this connection:—"You can scarcely meet two Karaites of one and the same mind in all matters: upon one point or another everyone has an opinion different from that of the rest." It is worthy of note to remark the point to which Qirqisânî once takes the opportunity of referring, namely, the want of attention among the Karaites to the Rabbinic literature—he means the Midrash. "Had the Karaites," he says, "obtained an insight into the flaws and discrepancies which disfigure this branch of literature they would have rendered the task of controversy with the Rabbis a much easier one." "It is only of late," he continues, "that some few among them occupy themselves with the study of that literature, and they soon light upon the weaknesses and contradictions referred to" (296, 3-6. In line 3, instead of אקאוילה̈, read אקאוילהם).

With remarkable candour does Qirqisânî lash the petty and selfish motives which often prompted the Karaite teachers in the expression of their opinions. In the first chapter, Qirqisânî sketches the character of Daniel al-Dâmegânî, also called Daniel al-Qumisî (אלקומסי), as the latest founder of a sect. He treats of him specially later on, in the eighteenth chapter. On the one hand he praises him as a person than whom no one was more honest and unreserved in the frank avowal of the results of his speculations in religious matters. He reports of him that he was in the habit of furnishing his followers who possessed copies of his works with verbal instructions concerning alterations which they were to mark in them in the event of any change which his opinions had undergone since the time his works first appeared. But, on the other hand, he reproaches Daniel Qûmisî for his unbounded hatred of the ʿAnanites. At an earlier period, so Qirqisânî relates, he used to style ʿAnan ראש המשכילים; but later on he never spoke of him else than as ראש הכסילים. This, he concludes, is one of the great scourges which is rife among our people, viz., the way they attack and bear hatred against one another. The motive in most instances is jealousy and ambition (ואכת̇ר מא יחמלהם עלי ד̇לך אלחסד וטלב אלריאסה̈, 280, 21).

In the same introductory chapter,[1] Qirqisânî directs his remarks also against those Karaites, who, like those residing in Tuster (Schuster, the ancient Susa), appear to accept the fundamental principle of Karaism, viz., independent enquiry and research, while in reality they find fault with the rational perception, viz., that of the demonstrative sciences, whether it be in Dialectics or Philosophy.[2] They adopt this course, says Qirqisânî, partly through dulness of the intellect and the difficulty of this sort of speculative enquiry, and partly through their insisting upon the idea that the application of the speculative methods of philosophy to religious matters is fraught with danger to their convictions. Our author cites also the said

[1] The beginning of the chapter, and consequently of the entire work, has, unfortunately, not been preserved.

[2] יעיבון עלי מן נט̇ר פי אלמעקול יעני בשי מן אלעלום אלברהאניה̈ אמא אלג̇דליה̈ ואמא אלפלספיה̈. (279.15)

Daniel al-Qûmisî as an example of an opponent to rationalism as applied to religion., He decisively combats the idea that reason opposes religious belief, and asks: Are there not many, who are not alone not weakened, but even strengthened in their faith by such knowledge, while many apostatise from their faith and become the worst heretics, who have kept aloof from rationalistic knowledge. Rationalism, says Qirqisânî—and this he wishes to prove in his work—is the foundation upon which every article of faith is based, and from which every knowledge flows (280, 7: אלמעקול אצל יבני עליה כל קול ויסתכרג̇ בה כל עלר).

He proceeds from a similar point of view as Saadyah in his chief philosophical work: and it is a particular worth mentioning, that the same verse, Psalm cxix. 18, with which Saadyah begins his introduction, is employed by Qirqisânî at the end of his introductory chapter (280, 30).

A large portion of Qirqisânî's history of the sects is devoted to polemics against the Rabbins. He regards these as a sect of Jews which sprang up at the time of the Second Temple. The real founder, however, of the school of thought introduced by the Rabbis, was no other than King Jeroboam I. He was "the first who brought dissension into the religious camp, and sowed the seeds of rebellion in Israel," "who altered the precepts of religion, and falsified them." We cannot here reproduce (as it would exceed the limits of this article) the reasoning by means of which Qirqisânî brings out this idea of identifying the principles of Rabbinism, as they appeared to a Karaite, with those of the seceding king, who was by no means an idolator (Vide p. 281, 1—282, 5; 286, 1-5). After giving in the second chapter a survey of the sects afterwards to be dealt with in detail (282, 16—285, 25), Qirqisânî devotes two long chapters (3rd, p. 285-297; 4th, 297-303) to the explanation of the points of difference between Rabbinism and the other Jewish sects. In the former chapter, he enumerates over sixty particulars, mostly of Halacha, in which the tradition of the Rabbis deviates from the proper explanation of Holy Writ, or in which it contradicts itself. At the head of this list, he places the reproach that the Rabbis in their work *Shiûr Kômâ*, שיעור קומה, represent God as a body (286, 8). A few more of these faults found with the Rabbis are :—that they do not pray the Psalms of David, but prayers composed by themselves, though in beginning their prayers they say, אשר בחר בדוד עבדו ורצה בשירי קדשו;[1] that the Psalms which they do adopt, they do not rehearse as prayers, but in a sitting posture, as though they were reading (286, 22 ; 287, 4); that they bow at the end of their prayer, in the manner of the Christians, to the right and to the left, presumably before the two angels appointed for man (287, 7); that in the prayer מכניסי רחמים they turn to the angels to bring their petitions before God's Throne, resting upon the Scriptural words of Koheleth x. 20 :—ובעל כנפים יגיד דבר and taking " winged ones " to mean angels, according to Isaiah vi. 2 (287, 10). They further explain that the laws of Cleanliness and Uncleanliness are abrogated during the exile, asserting : מיום שהרב בית המקדש אין טמאה ואין טהרה (289, 5); they omit an undoubted duty on the day of Atonement, viz., the saying of the prayer צלאה תמיד[2] in place of the daily morning sacrifice, commencing as they do with the recital of the confession of sin : while, on the other hand, they have made it a duty to repeat at the conclusion of the day an unknown prayer called by them נעילה (294, 10).

In the Fourth Chapter Qirqisânî gives us a similar list of Rabbinic teachings and expressions, but these belong

---

[1] In that part of the Prayer Book ברוך שאמר, which introduces the Psalms of the Morning Service, it is said : ובשירי דוד עבדך נהללך. The Benediction quoted by Qirqisânî is one formed after that employed in connection with the Haphtara (אשר בחר בנביאים טובים ורצה בדבריהם). It is a question whether such was actually in use at his time.

[2] *Vide* the same expression, 294, 21 ; what is meant is תפלת שחרית. The prayer in the Liturgy of the Day of Atonement called ת' שחרית, is not regarded by Q. as such, inasmuch as it has included in it the Confession of Sin.

to the Agada. In this chapter he also begins with the book שיעור קומה; then he adduces expressions from the pseud-epigraphic writings אותיות דר' עקיבא and כתבא ישמעאל (=היכלות), and from the Talmud. He reproduces in detail the legends of Rabba b. Nachmani (he consistently puts רבא) taken from *Baba-Mezia* 86*a*, and of Elieser b. Hyrcanus from *B. M.* 59*b*. He criticises most vehemently the Talmudic account of the origin of the Septuagint (*Megilla* 9*a*), which he places side by side with the Christian account. Lastly, he refers to the extraordinary appreciation by the Rabbis of the translation of the Pentateuch by Onkelos (אנקלוס הגר), selecting a few examples of renderings which he considers perfectly absurd, viz., that of Gen. xxviii. 21; xlix. 11; Exod. xii. 48;[1] Deut. xxiii. 18. Qirqisânî does not admit the defence put forth by some Rabbis that such passages of the Agada have to be regarded not as belonging to the general traditions, but as the opinions of individuals, or that they were the expressions of enemies of the Rabbis, which had become incorporated among their own (302, 16).

With apparent delight and avowed tendency does Qirqisânî include within the limits of his picture the well-known differences in matters of ritual, specially between the Palestinian and Babylonian Jews. He adduces this divergence within the folds of Rabbinic Judaism in the matter of religious opinion as a strong argument against the genuineness and truth of Rabbinic tradition, and as a weapon on his side against the reproach, so fondly levelled by the Rabbins at the Karaites, that of want of unanimity and certainty (*vide* 308, 24; 319, 27). According to Qirqisânî, these differences between the Jews of Palestine and Babylon are connected with the ancient feud between the schools of Hillel and Shammai (284, 2), and upon the strength of this assumption he refers, in the list of

---

[1] He quotes (as a translation of וכל ערל לא יאכל בו): כל משעמד לא יאכל מנה.

the various sects, to the said differences in chronological order in that part (ch. 10), in which we should have expected, according to the introductory survey of the Second Chapter, a mention of the Schools of Hillel and Shammai, concerning whose controversies he also introduces several notices (309, 2-18). He derives his knowledge of these differences between the Palestinian and Babylonian Jews, as he asserts at the end of the chapter dealing with them (311, 15), from the writings of the Rabbis themselves, one of their number having collected them in a separate volume. In the beginning of the Chapter (308, 20) he remarks that these differences amount to about fifty, and enumerates amid polemical expressions, sixteen of them. Of the fifty-five entries of differences found in Joel Müller's treatise,[1] we find quoted by Qirqisânî the following numbers: 3, 6, 7, 9, 11, 15, 16, 17, 18, 23, 31, 40, 41, 51. He includes two numbers which are missing in the sources from which Müller drew his materials.[2]

From what has already been stated, it will easily be seen that Qirqisânî studied with industry, for polemical purposes, the Literature of the Rabbis. In addition to the *Mishna* and *Talmud*, and those works of mystic and pseudepigraphic literature already mentioned, we learn from the text before us of the following works which he cites:—

1. A book, יראת חטא, from which he quotes this expression: "You will have no reward for studying and

---

[1] חלוף מנהגים בין בני בבל לבני ארץ ישראל (reprinted from Jhg. VII. and VIII. of השחר), Vienna, 1878.

[2] In a Hebrew translation the two numbers would have to run thus:— 1. (310, 11), אנשי בבל מתירים לשום את הקדרה אל התנור קודם בוא השבת כדי שתתבשל בשבת ואנשי א״י אוסרים; 2. (310, 5) אנשי בבל אין מתירים לקדש את האשה בשנה השביעית ואנשי ארץ ישראל מתירים זה. This latter number must undoubtedly be based upon some misunderstanding. In the original there occurred the word בשביעית (=בפירות ש׳ or בדמי ש׳), and Q. thoughtlessly took it to mean בשנה השביעית. Cf. the Commentary משנה למלך on Maimûni's *Mishne Torah*, *Hilch. Ishûth*, V. 3.

searching the Torah, but only for your searching the teachings of the Rabbis" (248, 10: וקאלוא פי יראת חטא ליס לך אגר אן תקרא ותדרס פי אלתוריה̈ אלא פי גמאר אלרבאנין).

The book is evidently the same that, as Azulai (ed. Benjacob, II. 62*a*) remarks, is referred to by Salomon b. Al-Kabez in his commentary to Ruth i. 21, by the name מס׳ יראת חטא. Harkavy (p. 298, note 10) is, therefore, wrong in saying it is quite unknown. It is an ethical treatise similar to מס׳ דרך ארץ. Two MSS. of the Bodleian (No. 120 and 380, vide *Neubauer's Cat.*, Col. 19 and 83) contain the tractate יראת חטא, between the tractates Aboth and Derech Erez. Qirqisânî's citation is a testimony to its age.

2. סדר גיהנם (298, 16), not identical with the מסכת גיהנם (published in Jellinek's *Beth-Hamidrash*, I. 147, 9), for Qirqisânî's quotation is not to be found in the latter.

3. תשובת אחאב, probably an Agadic work based upon the Biblical story of King Ahab's repentance (1 Kings xxi. 27-29). Qirqisânî quotes from this and the aforementioned work the Agada occurring in both, according to which God himself, in Isaiah xxii. 12, makes use of weeping and lamentation. This bold Agadic conception which presents God as weeping over the destruction of his sanctuary, is already met with in older Midrashic writings (Vide *Die Agada der Palästinensischen Amoräer*, I. 145; note 4).

4. An Agadic work known as תלמוד בני רבי (299, 4: אגדה להם תערף בתלמוד בני רבי). He quotes from the same an Agadic passage which, rendered into Hebrew, would probably run thus:—שלשה דברים למד הקב״ה ממשה · אחד במעשה העגל כאשר רצה להשמיד בני ישראל כמו שאמר ועתה הניחה לי ויחר אפי בהם ואכלם אמר משה לפניו ושמעו מצרים כי העלית בכחך וגו׳ אמר לו הקב״ה החייתני בדבריך שנאמר ואולם חי אני · והשני במעשה סיחון כשאמר הקב״ה למשה והתגר בו מלחמה לא ישר הדבר בעיני משה ולא עשה מה שצוהו הקב״ה שנאמר ואשלח מלאכים ממדבר קדמות אל סיחון וגו׳ ומה שעשה ישר בעיני הקב״ה ואמר לו משה

מבטל אני את דברי ואקיים את דבריך וזה שאמר אחר זה כי תקרב אל עיר וגו׳.

The third point, referred to in the opening words, which God learnt from Moses, is missing.

Qirqisânî adds the remark: "I think that this passage is taken from the Talmud" (ואחסב אן הדא אלהול מן אלתלמוד). Perhaps he was thinking of the passage in Berachoth, 32*a*, where we may read almost literally part of the first Agada based on Exod. xxxii. 10 and Numb. xiv. 13, 16, and 21. The second Agada, which brings into connection Deut. xx. 10 and Deut. ii. 24 and 26, is to be found in the Midrash Tanchuma in the frame of a similar three-fold Agada.[1] What the "Talmud of the Sons of Rabbi," as the title of an Agadic work, is to signify, is beyond even conjecture.

5. A work of Hâi, Chief of the College, in which he attributes to R. Jizchak Nappacha, the Palestinian Amora, the rules for fixing the Calendar (293, 5). This work of Hâi the elder (Hâi b. David), is known also to later Karaite writers, beginning with Jepheth b. Ali, as Pinsker has shown (*Likkute Kadmonijoth*, II., 94, 148-151). According to Levi b. Jepheth it was a controversial work against the Karaites.

6. Not from personal observation, but from the relations of others, Qirqisânî was acquainted with a translation made by the same Chief of the College, Hâi. It is said of the latter, that he in conjunction with his father (הו ואבוה, perhaps הו ואכוה, he and his brother) translated the book of 'Anan from Aramaic into Hebrew מן אלארמאני אלי אלעבראני). The two translators, as we are further told in this remarkable account, had found nothing in 'Anan for which there was not some support in the teachings of the

---

[1] *Tanch.* שופטים, fine: א״ר לוי שלשה דברים עשה משה והסכים הקב״ה על ידו · ואלו הן······ ואחת בימי סיחון ועוג א״ל הקב״ה לך הלחם עמו סכור אמת המים שלו ומשה לא עשה כן שנאמר ואשלח מלאכים · א״ל הקב״ה חייך עשית כראוי מסכים אני על ידך לפיכך משה מזהיר על ישראל ואומר להם כי תקרב אל עיר להלחם עליה וקראת אליה לשלום. Conf. *Deuteronomium Rabba*, c. V. *fin.*

Rabbins, with the exception of one ordinance concerning the firstborn of cattle. Ultimately they even found this point in the ritual of the Paitan Jannai (פי חזאנה̈ ינאי), 284, 17-22.

7. The ritual of Eleasar (אלעזר פי חזאנתה), *i.e.*, of Kalir, from which Qirqisânî quotes (300, 1-3) a piece belonging to the Liturgy of the Day of Atonement, and beginning לך ארץ ודריה. He cites from it the words וחיד חרמה אשר ברחט אסורה. This same quotation, probably derived from our author, is to be found several times in *Hadassi (vide* Zunz, *Literaturges. d. Syn. Poesie*, p. 63).

Qirqisânî in one place makes mention by name of a Rabbinic authority (312, 2). I asked—so he relates—Ja'qûb Ibn Ephraim, the Palestinian (אלשאמי): Why do you (Rabbis) attract to yourselves the 'Isavites (the adherents of 'Isa Isfahani) and intermarry with them, seeing that they (as you are well aware) ascribe the prophetic spirit to such individuals as were no prophets, namely, Jesus and Muhammed? His reply was:—Because they do not differ from us in the matter of the Festivals. Harkavy remarks that the person here named, Jacob b. Ephraim, is identical with the man whose Commentary to the T. Sabbath of the Jerusalem Talmud was brought from Palestine to Babylon by Salmon ben Jerucham (Pinsker, II., 14).

The most important authority whom Qirqisânî follows in his account of the sects, is one who, as a philosophical writer, is highly esteemed on the Rabbinic side since Bachja Ibn Pakûda, viz., David Almuqammeṣ (or, as his name was also pronounced Almiqmâṣ, אלמקמאץ). Concerning this personage, around whom there has gathered some inexplicable mystery, we learn from this work of Qirqisânî the most astounding particulars. In the chapter on Christianity he states that he is indebted for his statements on this subject to the accounts of David b. Merwân Al-Raqqî. He then proceeds: "This person, known by the name of אלמקמץ, was a philosopher. First he was a Jew, and then he became converted in Nisibis to Christianity, under the lead of a man named Nânâ (=Nonnus, *vide* p. 259, note 3). The latter was much esteemed among Christians, as he was a perfect philosopher and practised medicine. David Almuqammeṣ was for many years his pupil, and thus it was that he learnt the principles of Christianity so thoroughly, and distinguished himself in philosophy. Later on he wrote two books concerning the Christians, in which he attacked them; both works are known. He further translated from among their books and commentaries a Commentary upon Genesis, which he termed כתאב אלכליקה̈ (Book of Creation), and also a Commentary upon Koheleth" (306, 16-23). These data impress one with their own historic truth, and we have no reason to doubt their being facts. Qirqisânî seems to have spent some time in Raqqua, David's native place (*V.* Munk, *Mélanges de Philosophie*, p. 474), for he receives information from a scholar of this town concerning some particulars in the ritual of Jerusalem (310, 29: וחכי שיך̇ מן משאיך̇ אלרקה̈). He could thus have gathered from that place authentic details regarding the life of Almuqammeṣ. With reference to this surname, we have the ingenious suggestion of Harkavy, viz., "the leaper, jumper" (cf. Arabic קמץ, Aram. קמצא, grasshopper, *sauterelle*), this surname having been intended to point to the fact that David changed his religion twice, "jumped" from one to the other, seeing that he was converted to Christianity, and then returned to Judaism. David's Commentary on Genesis, to which reference is made, Harkavy found quoted in a fragment of an anonymous Arabic Commentary on Genesis. It is stated in this fragment (p. 261): "David b. Merwân Al-Raqqî, called Almuqammeṣ, wrote a book in explanation of Genesis, which he translated from the commentaries of the Syrians." The fragment lays stress upon a characteristic of this Commentary on Genesis by David b. Merwân, stating that it is now defective, now unnecessarily prolix.

The work of David b. Merwân, from which Qirqisânî

drew most of the materials for his chapter on Christianity (p. 305-307), he calls in another passage (308-316) כתאב אלצ̇ראה̈, Kitâb-al-Dharâ, Book of Fierce Attack, a characteristic title for a controversial work. He also refers in his accounts of individual sects (304, 9 and 16) to David b. Merwân as his authority, and we may infer that even in those parts in which he does not refer to him specially, he drew from him as his source. The same source supplied in later times (twelfth Century), Jehuda Hadassi with material for Nos. 97 and 98 of his Eshkol Hakkofer on Jewish sects. This account, hitherto regarded as the chief source of information on the subject, can now be controlled and supplemented with the assistance of Qirqisânî.

Qirqisânî sets to work chronologically in his accounts of the Jewish sects, as well in his introductory survey in the second chapter, as in the later chapters devoted to the individual sects. Here follows an enumeration of the various sects in the same order as he mentions them, with details of special interest or such as have been hitherto unknown.[1]

1. The Samaritans, "called by the Jewish people כותים" (282, 16). It is related of them, that to this very day, they revere the memory of Sanballat the Choronite as one of their princes (285, 21). During their prayers they turn to Shilo (303, 11). They reckon the new moon according to a calendar supposed to have been fixed by Jeroboam (עיבור ירבעם, 303, 15). They are divided into two sects, one called כושן, the other דסתאן (Dustân= Dositheos). One of these sects denies the Resurrection. They, having made a few alterations in the text of the Thora, accordingly add in Gen. iv. 8, קום נצא השדה (303, 18-22).

2. The Sadducees ((אלצדוקיה̈). Zadok, their founder, wrote books against the Rabbanites, without adducing proofs, in behalf of his views which were opposed to those of the Rabbanites (283, 11-13). Boëthus, the other founder,

[1] Concerning the Rabbanites, this has appeared in the foregoing remarks.

taught, as the ʿAnanites and all other Karaites, that the Feast of Weeks could only be held on a Sunday (283, 15; 304, 22). The Sadducees prohibited divorce, as Jesus did later (304, 3; 305, 12). They explained (according to the statement of David Almuqammes), the bodily attributes ascribed to God in Holy Writ in their literal signification (304, 9-16).

3. The Magârites (אלמגאריה̈). They are so called from the fact that their books were found in a cave (מגאר, Hebr. מערה). The "Alexandrine" belongs to them, whose work is known and famous; it is the best of the "Books of the Cave." Then comes a little work called ספר ידוע, also a beautiful book. The remaining works of the Magârites are mostly devoted to idle, senseless talk (283, 18-20). It is said that some of this sect held laughing as prohibited (304, 14). They explain several passages of Scripture in an improbable, senseless (allegorical) manner (304, 15). They insist upon the bodily attributes referred in Scripture to God being taken to have reference to an Angelic Being, to whom even the creation of the world is ascribed (304, 18-21). On this last point, Qirqisânî remarks, they agree with the view expressed by Benjamin Nehâwendi. By the term "Alexandrine" (אלאסכנדראני) we have to understand Philo, as Harkavy rightly assumes (p. 256, etc.). The title of the work ספר ידוע may be read ס׳ יָדוּעַ or ס׳ יַדּוּעַ (p. 257). The phrase "dwellers in caverns" reminds us, says Harkavy, of the Egyptian Therapeutæ. The references to the allegorical explanation of Scripture, and to the angels creating the world (Logos, Demiurgos) agree with the mention of Philo's name in connection with this sect, which, according to Qirqisânî's chronology, sprang up before the rise of Christianity. The existence of an account of Philo and his writings among Jewish circles (which may probably have been drawn from Christian literature, through David Almuqammes) is a highly interesting piece of information in the history of literature, which has become known through Harkavy's edition.

4. Jesus and the Christians. In the chapter on Christianity, Qirqisânî reproduces (as he states in the heading of the chapter) mostly that which he found in the work of David Almuqammeṣ. It is a short sketch containing the chief doctrines, and a few details concerning the history of Christianity, and it also includes a sort of criticism. The religion of the Christians, as at present existing, was introduced and diffused by Paul (פולץ). He ascribed Divinity to Jesus and the prophetic spirit to himself. He denied the necessity for carrying out the commands, and taught that religion consisted in humility (אלתואצ̇ע). All animals may be eaten, "from the fly to the elephant" (305, 14-19). The later Christian philosophers (אלמחדת̇ין מן פלאספה̈ אלנצארי) assert, that the religious ordinances were given to the Israelites in Divine wrath. The Israelites chose these ordinances for themselves because they resembled those of the Sabians; while those of the Egyptians, to which those of the Sabians were related, were known to them through their stay in Egypt (306, 4-7). The Nicæan Council, at which 318 bishops were assembled, determined upon precepts which occur neither in the Thora, nor the Gospel, nor in the articles of faith of Peter and Paul (פי קאנון פוטרוס ופולץ), (306, 29-32).

5. The Qar'ites (אלקרעיה̈), so called because they only made use of vessels fashioned out of gourds (קרע) (283, 28). They reside near the Nile, twenty parasangs from Fostât. According to one writer, they trace their descent to Jochanan b. Kareach (Jer. xliii. 4),[1] who emigrated to Egypt (283, 30). They are said to celebrate the Sunday in addition to the Sabbath, and this is an evidence of their leaning towards Christianity (308, 11). If David Almuqammeṣ be right, that Christianity is based upon the teachings of the Sadducees and the Qar'ites, then the latter must naturally have existed before Christianity (308, 14-18). The exclusive use by them of vessels made

[1] This is also the view of the Karaite lexicographer David b. Abraham (*vide* Pinsker, I. 166).

of gourds is explained by Qirqisânî (308, 2-10) by the assumption that the Qarʿites, like the Samaritans, avoided as unclean contact with other people, and consequently made use of gourd vessels fashioned by themselves. Qirqisânî found particulars concerning this sect in a book which he calls חכאיה אלמקאלאת (308, 14), which, according to Harkavy's ingenious conjecture, is the Kitâb al maqâlât (כתאב אלמקאלאת) of Abû ʿIsâ al-Warrâq, from which also Al-Bêrûnî derived many details regarding the Jews (*Revue des Etudes Juives*, XII. 258).

6. Obadja, known by the name Abû ʿIsâ Al Isfahânî. He declared himself a prophet in the days of the Chalif Abdulmelik b. Merwân. As the sign of his mission, his adherents regarded the fact which they alleged of his having been an ignorant tailor, who could neither read nor write, and yet composed books and scrolls without his having received instruction from anybody (284, 5-11; 311, 20-23). Relying on Ps. cxix. 164, he prescribed seven prayers daily; upon the strength of a revelation which he said was vouchsafed him, he prohibited the enjoyment of meat and wine, though having no Biblical evidence for it. He regarded the Rabbins as upon the same footing as the prophets, and insisted that he received a command from God to pray according to the prescription of the Rabbis, the Eighteen Benedictions, and the Shema' (311, 23-27). He recognised the prophetic mission of Jesus and Muhammed, and ordered the Gospel and the Korân to be read (312, 5-7).

7. Abû ʿIsâ Judgân. His followers call him the Shepherd (אלראעי), *i.e.*, the "Shepherd of the Nation." He is said to have been a disciple of Abû ʿIsâ Obadja (Isfahânî), and he also ascribed the spirit of prophecy to himself. His disciples look upon him as the Messiah (284, 12-14; 312, 16), and they await his return (312, 17). The Judganites prohibit meat and wine, and spend much time in praying and fasting. As regards Sabbaths and Festivals, they are but kept as memorials (312, 17-19).

8. ʿAnan the Exilarch. Qirqisânî enumerates over thirty lessons and precepts, mostly belonging to the Ritual, as those of ʿAnan (312, 23; 313, 30), the first point being an Halacha expressed in Hebrew אין משא אלא בכתף,[1] whereby it is permitted to carry on Sabbath articles of light weight. He states as a last point, that ʿAnan taught the transmigration of souls (אלתנאסך) and is said to have written a work on the subject.[2]

9. Benjamin Al-Nehâwendî. He was well versed in Rabbinic utterances and in the knowledge of Scripture. He is said to have been judge (דיאנא) for many years (285, 1-3). Qirqisânî attributes to Benjamin the second important founder of Karaism, about a dozen instructions, mostly bearing upon Religious Law (314, 3-24). At the head of these stands his well-known doctrine concerning the Demiurgos, which reminds us of Philo's Logos:—"God created an angel which created the entire universe. It is this angel which gave the prophets their commission, which allowed miracles to be performed, and gave commands and prohibitions."

10. Ismaîl al-ʿOkbarî (אלעכברי). He lived in the days of the Chaliph Almuʿtasim billâh (834-842). Most of his utterances border on insanity; nevertheless, he was full of self-admiration, and in his writings disparaged ʿAnan (314, 3). When on the point of death, he is said to have bidden his followers place upon his tomb the words:—רכב ישראל ופרשיו (284, 24-28). He did away with קרי and כתיב and insisted upon the Bible text being read as it is written. This is, however, contrary to what he himself is said to have asserted on several occasions, viz., that there are passages in Scripture which were originally different from what they appear in our present text: *e.g.* Gen. iv. 8, where the words נצא השדה were added; Ex. xx. 18, where, instead of רואים, there stood originally שומעים;

---

[1] Perhaps based on Numbers vii. 9, בכתף ישאו.

[2] *Vide* Schreiner, *Der Kalâm in der jüdischen Literatur* (Berlin, 1895), page 66.

in Exod. xvi. 35, where was יאׄכלו instead of אכלו; in Gen. xlvi. 15 there used to be שלושים ושנים instead of שלושים ושלוש: this is an error of the sacred text (גלט מן אלכתאב 314, 27—315, 7). As regards the first point, Qirqisânî remarks (319, 2) that it was also the custom of some Karaites in Chorâsân to read only according to the Kethib: in the same place (319, 3) he says of other dwellers in Chorâsân, that with regard to the pronunciation of the Tetragrammaton they hold that he who does not pronounce it as it is written (יהוה) but as אדני, is guilty of unbelief.

11. Musâ al-Saʿfrâni (אלזעפראני), known by the name of Abû ʿImrân al-Tiflîsi. He was a contemporary of Benjamin Nehâwendî and Ismaîl ʿOkbarî, and came from Bagdad. His surname he received on account of his having settled in Tiflis, a town of Armenia, where followers of his are yet to be found (283, 8-12). He wrote replies to questions attributed by him to Chiwi (Albalchî) (ולה גׄואבאת מסאיל ינסבהא אלי היויה), and also some leaves concerning the permission of enjoying flesh food (315, 21 *sq.*).

12. Malik al-Ramlî lived at Ramla. His followers are still called Ramlites or Malikites (285, 13-14). It is related of him that once during a stay in Jerusalem he swore that upon the altar of this sanctuary the cock was brought as a sacrifice (Cf. Pinsker, II. 84), (315, 23). Neither Malik al-Ramli nor Abû ʿImrân al-Tiflîsi wrote a work upon the precepts, and they differed only in a few minor points from the general body of Karaites (315, 17-19).

13. Mêshawaih (or Mêshuje, מישויה) al-ʿOkbarî lived, as the afore-named Ismaîl, in ʿOkbara (285, 15).[1] His opinions on Ritual Law savour of ignorance. An ʿOkbarite told Qirqisânî that Mêshawaih adopted and spread many of the customs of the Jews living in Gebâl (the Median mountain lands), among whom there exist many unwarranted innovations in the Ritual (316, 1-3). The Qibla

[1] Q. mentions nothing about Mêshawaih having lived in Baalbek, and having, in consequence, borne the name Baalbeki.

(facing at the time of prayer) should according to his opinion, always be to the west, even though in places situated to the west of Palestine, like Egypt and Maghreb, the back instead of the face would thus be turned towards Jerusalem (316, 11, 13).

14. Daniel al-Dâmegânî, known as Al-Qûmisî (אלקומסי), the last one who formulated a special doctrine, wrote a work and found adherents (285, 19, 20).[1] In his view upon angels, he deviates from that held by any of the Israelites (אל ישראל, Rabbanites as well as Karaites). He regards them, namely, not as living, reasoning creatures, entrusted by God with missions as prophets are; but he regards them as bodies, by means of which God produces effects, as fire, clouds, winds, etc. (316, 17-21). He is said to have taught that the obligation to carry out the precepts of religion only begins with the twentieth year of one's life (316, 25). He forbade certain things to be done on Sabbath, as *e.g.*, the washing of the hands with soap (316, 26). He declared as permissible the testimony of Mohammedans with regard to the observance of the New Moon (316, 28).

From the preceding survey we gain an insight into the multitude of Jewish sects, as they presented themselves in a chronologically arranged table to the imagination of Qirqisânî. The perspective from which these sects were viewed is that of a keen Karaite, to whom the large majority of the professors of Judaism appeared but as a sect, which had rebelled against the true principles of the Faith, represented as these were by the Karaites themselves.

In addition to this, small groups which clustered around the peculiar opinions of a certain teacher, are treated as real sects. It is surprising that only a passing reference is made to Chiwi Albalchi, and that he is not spoken of under a special heading. As we learn from Saadyah, he exercised a great influence, and his heretical opinions concerning the Bible had a far different scope from the Bible

[1] *Vide* above, p. 692 concerning him.

criticism—if we may use the term—equally remarkable, of Ismaîl al ʿOkbarî.

I regard it as superfluous to enter into details as to the value of Qirqisânî's work, made accessible to us by Harkavy, for the purposes of correcting and supplementing the accounts of Jewish sects which we have hitherto possessed, and which, in the main, are drawn from the self-same sources.

One thing is certain, the first part of Qirqisânî's *Book of Lights*[1] will have to be consulted as the most important

---

[1] Harkavy fixed the text upon the basis of two MSS. which mutually supplemented each other. Yet there are *lacunæ*, as both MSS. had them in the same places. The Arabic text is written in Hebrew characters; the Teshdîd sign is nowhere inserted, which, perhaps, would have done no harm here and there. I have found only unimportant printer's errors and other corrigenda, and I herewith place the list at the disposal of the editor and the readers of the book.

Page 279, line 5, *for* באלאמם *read* באלאמה̈
„ 279, „ 15, „ אלבראניח „ אלברהאניה̈
„ 280, „ 29, „ גדה „ ג̇ודה!
„ 281, „ 8, „ יד̇ה אד „ ידה אד̇
„ 281, „ 19, delete one אוהם.
„ 282, „ 5, in place of the words supplied by Harkavy in parentheses, הל קד, supply אפלא קד, or אפלים קד (cf. 301,5).

Page 284, line 10, delete the stop before פאט̇הר.
„ 284, „ 14, *for* ותלמיד̇ה *read* ותלאמידה
„ 285, „ 15, „ מישויה̈ „ מישויה
„ 285, „ 16, „ מע יחכי „ מא יחכי
„ 286, „ 16, „ מ „ מן
„ 288, „ 22, „ אגת „ אגת̇
„ 289, „ 21, „ ג̇לודה̈ „ נ̇לודה
„ 299, „ 30, „ בית אלמקדם „ בית אלמדרסה̈
„ 300, „ 24, after חתי, a verb has been omitted, say, שאהדוא.

Page 301, line 27, *for* שינעה̈ *read* שונעה̈ (=שְׁנַעָה), (cf. יובלג, p. 287, 19).

„ 302, „ 22, „ ויכ̇אבר „ ויכאבר (cf. p. 311, 17).

„ 315, „ 21, „ ג̇ואבה̈ „ גואבאת (Harkavy writes thus in *Studien und Mittheilungen*, V. 147, note 2).

Page 316, line 17, *for* יתבת *read* ית̇בת
„ 318, „ 36 „ זכר „ ד̇כר (cf. p. 312, 19).
„ 319, „ 29 „ ולך „ ד̇לך

source of information for this chapter of Jewish History, side by side with, or rather in preference to Jehuda Hadassi, Shahrestâni, and Makrisi. M. Harkavy deserves the thanks of all those who are interested in the history of the age of Saadyah, and of Judæo-Arabic literature in particular. May he have the good fortune to bring to light yet many such jewels out of those treasures of the St. Petersburg Library which are committed to his care and scholarship.

W. Bacher.

'ANAN'S LITURGY AND HIS HALF-YEARLY CYCLE OF THE READING OF THE LAW

By Jacob Mann,

It is only in recent years that the "Book of Commandments" of the founder of Karaism, wherein he embodied the laws to guide his followers in their daily life, both in private and in public, has been made accessible to us. In 1903 Harkavy published a part of this work from mss. in Petrograd.[1] Seven years later Schechter followed with the edition of fragments he discovered in the Genizah Collection at Cambridge.[2] Both publications contained sections of 'Anan's new arrangement of the service of the Synagogue in opposition to that of the Rabbanites.[3] But owing to their fragmentary state it was impossible to obtain from them a clear picture of this liturgy. While searching in that famous Genizah hoard at Cambridge, known as the Taylor-Schechter Collection, I have found more fragments of 'Anan's work which supplement those sections in both editions by Harkavy and Schechter, dealing with liturgy.

What is reproduced here as A (T.-S. 16, 365*a*, (2),), is from a piece of vellum, very damaged, the handwriting of which is similar to ms. III in ed. Hark. (see facsimile no. 3). B, (T.-S. 16, 365*a*, (1),), two joined parchment leaves, tops torn off), is of the same size and handwriting as T.-S. 16, 359-365 (ed. Sch., pp. 3-29). Between the leaves there is certainly a gap. Fol. 1 deals with the laws of pledges (משכונא). It most likely is a continuation of ed. Sch., p. 28. The leaf is so damaged that very little of connected text can be reproduced. It has therefore been left out here. But fol. 2 gives us a substantial part of 'Anan's

[1] *Studien u. Mitteilungen*, VIII, I. See also Pozn,, REJ, XLV, 51ff.

[2] *Documents of Jewish Sectaries*, Vol. II.

[3] Ed. Hark., pp. 17-21, 38-40; ed. Sch., p. 29.

service of the Synagogue. It will be noted that ed. Hark., p. 40, breaks off with the prescribed reading of the portion of the Law on Pentecost.[4] Where our leaf begins the same topic is continued as regards the Day of Atonement. The leaf is very likely a continuation of ed. Hark, and, had its top been preserved, we should have learned the still missing details for Pentecost and the New Year's Day.[5] Fragment C, (T.-S. 10 H 1'), reproduces in a complete form p. 29, l. 11ff. of ed. Sch. which is very damaged. We learn from it, for the first time, that 'Anan instituted a *half-yearly cycle* for the reading of the Pentateuch. We have also been able to reconstruct most of the divisions that formed this cycle. It should only be added that ed. Sch., p. 29, is probably the continuation of fragment B.

Now for a discussion of 'Anan's liturgy in detail, as far as preserved. We begin with the reading of the Law. "Every day before we pray we read in the scroll (the section dealing with) the day's sacrifice" (A. ll. 10-11), viz. פרשת התמיד, Num. 28, 1-8 (see ed. Hark., 38, Aram. l. 12ff.). 'Anan infers this from Neh. 8, 18. Though the whole argument is not preserved, as the fragment breaks off here, it seems that his deduction was that since Ezra read before the congregation on all the eight days of Tabernacles passages from the Torah, probably those prescribing the corresponding sacrifices, (Num. 29, 12ff.), hence the פ' התמיד is to be read on every day of the year. 'Anan's innovation consisted in the reading to be from the scroll of the Law, whereas Rabbanites, no doubt in his time already, recited this portion (either by heart or from a prayer-book) at the beginning of the morning service; (it is prescribed in *'Amram's Siddur*, I, 2*a*, top). On the whole 'Anan accepted the Talmudic principle that after the destruction of the Temple the actual sacrifices are substituted by the reading of the Biblical passages about them.[6]

4 עצרת is the last word of ms.

5 See however the attempt at reconstruction infra, p. 337 f.

6 See Ta'an. 27*b*.

Though not stated expressly, it appears that 'Anan prescribed the reading of פ׳ התמיד from the scroll also for the evening service, since he assigns an alternate section, Ex. 29, 38-41 (?), (also dealing with the Daily Offering), for Friday *evenings* and Sabbath morning (ed. Hark., l. c., ll. 14-16). It may be safely inferred therefrom that Num. 28, 1-8 was to be read from the scroll during the evening-service on weekdays. This would be quite in accordance with 'Anan's principle since the Tamid was offered up twice daily. Indeed, 'Anan rejected the מעריב-service, as being only a Rabbinic innovation (see Ber. 27*b*), and prescribed two daily services only in accordance with the times on which the Temidim were sacrificed.[7] The time fixed for the evening-service (corresponding to our תפלת מנחה) is not expressly indicated but from the expression בין השמשות) בי שמשי ed. Hark., l. c. l. 14; see also B., verso, l. 10) it can be inferred that the service was held close to nightfall. The whole question depends on the interpretation given to the expression בין הערבים (Num. 28, 8), which is a well-known point of dispute between Rabbanites and Karaites.[8] Later Karaites also inserted פ׳ התמיד in both services, but, differing from 'Anan, they did not recite it from the scroll.[9]

[7] See also גן עדן 69; והמעוט שאין למטה ממנו הם ערב ובקר שהם עתותי הקרבן. Cf. also Hark., l. c., 16 H, no. 9.

[8] Kirkisani in his *Kitab-al-Anwar* (ed. Harkavy, p. 318, ll. 13-15) tells us that 'Anan understood בין הערבים to belong partly to the day and partly to the following night, i. e. twilight (בין השמשות). In dealing with the difference of opinion amongst the Karaites. Kirk. writes ומנהם מן יזעם אן בין הערבים כלה מן אליום ומנהם מן יזעם אנה כלה מן אלגד. ומנהם מן יזעם אנה מן אליום ומן גדא עלי מא קאל ענן (cf. also Pozn., l. c., 177). See also Ibn Ezra to Ex. 12, 6 and Hadasi *Eshkol Hakkofer*, Alph. 135-6.

[9] See *Eshkol*, Alph. 15, letter מ׳ (for evening service) מזמורים על ענין התמיד וצו את בני ישראל . . . . את קרבני לחמי וגו׳; letter צ׳ (for morning service). Cf. also *Karaite Siddur* (ed. Vienna, 1854), I, 5, 19, 45, 56; II, 29, 56, etc.—In the Spanish rite פ׳ התמיד is also said at the Minhah-service before אשרי.

Following the general Rabbinic custom, 'Anan lays down the rule that benedictions should precede and follow the reading of the Law (ed. Hark., 17, Aram. l. 2ff.). But, of course, he would endeavour to deduce this rule independently from a Biblical verse. Since Ezekiel uses the expression "eating" for the reading of a scroll (3, 13-), therefore these two acts are to be alike as regards the duty of benedictions before and after. The analogy is further pressed by 'Anan so as to obtain a number of rules.[10] Only the reading from a scroll requires a benediction, but not reading by heart or from a book unlike a scroll in form.[11] Moreover, only the reading from a scroll in public needs benedictions before and after, while when in private only before. There must be in the benediction a reference to Zion. Accordingly, 'Anan lays down that the person called upon to recite in public from the scroll should begin with Ps. 99, 2: ד' בציון גדול הוא ורם על כל העמים[12]. The actual benediction, based on Neh. 8, 6, is ברוך ד' האלהים הגדול. The congregation, all standing, respond אמן אמן, raising at the same time their arms and bowing till their faces reach the ground. All those present remain standing till the portion is finished, whereupon the reader concludes with Ps. 99, 2, and the actual benediction (Ps. 106, 48) ברוך ד' אלהי ישראל מן העולם ועד העולם. The congregation respond אמן אמן הללויה perform-

[10] See also Harkavy, p. 199, note to p. 17.

[11] Ed. Hark., 17, Aram, l. 3 from bottom. See ibid., note 6.

[12] Ed. Hark, 19, Aram. l. 10—In the description of the ceremony it is not indicated who takes out the scroll from the ark and brings it to the almemor. Probably this was done by the שליח צבור (see infra, p. 15). It is only stated that the person called up for the reading of the portion, viz., the Kohen, as is shown farther on, on arriving where the scroll lies, stands still and as he opens it, all present rise from their seats. See also the description of "taking out the Law" in *Karaite Siddur*, I, 101; the verse of Neh. 8, 5 is also mentioned by 'Anan.

ing the same ceremony as before. Hadasi has 'Anan's concluding benediction as the one before the reading, and likewise the later Karaites.[13]

After the reading, שירה is said, whereupon "priest blesses Israelite" and the scroll is removed (ed. Hark., p. 20, Aram. ll. 1-3). This is obscure. But in B., recto, l. 13ff., we read, "And after we read in the scroll (about) the day's sacrifice, a Levite should recite the section of the שירה while the priests say המזכירים את י״י (Is. 62, 6*b*). Probably the verses in Is. were continued till the end of the chapter. 'Anan goes on to mention the Psalms for each day (l. 15ff.). By שירה he seems to have meant the corresponding Psalm for the day (שיר של יום) and also other verses from the Psalms. In ed. Hark., 40, Aram., ll. 7-9, we further read, "And before the priest says the concluding benediction for the reading of the scroll, he reads in the Book of Esther, etc." It thus appears that only a priest was called up for the reading of the Law, thereupon a Levite recited the "Psalm of the Day," while the priests said verses from Is. 62, 6*b* ff. This seems to be the meaning of the obscure expression "and priest blesses Israelite" (see also infra p. 341).

Now as to the various portions of the Law read throughout the year (ed. Hark., 38, Aram. l. 12 ff.).

(1). On every week day, morning and evening, Num. 28, 1-8.

(2). An alternate portion, Ex. 38, 38-41 (?), on Friday evening and Sabbath morning.

(3). On Sabbath morning the service was sub-divided into two parts, the first for the Tamid and the second in lieu of the additional sacrifices offered up on that day (מוסף). The readings for the second division were

[13] *Eshkol*, Alph.18, letter ח. See also *Kar. Siddur* I, 162—the concluding benediction is the doxology of the second book of Psalms (72, 18-19). Cf. also ibid. I, 36 (before the portion of New Moon's day), 86 bottom (the conclusion of Sabbath reading), 108; II, 33 (for Passover), etc.

Ex. 31, 12-17, 35, 1-3, Lev., 23, 1-3, Num. 28, 9-10. Of these portions the last only prescribes the additional sacrifices. Hadasi, as we have seen (note 13) mentions the sections Gen. 2, 1-4, Num. 28, 9-10, אלה החקים (Lev. 26, 46), and finally the Sidrah of the week (ופרשה של יומך). It is obscure which of these were read from the scroll. The Karaite Siddur (I, 86) gives תורה צוה (Dt. 33, 4), וזאת התורה (Dt. 4, 44), and אלה החקים (Lev. 24, 46) in the selection of verses recited before the reading of the Sidrah from the scroll (cp. also I, 162), while Ex. 31, 12-17, 35, 1-3, Lev. 23, 1-3, and Num. 28, 7-10, which 'Anan prescribes as readings from the Law, are said (but not from the scroll) earlier in the service (I, 68).[14] We see thus, as already noticed as regards פ׳ התמיד, how the later Karaites disregarded 'Anan's injunctions. True to his principle, 'Anan transferred Num. 28, 9-10, which are included in our 'Amidah, to constitute a portion of the Law to be read, adding other passages dealing with the Sabbath. Though they were from different parts of the Pentateuch, they were recited from one scroll. Here again he acted contrary to Rabbinic law, which, as is well-known, demands that, unless only one scroll is available, each portion be read from a different book (e. g. Sabbath ר״ח, etc.).

(4). If the Sabbath falls on New Moon's Day "we pray three times and we read, after the portion for the Musaf of Sabbath, one dealing with the additional sacrifices for New Moon's Day," viz. Num. 28, 11-15 (ed. Hark., 39, Aram. l. 2 ff.). It is evident that 'Anan subdivided the morning service on that day into three sections, each centering around the corresponding portion of the Law that prescribed the sacrifices for the occasion. On an ordinary weekday there was only the Tamid reading. On Sabbath morning (see sub 3) the service consisted of two sections

[14] Cf. also *Eshkol*, Alph. 18, beginning, where the same sections are given.

with readings for the Tamid and the Musaf, while on Sabbath and New Moon's Day a threefold division took place, viz. that of Tamid, Sabbath Musaf and Musaf of ר"ח. The most essential item in each section of the morning service on that day was the reading of the corresponding section of the scroll. No doubt three separate ceremonies of opening the Ark and taking out the scroll were performed. The same threefold division of the morning service took place also when a Festival fell on the Sabbath (ed. Hark., 39, Aram. ll. 5-6). This scheme 'Anan consistently applies as regards the Festivals. He thus still observed the distinction between תפלת שחרית and תפלת מוסף which became obliterated in in the service of the later Karaites.

(5). On every day of Passover, except the day when the 'Omer was offered up (see sub. 6), the morning service was divided into two parts. The corresponding readings were Num. 28, 1-8, for the Tamid, and Lev. 23, 4-8, Num. 28, 16-25, Dt. 16, 1-8, 16-17 for the Musaf of the first day of the Festivals. On the remaining days the order was alike, except that the portion from Num. 28 began from verse 19, (ed. Hark., 39, Aram. ll. 9-16).

(6). A threefold division of the morning service took place on the day of Passover when the 'Omer was offered up (in times of the Temple, ed. Hark., 39, l. 17ff). The readings were Num. 28, 1-8 (for the Tamid), Lev. 23, 4-8, Num. 28, 19-25, Dt. 16, 1-8, 16-17 (for Musaf) and Lev. 23, 9-15, Dt. 16, 9-12 as the portions for the 'Omer.[15] Now 'Anan does not indicate exactly when the 'Omer-day is to fall during the Passover week. But from his incidental statement that the portion from Num. 28 (in the Musaf-section) is to begin from v. 19 (והקרבתם, ed. Hark., 39, Aram., last line) it may be inferred that the 'Omer-day

[15] For וחדא דעולה דעומר ed. Hark., 40, Aram. l. 1, most likely read וחדא דעלה דעומר "and one (reading) about the 'Omer." Yet the text is essentially correct (see Lev. 23, 12).

could never be on the first day of the Festival, when this reading would begin from verse 16. Here we come to a knotty point. As is well known, the Karaites followed the Sadducees in the literal interpretation of ממחרת השבת (Lev. 23, 11) as being Sunday. Accordingly the Sunday in the Passover week, be it the first or any other day of the Festival, was the occasion on which the 'Omer was offered up.[16] Whether 'Anan already concurred with the Sadducees on this point is not stated expressly, but it should be taken as a matter or course in view of his general opposition to Rabbinic teachings. Now Kirkisani reports that if Nisan 15th fell on a Sabbath, 'Anan postponed the Festival for Sunday, Nisan 16th.[17] Did 'Anan then regard this Sunday, the first day of the Festival, as the 'Omer-day? If so, there ought to have been an indication in the above prescription of the reading of the Law.[18] This difficulty would tend to make one doubt whether 'Anan did not really accept the Rabbinic explanation of ממחרת השבת, hence the 'Omer day was always the second day of the Festival.[19] Let us hope that, as more of 'Aman's work becomes known, this point will be cleared up.

(7). 'Anan ordained a fast of 70 days, from Nisan 13th to Sivan 23rd, to commemorate the danger to which the Jewry in the Persian Empire was exposed in the time of Haman. On the former date the decrees ordering the destruction of the Jews were written (Esther 3, 12). From

[16] Cf., e. g., Ibn Ezra 23, 11, Hadasi, *Eshkol*, Alph. 222-24; *Gan Eden*, 50 ff.

[17] Hark., l. c., p. 130; see also Pozn., l. c., 17, 7, and my remarks in an article to be printed in JQR, N. S.

[18] Needless to say that 'Anan kept only 7 days of Passover, hence there would be no second Sunday as the last day of the Festival. He expressly mentions "7 days of מצה" (l. c. Aram. l. 7).

[19] The Karaite Solomon b. Aaron of Troki (end of 17th cent.) in his treatise אפריון עשה לו (printed in Neubauer, *Aus der Petersburger Bibliothek*), p. 11, bottom, deals with this dispute about the 'Omer day. As is well-known, the historic veracity of these later Karaite writers is very problematic. Solomon even antedates 'Anan more than a century.

that day till Sivan 23rd, when Mordecai had letters despatched permitting his people to arm themselves in self-defense (8, 9), a general fast was kept.[20] 'Anan also ordered that the two days of Purim, Adar 14th-15th, be observed as fast-days. Now during these 70 days the reading (beside Num. 28, 1-8 for the Tamid), during the morning service is from Ex. 17, 8-12, whereupon, before the Cohen says the concluding blessing (see above) a section from the Megillah (Esther 3, 8 to 4, 17) is recited.[21] Ex. 17, 8-12 is also the prescribed reading on the two days of Purim which will be discussed later on (sub 12).

(8). Ed. Hark. breaks off with Pentecost, while fragment B. begins with the Day of Atonement. But having in mind 'Anan's arrangement of the readings we would be able to reconstruct those for Pentecost, if only there were a certainty as to his explanation of ממחרת השבת, since this has, of course, a bearing on the fixing of the fiftieth day after the 'Omer. According to Sadducean and Karaite interpretation, Pentecost would always fall on a Sunday, seven full weeks after the Sunday of the Passover-week, and its date would vary from Sivan 5th till 11th in accordance with the variation of the Passover Sunday from Nisan 15th-21st. Thence Pentecost could not in any way be connected with the giving of the Law on Mount Sinai (מתן תורה) on Sivan 6th as the Rabbanites did. Assuming, as is very likely,[22] that 'Anan regarded Pentecost solely as the "festival of first-fruits," the morning-service was subdivided into two sections, while the readings were

[20] See ed. Hark. 130, 133 (no. 14), 149, (no. 27) and 157 (no. 7), and 164, (no. 7).

[21] Ed. Hark., 40, Aram., ll. 5-11.

[22] Even if 'Anan followed the Rabbanites as regards the 'Omer Day (Nisan 16th), and, accordingly, Pentecost on Sivan 6th, he probably rejected their coupling the Festival with "the giving of the Law."—Karaite opinion was not unanimous as to the day of Pentecost. Kirkisani (l. c., ed. Hark., p. 318, l, 33ff.,), mentions that early Karaites of Basrah thought that Pentecost always falls on a Sunday but did not know when.

Num. 28, 1-8 for the Tamid, and Lev. 28, 15-22, Num. 28, 26-31, Dt. 10, 9-12, 16-17 for the Musaf.

(9). The portions for New Year's Day probably were Num. 28, 1-8 for the Tamid, and Lev. 23, 23-24, Num. 29, 1-6 for the Musaf.

(10). We are on safe ground when coming to the Day of Atonement (B., recto, 1 ff.). 'Anan no doubt rejected the Neilah-service. There were the usual morning and evening services. The former consisted of three sections, and the corresponding portions of the Law were Num. 28, 1-8, for the Tamid, Lev. c. 16, for Musaf, while a third scroll was taken out for the reading about the day itself, viz. Lev. 23, 26-30 (?) and Num. 29, 7-11. (The words: "a third scroll was taken out" seem to be in contradiction to p. 334: "Here again he acted contrary, etc;" see p. 341.—*Editor*.)

(11). On the morning of the first day of Tabernacles the readings were Num. 28, 1-8, for the Tamid, and Lev. 23, 33-36, Num. 29, 12-16, Dt.16, 13-17 for Musaf. Likewise on the remaining seven days, except that the section in Numbers c. 29 began from v. 17ff. according to the number of the corresponding day. Just as in the case of Passover, 'Anan drew no distinction between יום טוב and חול המועד.

(12). Finally on the two days of Purim Ex. 17, 8-12 was read (besides, of course, Num. 28, 1-8 for the Tamid) and subsequently the whole book of Esther. 'Anan followed the Rabbinic tradition of reading the portion about 'Amalek's attack upon Israel, evidently because he regarded Haman the Agagite as the descendant of Agag, 'Amalek's king in Saul's time. For the same reason this portion was prescribed for the 70 fast-days, occasioned by Haman (no. 7). But 'Anan stopped at the end of v. 12, apparently without any reason, if this be not a whim of the sectarian. Later Karaites read (but not from the scroll) the whole portion till the end of the chapter (see karaite Siddur I, 15*a*, top) corresponding to the Rabbinic portion of the Law. The Rabbinic precept that no less than

10 verses should be read from the scroll was, of course, disregarded by 'Anan. Our portion on Purim, containing as it does only 9 verses, is discussed by Yehudai Gaon, 'Anan's contemporary.[23]

The readings for the other fast-days, as practised by the Karaites, and, presumably, prescribed already by 'Anan (see my remarks in a paper to appear in J. Q. R., N. S.), have not been preserved. They were probably enumerated in the missing part of B., recto, top. 'Anan also prescribed a fast for the seventh day of every month, as Kirkesani reports (in. Hark., l. c., 130). The reason for this fast is not indicated. Hence it is impossible to surmise what reading he fixed for that day.

It seems that at the end of every service Dt. 1, 1-11 was recited (but not from the scroll), whereupon the trumpet was sounded as a sign for the congregation to depart (B., r., ll. 12-13). This Biblical section was probably read because of verses 10-11 being blessings for the increase of those present. The blowing of the trumpet seems to have been preceded by נפילת אפים accompanied by supplication for God's mercy (רחמי). It is here that ll. 1-10 of H. are to be considered. 'Anan deduces from 1K. 8, 48-9 that "supplication" (תחנה) has to follow "prayer" (תפלה). He mentions in this connection the sounding of the trumpet (l. 7, cp. l. 9) which apparently concluded the ceremony נפילת אפים and the supplication for mercy. It was also the last item of the service.

We come now to the prayers following the reading of the law (B., r., l. 13 ff.). 'Anan laid down the rule that the prayers must consist solely of Psalms. He also fixed

[23] See ה"ג ed. Hildesheimer, 622. It seems that in order to make up the number of 10 verses some people began the reading, probably, from Ex. 17. See also *'Amram's Siddur* (ed. Frumkin, II, 185), and *Eshkol* II, 67 (in the name of Sa'adya). On the other hand some would read on, after the 9 verses, Ex. 18 ff. in order to lengthen the portion. The author of *Mas. Soferim* is against this practice (21, 6.)

certain chapters for the services on morning and evening (so Kirkisani, as cited in Hark., l. c., pp. 200 (note to p. 20) and 203 (note to p. 39)). These he called שירה, similar to the שיר של יום which the Levites sang in the Temple (Tamid c. 7, end.). However, 'Anan did not accept the Talmudic tradition and accordingly we have quite different an arrangement. After the Cohen recited the portion of the Law dealing with the day's sacrifice, the Levite, (as of yore in the Temple), says the corresponding song for the day while the priests chant verses from Ps. 62 (see above, p. 333). The psalms are c. 90 for Friday morning, c. 91 for the evening, and c. 92 for Sabbath morning. Here we have an illustration of 'Anan's way of reasoning. Because c. 92 is expressly assigned for the Sabbath, (מזמור שיר ליום השבת), hence the preceding two must be for the two services held immediately before. The Psalms for the other days are not preserved since the top of B., verso, is missing. Perhaps in B., v., l. 1, Ps. 76 is prescribed for Sabbath evening.

After the day's "song," seven other verses from Psalms, also called שירה, were recited. Priests and Levites took their stand on the mat (carpet) on the left side of the Ark while the right side was preserved for certain people (there is a lacuna here), probably those belonging to the "guard" (משמרא l. 13, to be discussed presently). They then recited the 7 verses, viz. 3 from Ps. 119, 2 from c. 1 and 2 from the שיר המעלות. Thereupon the priests and Levites advanced before the Ark, said Ps. 118, 35 ff., fell upon their faces in obeisance, and withdrew, half their number to a special place near the Ark, while the remainder went back to the "place of prayer" (i. e. the almemor, B., v., l. 8; see infra., note 25); where, it seems, they recited four verses, one each from Ps. 90, 98, 99, 100. Subsequently on Friday eve the one section of the priests and Levites (probably the latter) said Ps. 67, while the other Ps. 122. But on other days only Ps. 122 was recited, probably only the section remaining near the Ark. Finally both groups said in unison Ps. 118, 28 (and probably also v. 29).

On l. 13ff. we read, "And when the men of the 'guard' (משמרא) begin to say שירה (i. e. the Psalms), the congregation stop. And during the morning 'guard,' before the time of prayer, we say 7 verses, as we have written" (viz., in ll. 4-5). It is evident that together with the priests and Levites, a number of Israelites were selected, by a certain rota, to act in the service as representatives of the whole congregation. As is well-known, there existed 24 guards (משמרות) of priests and Levites for alternate service in the Temple. To each there was attached a "post" of Israelites (מעמד) stationed in Jerusalem while the corresponding "guards" of priests and Levites performed the Temple service (Ta'anit c. 4). Apparently 'Anan retained these divisions while arranging the service of his sectarian synagogue. It seems that there was a "guard" for the morning and also for the evening services.

Here B., verso, breaks off. We come to deal with C, wherein the half-yearly cycle of the reading of the Pentateuch is prescribed. Owing to the defective state of ed. Sch. p. 29, top, it is obscure whether this reading took place from the scroll or from ordinary copies. 'Anan, with his opposition to everything Rabbinic, may be credited to have abolished the reading from the scroll. According to his general principle, as evident from our remarks before, this should be reserved for the portions dealing with the sacrifices of the day. But in order to keep up a knowledge of the Torah amongst his followers, 'Anan ordained that it should be read in synagogue, in a half-yearly cycle, from ordinary copies.[24] It is not stated when during the service

[24] A parallel is supplied by the custom, prevalent at the synagogue of the Palestinians in Fustat since several generations before Sa'adya and continued into the 13th century, to read from ordinary Bible copies the portions of the Law according to the annual (Babylonian) cycle while those sections recited from the Scroll corresponded to those of the triennial (Palestinian) cycle. See my "*Jews in Egypt* and *in Palestine under the Fatimid Caliphs.*"

this was to be done, but probably it was quite at the end of the service. Thus Hadasi (in the passage indicated above, note 13), after describing the whole Sabbath morning service, states that the congregants sit, greet each other (the service being over) and the "section of the day" (ופרשה של יומך) is read, which evidently means the Sidrah of the week. However later Karaites altogether paid no heed to 'Anan's directions. They have adopted the annual cycle of the Rabbanites, taking out the scroll from the Ark and calling up 7 people for the reading of each Sidrah.[25]

'Anan states explicitly (C., T.-S. 10 H., 1^1, ll. 4-5), "And we complete (the reading of the Pentateuch) on Tabernacles, and we do it on Passover." The Jewish year consisting of 50 weeks, the Pentateuch had to be read through on 25 Sabbaths, hence every book had to be divided into 5 parts. The last section of Deuteronomy was read on the Sabbaths of Passover and of Tabernacles. We are able to reconstruct most of these sections. They are as follows (C., l. 1ff.):

(1). Gen., c. 1—?
(2). Gen., c. ?—?
(3). Gen., c. ?—?
(4). Gen., c. ?—40 (end)
(5). Gen., c. 41—50
(6). Ex., c. 1—c. 9 (end)
(7). Ex., c. 10—c. 17 (end)
(8). Ex., c. 18—c. 23, 19
(9). Ex., 23, 20—34, 26
(10). Ex., 34, 27, c. 40
(11). Lev., c. 1—c. 7 (end)
(12). Lev., c. 8—c. 12 (end)?
(13). Lev., 13, 1 ?—c. 17 (end)

[25] See the Damascus Karaite liturgies, described by Margoliouth, *Catal. British Mus.*, II, 450 ff. Cf. especially p. 451, col. 1. See further *Karaite Siddur*, I, 161-2, 172 ff. It would be of interest to know whether the Karaites in Jerusalem, in the early period, followed the Palestinian triennial cycle.

(14). Lev., c. 18—21, 16?
(15). Lev., 21, 17 ?—c. 27
(16). Num., c. 1—?
(17). Num., ?—c. 15 (end)
(18). Num., c. 16—20, 13
(19). Num. 20, 14—c. 29 (end)
(20). Num., c. 30—c. 36
(21). Dt., c. 1—6, 3 (or c. 8, end)
(22). Dt., 6, 4 (or 9, 1)—14, 21
(23). Dt., 14, 22—22, 5
(24). Dt., 22, 6—29, 8
(25). Dt., 29, 9—c. 34

It is difficult to ascertain exactly what principle guided 'Anan in making these divisions. It will be noted that several times he follows the division of the Sidrot according to the Babylonian Rabbinic yearly cycle (so in nos. 5, 8, 18, 20, and 25; in the last instance even where the chapter is split up, Dt. 29, 9). In no. 8, Ex. 23, 17 is a logical ending as it concludes the laws of פ"משפטים. Now since, Ex. 23, 18-19 are repeated in 34, 25-26, it suggested itself to 'Anan to conclude no. 9 with the latter verses. A well-known portion of the Law read by the Rabbanites on Festivals, עשר תעשר, became the beginning of a new division, (no. 23). No. 11 ends with the first section of Leviticus (see especially 7, 37-38). Likewise No. 13 concludes the section dealing with the laws of purity and impurity (15, 32-33). It is altogether unknown who and how many read each weekly section before the congregation. The whole cycle, accepted no doubt by 'Ananites, but abandoned by the other karaites, became entirely forgotten till the Genizah disclosed portions of the "Book of Commandments" of the founder of Karaism.

Special prayers are prescribed for the fast-days (C, T.-S. 10 H. 1[1], r., l. 5 ff.). On the 70 days of fasting verses of supplication are recited from Neh. 9, 5-37, Ps. 100, 47 (7 times), Ps. 106, 48 ,(4 times). Thereupon priests, clad in "holy garments" (i. e. special robes), approach the space in the synagogue "between the אולם and the bench of the priests" (l. 9) and recite 7 times Joel 2, 17 whereupon the congregation respond Ps. 115 (probably the whole chapter.) It seems that 'Anan divided his sectarian synagogue into compartments corresponding to those of the Temple. Where the Ark was deposited was the "holy of holies" (קדש הקדשים, or the Biblical דביר), while the space before it was similar to the היכל (probably identical with קמי ארון B., v., l. 7). The remainder of the synagogue was the "hall" (אולם).[26]

Now Joel (2, 17) makes the priests stand between the "hall" and the "altar." In 'Anan's synagogue the "bench of the priests" corresponds to the latter. Hence the priests, while reciting Joel 2, 17, had to stand in a space corresponding to the one in the Temple.

Instead of ברכו in our ritual the Karaites recite קומו ברכו, Neh. 9, 5 (so in Karaite Siddur at each

[26] The "hall" in Solomon's Temple corresponded to the "court-yard of the Tent of Assembly" in the Wilderness (חצר אהל מועד). In ed. Hark., 35m Aram., l. 19 ff., 'Anan expressly compares the synagogue, "wherein the priests bless the Israelites," to this court-yard. By his benediction the priest causes the Shekkinah to dwell in the synagogue. Moreover prayer is like the burning of incense. Thence the worshippers have to wash their hands and feet before entering here. The service itself is to be preceded and followed by the ablution of hands, limbs, legs and knees on the part of all present.—Kirkisani reports that 'Anan commanded the service to take place in a special place called חצר (Hark., l. c., 129). Already Harkavy (note 3) suggested that 'Anan called the synagogue so owing to having compared it with "the court-yard of the Tent of Assembly." But we can now go further in suggesting that, according to 'Anan, the worshippers who were Israelites had to be seated in the compartment called אולם (or חצר). It is there that the almemor was situated (מקום תפלה, B., v. l. 8). The "bench of the priests" was higher between the אולם and the place before the Ark (corresponding to היכל). Only those Israelites who formed the "guard" and participated in the service (above, p. 340), were permitted to proceed from the "hall" to the space before the Ark. In this manner 'Anan endeavored to make the synagogue resemble the Temple as much as possible.

service before the Shema', I, 2 top, 15, 51, etc.). This has been adopted from 'Anan's practice, as he tells us (l. 10 ff.), "When the reader (שלוחא) draws near (the almemor) to say קומו ברכו," he adds (on the 70 days of fasting) the doxologies at the end of the first 4 books of Psalms, viz. 41, 44, 72, 18-19, 89, 53, 106, 47-48. Then he continues from Neh. 9, 6 (till v. 37?); on the 7th day of the month (also a fast day, see above p. 10) 7 verses from Ps. 106 are recited before Neh. 9, 5-37, probably by the reader. At the conclusion of the verses from Neh. the congregation perform נפילת אפים. Likewise at the end of each of the following Psalms, 113, 114, 116, 117, 118. Whenever the verses from Neh. (9, 5-37) are recited, viz. on the Day of Atonement, the 7th of each month, the two days of Purim and the 70 days of fasting, the "curtains" (פרכת) are removed from the ark and "we put ashes on the fast" (verso, 11, 3-5). Unlike the Rabbanites who regarded Atonement Day as יום טוב, 'Anan, followed by the later Karaites, invested it with a sad and mournful significance (see my remarks, J. Q. R., N. S.).

This is the account of 'Anan's liturgy, as far as preserved. It is evident from the above remarks that he endeavoured to imitate the service in the Temple, as he conceived it, modified, of course, by the alterations in consequence of the cessation of sacrifices. The services were limited by the number and the times of the sacrifices for the day. The readings from the Law were the substitutes of the actual offerings.[27] The priest had to do the reading just as if he offered up the korban in the Temple. The Levite was to recite the Psalm of the day just as his ancestor chanted it in the sanctuary at Jerusalem. The synagogue had compartments corresponding to those of the temple and the seats of the priests were arranged so as to remind one of the altar. They had also to wear special garments.

[27] A responsum by R. Hai (cited in האשכול, II, 1) contains a *veiled* polemics *against 'Anan's* principle.

A remnant of the "guards" and "posts" (משמרות ומעמדות) was preserved. The Ark with the scrolls took the place of the Holy of Holies and was venerated by kneeling and bowing till one's face touched the ground. We now understand against whom the Karaite settler in Jerusalem writes in his tract (to be printed in J. Q. R., N. S.): "And if you have a box to deposit within a scroll, leave the Torah in one of your synagogues, but do not place it before you to bow down, as (was) the custom of the *early Karaites* (כמנהג ראשונים), who made an ark, with a scroll of the law therein, putting a cover on it like the Ark of the Covenent. You must not do so, for it is not permissible. Know you that in the whole of Palestine there was no Ark to worship God before it, except the Ark of the Covenant inside the Temple. Now, our brethren, turn back from your ways and act not so, for God will not favor this." Our author goes on to emphasize that whoever call any place but the Temple a sanctuary is like worshipping idols. Prayer is not like sacrifice. The latter must be offered up by a priest clad in holy garments and being in the sancturay. But prayer can be said by every man, if in a pure state, and in any garment, "clean but not *holy*." It is manifest that here this later Karaite argues against the service organized by 'Anan as described above. This opposition, no doubt developed by other Karaite spokesmen, resulted in 'Anan's liturgy being disregarded in several essential points. Altogether the principles that guided 'Anan in his arrangement of the service of his synagogue became obliterated in the rite which his fellow-sectaries evolved in the course of centuries.

In conclusion, a few more liturgical items, found in 'Anan's "Book of Commandments," should be mentioned, The benedictions, before and after meals, (cf. above, p. 332). are as follows (ed. Hark., 17-19):

(1). Before the meal, (Ps. 135, 21) ברוךְ ד׳ מציון שוכן ירושלם הללויה שעיני כל אליךְ ישברו והוא

נותן להם את אכלם בעתו ככתוב עיני כל אליך ישברו ואתה נותן להם את אכלם בעתו

(2). After the meal, (Ps. 145, 15) ברוך ד' מציון שוכן ירושלם הללויה׃ שפתח את ידו ומשביע לכל חי רצון ככתוב פתח את ידיך ומשביע לכל חי רצון

Only a fixed meal requires grace after it.

(3). The benediction before drinking water was, (Ps. 145, 15) ברוך ד' מציון שוכן ירושלם הללויה׃ שמברך את לחמינו ואת מימינו ומסיר מחלה מקרבינו ככתוב ועבדתם את ד' אלהיכם וברך את לחמן ואת מימין והסרתי מחלה מקרבן

(4). Finally four classes of people who were saved from imminent danger, viz., travelers in the wilderness and on the sea, released prisoners, and convalescents (see Ps. 107), had to offer up thanks to God privately and in public (ed. Hark., Aram., l. 2 ff.). The private thanks consisted in אודך ד' אלהי בכל לבבי ואכבדה שמך לעולם׃ כי חסדך גדול עלי והצלת נפשי משאול תחתיה׃ ברוך אתה ד' למדני חקיך (Ps. 86, 12-13 119, 12).

The public thanks (in lieu of the Rabbinic ברכת הגומל) found expression in the following verses: Ps. 86, 13; 34, 4; 103, 10; 40, 6; 72, 18-19. From וימלא the congregation joins in. 'Anan does not mention that this is to be said in the synagogue, and in particular when the person concerned finishes the concluding benediction subsequent to having been called up for the reading of the Law, (as is our custom). 'Anan only states "before people" (קמי אנאשי). However, since he calls them ציבורא (l. c., 38, Aram., l. 10), it can be inferred that it took place in the synagogue during the service. But further details are lacking.

A

(Recto, top torn off and faded)

....

..........................ו וג׳ וא.......................................

.........................ומשתהוים לי״א..................................

ביתו דכתיבי והתפללו אליך דורך ארצם אשר נתתה לאבותם]

[ה]עיור א]שר בחרת והבית אשו֗ר בניתי לשמך ושמעת]

[השמים מכון שובתך את תפלתם וא]ת תחנתם] ועשית משפו֗טם]

[קא אמא את ת]פלתם ואת תחנתם לאודועך דצריכינן........

רחמי נאמרה לתרועה בתר תפלה לאודעך דרחמי........

בעונן הילכך מצלונן ובעונן רחמי ו֗נפלינן על אנפ֗יננ]....

רחמי דמנפל על אפין נמי כי צלותא חשיב דתר[ו]עה]......

אמרינן להו ◦ וכל יומא מיקמי דמצלינן קרינן [בסיפרא]

קורבנא דיומיה דכתיב [2]ויקרא בספר תורת האלהים

(verso is very faded and illegible)

B

(Fol. 2, recto)

....[וביום הכפורים]

מ]צלונן ג׳ חדא ד]תמיוד] קורונן [את קרבני לחמי [3]והדא דמוספי]

בהדי חטא]ת יום הכ]פורים קרי מרישא דאחרי מות עד סוף פיסקא[4]

וחדא דעלה [ד] יום הכפורים קרי הש [5]....[וכאריך סיפרא]

לזאת [6]וקרי [ובע]שור[7] ומסליק סיפרא ◦ ו[בהג הסכות מצלונן]

[1] I K. 8, 48-9.

[2] Neh. 8, 18.

[3] Num. 28, 2.

[4] Lev. 16, 1 ff.

[5] Probably Lev. 23, 26-30 is meant here.

[6] i. e. the second half of Num. beginning with זאת חקת התורה (c. 19). This was the general custom in the East in the Middle Ages to divide each book of the Pentateuch into two halves (see my remarks in the above-mentioned paper, to appear in JQR, N. S.). Thus Genesis into בראשית (1, 1 ff.) and ויצא (28, 10 ff.), Exodus into שמות (1, 1 ff.), and ואלה המשפטים (21, 1 ff.), Leviticus into ויקרא

בׄ חדא דתמי[ד] את קרבני [ו]חדא דמוספי קרונן באחרי מות[8] דבר אל בני ישׂ [לאמ]ר בחמשה עד סוף פיסקא וכריךְ סיפרא לזאת וקרי בקרבנות ובחמשה עשר ועד סוף פיסקא[9] ובאריךְ סיפרא לאלה הדברים וקרי הג הסכות שלוש [פ]עמים איש כמתנת[10] ומסלי סיפרא ובשאר ימי סוכה מצלונן כל יו[מ]א תרתין חדא דתמיד צו [וחד]א דמוספי קרונן פיסקא דיומי[11]....פיסקי לתמניה יומי ובפוריא תריז יומי קרונן קרו [וי]בא עמלק ועד בא השמש[12] וקרונן מגלה כולהֿ ∘ וכד נפקין לדב[ר]א קרונן מרישא דאלה הדברים ע[ד]ויברךְ אתכם[13] ותקעינן ופטרינן ולבתר דקרונן בסיפרא קרבן יומיה י[קרא] לוי פיסקא דשירה[14] כד אמרין כהנים המזכירים את ייי[15] אמא בצ[פר]א במעלי שבתא תפלה למשה ו[ב]בי שמשי אמ יושב בסתר עלי[ון] ובצפרא דשבתא אמר מזמור שיר[16] לאפוקי

(1, 1 ff.) and אחרי מות (16, 1 ff.), Numbers into וידבר (1, 1 ff.), and זאת חקת (19, 1 ff.), and finally Deuteronomy into אלה הדברים (1, 1 ff.), and שפטים (16, 18 ff.). Thus a passage in פ׳ פנחס (Num. 29, 7) is cited here by 'Anan as being in זאת חקת, i. e. the second half of Numbers. Likewise in l. 5 f. a passage in פ׳ אמר (Lev. 23, 33-36) is quoted as in, אחרי מות viz., the second half of Leviticus. See also ed. Harkavy p. 38 (Aramaic l. 15) where Ex. 29, 38 (in פ׳ ואתה תצוה) is given as in אלה המשפטים, i. e. second half of Exodus. Harkavy (note 9) did not understand this fact and therefore deduces that 'Anan had a different arrangement of the weekly sections. This is perfectly true, as is evident from our fragment under III, but here the division of the books of the Pentateuch is meant which was the general practice.

[7] Num. 29, 7-11.

[8] Lev. 23, 33-44.

[9] Num. 29, 12-16.

[10] Dt. 16, 13-17.

[11] i. e. Num. 29, 17-19, etc.

[12] Ex. 17, 8-12.

[13] Dt. 1, 1-11.

[14] Probably the "song" for the corresponding day (שיר של יום)

[15] Is. 62, 6.

[16] As Ps. 92 is evidently for the Sabbath, the two preceding ones (90, 91) must, according to 'Anan's logic, be said on Friday morning and evening, respectively.

(Verso)

....

.... השבת אמר נודע ב[יהוד]ה[17] ובתרה ....[אמר]ין ז׳ פיסקין שירה כד קי[מו]נן בתרין ....[ב]צפא[18] לשמאל דארון קימ[י]ן [כה]ני וליואי ובצפא לימין דארון קימין···[וא]מרין ג׳ [פיס]קי משרי[19] תמימי דרך ותרין פיסקי מראש ספר דתהלים והרי[נן] פיסקי משיר המעלות ולבתר דמסימינן עד ז׳ פיסקי קרבי כהני וליואי פסקי לקמי ארון ואמרי[ן] אנא יי הושיעה נא וג׳[20] עד דמסימין ומפלוין[21] על [אפיהון] ופסקי והדרי פל[גא] למקום ארון ופלגא למקום תפלה ואמרי פ[ס]וקי קמ[י] אילין···[תפ]לה למשה ומזמור שירו ליי׳ יי׳ מלך [ירגזו] ומזמור לתודה[22] ולבתר [דמס]יימין הלין ה׳[23] ארבעה פיסקין בבי שמ[ש]י אמרין מזמור שיר[24] וה[לין] אמרין שיר המעלות לדוד שמחתי[25] ובשאר יומי אמרינן שיר המעלות לדוד שמחתי ו[ל]בתר דמסיימין אמרין כולהון בהדו[26] הדדי אלי אתה ואודך[27] ו[כד מתחלין] אנשי דמשמר[א] בשירה [פס]קין קהלא ובמשמרא דצפרא מ[קמי] עידן צלותא אמרינן ז׳ פ[י]סקין כי היכ[י] דכתבנן ד···[ומ]סימינן בשיר המעלות ומקמי דקרב[ונן ל]מימר שירה בי [שמשי····

[17] Ps. 76.

[18] Probably "mat", i. e. carpet on both sides of the Ark. Cf. Syriac צפא.

[19] Read מאשרי, Ps. 119.

[20] Ps. 118, 25.

[21] Probably read ונפלין.

[22] Pss. 90, 98, 99, 100.

[23] This ה׳ is unintelligible here and should probably be deleted.

[24] Probably Ps. 67.

[25] Ps. 122.

[26] = בהדי.

[27] Ps. 118, 28.

C

[Schechter, Documents of Jewish Sectaries, II, 29, ll. 1-11, as re-examined by me.]

..............................פרש...............ייתר
....יבי ומן.......
....הי עד ויגד ומן
.........[עד ויהי] מקץ[28] ומן מ[קץ] עד רישיה ד[חו]משיה
[ד]ואלה שמות[29] ומן ואלה עד כי אני הכ[ו]בדתי[30] ומן כי אני עד וישמע יתרו[31]
[ו]מן וישמע עד ראשית בכורי[32] ומן רא[ו]שית עד כתב לך[33] ומן כת[ו]ב עד
[ו]רישיה דהו[מ]שיה דויקרא[34] ומן ויקר[א] עד קח את אהרן[35]: ומן [ו]קח עד
[ו]אדם כי יהיה[36] ומן אדם עד כמ[ו]עשה ארץ[37] ומן כמעשה ע[ו]ד [ח]בר
[ו]אל אהרן[38] ומן דבר עד רישיה ד[ח]ומשיה וידבר[39] ו[ומ]ן וידבר ע[ד][40]....
...............[ו]עד וי[ק]ח קרח[41] ומן ויקח עד וישלח משה[42]
[ו]מן וישלח ע[ד] וכו'

[T.--S. 10 H 1^1, vellum, square writings, recto]

ראשי המטות[43] ומן ראשי המטות [ו]עד ר[ו]אש חמשה ראלה
הדברים[44] ומן אלה הדברים ועד שמע ישראל[45] ומן שמע

[28] Gen. 40, 43.
[29] Gen. 41, 50.
[30] Ex. 1-9, 35.
[31] Ex. 10-17.
[32] Ex. 18-23, 19.
[33] Ex. 23, 20-34, 26.
[34] Ex. 34, 27—40.
[35] Lev. 1-7.
[36] Lev. 8-12 (?)
[37] Lev. 13, 1 (?)-17
[38] Lev. 18-21 (?)
[39] Lev. 21, 17 (?)—27.
[40] Num. 1—?
[41] Num. ?—15.
[42] Num. 16-20, 13.
[43] Num. 20, 14-29.
[44] Num. 30-36.
[45] Dt. 1-6, 3 (or 8, 20)

ועד עשר תעשר[46] ומן עשר ועד כי יקרא קן[47] ומן כי יקרא ועד אתם נצבים[48] ומן אתם נצבים ועד לסופה[49] ומסימינן בחג הסכות ומסימינן בפסחא וכל ישבעין יומין דצומא בעינן רחמי ואמרינן פסוקי דעזרא ומן קומו ברכו עד ותבואתה[50] ואמרינן הושיענו[51] ז׳ זמני וברוך יהוה אלהי ישראל[52] ד׳ זמני וקריבין כהני דלבישין מאני דקדש וקימין בין האולם לתכתיא[53] דכהני ואמר ז׳ זמני חוסה יי על עמך[54] ואמרין קהלא לא לנו[55] וכד קריב שלוחא למימרן קומו ברכו[56] אמר ברוך יהוה אלהי ישראל[57] ברוך יהוה אלהים אלהי ישראל· וברוך שם כבודו·[58] ברוך יהוה לעולם·[59] וחושיענו· ברוך יהוה·[60] והדר אמא אתה יהוה לבדך·[61] ובשבעא בירחא וביומא דכיפורי אמרינן מיקמין פסוקי דעזרא שבעא פסוקי מן ספר תלים הודו ליהוה מי ימלל·[62] ועד דמסים ליה לפסוקא כוליה ונפלין על אנפיהון ואמר הללויה הללו את שם יהוה[63] עד דמסים לה ונפלין על אנפיהון ואמר הללויה הללו עבדי יהוה[64] עד דמסים

[46] Dt. 6, 4 (or 9, 1)—14, 21.

[47] Dt. 14, 22—22, 5.

[48] Dt. 22, 6—29, 8.

[49] Dt. 29, 7—34.

[50] Neh. 9, 5-37.

[51] Ps. 106, 47.

[52] Ps. 106, 48.

[53] Bench.

[54] Joel, 2, 17.

[55] Ps. 115.

[56] Neh. 9, 5.

[57] Ps. 41, 14.

[58] Ps. 72, 18-19.

[59] Ps. 89, 53.

[60] Ps. 106, 47-48. Thus the Doxologies at the end of the first four books of Psalms.

[61] Neh. 9, 6.

[62] Ps. 106.

[63] Ps. 135.

[64] Ps. 113.

ונפלין על אנפיהון ואמר בצאת ישראל[65] ונפלין על אנפיהון ואמר אהבתי כי ישמע[66] עד דמסים ונפלין על אנפיהון

(Verso)

ואמר הללו את יה[ו]ה [כל] גוים[67] ונפלין על אנפיהון ואמר הודו ליהוה יאמר נא ישראל[68] עד דמסים ונפלין על [וא]נפיהון ובכל דאמרינן פסוקי דעזרא בין ביום הכפרים [ובין] בשבעה בירהא ובין בתרין יומי דפורים ובין בשבעין [יו]מי דצומא מכסונן פראסי[69] ושדונן קיטמא דצומא ०

[Follow scribblings of Biblical verses in different handwritings]

[65] Ps. 114.

[66] Ps. 116.

[67] Ps. 117.

[68] Ps. 118.

[69] Curtains, i. e. the veil (פרכת) in front of the Ark.

LEON NEMOY

ANAN BEN DAVID

— A re-appraisal of the historical data —

Forty-five years have passed since Samuel Poznanski published his essay „Anan et ses écrits",[1] in which he re-examined anew all the data then available as to Anan's life and teaching. Since Poznanski, with his customary conscientiousness, distincly acknowledged his dependence upon the earlier researches of Abraham Harkavy,[2] this essay has been rightfully regarded as the mature judgement ot both these eminent scholars together.

Since that time much new information on Anan's teaching has come to light, notably Harkavy's,[3] Schechter's,[4] Mann's,[5] and Sokolov's[6] publications of portions of Anan's ספר המצות, and the additional data on Anan's views contained in the *Kitāb al-anwār* of al-Qirqisānī.[7] No new facts about Anan's life and personality, however, are contained in all these documents, so that our knowledge of the personal history of the Karaite *pater ecclesiae* remains still the same; and subsequent articles on Anan (notably in the several Jewish encyclopedias) follow the conclusions reached by Harkavy and Poznanski fairly closely. In fact, I myself have done the same in my short sketch of Anan in the *Universal Jewish Encyclopedia*,[8] published only a few years ago.

The summation reached by Poznanski, coinciding fully with that reached by Harkavy, was „que les documents caraïtes sont altérés à dessein d'une façon invraisemblable; que les documents rabbanites, au contraire, s'insèrent logiquement dans le cours des choses et peuvent, par conséquent, revendiquer une plus grande vraisemblance".[9] Such categorical statement by two major authorities in the field of Karaitology, backed by their vast erudition in both Karaite and Rabbanite literature, is obviously not a matter to be disagreed with lightly, nor one to be questioned without serious and compelling motives. And yet, as I read and re-read the earliest accounts of Anan's life available to us, I could not suppress an increasingly uncomfortable

[1] *REJ*, XLIV (1902), pp. 161—187; XLV (1902), pp. 50—69, 176—203.
[2] *REJ*, XLIV, p. 161: „Comme on le verra . . . je m'appuie souvent sur Harkavy.".
[3] *Studien und Mitteilungen aus der Kaiserlichen Oeffentlichen Bibliothek zu St. Petersburg*, VIII Teil, St. Petersburg, 1903.
[4] *Documents of Jewish Sectaries*, vol. II, Cambridge, 1910.
[5] *Journal of Jewish Lore and Philosophy*, I (1919), pp. 329—353.
[6] *Bulletin (Izvestiya) of the Russian Academy of Sciences, Section of Humanistic Studies*, VII (1928), pp. 243—253. The codex from which this portion was taken is an exceedingly curious one, from a paleographical point of view.
[7] Edited by L. Nemoy, New York, 1939—43, 5 volumes.
[8] 1939—43, vol. I, p. 293.
[9] *REJ*, XLIV, p. 161.

feeling that both Harkavy and Poznanski have overlooked a number of inner contradictions and logical improbabilities which should not, in all justice, be ignored, if we propose to arrive at even an approximation of the historical truth. My discomfort was, and still is, enhanced by the fact that, as noted above, no new documentary information on Anan's life unknown to Harkavy and Poznanski has as yet been uncovered, and that consequently it is impossible to *prove* that any part of their conclusions is patently contrary to fact. All I can do, therefore, in the following lines is set forth the doubts which have beset me, and show where these doubts might possibly lead.

II.

What are the sources available to us on the facts of Anan's life? There is a plethora of them, and as we go along the centuries down to modern times, their detail and the fancifulness of their narrative increases by leaps and bounds, particularly in the works of the Sultansky—Firkovitch school of official Karaite historiography. The later Rabbanite accounts are less detailed and less fantastic, but equally valueless. In the older Rabbanite literature, short mention of Anan is fairly frequent,[10] sometimes accompanied by a few choice epithets in condemnation of his heresy, which, however, convey no exact facts. The accounts found in Muslim-Arabic works (by al-Balkhī, al-Bīrūnī, al-Shahrastānī, and al-Maqrīzī) are patently based on Karaite information drawn from, or through, al Qirqisānī, and augmented with fancy details. We need, therefore, have no hesitation in leaving all these sources entirely out of our consideration, and limiting ourselves to the four earliest extant narratives, one Karaite and three Rabbanite — a rather uncomfortable disparity in numbers.

III.

The earliest of these four sources is a Rabbanite one, contained in the *Siddūr* of Rab Amram[11] and ascribed to the Gaon Natronai who flourished about the year 860. It reads as follows:

„These men[12] are heretics (מינין) and scoffers who hold in contempt the words of scholars (חז"ל), and who are disciples of Anan — may his name rot — the grandfather of Daniel[13] . . . who said to those who strayed and were seduced to follow him, 'Forsake ye the words of the Mishnah and of the Talmud, and I will compose for you a Talmud of my own!' To this day they remain in their error, and have become a people[14] unto themselves, whilst he[15] fabricated an evil and

[10] An excellent list of these references is given by Poznanski, *REJ*, XLV, pp. 191—203.

[11] Frumkin's edition, Jerusalem, 1912, vol. II, pp. 206—207. It must be borne in mind that the text of the *Siddūr* has undergone considerable modifications in the course of time, and that the account of Anan contained in it may have been somewhat different originally.

[12] The context deals with those who deviated from the Rabbanite form of the Passover liturgy.

[13] Daniel was the son of Anan's son Saul; cf. Mann, *Texts and Studies*, Philadelphia, 1935, vol. II, pp. 129—130.

[14] *i. e.*, a congregation, or sect.

[15] *i. e.*, Anan.

wicked Talmud for himself. My master Eleazar Allūf[16] has seen this abominable book of his, which they call ספר מצות; it contains many (heretical) tricks (תחבולות)".

In other words, barely 75 years or so after Anan's death all that Gaon Natronai — who lived in the very center of Anan's activity and who belonged to the circle of society which should have possessed the greatest and most authentic amount of information on Anan's personal history — all that Gaon Natronai knew of Anan was that he had seceded from the Rabbanite synagogue and had written his ספר המצות, which Natronai himself had no access to, but which had been examined by Eleazar Allūf who quite naturally judged it to be an heretical concoction. Did Anan actually say to his followers „I will compose for you a Talmud of my own"? Perhaps he did, in a moment of anger; yet his alleged outburst is curiously reminiscent of Jeroboam's exclamation to the Israelites, after he had made the two golden calves, „Behold thy gods, o Israel!" (I Kings 12 : 28), and might conceivably represent a quite understandable attempt to turn to Rabbanite advantage the ancient and well known Karaite accusation that Rabbanism was not true traditional Judaism, but the fruit of the schism initiated by the wicked mind of the first ruler of the Israelitish kingdom. Moreover, is it logical to suppose that Anan, to whom the Talmud was an ungodly makeshift, a מצות אנשים מלומדה, would offer to compose for his followers the exact counterpart of the work he was so completely opposed to? And does it square with his reputed motto, חפישו באורייתא שפיר ואל תשענו על דעתי?[17] Clearly it does not, for it would have been an absurd contradiction, evident even to the most ignorant of his followers, were he to claim for his ספר המצות the same divine inspiration and the same authority as that which attaches to the Talmud.

It seems just as significant to consider what Natronai's account does *not* say. It does *not* say a word about Anan's aristocratic (Davidic) descent, nor his rôle in the contest for the office of exilarch, nor his rejection for that office because of his unorthodoxy. Assuming that Natronai knew all these things, what possible reason could he have had for suppressing them? It seems to me that, on the contrary, he had every reason, from his point of view, *not* to suppress them. What stronger proof of Anan's unworthiness could he have desired than the fact that the Geonim who represented the highest learning and piety in Israel had unanimously found him unfit? If he was of Davidic descent, and if he was the older of the two candidates for the exilarchate, so much better for Natronai's purposes, for surely the Geonim would not have dared to defy such high qualifications for purely personal and partisan reasons, and without any motive of a

[16] An eminent Rabbanite scholar.

[17] Quoted first, so far as now known, by Yefeth ben 'Alī (last quarter of the 10th century) in his commentary to Zech. 5 : 8; there appears to be no reason to doubt its authenticity — the phraseology is certainly such as Anan would have used. To be sure, al-Qirqisānī does not mention this motto; but then, it is not clear from the *Kitāb al-anwār* whether al-Qirqisānī had access to a copy of the ספר המצות, or whether he drew his information about Anan's teaching from secondary sources.

higher order. Since they did reject him, nonetheless, clearly his schismatic tendencies must have been flagrant and serious indeed, too serious to allow of any leniency or of any hope that Anan might discard them on entering upon his high office. If one should reason that Natronai must have been inclined to think that the less said about the presence of such a black sheep in the illustrious exilarchic line, the better — the obvious rejoinder would be that this argument would hold if there had been any physical chance of keeping this embarrassing skeleton-in-the-closet secret. As a matter of cold historical fact, there was no such chance: so far as we can tell, Anan himself and his lineal descendants after him were openly called ריש גלותא (in Arabic, rās al-jālūt) by their co-sectarians, first by the Ananites, and later by the Karaites. There could not be any secrecy about it.

But let us pass on to the next source on our list.

IV.

The next account to be sonsidered is that contained in the *Kitāb al-anwār* of Ya'qūb al-Qirqisānī, composed in the second quarter of the 10th century. It is the oldest Karaite account so far available, and being the work of an exceedingly learned and accurate scholar carries considerable weight. Its reliability is further enhanced by the fact that al-Qirqisānī, far from being an Ananite, differed from Anan in several major points of law and repeatedly criticized him, occasionally in a most sarcastic and irreverent manner. It runs as follows:[18]

„Anan's appearance took place in the days of (the Caliph) Abū Ja'far al-Manṣūr.[19] He was the first to make clear a good deal of the truth about the (Scriptural) ordinances. He was learned in the lore of the Rabbanites, and not one of them could gainsay his erudition. It is said that Hai, the president of the (Rabbanite) academy,[20] together with his father translated the book of Anan[21] from the Aramaic into Hebrew and encountered nothing in it of which they could not discover the source in Rabbanite lore ... The Rabbanites tried their utmost to kill Anan, but God prevented them from doing so".

The additional data supplied here, to supplement Natronai's account, are the exact time of Anan's activity,[22] his learning in Rabbinics,[23] and the divinely thwarted attempt of the Rabbanites to take his life. Of the last, al-Qirqisānī unfortunately gives no details; of the second, Anan's learning in Talmudics, the ספר המצות itself supplies ample evidence. Once more, we are compelled to consider what al-Qirqisānī does *not* say, and why.

Once more, we observe a complete silence as to Anan's noble

[18] Nemoy's edition, I, p. 13.

[19] Reigned 754—775.

[20] Variously identified with Hai ben Nahshon, gaon at Sura in 886—896, and Hai ben David, gaon at Pumbeditha in 890—898.

[21] *i. e.*, the ספר המצות.

[22] A more exact *terminus a quo* is supplied by Ibn al-Hītī (15th century) who states, presumably on good authority, that Anan lived at Baghdad (*JQR*, IX (1897), pp. 432, 436); the building of the city began in 762.

[23] We may assume, however, that Natronai, too, silently implies it.

descent and the contest for the exilarchate which is supposed to have been the immediate cause of his break with the Rabbanite synagogue. Would al-Qirqisānī have suppressed this information had he had it? Hardly, it seems to me; for while he was not an Ananite, he had no hesitation in freely acknowledging his realization of Anan's major rôle in the Anti-Rabbanite movement. It surely would have been a feather in his cap had he been able to point out that Anan was not just an ordinary obscure run-of-the-mill sectarian, like all the other schismatics mentioned in the *Kitāb al-Anwār*, but rather a senior member of the *crême de la crême* of the Rabbanite aristocracy, who would have stood at the helm of the Rabbanite synagogue had he not become the victim of a dastardly and ungodly intrigue.[24] To be sure, there is that cryptic reference to the Rabbanite attempt to have Anan assassinated. Again we must ask why it is so short and so cryptic. If al-Qirqisānī knew the details, even the very barest ones, it was assuredly to his advantage to set them forth, in order to illustrate the extent of Rabbanite villainy. Is this reference, then, an interpolation, perhaps inspired by the statement in an earlier paragraph of the same chapter that „the Rabbanites schemed against Jesus until they put him to death by crucifixion"?[25] We have no choice but to let the question-mark stand — the true facts are beyond our reach.

And now we come to the third source, apparently independent of the preceding two, in which for the first time the story of Anan's secession from Rabbanism appears in its conventional form.

V.

This account, a Rabbanite one, is quoted in the חלוק הקראים והרבנים, written by a Karaite author named Elijah ben Abraham who appears to have lived in the 12th century.[26] Pinsker was the first to assume that this account was taken from the lost *Kitāb al-radd ʿalā ʿĀnān* of the Gaon Saʿadiah (882—942), on the ground that Saʿadiah seems to be the only gaonic author to have written a separate work against Anan. This would make it some twenty years earlier than al-Qirqisānī's account. Although this hypothesis has received the blessing of Poznanski,[27] I cannot help but question it. The story is quoted perfectly anonymously and is ascribed to „a member of your (*i. e.*, Rabbanite) persuasion (בן דתכם), who has cast opprobrium on Anan (אשר חרף לענן) ... and wrote (it) down in his lying narrative (וכתב בספור שקרותיו)" The wording certainly does not imply with any degree of clarity that the author was Saʿadiah, or that the work from which the account was taken was devoted in its entirety to the confutation of Anan; it may have been, for all we know, a general chronicle or an halakhic tract Nor does Elijah ben Abraham even imply that the work was one of great antiquity — it would have been some

[24] Which is precisely why later Karaite writers go into such lurid details about this story.

[25] Nemoy's edition, I, p. 12.

[26] *Cf.* Poznanski, *The Karaite Literary Opponents of Sa'adiah Gaon*, London, 1908, pp. 72—74.

[27] *REJ*, XLIV, p. 166; XLV, p. 192.

200 years old, if Sa'adiah were the author. In short, there seems to me to be no evidence that this account is older than that of al-Qirqisānī; the likelihood is rather that it is of a later date, perhaps of the 11th or even early 12th century.

Be that as it may, the account reads as follows:[28]

„Anan had a younger brother named Hananiah. Although Anan excelled this brother both in learning (בתורה) and in age, the contemporary (Rabbanite) scholars refused to appoint him exilarch because of his excessive freethinking (or lawbreaking, ויתור פריצות) and lack of piety וחסרון יראה. They therefore turned to his brother Hananiah, for the sake of his great modesty ענוה, retiring disposition (ביישנות), and fear of Heaven, and set him up as exilarch. Thereupon Anan was seized with a (wicked) zeal — he and (with him) all manner of evil and worthless men from among the remnants of Zadok and Boethus.[29] They set up a dissident sect — in secret, for fear of the (Muslim) government which was then in power — and they appointed Anan as their (own) exilarch. On a (certain) Sunday, however, the affair was discovered by the government, and the order was issued to have Anan imprisoned until the (following) Friday, when he was to be hung from the gallows as a political rebel (כי מרד במלכות). In prison Anan came upon a Muslim scholar[30] who was also confined there and was likewise due to be hung on (the same) Friday, as a violator of the Muhammadan faith.[31] This scholar advised Anan, saying, 'Are there not in the Torah ordinances admitting of two (contradictory) interpretations?' 'Indeed there are', answered Anan. 'Observe then', said the Muslim scholar, 'the interpretation accepted in the teaching of those who follow thy brother, and take thou the other interpretation, providing that those who follow thee will back thee up in it. Then give a bribe to the viceroy,[32] so that thou mightest perchance be permitted to speak (in thy defence); then prostrate thyself and say ‚My Lord the King! Didst thou set up my brother over one religion or over two? Upon his replying, over one religion (only), say to him further' But I and my brother belong to two (different) religions! Of a certainty thou wilt save thyself, providing thou wilt explain to him the differences[33] between thy religion and the religion of thy brother, and providing thy followers will back the up. Say these things, and when the King hears them he will say nothing (further about thine execution)'. Anan undertook also to deceive his own followers and said to them, 'Last night Elijah (the Prophet) appeared before me in a dream

[28] S. Pinsker, לקוטי קדמוניות Wien, 1860, p. 103.

[29] *i. e.*, from among the Sadducees.

[30] Identified in another Karaite work as Abū Ḥanīfa al-Nu'mān ibn Thābit, the founder of the Ḥanafī school of Muslim jurisprudence (*REJ*, XLIV, p. 167, footnote 2), who is said (according to a none too reliable tradition) to have died in prison in 767. The ground for this identification is not known, and one may well ask if it might not be an *ex post facto* inference.

[31] בדת מחמד — it seems difficult to believe that Sa'adiah would have used this particular expression.

[32] למשנה — presumably the vezier.

[33] The following 'והכתו makes no sense and is presumably a scribe's error which he failed to cross out.

and said to me, Thou deservest to be put to death for violating that which is written in the Torah'[34] — he spoke to them thus (in orde to entice them) with his crafty argamentation (והוציא להם אלו הדברים מתוך פלפולו), and out of fear for his life, so that he might save himself from a cruel death and perpetuate his name in eternity.[35] He also expended a great sum of money in bribes, until the King gave him permission to speak, whereupon he said, 'The religion of my brother employs (a calendar based upon) calculation (of the new moon) and intercalation (of leap-years) by cycles (תקופות), whereas my religion depends upon observation of the moon and intercalation (regulated) by (the ripening of) new grain. Since the King('s religion), too, employed observation of the moon and (the ripening of) new grain, Anan thus gained his favor and goodwill".

Here, then, we have for the first time the full traditional Rabbanite account of Anan's secession from the Rabbanite synagogue. Before examining it in detail we must call to mind the fact that the exilarchate was essentially a secular office, that of the *princeps Judaeorum* who acted as the political representative of Jewry before the Muslim court and who had charge of the administration of justice and the collection of taxes. The principal reward of the exilarchic office was not the aura of the *pontifex maximus*, or the respect accorded to the most learned man in Jewry, but rather the temporal power and the princely income which enabled the exilarch to live in a style comparable, *mutatis mutandis*, to that of his Muslim counterpart, the Caliph. If we are, therefore, to conceive of Anan as a man of ruthless and unscrupulous lust for political power, we must suppose that inasmuch as he had known all along — there could not possibly have been any secrecy about it — that he was the next in line for the exilarchate, he would have been exceedingly careful to keep his name clear of the slightest taint of unorthodoxy and he would not have joepardized his political future by openly professing schismatic doctrines; in other words, like King Henry of France he would have regarded the exilarchate as well worth a Talmudic Mass. That according to this Pseudo-Sa'adian account he did the exact opposite, seems psychologically inexplicable. Nor do the known facts of Anan's teaching square with this conception of him as a power-hungry intriguer. A man who instituted a yearly fast of seventy days' duration, who prohibited all medical treatment, whose entire teaching is permeated by a spirit of ascetic rigor and self-denial — such a man makes a poor actor for the rôle of an ambitious and vengeful politician. And even if we assumme that he was so abysmally stupid as to deliberately ruin his chances for the exilarchate, what possible gain would there have been for him in becoming the leader of a minute and obscure group of schismatics?[36] On the contrary, as far as material wealth and social

[34] Meaning — I take it — for continuing outwardly as a Rabbanite, as it were worshipping a false god, instead of openly seceding from the Rabbanite synagogue.

[35] In other words, in order to supply an honorable excuse for his secession from the Rabbanite synagogue.

[36] The problem of the social and economic motives in the early sectarian and Karaite movements is undoubtedly of great importance, as is the influence upon them

rank are concerned, Anan would have been vastly better off if he had swallowed his chagrin[37] and remained, if not the exilarch, at least the senior member of the Davidic aristocracy, accorded the full honors and emoluments connected with his noble rank.

But let us proceed further. No sooner was Anan's candidacy rejected than all the scattered and disunited schismatics of the Sadducee taint suddenly united in electing him their leader. Why and how did this miracle happen? It must have been a miracle, if we are to believe al Qirqisānī's account of the chaotic conditions of his time when, as he picturesquely puts it, it was impossible to find two Karaites who agreed completely with one another; and this state of affairs prevailed, let us not forget, some 150 years after Anan's death! Not to speak of the fact that al-Qirqisānī knows nothing of Anan's having been acknowledged by Sadducees or any other sect, in addition to the Ananites whose sect he had himself founded.

This secession of Anan, we are told further, took place in secret, as did his election to be exilarch of the Ananites. When the affair reached the ears of the Muslim authorities — note that the Rabbanites are not accused here of having denounced Anan, which seems to lend support to the aforementioned doubt of the authenticity of al Qirqisānī's statement that the Rabbanites tried to assassinate him — he was arrested and sentenced to the gallows on the charge of sedition. Once again, the psychology of this story defies explanation. Why the secrecy, and what did sedition against the Muslim state have to do with Anan's becoming the leader of a Jewish schism? Was it a crime in Muslim law for a Jew to found a dissident Jewish sect? There were then, as we well know, a number of non-Rabbanite schisms and their adherents not only were permitted by the Muslim authorities to live undisturbed, but even the Rabbanite authorities preferred not to molest them.[38] To be sure, the newly elected Rabbanite exilarch was customarily confirmed by the Caliph, and if Anan had set himself up as a rival *Rabbanite* exilarch he might possibly have laid himself open to the charge of defying the Caliph. But we are not told anything of the kind, since Anan is explicitly stated to have been elected by sectarians to a purely sectarian post.

The story of Anan's supposed conversation with Abū Ḥanīfa is so patently fantastic that it needs little discussion. Any such collabo-

of the contemporary social and economic stresses amongst the various classes of the Muhammadan population. Our lack of sufficient documentary evidence makes an answer to this question impossible. What few bits of information we posses tend to indicate that, with the possible exception of Anan, the leaders of the schisms and their followers belonged predominantly to the lower and poorer classes of Jewry, who engaged in petty agriculture and manual trades. It is only much later, in Egypt and Syria, that we encounter Karaite individuals in high government service, in the professions (mainly medicine), and in big business. An exceedingly interesting paper in this connection was recently published by Dr. Raphael Mahler, in Yiddish, „Di soziale tendenzn un welt-banem fun der karaimisher bawegung," *Gedank un Leben*, New York, I (1943), pp. 185 - 206; his conclusions are in my judgment rather premature, because of the lack of sufficient historical data, but the article is certainly thought-provoking.

[37] None of the portions of the ספר המצות so far discovered contain a word of polemic against the Rabbanites.

[38] *REJ*, XLIV, p. 164.

ration between a pious[39] Muslim divine and a Jewish schismatic is, in the nature of things, a highly improbable event, and the only advice Abū Ḥanīfa might possibly have been expected to offer to a despised „unbeliever" would have been to give up his „false" faith — whatever his quarrel with Rabbanism might be —, pronounce the *shahāda*, and become a good Muslim. But aside from this, and assuming that this curious cvnversation did actually take place, it would have been a furtive and private affair, and Anan would have taken very good care that no one else got an inkling of it, and would have carried the secret to his grave. Certainly there is nothing in the record of early Karaism to suggest that such collusive scheming between Anan and Abū Ḥanīfa would have evoked anything but emphatic condemnation on the part of the Ananites; however bitter their feelings were against the Rabbanites, they remained, as far as we know, perfectly staunch in the essential Jewishness of their faith.

Nor is the concluding portion of the account — about Anan's use of prevarication in order to induce his followers to join him in secession from the Rabbanite synagogue — any more *vraisemblable*. They already *had* seceded, more or less formally, before Anan had ever joined them, and required no such devious inducement. As for the naive explanation that the Caliph favored Anan because of the latter's method of calendation, which stood nearer to Muhammadan practice than did the Rabbanite one, it is not easy to believe that any Caliph, certainly not al-Manṣūr, would have commuted a death sentence on a charge of sedition for any such flimsy reason. And there is certainly no evidence that Anan himself, or the Ananites as a group, had anything material to show in the way of high royal favor on the part of the Muslim sovereigns.

VI.

The fourth, and last, of the early accounts of Anan's secession is the one given by Abraham ibn Dāūd in his chronicle composed in 1161. It reads as follows:[40]

„In the days of the Gaon Yehudai[41] lived Anan and his son Saul . . . This Anan was (a scion) of the family of (King) David. He was at first an orthodox scholar(תלמיד חכם), but (later) there became evident in him traces of heresy (פיסול) for which reason he was not named gaon, nor was he vouchsafed any Heaveninspired help to become exilarch. Moved by envy and hatred which took hold of his heart, he proceeded to build up a sand-hill (of heresy) and to seduce Israel from the tradition of the learned . . . He composed books and set up (his own) disciples, and invented out of his own heart laws which were not good and judgments by which men could not live (in righteousness)."

The dependence of this account upon the Pseudo-Saʿadian one is sufficiently clear. The new embellishments are Anan's alledged can-

[39] Whatever Abū Hanīfa's quarrel may have been with the theology favored by al-Mansūr, there can be not a shadow of a doubt that he remained a staunch and fanatical Muslim.

[40] A. Neubauer, *Medieval Jewish Chronicles*, I. pp. 63—64.

[41] Gaon at Sura, 757—761.

didacy for the gaonate, and his autorship of books — in the plural.[42] The historical value of these additions is patently negligible.

VII.

The reader who has been patient enough to follow our analysis of the source-material this far will observe at this point that, as was stated at the outset, the results are purely negative: there is no way of *proving* that any statement contained in the four earliest accounts is definitely false. All, if anything, that we may have succeeded in showing is that up to the 10th century — or more likely, up to the 11th or even the 12th century — the story of Anan's Davidic descent and of his unsuccessfull candidacy for the exilarchate appears to be totally unknown, and that moreover this story contains within itself the seeds of such serious contradictions and psychological improbabilities that its historicity cannot but become subject to grave doubt. The only choice remaining for us, therefore, pending the possible discovery of genuine documentary proof to the contrary, is to assume that the wole tale is an *ex post facto* inference, invented in the 11th or 12th century in order to explain the hereditary assumption of the exilarchic title by the senior descendant of Anan in each generation. The logical explanation of Anan's rôle as a rallying point for the various schismatic movements of his time would thus be not his alleged aristocratic descent, but his great learning and his pioneering rôle as the first non-Rabbanite theologian to compose a complete systematic handbook of schismatic teology and jurisprudence. The various non-Ananite schisms felt free to disagree with him in individual points of canon law, but in the main the ספר המצות of Anan remained for them the keystone of non-Rabbanite theology. It would seem, then, that it is this consideration, and not Anan's supposed high social rank, which prompted the Karaites as a group to elevate him to the position of the father of their synagogue. In this they were undoubtedly right, in the sense that without the unifying impulse supplied by the ספר המצות Karaism would never have come into being, at least not in the form in which it proved capable of enduring through the centuries down to the present day.

Whether the considerations offered above are or are not convincing, they do, I believe, supply one more proof — if any is needed — of our abysmal ignorance of the true history of early sectarianism and early Karaism, and of the urgent need for a thorough search in the Karaite manuscript collections, both in the Western libraries and in the Genizas and other storehouses of the East, for every bit of genuine early material that might shed the least bit of true historical light on Anan and his immediate followers. Until this gigantic task is performed, completely and thoroughly, we shall only continue to grope in the dark of uncertainty and doubt.

[42] The only other work, aside from the ספר המצות, ascribed to Anan is a tract on metempsychosis, which al-Qirqisānī mentions on the basis of hearsay („wa-hukiya 'anhū annahū kāna yaqūlu bil-tanāsukh wa-annahū dawwana fīhī kitāban"): al-Qirqisānī clearly is doubtful of Anan's authorship of the tract, and even of his belief in the transmigration of souls. Poznanski's arguments (*REJ*, XLV, pp. 190—191) for the historicity of this rumor seem to me to be unconvincing.